POLITICAL SCIENCE LABORATORY

Oliver Benson

University of Oklahoma

Charles E. Merrill Publishing Company
Columbus, Ohio
A Bell & Howell Company

Merrill Political Science Series

Under the Editorship of
John C. Wahlke
Department of Political Science
The University of Iowa

International Standard Book Number: 0-675-09593-X

Library of Congress Catalog Number: 69–10596

75 / 10 9 8

Printed in the United States of America

To my wife
June

Note to Teachers

Gaps have developed between teaching and research in political science. Typically the undergraduate textbook avoids quantification and the methodology of most contemporary political research. Typically the professional journals of the discipline increasingly emphasize these techniques. The gap is partly between the generations, sharpened by the new behavioral approaches, and partly between institutions—the large, well-equipped installations of a few centers affording advanced research facilities not commonly available.

This manual is the result of an experimental "laboratory" course designed to reduce the gap. Used originally in connection with a graduate methods course, it is easily adaptable to the enrichment of other existing courses. None of its content should be beyond the capacity of undergraduate students, even at the level of the introductory course in "Principles of Political Science." On the other hand it should be useful to any political science student, at whatever level of advancement, who has not been exposed to such material.

The topics are organized for either a quarter or a semester course. In a quarter course, the ten weekly sessions needed to cover the workbook may be followed by from one to three sessions devoted to student reports, as time permits. In a semester course, the units on statistics, scaling, and content analysis should be expanded to two sessions each.

For a new course built around the laboratory, the appended "List of Lecture Sources" is keyed to the topics of the manual.

Note to Students

In this course you are to take part in an experimental new departure in political science teaching. Except for a few institutions, college work in political science has consisted largely of the textbook-lecture-library approach, with little in the way of "do-it-yourself" homework assignments. Here you are thrust into the midst of the real political science laboratory—the world around us—and are asked to draw your own conclusions about some of its political patterns.

The methods you will apply in the exercises emphasize several quantitative techniques, but advanced statistical or mathematical concepts are avoided. Common sense and attention to the "cookbook" worksheets should see you through. A social science article or book using mathematics often assures the reader that "high school algebra" is a sufficient background; we are fairly confident that the exercises here can be handled with a knowledge of grade school arithmetic (not the "new math"), plus a few manipulative procedures which are carefully explained. This does not mean the exercises are easy. The aim of the workbook is to make things clear and—we hope—interesting, but as always, your own effort is required.

Relevance of these topics to modern political science research is clear from the illustrative tables, many of which are drawn from recent important literature of the field. The course should equip you to read intelligently the journals and scholarly works which more and more depend on such methods as these.

Acknowledgments

This book has drawn so heavily on the help of others that at times I have had the feeling I was more its coordinator than its author. The greatest debts are owed John Wahlke and James N. Rosenau, whose help, encouragement, and line-by-line critical reading and emendation of the entire manuscript are reflected on every page. It is not their fault that this is not a better book; they have labored valiantly to make it so. Francis B. May lent his professional statistical eye to a critique of the materials of Chapters 5 and 9. Harold Bradbury contributed his computer programming skill, so that the FORTRAN programs of the Appendix will actually run and do problems.

In launching the experimental Political Behavior Laboratory course from which the exercises grew, valuable help was given by Carolyn Pratt, A. K. Basu, and Kenneth Meyer. Miss Pratt served as coordinator of the planning committee and advised at all the sessions.

A special stimulus has been the unsolicited interest and encouragement of some who have seen portions of the manuscript by chance. I must mention two in particular. Irving Crespi, vice-president of the Gallup Organization, to whom I wrote for permission to quote, read the pages in which his table was embedded, and took time to prepare a detailed and clarifying comment on survey research. A chance encounter with Karl Deutsch led to his perusal of the outline and to several of his typically discerning suggestions.

For general encouragement and opportunities to explore some of these topics in the company of specialists, thanks are due Richard Snyder, Harold Guetzkow, George Blanksten, Ithiel de Sola Pool, Charles McLaughlin, William Flanigan, and Charles McClelland. The Social Science Foundation of the University of Denver, through a fellowship for the academic year 1964–1965, made possible a year of concentrated work on another project from which this one has profited.

My students in Political Science 399, struggling with unaccustomed tools, have sharpened the notes and exercises. Typists who have worked faithfully on the many tables and arrays include Erna Zeigler, Darla Boswell, and Coleen Ewy Sheline. Carol Takacs and Polly Beese helped prepare the index.

Oliver Benson

Kingscourt
Allenspark, Colorado

Permissions

Grateful acknowledgment is made to the authors, artists, and publishers who have generously granted permission to reproduce tables, graphs, and drawings. Without their kind cooperation the workbook would not have been possible. Listing is by authors and artists. Page citations are to this book. A few permissions were obtained directly from the publishers. All rights to the further use of this material are reserved by the copyright owners.

Mark Abrams and the *British Journal of Sociology* for Table 6-J, "Social Class and Inter-Generation Voting Behavior: London University Students," p. 225.

Hayward R. Alker, Jr., and the Macmillan Company for Table 5-H, "Voting, Governmental Expenditures, and Level of Economic Development," p. 169, from *Mathematics and Politics* (1965).

Gabriel A. Almond, Sidney Verba, and Princeton University Press, for tables from *The Civic Culture* (1963) used in Exercise 2–7, "Estimated Degree of Impact of Local Government on Daily Life"; Exercise 2–8, "Character of Impact of National Government"; Exercise 2–9, "Percentage Who Discuss Politics; by Sex and Education"; Exercise 2–10, "Percentage Who Acknowledge Duty to Participate in Local Community; by Sex and Education," pp. 51–57; and for extracts of data used in Table 5-J, "Pride in Governmental System and Confidence in Redress of Grievance," p. 175; Table 5-K, "Pride in Governmental System and Lack of Interest in Election," p. 175; Table 5-P, "Exposure to Political Communications and Community Activity," p. 181; and Exercise 5–3 (4), "Lack of Pride in Nation for Respondents of Low Civic Competence," p. 191.

Charles H. Backstrom, Gerald D. Hursh, and Northwestern University Press, for the "bad question" typology adapted from *Survey Research* (1963), pp. 204–205.

Arthur S. Banks, Robert B. Textor, and Massachusetts Institute of Technology Press, for Table 1-1, "Literacy by Former Colonial Status and Literate Nature of Predominant Religion," p. 4, from *A Cross-Polity Survey* (1963).

James O. Bennett for his "Racial Conservatism Scale," p. 237.

Bernard R. Berelson, Paul F. Lazarsfeld, W. N. McPhee, and the University of Chicago Press for Figure 3–7, "Religion as a Factor in Party Vote Choice in Elmira, New York, 1948," p. 69; and Table 5-G, "Respondent's Vote Intention by Usual Vote of Father, and for Usual Vote of Father Controlled for Spouse's Vote Intention, Elmira, 1948," p. 169, from *Voting* (1954).

Emory S. Bogardus and the Antioch Press for the Racial Distance Scale, p. 239, from *Social Distance* (1959).

Morrie Brickman and the Washington Star Syndicate, for the *Small Society* cartoons, pp. 149 and 312.

David Bromley, Allan Kornberg, and Joel Smith, for Table 6-K, "Relation of Age of First Party Identification to Parental Agreement in Political Party Support for Women Party Officials and League of Women Voter Members," p. 225.

Robert Calvert, Jr., and the American Academy of Political and Social Science, for Table 5-I, "Goals of Peace Corps Volunteers Before and After Service," p. 171.

Angus Campbell, Gerald Gurin, Warren E. Miller, and Harper & Row for the table of Exercise 2–1, "Party Preference as a Function of Parental Party Preference," p. 39, from *The Voter Decides* (1954).

Angus Campbell, Philip E. Converse,

Warren E. Miller, Donald E. Stokes, and John Wiley and Sons, Inc., for the table of Exercise 2–5, "Relation of Perceived Closeness of Election and Intensity of Partisan Preference to Voting Turnout, 1956," p. 47; Figure 3–13, "Relation of Attitude toward Eisenhower to Party Vote, 1956," p. 74; Table 6-L, "Relation of Degree of Concern About Election Outcome to Voting Turnout, 1956," p. 227; and Table 6-M, "Postelection Preference of Nonvoter, 1948 to 1956," p. 227; from *The American Voter* (1964).

Congressional Quarterly, Inc., for roll-call data used in Exercise 5–3 (7), "Freshmen Democratic Congressmen and Support of President Johnson," p. 195, and in the scalogram illustrations and exercises of Chapter 7, pp. 242, 251, and 259.

Irving Crespi and the *Public Opinion Quarterly*, for Table 5-E, "Pre-Convention Goldwater Support, by Region and Religion, 1964," p. 165; and brief extracts of data used in Exercise 5–3 (3), "Goldwater Support by Region," Exercise 5–3 (5), "Religion as a Factor in Pre-Convention Goldwater Support: The South," and Exercise 5–3 (6), "Religion as a Factor in Pre-Convention Goldwater Support: The Midwest," pp. 191–193.

James C. Davies and the *American Sociological Review,* for the two graphs used in Figure 3–15, "The Davies J-Curve of Revolution," p. 76.

Leon D. Epstein, Austin Ranney, and the *Political Science Quarterly* for Exercise 2–2, "Education and Presidential Vote," Exercise 2–3, "Age and Presidential Vote," and Exercise 2–4, "Party Activists and Presidential Vote," pp. 41–45, from their article, "Who Voted for Goldwater: The Wisconsin Case."

Heinz Eulau, John C. Wahlke, William Buchanan, LeRoy C. Ferguson, and the *American Political Science Review,* for Table 6-E, "Political Character of Electoral Districts and Areal Role Orientations in Three States," and Table 6-F, "Areal-Focal and Representational Role Orientations in Four States," p. 221.

I am indebted to the Literary Executor of the late Sir Ronald A. Fisher, F.R.S., to Dr. Frank Yates, F.R.S., and to Oliver & Boyd Ltd., Edinburgh, for permission to reprint the abridged table of critical values of chi-square, Appendix G, p. 394, from their book *Statistical Tables for Biological, Agricultural and Medical Research* (6th edition, 1963).

Johan Galtung and the Free Press (a division of the Macmillan Company) for Exercise 2–12, "Favorable Attitudes Toward Religious Belief, Religious Practice, United Nations Forces, and Service in International Forces, by Social Position, Norway, 1966," p. 61, from James N. Rosenau (ed.), *Domestic Sources of Foreign Policy* (1967).

Norbert Ginsberg and the University of Chicago Press for Figure 3–12, "Percentage in Secondary and Higher Education," p. 73, from the *Atlas of Economic Development* (1961).

Daniel Goldrich, Edward W. Scott, and the *Journal of Politics* for Table 6-I, "Attitudes of Panamanian Students toward Cubans, North Americans, and Russians," p. 225.

Fred Greenstein and Yale University Press for Table 6-G, "Children's Evaluations of Three Political Executives Contrasted with Adult Evaluation of President Eisenhower During the Same Time Period," and Table 6-H, "Children's Images of the Mayor and President, by School Year," p. 223, from *Children and Politics* (1965).

Orlando M. Hernando, for Table 10–2, "Attitudes on Right to Counsel, by Occupation and Nation," p. 363.

Herbert H. Hyman, Paul B. Sheatsley, and the *Public Opinion Quarterly* for Table 5-F, "Effect of Education Campaign on Attitude toward U.S. Loan for Britain as Related to Respondents' Trust in England's Cooperation," p. 167.

Arnold Kaufman, for Table 10–1, "Student Agreement on Democratic 'Rules of the Game,' by Political Orientation, Controlled for Frame of Reference," p. 361.

Yasumasa Kuroda and the *Public Opinion Quarterly* for Table 5-B, "Political Activity in a Japanese Community, by Sex"; Table 5-C, "Party Preference of Leaders and Advisors in a Japanese Community"; and Table 5-D, "Party Preference in a Japanese Community, by Role and Sex," pp. 161–163.

Robert E. Lane and the *American Political Science Review* for Table 6-C, "Perceptions of Life Now, Earlier, and Later," and Table 6-D, "Changing Attitudes Toward Integration," p. 221.

The League of Women Voters of Pennsylvania for the "Score Card for Citizen Political Action," p. 237.

George S. Lokken, for Table 10–3, "Militancy of Graduate Students and Military Officers Compared with Respondents' Self-Identification, by Career and Party Preference," p. 365.

Herbert McClosky, Harold E. Dahlgren, and the *American Political Science Review* for Table 2-9, "Relations between Voter Stability, Family Preference, and Social Distance," p. 31, which is also the basis for Figure 3–6, "Voter Stability, Family Preference, and Social Distance," p. 68.

Herbert McClosky, Paul J. Hoffman, Rosemary O'Hara, and the *American Political Science Review* for Table 6-A, "Comparison of Party Leaders and Followers on Reliance on the United Nations," and Table 6-B, "Comparison of Party Leaders and Followers on Public Control of Atomic Energy," p. 219.

W. Miller and the *New Yorker* Magazine for the cartoon on survey research, p. 201.

Robert C. North, Ole R. Holsti, George Zaninovich, Dina A. Zinnes, and Northwestern University Press, for the U-2 and Korea examples of unit themes in Chapter 8, p. 271, and permission to adapt their discussion of the Q-Sort technique for content analysis, pp. 272–3, from *Content Analysis: A Handbook with Applications for the Study of International Crisis* (1963).

The University of Oklahoma Bureau of Government Research, for Table 5-N, "Does a Close Runoff Primary Hurt the Party in the General Election?" p. 179, and Table 5-O, "Relation of Type of Agriculture to Normal Party Preference," p. 181, from *Oklahoma Votes, 1907–1962*.

Paul R. Petty for Table 10–5, "Responses of U.S. and Swiss Students on Questions of Internationalism," p. 369.

Leroy N. Rieselbach and *International Organization* for Table 7–9, "Scalogram of Colonial Questions in General Assembly, 1956–1957," p. 247, and data used in Table 7–10, "Voting Agreement Matrix for Sixteen Selected States on Colonial Issues in the United Nations General Assembly, 1956–1957," p. 248.

Bruce M. Russett, Hayward R. Alker, Jr., Karl W. Deutsch, Harold D. Lasswell, and Yale University Press, for permission to use data from the *World Handbook of Political and Social Indicators* (1964) in Table 5-L, "Does a Strong Socialist Party Tend to Weaken the Appeal of Communism?" p. 177; Table 5-M, "Communist Electoral Success and Strength of Catholicism," p. 179; Table 5-R, "Tests of Marxist Theory I: Industrial Labor Force and Unemployment," p. 183; and Table 5-S, "Tests of Marxist Theory II: Industrialization and Working-Class Awareness," p. 185.

Gerhart H. Saenger and the *American Journal of Sociology*, for Exercise 2–6, "Proportion of Voters in Six Status Groups who are Members of Political Organizations, by Roosevelt and Dewey Voters," p. 49.

S. Sidney Ulmer and the *American Behavioral Scientist* for Table 7–8, "Scalogram Analysis of Non-Unanimous Civil Liberties Cases, U.S. Supreme Court, 1957 Term," p. 246.

Roberto E. Villarreal for Table 10–4, "Attitudes of Oklahoma and Florida College Students on United States Cuban Policy, by Party," p. 367.

William E. Wright, the *Midwest Journal of Political Science*, and Wayne State University Press, for Exercise 2–11, "Ideology-pragmatism Orientation of West Berlin Party Officials, by Age Groups, with Party Controlled," p. 59.

Contents

1 POLITICS AND DATA: The Use and Limits of Numbers   1

Some Philosophic Terms, 1; An Example of Hypothesis Testing, 3; Objections to a Science of Politics, 4; Quantification: Pro and Con, 6; Derivation of a Simplified Gini Index, 8; Exercise Set 1, 13; Reading List, 21.

2 HOW TO READ A TABLE: The Variety of Variables   22

What a Table is For: Look for the Key Relationship, 22; Anatomy of a Table, 23; Problems of Percentages: Which Way Do They Add Up? 26; Variables and Variation, 28; A More Complex Example: Voter Stability, 31; Multiple Causality, 33; Constructing a Table: the Concept of Property Space, 34; Exercise Set 2, 39; Reading List, 63.

3 GRAPHS AND CHARTS: Mapping Your Data   64

Qualities of a Good Graph, 64; Types of Graphs Useful in Political Research, 67; The Bar Graph, 67; Coordinate Graphs, 71; Circle and Half-Circle Graphs, 79; Pure Relationship Graphs, 81; A Word on Mechanics, 88; Exercise Set 3, 91; Reading List, 109.

4 DATA PROCESSING: Do Not Fold, Spindle, or Mutilate!   110

Coding Your Information, 110; Sorting Your Data, 115; Searching for New Variables: A Return to Property Space, 119; Automatic Data Processing, 121; The Keysort Cart—A Compromise, 123; Exercise Set 4, 127; Reading List, 147.

5 STATISTICS: A Little Dab'll Do You   148

Inference, 148; Sample and Population: Statistic and Parameter, 149; Testing of Hypotheses, 150; Errors, 151; Yule's Q Test for Two Dichotomous Variables, 151; Spearman's Rho (ρ): A Coefficient of Rank Correlation, 152; The Chi-Square (χ^2) Text, 154; Other Statistics, 158; Exercise Set 5, 161; Reading List, 197.

6 SURVEY RESEARCH: How to Ask Questions   198

The Sample, 198; The Questionnaire, 200; Structure of Questions, 202; To Structure or Not to Structure? 203; Bad Questions, 204;

Planning Your Own Survey: An Adventure in Discovery, 205; A Note on the Exercises, 208; Exercise Set 6, 209; Reading List, 233.

7 INDEXES AND SCALING: Light from the Political Spectrum 235

Qualities of a Good Index, 235; Kinds of Index Values, 236; A Simple, Untested Index: Citizen Political Action, 236; A Racial Conservatism Scale, 237; A Social Distance Scale, 239; Guttman Scaling, 240; Scaling Roll-Calls, 241; An Example from Senate Roll-Calls, 242; Cluster Analysis and Scale Analysis, 245; Other Applications, 246; Exercise Set 7, 251; Reading List, 267.

8 CONTENT ANALYSIS: Who Said What, When, and How? 268

Political Uses of Content Analysis, 268; Category Identification, 270; Coding, 270; Affect and Action Statements Separated, 271; Scaling: The Q-Sort Scale, 272; A Content Analysis Project Using Q-Sort, 273; Exercise Set 8, 275; Reading List, 301.

9 EFFECTS OF A CONTROL VARIABLE 302

An Example: The "Nothing Happens" Effect, 302; The Independent Effect, 305; The "Stretch and Shrink" Effect, 307; The "Half-True" Effect, 308; The "Plus and Minus" Effect, 310; The "Now You See It and Now You Don't" Effect, 312; The "Something from Nothing" Effect, 314; The "Flip-Flop" Effect, 315; Spuriousness, 316; Exercise Set 9, 319; Reading List, 353.

10 REPORTING YOUR PROJECT: What Have You Proved and What Difference Could It Make? 354

Your Prefatory Statement, 354; The Procedural Statement, 354; Analysis of Your Results, 356; Tabular Presentation, 357; Statistical Test, 357; Conclusions, 358; Exercise Set 10, 359; Reading List, 373.

APPENDIX 375

A List of Lecture Sources, 375
B Speed in Computations, 377
C Computer Programs, 381
D Table of Reciprocals to 100, 392
E Values of Q for Percentage Deciles, 392
F Significance Levels for Spearman's Coefficient of Rank Correlation, 394
G Abridged Table of Critical Values of Chi-Square, 395

POLITICS AND DATA:

The Use and Limits of Numbers

Political science uses empirical data as a means to help us understand political relationships. On the basis of such discovered relationships, political scientists are interested in developing, though cautiously, a theory of the political process that will have general validity. This is the central purpose of the new school of political behavioralism and the reason for its emphasis on empirical work.[1]

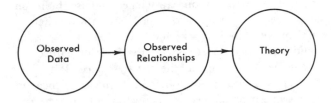

The word "data" as used in the diagram means all sensed information which comes to us from the world about us—from "nature." Some of this information can be counted, sorted, measured, weighed, located, arrayed by magnitude, or scaled and assigned an index value. Speed of movement and other rates of change can be recorded. These human mental operations result in a variety of quantitative descriptors or indicators about some of the data in nature.

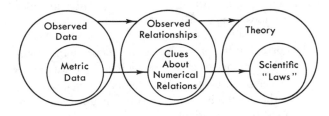

---

[1] The "behavioral-institutional" controversy in political science has stimulated much of the discipline's development since the second World War. Good short introductions to the topic are: James Charlesworth (ed.), The *Limits of Behavioralism in Political Science* (Philadelphia: American Academy of Political and Social Science, 1962); Heinz Eulau, *The Behavioral Persuasion in Politics* (New York: Random House, 1963); and Albert Somit and Joseph Tanenhaus, *The Development of Political Science: From Burgess to Behavioralism* (Boston: Allyn and Bacon, 1967).

Sometimes examination of these quantitative indicators yields clues to relationships, and eventually to general principles or scientific laws. Sometimes it does not, and even when it does the clues often prove misleading or wrong, so that we must go back to nature for another look.

The process of measuring data depends upon application of the human mind—upon "intellectualization" about the data. The mental approach to data may involve not merely a kit of measuring instruments and knowledge of how to use them, but a great variety of non-quantitative ideas, principles, concepts, and knowledge of prior discoveries. Just as measuring instruments may be inaccurate or unskillfully used, so may these non-quantitative ideas and principles be poorly founded, vague, or mistakened. The point is that, for better or worse, observation of data is never devoid of the human conceptualization. We may term the set of mental concepts within which data are observed a "conceptual framework" and note that it derives from some level of theory.

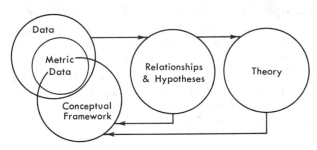

1-1 Some Philosophic Terms

Scholars are by no means agreed as to how we become aware of information about the world—about nature. The study of human knowledge—known as *epistemology*—has developed a variety of conflicting theories. At one extreme is the theory of *phenomenology,* which contends that we can be aware only of sensed data. Less extreme than phenomenology is *empiricism,* which still puts the emphasis on sensed data, but allows for the work of the human mind as well. Empiricists contend that knowledge develops primarily (or entirely) from observation of nature: the data come first, and only on the basis of data can the human mind build explanations, principles, or general laws. The great social philosopher F.S.C. Northrop uses the term "radical empiricism" to describe the view that we must always start first with data, that scientific principles derive only from the "empirical world." He contrasts it with "logical realism," the more usual scientific approach which puts greater emphasis on maximum intellectualization—on use of the human brain to reason and draw logical conclusions about reality. Northrop feels that knowledge grows from what he calls "epistemic correlations," operations by which the theorems derived from scientific theories are found by experimentation to correspond with the purely empirical world. The most adequate epistemology of science, Northrop feels, is "logical realism in epistemic correlation with radical empiricism." Adequacy of the operation of epistemic correlation is tested by whether the theory accounts for natural "facts." In political theory, for example, certain doctrines emphasizing elitist and racist principles simply do not correlate with the findings of modern biology. Thus the operation of epistemic correlation results in "disproving" them.[2]

The controversy in contemporary political science between behavioralism and traditionalism to some extent parallels the more general conflict between pure empiricism and logical realism. Actually most scientific knowledge has developed by a combination of empirical observation and logical analysis. Political behavioralism focuses on individual and group behavior related to the political system, rejecting as insufficient the traditional emphasis on formal political institutions, laws, and theories. It stresses rigorous empiricism—intensive use of quantitative methods, and the development of technical terms to identify and analyze general features of political processes. As Professor Sorauf puts it,

> The new mood in political science seeks to impel the discipline toward generalizations which will explain relationships within the political system. It is the old goal, more cautiously presented, of a science of politics. The behaviorists have brought the hypothesis and theoretical proposition back into even narrowly circumscribed research. At the same time they con-

tinue the search for the towering, over-all theoretical edifice which will integrate and unify the more specific findings and propositions of the discipline.[3]

Deduction, Induction, and Scientific Methods. Deduction is reasoning from the general to the particular. Induction is reasoning from the particular to the general or from the individual to the universal. In a way the contrast is that between pure empiricism and logical realism: on the one hand, we establish deductively the validity of a specific point by reasoning from a general principle; on the other, we are led from specific findings to a generalization. But these terms are more strictly applied to the reasoning process itself. We speak of deductive sciences, of which the chief examples are mathematics and logic (now tending to merge), wherein the only test of valid conclusions (or laws) is that of consistency with premises. But we do not speak of deductive sciences in contrast with inductive sciences but rather in contrast with empirical sciences—those built on extensive use of empirical data from nature: chemistry, physics, biology, geology, wherein the test of valid laws is consistency with the facts of nature.

Into which group do the social sciences fall? The answer is by no means obvious. Political science, to take our particular field, depends on both reason and fact. The question of which came first is much like the folk paradox "which came first, the chicken or the egg?" Rulers and their advisors, popular leaders and successful administrators—all participants in the political process—have always been creatures both of the mind and of reality.

Indeed the basic method of science involves a constant interplay of deduction and induction. Although probably no individual scientist follows precisely the routine usually set forth as a description of "the scientific method," all scientific investigation includes these various operations:

1. Formulation of a question about some phenomenon or group of phenomena (Induction).
2. Development of a preliminary or general hypothesis which might furnish an answer to the question (Deduction).
3. Elaboration of the hypothesis into a proposition or group of propositions which can be shown to be true or false by testing them against relevant data (Deduction).

---

[2] For a lucid essay relating Northrop's philosophy to political theory see Joyotpaul Chaudhuri, "Philosophy of Science and F.S.C. Northrop: The Elements of a Democratic Theory," *Midwest Journal of Political Science*, Vol. XI, No. 1 (February, 1967), pp. 44–72.

[3] Frank J. Sorauf, *Perspectives on Political Science* (Columbus: Charles E. Merrill Publishing Company, 1965), pp. 15–16.

4. The actual testing of the hypothesis against relevant empirical data, resulting in its acceptance, rejection, or modification (Induction).

5. Rather than stopping, the process then enters a new cycle with new or modified questions, new or modified hypotheses, and new testing.

Some of the terms used in this outline of "the scientific method" require brief definition and comment:

Phenomenon—any fact or event known through the senses rather than by thought or intuition. We cannot say that a phenomenon is "true" or "false." We simply sense that it exists. Of course our sensory perceptions may be faulty, so that we think we sense a non-existent phenomenon, or fail to observe one that does exist, or sense a real phenomenon inaccurately. The recurrent controversies over flying saucers and other "Unidentified Flying Objects" illustrate the range of discussion appropriate for phenomena.

A phenomenon may be contrasted with a purely mental *concept*—such as the concept of political stability or political socialization. It is also inappropriate to call a concept "true" or "false." Being only a product of someone's intellectualization, its existence cannot really be challenged. We may argue that it exists "only in the mind," but that is the very definition of a concept. Logical discussion about a concept concerns rather such questions as whether it is useful or useless, clear or fuzzy, well-structured or not, relevant or irrelevant.

Proposition—a meaningful statement in words or symbols of something that can be believed, doubted, or denied. Propositions may be logically true or false, or empirically true or false, or purely speculative. Not all propositions are subject to verification nor are they meant to be. A proposition may be an expression of belief or a simple assertion admittedly without proof. When Jefferson declared that "all men are...endowed by their Creator with certain unalienable rights," he did not imply that this assertion was subject to empirical verification—the empirical evidence would certainly have been against it. When Spengler asserted that "there is higher man and lower; I will say it again and again," he helpfully included in his second clause an admission that the statement was not subject to any but rhetorical argument.

Hypothesis—a proposition worded so that its truth or falsity can be verified by empirical obser-

vation. In a scientific investigation we usually have a "working hypothesis" or "test hypothesis," a tentative answer to the question we have formed about some phenomena. It is important to understand that a hypothesis is a tentative explanation meant to be tested. It is this feature which distinguishes it from a dogmatic statement or an assertion based purely on mental processes. One might assert, for example, that a legislator elected from a district in which party competition is high will be more alert to his constituents' demands than another legislator from a safe district. It seems "logical" that the danger of defeat would have this effect. The same proposition, worded as a tentative explanation of how some legislators interpret their roles, was set up as a working hypothesis in an empirical study by Eulau and Wahlke (see Chapter 6 for some of their results). Rather than simply accepting a plausible idea, they developed a research plan to test it.

Relevant data—data are relevant to an investigation if they can be described in propositions which supply evidence for or against the hypothesis which is being tested.

1-2 An Example of Hypothesis Testing

This sequence of reasoning about a hypothesis and testing it with data is illustrated by an example drawn from the elaborate statistical study *A Cross-Polity Survey,* whose authors investigated available data for 115 independent states on 194 characteristics (such as literacy, stability of government, date of independence, communication facilities, types of culture, law, and government). One group of states shared the common characteristic of having recently emerged from colonial status—nineteen had been British colonies and twenty had been French colonies. A table on literacy revealed that most of the former British colonies fell in the higher literacy category (fifteen had literacy rates above 10 per cent, while only four had rates below 10 per cent). In contrast, most of the former French colonies fell in the lower literacy category (thirteen below 10 per cent, only seven above).[4]

---

4 Arthur S. Banks and Robert B. Textor, *A Cross-Polity Survey* (Cambridge: M.I.T. Press, 1963). The authors' account of these data (pp. 14–16) is inconsistent with the computer printouts of characteristics 46 (literacy 10 per cent and above) and 56 (literacy of predominant religion). Ghana, Ireland, Jordon, Tunisia, Laos, Lebanon and Syria are omitted; Guinea and Mauritania (classed as "Not Ascertained" by the printout) are added. Table 1-1 was therefore prepared directly from the computer printouts reproduced in the volume.

Formulation of a question about this collection of data (Step 1 in the process described on p. 2) is fairly obvious: Why do the states formerly under British rule have higher literacy rates than those formerly under French rule? Development of a preliminary hypothesis (Step 2) is more difficult; in fact, for this problem we essentially pass over Step 2 to Step 3 and set up two testable hypotheses. Either the British did more to promote literacy than did the French, or the peoples of the British colonies were more literate to start with. Since the data were more readily at hand, the authors tested the second of these alternative hypotheses, classifying the states on the basis of whether the prevailing religion was predominantly literate or non-literate (Step 4). The new classification yields the following:

TABLE 1-1. *Literacy by Former Colonial Status and Literate Nature of Predominant Religion*[a]

Literacy Rate	States Formerly British Colonies		States Formerly French Colonies[a]	
	Religion Literate	Religion Non-Literate	Religion Literate	Religion Non-Literate
Above 10%	11[b]	4[b]	5	1
10% and Below	0	4	0	13

[a] South Vietnam, included in the French group with literacy over 10 per cent, is omitted here because predominant religion not ascertained.
[b] Jamaica and Trinidad have literate religion now but probably did not at time of colonization and are classed here with the non-literate religion group.
Source: *A Cross-Polity Survey.*

We are now in a position to test the hypothesis that literacy of the predominant religion is a significant factor in accounting for the former French colonies' falling in a lower literacy class than the former British colonies. Our conclusions (Step 4) are readily drawn. Obviously[5] the French colonial empire included many more polities in the non-literate religion group. We note that not a single state with a literate religion falls in the low literacy category, regardless of whether France or Britain ruled. A further check of the authors' world data discloses that of the 106 states for which data were available on the two factors, 76 fall in the literate religion class and of

these 92 per cent (70 states) have literacy of 10 per cent or more. Of the 30 states which fall in the non-literate group, 67 per cent (20 states) have literacy of less than 10 per cent. With this additional confirmation we may state confidently a general principle that literacy of a religious tradition is strongly associated with literacy of a country.

Our brief examination of these thirty-nine countries has moved through the five prescribed steps, although in a somewhat contrived fashion. You may feel uneasy about the pattern being so orderly, and your feeling is soundly based. Most actual investigations do not follow this idealized sequence, and some scientists object strenuously to the term "scientific method" itself. It is true that hunches, guesses, and plain luck play an important role in scientific discovery, but the elements of systematic investigation are always found to be at work as well. One perceptive social scientist has expressed the whole concept of scientific method more concisely as consisting of three basic processes: (1) forming a question, (2) guessing at an answer, and (3) testing the answer.

1-3 Objections to a Science of Politics

Since this book is planned to equip you to apply the rudiments of the scientific method to the investigation of political questions, it is important for you to be aware of some of the criticisms commonly leveled against empirical work in political science, and quantitative work in particular. These objections and criticisms are included not merely to be argumentative, but because most of them are part-truths, containing important cautions for empirical research and emphasizing some of its basic limitations.

Some of the objections raised:

1. That most empirical research is trivial—that it elaborates the obvious and derives conclusions which the ordinary rational man already knows on the basis of his general observation and common-sense reasoning.

2. A criticism contradictory to the first is that man is an irrational being, so that human behavior cannot under any circumstances be explained or predicted (this charge may be dismissed briefly; irrational behavior itself can be treated as researchable data, as in studies of the psychotic).

It is true that much empirical research is apparently trivial, but the same is no less true of the hard sciences than of the social sciences: most scientific development has come by gradual building, by piecemeal findings. As for "common-sense" reasoning, it

---

[5] "Obviously" is a rather unscientific term. Statistical tests provide methods and rules which permit us to say just how "obvious" such a conclusion is, as well as to draw conclusions in cases that are not "obvious."

is unfortunately true that common-sense plausibility can support quite contradictory conclusions. Paul Lazarsfeld once gave an excellent demonstration of the "common-sense fallacy" in a review of the intensive World War II study of *The American Soldier*—one of the classics of modern social research.[6] He listed a series of findings from the study which he assumed would appear "obvious" by common-sense reasoning, and paired the findings with the "common-sense" explanations. Two examples will suffice:

White privates were more eager to become noncoms than were Negroes. (The lack of ambition among Negroes is almost proverbial.)

Southern Negroes preferred Southern to Northern white officers. (Isn't it well known that Southern whites have a more fatherly attitude toward their "darkies"?)

The only trouble with these common-sense explanations is that Lazarsfeld had deliberately reversed the actual findings: "common-sense" led to exactly the wrong conclusion in each case! On the other hand, assuming the correct findings were reported, you can easily find equally plausible common-sense arguments in support: "obviously" Negroes would be more eager to advance because they had so much more to gain; obviously they would prefer Northern white officers, who would presumably be more likely to treat them as equals.

The charge of triviality in political research deserves to be taken seriously. It is made in strong language by some of the most eminent scholars of the discipline. Professor Leo Strauss feels that empirical political scientists can never discover significant political truth by their methods, and deplores the squandering of time and resources on trivial investigations, time and resources which might be devoted far better to the crucial problems of modern society. His now famous dictum about the new political science is memorable: "One may say of it that it fiddles while Rome burns. It is excused by two facts: it does not know that it fiddles, and it does not know that Rome burns."[7]

3. That much political behavior is decided within the individual's mind, and so is not researchable, or is the product of a variety of causes so complex that they are inherently not susceptible to explanation or prediction.

[6] Paul Lazarsfeld, "The American Soldier—An Expository Review," *Public Opinion Quarterly*, Vol. 13, No. 3 (Fall 1949), p. 380.
[7] In Herbert J. Storing, ed., *Essays on the Scientific Study of Politics* (New York: Holt, Rinehart and Winston, Inc., 1962), p. 327.

The two propositions contained in this criticism are significant limitations on political research, and point to the importance of appropriate precautions in designing an investigation and due modesty in drawing conclusions from findings. They are not, of course, unanswerable objections to doing any empirical political research at all. Being alert to the problem of the complexity of political influences, we can take care to isolate the significant variables and be cautious in assertions based on a single investigation. Being alert to the privacy of human political decisions, we can be appropriately careful to insulate that privacy, for example, by assuring respondents of the confidential nature of their answers to questionnaires.

4. That the social or political scientist is bound to his own society's culture, and therefore incapable of truly detached scientific objectivity in the study of society.

This objection points to an important danger in political research, which careful scholars are well aware of and call the "cultural fallacy." Cultural fallacies abound in both empirical and traditional political science, but one can argue that empirical methods permit greater care in eliminating them than is possible for the conclusions of sheer deductive reasoning about politics. As Heinz Eulau has pointed out, empirical methods allow for cross checking, for replication of investigations by others, for criticism by colleagues, for team research by scholars from different cultures, for empirical investigations explicitly built on theoretical propositions, for use of empirical data to develop new theoretical propositions, for theoretical conceptualization to extend the range of empirical research, and for cumulative building of consistent empirical research findings from many investigations.[8]

5. That social events are so complex in causation as to be unique and non-recurring—hence unpredictable. In contrast to this criticism is the related one that a social or political prediction itself influences behavior, so that it is impossible to tell whether fulfillment of a prediction is due to the factors analyzed or to the sheer fact of the prediction itself.

It is true that political and social events can be defined as unique, but so can events in nature as studied by the hard sciences. The job of empirical research is to identify the typical and to eliminate the unique in each experiment. The example from *A Cross-Polity Survey* illustrates the point. Certainly

[8] Heinz Eulau, ed., *Political Behavior in America: New Directions* (New York: Random House, 1966), pp. 5–10.

no one would deny that each of the thirty-nine countries included in the tabulation has many unique characteristics. The significance of the study lies, however, in the common factors of literacy and literate nature of the religious culture. On the other hand, attention to unique (or atypical) cases may have important research payoffs. In the tabulation, there were five such deviant cases—Jamaica, Trinidad, Malagasy, Ghana, and Nigeria all fell in the higher literacy group though their religious culture at the time of colonization could be classed as non-literate. Examination of these deviant cases reveals that three of them—Jamaica, Trinidad, and Malagasy—are island countries located on important trading routes and so exposed for a long time to literate influences associated with commerce. Thus a new factor is suggested for further investigation.

As for the impact of a prediction on events, this is quite possible. Marx predicted social revolution to redress the class inequities of the capitalist system, and certainly his writings and activities helped to bring about social revolutions in some countries, as well as to bring about measures to redress inequities and so avert revolution in others. In the one case we have a self-fulfilling prediction; in the other a self-defeating prediction.

On a less grandiose scale than Marx and world revolution, an industrial psychology experiment at Western Electric in the 1920's introduced a variety of controls for testing the relationship of worker productivity and working conditions, including better lighting, less lighting, more rest periods, fewer rest periods, shorter work days, shorter work weeks, snack breaks, and increased pay. At each stage of the experiment and for both experimental and control groups, worker productivity increased, reaching an all-time high at the final stage which involved a return to all the original conditions. The only common factor which could possibly account for the results was the fact that the workers knew the experiment was being conducted—that management was trying to do something about their conditions of work.

Impact of political polls on the outcome of elections is a recurrent topic of controversy, though mitigated in part by such spectacular errors as that of the Literary Digest poll of 1936 and of all the supposedly more "scientific" polls of 1948. Most scholarly empirical research in social and political science does not reach so large a public, but the impact of the test instrument or "laboratory" on the subject of investigation remains a problem. The whole difficulty is parallel to that of the Heisenberg uncertainty principle in quantum mechanics—that it is impossible to determine for a given instant of time both the location and the speed of a subatomic particle, because of the necessary impact of the testing apparatus on the subject of the test.

Actually, of course, society and government constantly act on the basis of predictions. The recruiting and organization of armies, the planning of industries, the development of school systems, programs of land reform, and the conduct of parliamentary assemblies are a few of the better known sociopolitical processes which involve more or less accurate forecasting that given results will flow from given conditions. The developments of nuclear weaponry and space technology were sociopolitical achievements as well as scientific achievements. If schools are provided, literacy will increase; if firearms are freely sold, more people will get shot; if government guarantees home mortgages, interest rates will be lower and so more homes will be built; if a country goes to war, taxes will go up; if speed limits in dangerous traffic areas are too high, there will be more smashups. Usually government takes action not on the basis of scientific testing of relationships but merely on the strength of plausibility. To an increasing degree, however, the specialist or technician in social science—the economist, the sociologist, the psychologist, and even the political scientist—is called on to advise and consult on public policy.

1-4 Quantification: Pro and Con

It is important that examples of research using numerical data not be taken to suggest that all worthwhile research in political science is quantitative. Quantification is only one way to study political phenomena and can easily lead us astray. A purely quantitative assessment of the military capabilities of Israel and her three hostile Arab neighbors (Egypt, Syria, and Jordan) in May 1967 would have revealed Israel to suffer a 4 to 1 disadvantage in size of armed forces, a 14 to 1 disadvantage in population, a 2 to 1 disadvantage in combat aircraft, and a 3 to 1 disadvantage in gross national product—all factors deemed significant ingredients of military strength. Such an assessment would have proved completely worthless as an indication of actual comparative military capability. The illustration furnishes a salutary reminder that qualitative judgment and substantive information about the universe we are examining are indispensable to sound reasoning about it. It is relatively easy to run computations. Moroney reminds us that it is also "an easy and fatal step to think that the accuracy of our arithmetic is equivalent to the accuracy of our knowledge about the problem in hand."[9] The great mathematical economist Oscar Morgenstern (co-author with John von Neumann of *Theory of Games and Economic Behavior*) quotes an old Latin proverb to this point: *Qui numerare incipit, errare incipit* ("When you start to count, you start to make mistakes"). There is no substitute in numbers for political wisdom and substantive comprehension of our subject.

Though quantification is only one way to study politics, it is nevertheless an important and useful way, provided always that we not become so enamored of quantitative techniques that we overlook the importance of political information outside the realm of numbers. For certain investigations, quantitative methods supply the best way to examine political problems: indeed for certain problems they are the only way. In general, we need quantitative methods when we search for (1) the typical, (2) variations from the typical, or (3) patterns of change. In order to answer the question "How typical is this case of the group to which it belongs?" we must count, average, and establish equivalences. To answer the question "What kind of case is this?" we must develop discriminations and classifications. To study causal relationship or association we must distinguish, usually by counting, different effects which occur under different conditions. To study change, we need a base point and a way to measure rate and direction of movement. Kaplan makes a useful distinction between numbers and numerals: numbers imply *measurement;* numerals assign orders of *magnitude* or degree of relationship.[10] We must quantify to use either.

The problems of legislative and congressional reapportionment, for example, can hardly be solved in terms of the Supreme Court's mandate for "one man, one vote" without considerable quantitative analysis. Other topics requiring quantification include analyses of cross-national political and socioeconomic data, studies of roll-calls and voting blocs in legislative and international bodies such as the U. S. Congress and the United Nations, investigation of electoral data on voting behavior, probing into voter motivation and other political attitudes by the methods of survey research, examination of the internal structure of significant political groups like political parties and influential pressure organizations, small group simulation studies in which real political decision-making situations are re-created in miniature for step-by-step investigation, and public policy problems which involve budgetary data, economic information on resources, and international trade.

Thus students of politics need to know something of the discipline required by quantification even if later they come to prefer other modes of analysis—historical or theoretical. Without quantitative measurements we will not be able to study very effectively such topics as those just listed. Of course, knowledge of political reality must go hand-in-hand with quantification. Some topics of the utmost importance to political scientists require especially great depth of background in history, philosophy, and law—fields which have used quantification little or not at all. With quantitative methods alone we will not be able to study very effectively such important political themes as the role of political leaders, the legal bases of government, the history of political thought, or the niceties of international diplomacy.

There is a relation between what is known about politics and how we go about knowing it. Remember Northrop's emphasis on the need for "epistemic correlations" between your empirical data and analysis. The world is full of data; the research problem is to isolate those which are relevant and typical of some relationship. The pure empiricist who insists on putting almost all emphasis on data from the "real world" is sometimes answered by a reference to the scientific study of falling bodies. Had Galileo and Newton limited their data to records of the motions of falling bodies in "nature" (over 99 per cent of which are raindrops, snowflakes, dust particles, and dry leaves), they would have found themselves confronted with an unwieldy mass of complex data, practically all irrelevant to their basic problem. Either a very strange theory of falling bodies would have emerged, or perhaps Galileo and Newton would have become meteorologists.

Political Values. Least subject to quantification among the themes usually studied by political scientists is the study of normative questions, of what is "good," "right," or otherwise evaluated by some ethical standard. Quantitative methods may treat values as data: the aspirations people hold may be identified, the intensity with which they are held may be measured, and the conditions in which they change may be explored. But quantification has no answer to the

---

9 M. J. Moroney, *Facts from Figures* (Baltimore: Penguin Books, 3rd edition, 1956), pp. 36–53.
10 Abraham Kaplan, *The Conduct of Inquiry* (San Francisco: Chandler, 1964). Chapter 21, "The Structure of Measurement," is an excellent summary of the role of quantification in behavioral research.

ultimate value question of what "ought to be." What form of government is "best"? Is human equality desirable? What are the optimum goals of the political process? In practical politics, what priorities should control the "authoritative allocation of values" (David Easton's definition of the political process)? What is the proper budgetary balance between the war in Vietnam and the war on poverty?

We cannot measure an ethical value, but we can often measure the extent to which it has been achieved or to which it is held. Take the concept of "equality," which underlies much of democratic theory. We cannot determine empirically how much equality "ought to be" but for a given factor in human society we can, given enough data, say with fair precision what degree of equality actually exists or is desired. One measure of equality is the Gini index. This index moves from a base of zero (perfect equality), and approaches 1.00 as inequality in distribution of a value increases. Used by economists to measure distribution of land, income, and other economic values, it has recently been adapted by Hayward Alker as a measure of the distribution of such political values as voter representation, degree of racial imbalance in schools, and impact of income taxation.[11] It could be further adapted to measure equality of such other political distributions as size of armed forces, burden of the military draft on various groups, communication facilities, or indeed any sociopolitical indicator for which adequate data are available. The basic concept of the Gini index is easy to grasp though its derivation requires integral calculus. We conclude this introduction by a brief description of the index in simplified form, as an example of how quantification may serve a purpose even in the study of so abstract an idea as political equality.

1-5 Derivation of a Simplified Gini Index

To find the value of the index we need a square graph grid, each axis of which is measured from zero to unity (1.00), and two curves on the graph. You may think of the measurements on the graph's axes as percentages, but in doing computations you must translate percentages into decimal fractions of 1.00—for example, 50 per cent becomes .5, 100 per cent is 1.00.

1. On our graph grid the X (horizontal) axis is used to locate the proportion of population receiving a given proportion of value—such as voting power

or income—and the Y (vertical) axis is used to locate the proportion of the value received by that proportion of people. To locate a point on the graph we use algebraic notation for the (x, y) values: the point (.2, .1) would mean that 20 per cent of the people receive 10 per cent of the value. A "curve" on the grid, showing distribution of proportions of value among proportions of people, will always begin at (0, 0)—zero people has zero value—and end at (1.00, 1.00); whatever the distribution in detail, all the people as a whole have all the value. If all given proportions of people have exactly the same proportions of value, the curve is a straight line rising at a 45° angle from (0, 0) to (1.00, 1.00). This "curve of perfect equality" is our first, or base line on the graph (see Figure 1–1).

2. Our second curve is plotted to show the actual distribution of the value. For example, if 20 per cent of the people have only 10 per cent of the income or other value, we plot this datum on the graph of Figure 1–2 at point A (.2, .1). If the lowest 40 per cent have 20 per cent of the income, this is entered as point B (.4, .2). If the lowest 60 per cent have 30 per cent of the income, this is entered as point C (.6, .3). If the lowest 80 per cent have 40 per cent of the income, this is entered as point D (.8, .4). The remaining 20 per cent of the people obviously must have the remaining 60 per cent of the income.

3. The Gini index measures the proportion which the *area of inequality* (the region between the two curves) constitutes of its maximum. If the second curve (showing actual distribution of values) is exactly the same as the first curve (showing perfect equality), the area of inequality is zero. The Gini index of course also is 0.0, since zero area is a zero proportion. Thus a Gini index of 0.0 means perfect equality in distribution of the given value: everyone has exactly the same income, or exactly the same voice in choice of legislative representatives. As the space between the second and the first curve increases, the area of inequality becomes greater and the Gini index becomes higher. A curve of perfect *inequality* (a theoretical, not an actual limit in our example) would yield an index of 1.00, as the curve of actual distribution approaches its maximum.

The maximum area of inequality is exactly one-half, or .5, of the entire unit square, since the diagonal "curve of perfect equality" cuts the grid exactly in two. To obtain the area of inequality we will find it simpler to calculate the area *below* the second line, and then subtract this quantity from .5, since we will be dealing with regular right triangles and

11 Hayward R. Alker, Jr., *Mathematics and Politics* (New York: Macmillan, 1965), pp. 36–53.

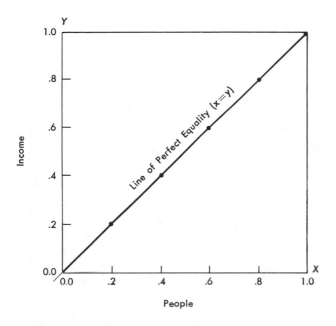

FIGURE 1-1.

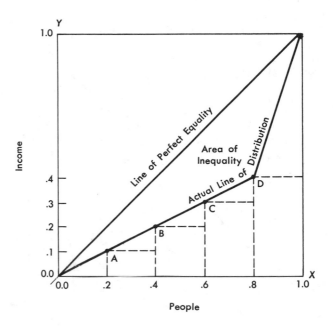

FIGURE 1-2.

rectangles (see Figure 1–2). The formula for the index may be expressed:

$$G = \text{Area of Inequality}/.5$$

or, since dividing by one-half is the same as multiplying by two:

$$G = 2 \times \text{Area of Inequality}$$

For any number N of points (past zero) entered on the graph, there will be N triangles and $N - 1$ rectangles. The computation for the distribution in Figure 1–2 is shown in detail as follows (recall your formulas from geometry: for a triangle, $A = hw/2$; for a rectangle, $A = hw$):

Area of the 5 triangles:
    (1) 4 triangles measuring .1 × .2
        $A = 4(.1 \times .2)/2 = .04$
    (2) 1 triangle measuring .6 × .2
        $A = (.6 \times .2)/2 = .06$
Area of the 4 rectangles:
    (1) 1 rectangle measuring .1 × .2 A = .02
    (2) 1 rectangle measuring .2 × .2 A = .04
    (3) 1 rectangle measuring .3 × .2 A = .06
    (4) 1 rectangle measuring .4 × .2 A = .08
Total Area =   .30
Area of Inequality = .50 − .30 =   .20
Gini Index = (Area of Inequality/.5)
        = .20/.5 = 2 × .20 = .40

What does it mean that the Gini index for this society's income distribution is .4? A possible verbal translation is that this society has moved a little more than halfway toward perfect equality insofar as distribution of the value measured on the Y-axis is concerned. One useful feature of the index is that it reflects all of the data we have available. On the other hand, the index has its limitations. The same value may result from quite different detailed distributions. For example, to show the maximum of inequality possible for our given five groups, we could assume zero income for the lower 80 per cent of the people, the upper 20 per cent receiving all the income, as in Figure 1–3. Such a situation might be true of a society in which 80 per cent of the population were slaves—approximating some of the ancient Greek "democracies." This distribution yields a Gini index of .8 (verify the computation). It is intuitively satisfying that the higher index shows more inequality— though it is impossible to convince ourselves that there is exactly *twice* the inequality in Figure 1–3 as in Figure 1–2. If in a society of 10,000, one billionaire had 80 per cent of the income, all the others sharing equally in only 20 per cent of the total, the graph would be somewhat like that of Figure 1–4, yielding a Gini index of .8002, about the same as Figure 1–3 though the character of the two societies would obviously be quite different. Confirm for yourself the value .8002 for Figure 1–4.

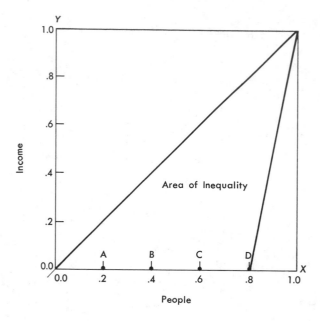

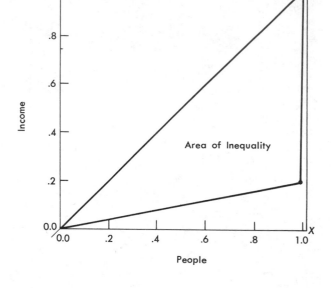

FIGURE 1-3. *Gini Index = 2(.5 − .1) = .8*

FIGURE 1-4. *Gini Index = 2(.5 − .0999) = .8002*

4. *More points.* For all the people in an actual society there would be so many points to locate on the curve of distribution that computation of the index by this hand method of measuring triangles and rectangles would become impossibly laborious. Mathematical economists use integration formulas, each representing an approximate pattern of inequality shown by the available data. A graph with ten points is shown in Figure 1–5, in which we consider votes in the United Nations General Assembly to be "values" and population of the member states to be "people." Calculation of the Gini index is shown below the graph (points being located for each 10 per cent of the 120 votes, the total membership at the time these data were compiled).

Figure 1–5 brings out two additional features of the graph which are often useful. First, by plotting a point for a given percentage of the value which has substantive significance (a majority, or a two-thirds majority when those are significant voting shares), one can see at a glance the percentage of the people who control such shares or who may block action requiring such shares. Second, the point on the plotted actual curve at which the line begins to rise more steeply than 45° (when width of a triangle becomes less than its height), is the point of division between those receiving more than an equal share and those receiving less than an equal share.

Of what use in political analysis is the Gini index? Like other quantitative measures it has both advantages and limitations. Figure 1–5 certainly does not mean that there is any basic assumption that UN voting *should* be proportionate to population; it merely shows precisely how far from proportionate it actually is. It is true that so high a Gini index (over .70) is extremely rare, perhaps suggesting a reason why some UN decisions are far from reality.

Use of this measuring device has been unusual in political research, although since Alker has called it to the attention of political scientists, we will probably see it more frequently in the future. It offers excellent possibilities for making meaningful comparisons of cross-national data—index values for world literacy, access to communications, political participation, and the like, both for individual political systems and for given groups of political systems. It could be used for cross-factor comparisons—equality of distribution of consumer goods as compared with equality of distribution of voting participation. It permits comparison of a given factor across time (balance or disparity of military forces in 1950 compared with 1967). Finally it affords a means for making hypothetical comparisons of the probable results of alternative policy decisions (Alker has shown this application for alternative plans of school integration and income tax changes).

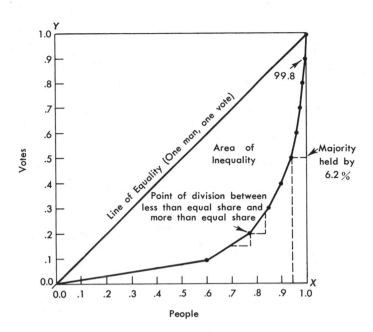

FIGURE 1-5. *Graph for Gini Index of UN Voting*

Computation of Gini Index for UN Voting

This per cent of the people	Have this per cent of the votes	Area of Triangles			Area of Rectangles		
		h	w	A	h	w	A
61.7	10	.1	.617	.03085	—	—	—
77.2	20	.1	.155	.00775	.1	.155	.0155
85.1	30	.1	.079	.00395	.2	.079	.0158
90.1	40	.1	.05	.0025	.3	.05	.015
93.8	50	.1	.037	.00185	.4	.037	.0148
96.2	60	.1	.024	.0012	.5	.024	.012
97.8	70	.1	.016	.0008	.6	.016	.0096
99.0	80	.1	.012	.0006	.7	.012	.0084
99.8	90	.1	.008	.0004	.8	.008	.0064
100.0	100	.1	.002	.0001	.9	.002	.0018
Totals				.05000			.0993

Total Area = .0500 + .0993 = .1493
Area of Inequality = .5 − .1493 = .3507
Gini Index = .3507/.5 = 2 × .3507 = .7014

Consideration of such possibilities for use of the Gini index reminds us again that it is important to have some kind of grounding in theory before applying a quantitative technique—the choice of a technique is partly determined by the substantive theory. In other words, it is important that you know not only *how* to use a technique, but also *when* it is appropriate to the problem at hand.

If you have followed this exposition carefully, you should now be prepared for the exercises which follow this chapter. Frankly, we have included the account of this one quantitative technique in what perhaps should have been a completely general introductory discussion because we felt it desirable to put you in a quantitative frame of mind as part of your preparation for a quantitative workbook. Despite the quite proper emphasis we have given to the limits of quantitative methods, it is these methods which this book is all about. We turn now to Exercise Set 1, and get to work.

1–1. Explain briefly the following terms. Use as sources the discussion in this chapter, a good dictionary, and any other readings assigned or available.

data	deduction
nature	induction
index	proposition
indicator	hypothesis
conceptual framework	relevant data
relationship	variable
theory	cross-tabulation
epistemology	hard sciences
phenomenon	cultural fallacy
phenomenology	uncertainty principle
empiricism	*qui numerare incipit, errare incipit*
logical realism	simulation
epistemic correlations	political values
behavioralism	norms
scientific method	Gini index

1–2. Define in a short paragraph:
political science
political behavior

1–3. Comment on the uses and limits of quantitative methods in political research. Use illustrations of your own for both uses and limits.

1–4. Revise the Gini index of Figure 1–5 by breaking down the first group into two: (1) India, with 20 per cent of the population, and (2) the states holding the other 11 votes in this first group, with 41.7 per cent of the population. *Note.* Coordinates for India are (.2, .008), since one vote is approximately 0.8 per cent of the total of 120 votes. The revision requires that we plot this point between (0, 0) and the first plotted point of Figure 1–5.

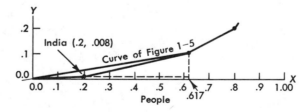

As a result of the additional point, the first triangle listed in the computation table below Figure 1–5 will become two triangles and one (very small) rectangle. The first line of the computation table will become two lines:

This per cent of the people	Have this per cent of the votes	Area of Triangles			Area of Rectangles		
		h	w	A	h	w	A
20.0	0.8	.008	.2	.0008	—	—	—
41.7	9.2	.092	.417	.0192	.008	.417	.0033

The sum of these three areas is substituted for the area of the first triangle in the computation table. All the other areas remain unchanged. You now complete the revision in the following steps:

(1) Total Area computed in Figure 1–5:   .14930
(2) Less Area of first triangle: −.03085
                                       .11845
(3) Plus sum of three substituted areas: _____
(4) New Total Area   _____
(5) New Area of Inequality = .5 − New Total Area = _____
(6) New Gini Index = 2 × New Area of Inequality = _____
Your work should confirm that the new index is .7165

1–5. Daily newspaper circulation in the four large states of Western Europe totals about 60 million, divided as shown in the table below. Compute the Gini index for distribution of newspapers among the peoples of these four countries. Since the countries are nearly equal in population, we plot them on the X (horizontal) axis at equal intervals of .25.

Daily Newspaper Circulation in Four Western European States

State	Circulation in millions	Per Cent of Total	Cumulative Per Cent
Italy	4.8	8	8
France	12.0	20	28
Germany	16.8	28	56
Britain	26.4	44	100
Total	60.0	100	

Source: *Britannica Book of the Year, 1967;* p. 460.

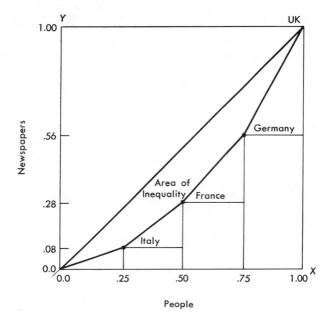

Computation of Gini Index

	This per cent of states	Have this per cent of newspapers	Area of Triangles			Area of Rectangles		
			h	w	A = hw/2	h	w	A = hw
	25	8	.08	.25	.01	—	—	—
	50	28	.2	.25	.025	.08	.25	.02
	75	56	.28	.25	.035	.28	.25	.07
	100	100	.44	.25	.055	.56	.25	.14
Totals			1.00		.125			.23

Total Area = .125 + .23 = _____
Area of Inequality = .5 − _____ = _____
Gini Index = 2 × _____ = _____

Your work should confirm that the Gini index is .29.

1–6. Data of the Institute of Strategic Studies show that in 1966 there were exactly ten states with armed forces of more than 400,000 men. Ignoring populations, and using the X (horizontal) axis to show simply proportions of this universe of ten states, we will plot them at equal intervals of .1. The Y (vertical) axis will be used to plot proportions of the total forces of this group.

Ten Largest Military Forces in 1966

State	Forces in Thousands	Per Cent of the Ten Forces	Cumulative Per Cent
United Kingdom	437	3.5	3.5
West Germany	440	3.5	7.0
Turkey	450	3.6	10.6
France	535	4.2	14.8
China (Formosa)	544	4.3	19.1
South Korea	561	4.5	23.6
India	879	7.0	30.6
China (Mainland)	2486	19.7	50.3
United States	3093	24.6	74.9
USSR	3165	25.1	100.0
Total	12590	100.0	

Source: *The Military Balance 1966/1967* (London: Institute of Strategic Studies, 1966).

Sketch the actual line of distribution of forces among these ten states on the graph and compute the Gini Index, using the worksheet provided but only partly filled in. A comparison of this computation with that of Exercises 1–4 and 1–5 shows two things about the area of the triangles: (1) the more intervals we plot, the smaller the sum of the triangle areas, and (2) if *equal* intervals are used on either axis, the sum of the triangle areas (expressed as a decimal fraction of the unit square) is exactly equal to half the value of one interval expressed as a decimal fraction of its unit axis. For a very large number of intervals, the sum of the triangle areas approaches zero as a limit, and the curve becomes "smooth." It is this feature of the graph which permits the use of integral calculus for standard patterns of distribution.

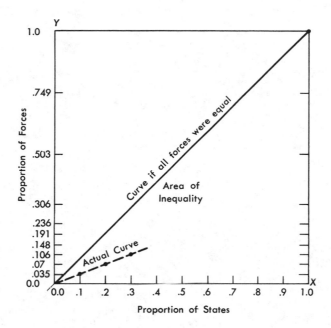

WORKSHEET FOR COMPUTATION OF GINI INDEX

This per cent of states	Have this per cent of forces	Area of Triangles			Area of Rectangles		
		h	w	A	h	w	A
10	3.5	.035	.1	.00175	—	—	—
20	7.0	.035	.1	.00175	.035	.1	.0035
30	10.6	.036	.1	.00180	.070	.1	.0070
40							
50							
60							
70							
80							
90							
100							
Totals							

Total Area = _____ + _____ = _____
Area of Inequality = .5 − _____ = _____
Gini Index = 2 × (Area of Inequality) = 2 × _____ = _____

Reading List

The capsule bibliographies which appear at the end of each chapter are planned to guide your further reading. Except for a few items noted as difficult, the books listed do not require special background either in quantitative methods or in political science.

1. *Books about Political Science*

Charlesworth, James C., ed., *Contemporary Political Analysis*. New York: Free Press, 1967.*

_____, *A Design for Political Science: Scope, Objectives, and Methods*. Philadelphia: American Academy of Political and Social Science, 1966.*

_____, *The Limits of Behavioralism in Political Science*. Philadelphia: American Academy of Political and Social Science, 1962.*

Crick, Bernard, *The American Science of Politics*. Berkeley: University of California Press, 1959.

Dahl, Robert A., *Modern Political Analysis*. Englewood Cliffs, N.J.: Prentice-Hall, Inc., 1963.

_____, and Deane E. Neubauer, eds., *Readings in Modern Political Analysis*. Englewood Cliffs, N.J.: Prentice-Hall, Inc., 1968.*

Easton, David, *The Political System*. New York: Alfred A. Knopf, 1953.

Eulau, Heinz, *The Behavioral Persuasion in Politics*. New York: Random House, 1963.*

Hyneman, Charles S., *The Study of Politics*. Urbana: University of Illinois Press, 1959.

Lasswell, Harold, *The Future of Political Science*. New York: Atherton Press, 1964.

Somit, Albert, and Joseph Tanenhaus, *American Political Science*. New York: Atherton Press, 1964.

_____, *The Development of Political Science: From Burgess to Behavioralism*. Boston: Allyn and Bacon, 1967.

Storing, Herbert, ed., *Essays on the Scientific Study of Politics*. New York: Holt, Rinehart and Winston, 1962.

Van Dyke, Vernon, *Political Science: A Philosophical Analysis*. Stanford: Stanford University Press, 1960.

2. *Books about the Use of Data*

Alker, Hayward R., Jr., *Mathematics and Politics*. New York: The Macmillan Company, 1965.*

Hawkins, David, *An Essay in the Philosophy of Science*. San Francisco: Freeman, 1964.

Kaplan, Abraham, *The Conduct of Inquiry: Methodology for Behavioral Science*. San Francisco: Chandler, 1964.

Ross, Ralph, *Symbols and Civilization*. New York: Harcourt, Brace, and World, 1962.*

---

* Paperback edition available.

HOW TO READ A TABLE

The Variety of Variables

Quantitative methods should be kept in balance with other approaches, but there is still no skill more needed and more often lacking in modern political science research than the ability to handle numbers. The political conditions, relationships, and problems of man-in-society are increasingly expressed in quantitative language—numbers, percentages, indexes, ratios, and proportions. Public and private data sources constantly pour out great volumes of statistical information. The published scholarly research of political scientists shows a steeply rising trend toward increased reliance on tabular displays to supply empirical reinforcement for verbal analysis of political reality (Table 2–1).

These lessons will not make you an expert in statistics, data processing, or survey research, but they should increase your competence to cope with the published product of research done with those useful tools, and your confidence that you understand what a tabular array actually says (as well as what it does not say). We begin with a brief look at mechanical format.

2-1 What a Table is For :
Look for the Key Relationship

In studying a table you should always keep in mind that it was prepared for a purpose—to convey not merely a set of numbers but substantive information about a process or a relationship. Everything presented in a table can be expressed (though at much greater length) by verbal discussion and analysis.

Even the simplest table represents a considerable amount of work—counting, arranging, often cross-tabulation of items and computation of an index—intended to give the reader as much information as possible in compact form. Examine for a moment the data reported in Table 2–1. Try to extract as much meaning from it as you can, and to put some of this meaning into words. Do not simply stare at the numbers; ask yourself such questions as "Why was

the table prepared?", "What is the author's reason for including it at this point in his text?", "What actual units do the numbers represent?", "What is the most obvious relationship disclosed by the numbers?"

TABLE 2-1. *Number of Tabular and Graphic Displays in the* American Political Science Review, *by Annual Volumes for Selected Years*

Year	Number	Index[a]
1908–1915	0[b]	0.0
1916	1	3.8
1917	15	57.7
1922	11	42.3
1925	28	107.7
1928[c]	26	100.0
1938	27	103.8
1948	26	100.0
1958	52	200.0
1966	204	784.6

[a] Base: 1928 = 100.0.
[b] Volume 1 (1908) contained a brief rate table from an administrative regulation.
[c] Base year chosen as midpoint.
Source: Original tabulation.

Some things are clear at once. Considering the questions just listed, you find the answer to the first one in the title: the table was prepared to show the use of tabular and graphic material in the *American Political Science Review* (the table does not tell you, but you either know or can readily assume that this is the official journal of the professional association of political scientists in the United States). The author included it here in support of his statement in the first paragraph that published work by political scientists increasingly makes use of such material. The entries in the second column represent the actual number of tables used in the year indicated; entries in the third column seem to represent some kind of computed index—examination of footnotes a and c discloses that the index is actually a percentage of 26, the number of tables used in the *Review* during the year 1928. Apparently the author chose 1928 because it was nearest to the halfway mark of the time period covered (actually 1927 is the median year, but perhaps he lacked the data for 1927—there seems to be no orderly plan behind his choice of years). The most obvious relationship is found, as is true in many tables, by looking for the greatest range of variability. In this "unidimensional" table, the greatest variability is easy to find: the *Review*'s use of tables ranged from zero during its first eight years to 204 in 1966.

Subsidiary relationships are found by closer examination. We suggest six guides to a preliminary systematic analysis:

(1) *The greatest range of variation*—here the values range from zero to 204.

(2) *The overall consistency of the pattern*—here the trend is steadily upward, though with an apparent plateau (with a few ups and downs) for about a quarter of a century from the mid-1920's to the late 1940's.

(3) *Intermediate ranges of variability*—the plateau just mentioned is one of these, as are the first appearance of a table in 1916, the noticeable increase in 1917 (could this be related to other developments, such as World War I?), and the substantial rise in 1958.

(4) *Inconsistencies and abnormalities*—the spectacular increase of 1966 strikes us at once.

(5) *Omissions*—several omissions are rather glaring. Data are shown for only seventeen of fifty-nine annual volumes, and we are not told why these were selected. There is no indication of how many articles or pages each volume contained; assuming the *Review* grew substantially in size, as have most scholarly journals, perhaps the larger numbers do not represent quite so high a relative increase as the index suggests. A table comparing "quantitative" articles and "non-quantitative" articles might be interesting. We would like to know more about that first table in 1916. The enormous jump from 1958 to 1966 shows too big a gap for the general trend; there should be a more detailed look at other years in this significant period.

Sometimes omissions may be included or explained in the accompanying text, but you (or the reader of your own tables) should not need to look there. The table should be self-contained as a display of information.

(6) Finally, *reliability of the figures*—the author is his own source; you would want to do the count yourself before depending on the data in your own work.

2-2 Anatomy of a Table

Our work will go more smoothly if we become familiar with some of the technical terms used for the component parts of a table. These include the items in the accompanying editorial apparatus as well as the main elements in the box. The list below refers to Table 2–2, which contains more of these features than does Table 2–1.

Editorial Apparatus. We use this term for all the descriptive information essential to understanding the table but which appears outside the main body, or *box,* of the table.

(1) *Table number.* Styles vary widely, the only indispensable requirement being unique identification of each table in a given publication, either by number alone or together with chapter number. The style "2–2" used here (some prefer 2.2) is convenient, meaning the second table in chapter two. Consecutive numbering in Arabic numerals (often still in the older style Roman numerals) is most common—the 1966 *Statistical Abstract of the United States,* published by the Bureau of the Census, proceeds logically from No. 1 to No. 1312 through its 33 major sections. An interesting variation by Wallis and Roberts in their volume *Statistics: A New Approach* is to assign each table the number of the page on which it appears in the book, a convenient reference device for a work containing many tables frequently mentioned in text. If two or more tables appear on the same page, they are identified by the page number followed by A, B, C . . . (e.g., Table 303A, Table 303B, Table 303C). More commonly the use of letters following a table number identifies a close association of the material—separate parts of the same basic display, or the same data in a different form—expanded, collapsed, reduced to percentages, computed into an index, summarized for a statistical test, or with rows and columns reversed. Letters alone should be reserved for graphs and drawings (Figure A, B, C . . .) and even for graphs the trend is to use numbers instead of letters.

(2) *Title.* The reader should be able to understand the title without referring to the accompanying text. The table should be a self-contained unit for con-

TABLE 2-2. *Civilian Population of Voting Age—Participation in National Election, by Region: 1964*

(As of November 1. Covers non-institutional population 18 years old and over in Georgia and Kentucky, 19 and over in Alaska, 20 and over in Hawaii, and 21 and over elsewhere. Includes aliens. Based on sample; see Source, p. 1)

Participation	Region									
	Northeast[a]		North Central[b]		South[c]		West[d]		Total US	
	1000's	Per cent	1000's	Per cent	1000's	Per cent	1000's	Per cent	1000's	Per cent
Voted	21,677	74.4	23,735	76.2	18,389	56.7	12,871	71.9	76,671	69.3
Did Not Vote	7,184	24.7	7,132	22.9	13,755	42.4	4,869	27.2	32,939	29.8
Not Reported	265	0.9	273	0.9	286	0.9	170	0.9	994	0.9
Total	29,125[e]	100.0	31,139	100.0	32,429	100.0	17,910	100.0	110,604	100.0

[a] New England and Middle Atlantic Census Districts.
[b] East North Central and West North Central Census Districts.
[c] South Atlantic, East South Central, and West South Central Census Districts.
[d] Mountain and Pacific Census Districts (Pacific District includes Alaska and Hawaii).
[e] Because of rounding, entries do not always sum to totals.
Source: Adapted from U.S. Bureau of the Census, *Statistical Abstract of the United States* (Washington: Government Printing Office, 1966. 87th Edition), Table No. 530. CIVILIAN POPULATION OF VOTING AGE—PARTICIPATION IN NATIONAL ELECTION, BY SELECTED CHARACTERISITICS: 1964, p. 382. Original source cited: Bureau of the Census, *Current Population Reports*, Series P-20, No. 143.

veying information, and the title is the most important key to the contents. Subjects, time, and place are included (or if omitted, only with good reason, such as previous use in a series of related tables). For analytical tables, of the sort represented by most of the tables in this book, we like the style of wording the title so that the dependent variable is mentioned first, followed by the independent or causal variable (see the discussion in Section 2–4 below and in Chapters 9 and 10 for an explanation of these terms). If more than one causal variable is involved, a good style for uniformity is to list them in the *reverse* order of their appearance in the table itself, perhaps including the phrase "controlled for" if suitable. Thus:

TABLE 1. PARTY PREFERENCE BY SEX AND INCOME

(or) TABLE 1. PARTY PREFERENCE BY SEX, CONTROLLED FOR INCOME

(or for four variables)

TABLE 1. PARTY PREFERENCE BY SEX, INCOME, AND REGION

(or) TABLE 1. PARTY PREFERENCE BY SEX, CONTROLLED FOR INCOME AND REGION

(3) *Headnote.* This appears immediately under the title, and contains information essential to understanding the data presented in the table or in further explanation of the title. In Table 2–2 the title uses the term "civilian population of voting age," which the headnote carefully defines to mean (a) persons of the voting age variously fixed by law in the fifty states, (b) as estimated by a sampling technique described elsewhere in the book, (c) to have been living on November 1, 1964, and (d) including aliens. The headnote may be used to identify the units used in the table (1000's, $1,000 US, per cent, million kwh), details regarding a survey sample, the method of constructing a scale whose values appear in the table, or indeed any relevant information.

(4) *Footnotes.* Use of lower-case letters (a, b, c . . .) is now usual in footnoting tables, unless a very large number of footnotes is necessary (the U.S. Census and the Statistical Office of the United Nations often exceed the limit of 26 footnotes for which letters are adequate, and use instead the same small numerical superscripts as for regular text: 91 notes appear after Table 1300 [LABOR FORCE, ENERGY, MANUFACTURING, IMPORTS, AND EXPORTS] in the *Statistical Abstract* for 1966). Special symbols (NA = not available or not ascertained) should appear above the sequential list of notes, whether these be numerical or alphabetical. In your own work, the lower-case alphabet should be adequate, and is preferred because it is the simplest way to distinguish the footnote apparatus from the numbers in the tabulated data and from other numbered footnotes in the accompanying text. For a study in which all tables will have very few footnotes, the old style of asterisk-dagger-double dagger-double S . . . (*, †, ‡, §,) is still occasionally seen.

Footnotes appear immediately under the table, *not* within the box nor at the bottom of the page unless the table has the entire page to itself. They explain exceptions and any omissions, idiosyncracies, or special features of individual items in the table as well as insufficiently explicit words or phrases in the title or captions.

(5) *Source.* Unless the data are original, the source should always be shown, and listed immediately after the footnotes. In fact, the "Source" entry is also employed to show that the data or computations are the author's, unless this is obvious from the article or report in which the table appears (as in a student survey report). You can use the source entry to check on the data, to seek out additional related data, and to decide for yourself how much reliability to place in the information reported. Table 2-2, for example, comes to you third-hand; it is adapted in this book from the *Statistical Abstract,* which in turn cites it from an original Census Bureau publication. You should exercise due caution in using it in your own work; if you use it without checking the original source, the only safe rule is to state in your own "Source" entry the details of this roundabout way you obtained it.

Elements in the Box. These include all parts of the table proper—those elements enclosed by the ruled lines at the top and bottom.

(1) *Boxhead.* All descriptive information about the actual data in the columns of the table is contained in the boxhead at the top. The boxhead is usually ruled into compartments, the most general categories appearing on the first row and subordinate categories on the row or rows just below. The boxhead of Table 2-2 contains seventeen compartments.

(2) *Column Captions.* Each separate column of the table should be clearly explained by its column caption. Clarity is often difficult because of the limited space available, so considerable latitude is permissible in using devices to compress this crucial information: abbreviations, footnotes, or prior explanation in the title and headnote. In Table 2-2, the first caption, "Participation," is unclear when taken alone, but the reader has already seen the fuller description in the title; the overall caption above the data, "Region," is not really necessary, considering the footnoted detail defining the regions themselves; the third row of captions consists of terms defining the units, and could have been avoided by headnote description and use of the "%" symbol. Terms defining units are sometimes entered just below the boxhead at the top of each column, often in parentheses or small type.

(3) *The Stub,* or lefthand column, contains the list of categories in which data are presented in the *rows* of the table (compare its location with that of the stubs in a checkbook).

(4) *Row Captions.* Labels for row categories contained in the stub are usually called "row captions." As for the columns, each row should have a clear identification. Both row and column captions are essentially *verbal*—where numbers are used (for years, income brackets, or categories of other quantitative measures of weight, distance, or volume), they nevertheless have semantic rather than numerical value.

At the intersection of the stub and boxhead is the compartment in the upper left corner, which contains a general term descriptive of the list of row captions in the column below it. This cell is sometimes empty if the row categories are obvious, or it may contain a footnote reference if a general term for the row categories is so awkward and lengthy as to require more space than is available.

The cell is sometimes split by a diagonal line to allow *two* general terms, describing both row and column captions—as in a statistical table displaying probabilities in the columns and "degrees of freedom" in the rows:

(5) *Totals.* Column totals are entered at the foot and row totals in the righthand column (or more rarely in the first column to the right of the stub if there is a special interest in them). When the basic data of the table are translated into an index, as in Table 2-1, or percentages, as in Table 2-2, more than one column may be needed for the row totals. Often the row totals, the column totals, or both, are omitted; the table may present incomplete data (as does Table 2-1) so that a total is meaningless, or the special purpose of the table may focus on only one set of totals.

When both row and column totals are shown as sums, each set can be thought of as a separate unidimensional table, related to but less detailed than the full table. From Table 2-2, for example, we can extract the two short displays of Table 2-3 and Table 2-4. These are called *marginal frequency distributions,* or more briefly, *marginals,* since the entries come from the totals in the right hand and bottom "margins" of the source table. We will find

TABLE 2-3. *Civilian Population of Voting Age by Region: 1964*

Region	Number in 1000's
Northeast	29,125
North Central	31,139
South	32,429
West	17,910
Total US	110,604

Source: Table 2-2.

TABLE 2-4. *Civilian Population of Voting Age— Participation in National Election: 1964*

Participation	Number in 1000's
Voted	76,671
Did Not Vote	32,939
Not Reported	994
Total	110,604

Source: Table 2-2.

valuable use for marginals in a later topic dealing with statistical tests. Notice that each set of marginals adds to the same grand total (they *crossfoot*), which is entered at the foot of the column containing the row totals. This value, when compared to the separate marginal frequencies in the two sets of marginals, is also of crucial importance in statistical tests.

(6) *Rules,* or rulings (a printer's term), are the ruled lines used to mark off the table itself from the accompanying text and editorial apparatus, as well as to mark off the compartments within the table. A double or a single heavy horizontal rule is used at the top. Single light horizontal rules appear (a) *below the boxhead,* separating the explanatory captions from the tabulated entries; (b) *within the boxhead,* to distinguish multiple orders of captions; (c) *above the column totals;* and (d) *at the bottom of the table.* Vertical rules are used (a) *to set off the stub* (this one runs the entire height of the table); (b) *to separate columns* of data (these run from the boxhead to the bottom of the table); and (c) to separate compartments within the boxhead where needed. Notice that no vertical rule is used at the sides of the table—the last column on each side is left open to the margin. For convenience or clarity either in very simple or very complex tables, some or all rules are often omitted—especially the vertical rules, which present special problems for both typist and printer.

2-3 Problems of Percentages: Which Way Do They Add Up?

Percentages are a useful shorthand for comparing several sets of disparate figures by reference to the common base of 100. The relationships in Table 2–2 would not be nearly so clear without the percentage columns; for example, it is not immediately obvious whether the voter turnout ratio in the Northeast (21,677/29,125) is greater or less than in the West (12,871/17,910). The percentages 74.4 and 71.9, representing the same ratios, tell us at a glance which of the two regions had the higher relative turnout. (Without doing the complete computation, you should satisfy yourself that 74.4 per cent is indeed the same value as 21,677/29,125.) Percentages further permit comparisons over time (increases or decreases) either for one set of figures—voter turnout in successive elections—or among several sets of figures—each party's share of the total vote in successive elections.

Quite commonly the data in a table are shown more concisely by omitting the actual numbers and substituting percentages for most of the entries. For analytical tables use of both numbers and percentages clutters the display unnecessarily and interferes with the reader's comprehension. If only percentages are included, the table can be read more quickly and comparisons between pairs of items made more easily. The practice is almost universal in tables reporting results of survey research, since the primary purpose of such tables is to facilitate examination of the relationships among various attributes of a sample population, rather than to report gross census findings or "macrodata." Such a percentage table should always include the actual numerical totals (or *N*'s) to which the percentages refer, as in Table 2–5. Without the total *N*'s the reader cannot judge the dimensions of the material involved; with the *N*'s available as totals he can derive any specific figure which interests him. Moreover, statistical significance in general depends on the size of the sample so that most statistical tests can be performed only with the actual "frequencies"—the numbers which the percentages represent.

Related to the same problem of retrieving frequencies from a percentage table is the question of how many decimal places should be used. While ordinarily in political science research whole numbers are sufficient for the degree of accuracy we can hope to achieve, the answer depends on the material involved. Certainly for gross differences a percentage

TABLE 2-5. *Civilian Population of Voting Age— Percentage Participating in National Election, by Region: 1964*

(Based on sample of non-institutional population; "voting age" is defined in Table 2-2. "Not reported" group omitted)

Participation	Northeast	North Central	South	West	Total US
Voted	75	77	57	72	70
Did Not Vote	25	23	43	28	30
N (1000's)	29,125	31,139	32,429	17,910	110,604

Source: Table 2-2.

without decimal places is adequate; in certain circumstances— say, the Kennedy-Nixon election—one or even two additional digits may be useful. A cautious rule for survey samples is to retain enough places to permit certain retrieval of frequencies by multiplying the percentage entry by the N. For example, if your total N is six or sixty, the entry 67 per cent must mean 4 or 40. But for a survey of 600 respondents, 67 per cent means 402. The entry 66.7 per cent is needed to obtain 400. If the percentage entry contains as many digits as does the N, no error will arise, though for very large samples such as those of the Census Bureau, it would be pointless to follow the complete logic of this rule.

Reading Percentages. Several safeguards are necessary in the arrangement and interpretation of a percentage table. If these are not observed, it is quite easy to make serious mistakes and to draw invalid conclusions.

(1) *Direction of Computations.* In almost all tables the percentages are computed only in one direction: by columns or rows. Either the percentages in each column add to 100 per cent, or the percentages in each row add to 100 per cent. The first imperative rule in reading a percentage table is to make certain you realize clearly which direction the compiler has selected. If the "N's" are given for only one direction as in Table 2-5, this is presumed to be the direction of computation. It is good practice to enter the actual figure "100" or "100%" at the foot of the column or the end of the row, but many tables omit it, as does Table 2-5, so that you must do at least a cursory mental addition to make sure. For a simple table with few categories, this is an easy task, but it is progressively more difficult for tables with larger numbers of categories. In your own tables you should

always enter the 100's. Another source of confusion on this point is that to save space many tables omit one set of percentages in a dichotomous distribution. The same information would be supplied in Table 2–5, for example, if either the "Voted" row or the "Did Not Vote" row were omitted, since the assumption would be that all those reported in the table fell into one group or the other.

(2) *Reason for Choice of Direction.* The usual rule for choice of direction for computation of percentages is to run them in the direction of the "explanatory" factor, or (as we shall see) the "independent variable." The reason for computing percentages is to provide a basis for comparisons among categories of the more important factor under examination. In Table 2–5 the compiler centers our attention on the factor of voter turnout, so the percentages are computed to permit comparison of proportions of voters and non-voters. We are not primarily interested in the distribution of population among the four regions: that information is available from more accurate census sources than the sample on which this table is based. We are interested in the regions because the regional cross-tabulation of voters and non-voters may furnish a more detailed explanation of the turnout factor (the original source table also presented comparisons by sex, color, age, urban-rural residence, education, employment status, and family income).

When we use the word "explanatory" or "causal" for the factor whose categories each add to 100 per cent, we do not presume that this factor literally "explains" or "causes" the variation in the factor under study. Usually we mean merely that the factor is so arranged in the table as to afford a tentative or partial aid in a more extended examination of the basic problem (in this case, voter turnout). The convenience of such phrases as "explanatory factor" and "causal variable" as terms to make this technical distinction between the two cross-tabulated factors often results in their use in verbal discussion of tables and surveys, and it is not always clear to the reader that they have this limited meaning. There is an air of dogmatism about them, sometimes irritating to a reader who does not think of them as simply technically convenient labels. For this reason you should exercise caution in using such terms in a written account of a quantitative project of any kind.

(3) *Verbal Statements about Percentages.* It is by no means desirable to translate every item in a table into words—the very purpose of a table is to summarize information. Ordinarily you will choose for

verbal discussion only the data most important to the theme you are developing. In making verbal statements about such selected data, however, care must be taken not to misread your own figures. Three basic types of statements may be made about data in a percentage table. For complex tables, quite complicated patterns of verbal translation are possible, but they all reduce to the three basic patterns.

1. *Statements about individual entries.* With reference to Table 2–5, we can say: "For the Northeast, 75 per cent of the civilian population of voting age actually voted in the national election of 1964." Similarly: "Twenty-five per cent of those of voting age in the Northeast did not vote in 1964." For Table 2–5 we can make ten of these valid if rather unremarkable statements. By combining them in compound sentences we may imply comparisons without making the comparisons explicit: "Thirty per cent of the total civilian population of voting age in the United States did not vote in 1964, whereas in the South 43 per cent did not vote."

2. *Comparisons within columns.* For Table 2–5 we can say: "Seven out of ten persons of voting age in the United States voted in 1964"; "In the Northeast, voters outnumbered non-voters by a ratio of three to one"; and "Southerners of voting age are divided relatively equally between voters and non-voters; the ratio is closer than 6 to 4." Such comparative statements may also be combined into compound sentences, implying without explicitly making comparisons across columns.

3. *Comparisons across columns.* These must be made with care, since we are dealing with percentages which refer to different numerical totals. For a simple table, two rules will help keep us safe: first, *word the statement in terms of percentages or ratios, not numbers;* and second, *word the statement in terms of the columnar captions* (assuming the columns add to 100 per cent). Thus: "Those of voting age in the Northeast, North Central and Western census regions voted in 1964 in proportions which exceeded the national average"; "In the South the proportion of non-voters was highest of the four major census regions."

Invalid Comparisons. Violation of the two rules just given will lead to trouble. For example, we cannot say "There were more voters in the West than in the South." Even though 72 per cent voted in the West and only 57 per cent voted in the South, the different numerical totals to which these percentages refer make the statement invalid. Actually, Southern voters

outnumbered Western voters by a ratio of 3 to 2, as shown in Table 2–2. The point seems almost too obvious to need emphasis in this example, but notice that it is *equally invalid* to say that "There were fewer non-voters in the West than in the South," *if we rely only on the percentage table.* The latter statement is in fact true, but can be established only by recomputing the data. Moreover, even though true, it has no inherent significance, since there are almost twice as many Southerners as Westerners of voting age. Always remember that *percentages are not numbers, and we cannot compare percentages based on different numerical totals.* The statement that "There were fewer non-voters in the West than in the South" is just as meaningless as the observation that "There were fewer voters in the South than in the United States," a truism so obvious that no one would say it, but which illustrates the common error of comparing percentages which refer to different numbers.

2-4 Variables and Variation

Research in political behavior is concerned with the examination and, if possible, the explanation of variation in political phenomena. At the descriptive level, we may be interested in measuring merely *how much* variation there is, for example, between the number of voters and non-voters or between Democratic and Republican votes in a given election. At the explanatory level, however, we seek some causal relationship between turnout or vote choice and other factors. A tabular display of the results of a political survey is meant to show some key relationship between two or more sets of categories. The first step in examination of a table should be the determination of just what key relationship is being examined.

Kinds of Variation. In the arrangement of data in a table, your first problem is the selection of significant characteristics into which your results are to be sorted out. Such characteristics are usually called "variables." A variable is any attribute, property, opinion, behavior pattern, or grouping, which may be used to describe or locate an individual or other entity of political interest on some kind of scale, or in some kind of classification. In reading a table, you should be familiar with the following concepts about variables:

1. Measurement of a variable may be on a *continuous* or *discontinuous* (discrete) scale. Age,

weight, and height are examples of naturally continuous characteristics—that is, there is an infinite number of points on the measurement scale, though for convenience we usually establish artificial discrete points for reporting such data (years, pounds or kilograms, inches and feet or meters, etc.). Income, vote returns, size of farms, newspaper circulation are examples of discontinuous variables.

2. A variable may be *ordered* or *unordered*. That is, a characteristic in which we are interested may have a rank-ordering, such as military rank, or an ordering which is unranked, such as state or country of birth. Some unordered variables, such as occupation, may be classified into rank-ordered sets (as by status, average income, white-collar or blue-collar, etc.). State or county of birth might be rank-ordered into such categories as average income, percentage of farm-ownership, percentage of Democratic voting, level of industrialization, voting turnout, or attitudes toward racial integration. The terms *ordinal* and *nominal* are sometimes used for ordered and unordered variables.

3. Use of *dichotomous* variables is frequent in political and social research. Some variables are naturally dichotomous (sex: male, female; military rank: officers, enlisted personnel; voters and non-voters; students and non-students; in a pure two-party electorate: Democrats and Republicans). Categories of other variables are sometimes *collapsed* into a dichotomous division for convenience in study: income categories may be divided into two—above or below average; age categories may be divided at 21 years, or voting age, or 65 (retirement age), or some other point meaningful to the study. When data are presented in a collapsed dichotomy, another researcher may be interested in *expanding* the dichotomous breakdown for closer examination, so the original data should be kept available. A collapsed dichotomy loses information which may turn out to be crucial. If we classify vote intention for two candidates, it may turn out that a third category—Undecided—is the most important in the actual election. In other words, you should never dichotomize merely for convenience in sorting data. Relevance to your problem should govern a decision to dichotomize; for that matter relevance is the proper key to all handling and presentation of variables. Dichotomization is least appropriate for a scale of intensity of attitude. If we want to use mean scores or scales, then five categories of intensity are often most desirable (Strong Support, Moderate Support,

Indifference, Moderate Opposition, Strong Opposition), though constructing a five-class scale (especially deciding on the middle category) can be difficult.

4. Variables may be *subjective* or *objective*. In opinion surveys and psychological tests we are often interested in political or social attitudes, a vaguely defined emotional or personality attribute, or other subjective qualities about which complete precision is impossible. Authoritarianism, perception of involvement in the political system, cooperativeness are examples of such subjective variables. Party membership, occupation, vote choice, age, residence are examples of objective variables.

5. In addition to the categories we have listed, variables may be identified by the kinds of measurements suitable to them as *nominal, ordinal,* or *interval.* A nominal variable (sex, party, occupation) has only named classes. For an ordinal variable (socioeconomic status, strength of partisanship), numbers may be used but refer only to the rank orders and have no true measurement values. In contrast a variable measured on an interval scale is inherently capable of being measured in some kind of meaningful numerical unit such as dollars, megawatt hours, number of people, or radiation units of atomic fallout.

Basic Variables in a Table. Any of the above kinds of variables may be used to display data in tabular form, but knowledge of three additional terms is essential when examining the actual table. These have to do with the *relationship* between two or more variables in the research model.

1. *The dependent variable* is what we are trying to explain. It is the variable attitude, vote choice, attribute, or action, which is thought to be *influenced by,* to *depend on,* or to be *explained by* some other factor (variable) or combination of factors. It is the usual practice (though not always followed) to list the categories of the dependent variable in the rows of the stub, or first (left-hand) column.

2. *The independent variable* is the factor with which we seek to explain the variation in the dependent variable. It is usual practice to display the categories of the independent variable in the boxhead at the top of the columns of the table. As we learned in Section 2–3, if this practice is followed each column should add to 100 per cent. Whatever pattern of display is followed, each category of the independent variable should add

to 100 per cent, or a note should explain slight losses because of rounding or larger ones because of omission of some cases.

Most research projects involve the use of several independent variables, since rarely does it seem reasonable to explain a political phenomenon by a single factor. However, for clarity, the report of the research project will often use a series of small tables, each displaying a single independent variable, such as sex, religion, education, or occupation. 3. A *control variable* is a second independent variable used in the same table, values of which are held constant in order to examine some alternative explanation for variation in the dependent variable. For example, if you have polled a sample of students and non-students, who also divide into Democrats and Republicans, concerning attitude toward U. S. policy in Viet Nam, you might arrange the results as in Table 2–6.

By re-tabulating our data under a control variable, we may determine whether a given independent variable is more significant than another. In the above example, it might turn out that initially the Democratic-Republican breakdown might seem significant, but this variation might disappear when controlled for student status.

Another use of controls is illustrated by the re-examination of the *Cross Polity Survey* data on former French and British colonies in Table 1–1. Essentially what that table did was to challenge the initial statement that "former French colonies have much lower literacy rates than former British colonies," the presumption being that "Colonial Ruler" was the significant factor in determining literacy. After tabulating High Literacy and Low Literacy

TABLE 2-7. *Literacy in Former British and French Colonies, Controlled for Literacy of Religious Tradition (in percentages)*

Literacy Rate	Former British	Former French	Religious Tradition Literate		Religious Tradition Non-Literate	
			Former British	Former French	Former British	Former French
High	79	32	100	100	50	7
Low	21	68	0	0	50	93
Total (*N*)	100 (19)	100 (19)	100 (11)	100 (5)	100 (8)	100 (14)

Source: Table 1-1.

states by "Colonial Ruler," we then introduced "Literacy of Predominant Religion" as a control variable, with the results of Table 2–7, which translates the data of Table 1–1 into percentages for both uncontrolled and controlled tabulations.

In this example, we see that most of the difference between the two literacy groups is accounted for by the literate character of the predominant religion. If the religious tradition is literate, the country is always in the higher literacy category, although "Colonial Ruler" still has some influence for countries in which the religious tradition was non-literate. By *controlling* for religion we have placed the "Colonial Ruler" variable in more complete perspective.

The Importance of N. In an earlier comment on percentage tables, we deplored the fact that some tables give only the percentage breakdown, omitting the essential information as to *how many* cases were involved in the survey. Sometimes this information may be obtained from the textual account of the survey or other project. In your own projects, the *N*'s—the numerical totals—should always be given. It makes a great deal of difference whether the number of cases reported is sufficient to establish reasonable confidence in the generality of the results. The U.S. Census survey on which Table 2–2 was based covered a national sample of about 80,000.

TABLE 2-6. *Attitudes toward U.S. Policy in Viet Nam, by Student Status and Reported Party Preference (in percentages)*

Dependent Variable: Attitude	Control:	Student		Non-Student	
	Independent Variable:	Dem.	Rep.	Dem.	Rep.
Support		75	80	73	67
Oppose		25	20	18	22
Don't Know		0	0	9	11
Total (*N =*)		100 (24)	100 (20)	100 (22)	100 (18)

Source: Adapted from a class project at the University of Oklahoma, May, 1966.

TABLE 2-8. *Protein Food Preference, by Sex of Consumer (in percentages)*

Food Preference	Male	Female
Non-fat	100	0
Non-lean	0	100
Total *N =*	100 1	100 1

In contrast, a familiar "survey report" on eating habits yields the information that "Jack Spratt could eat no fat; his wife could eat no lean." Results of this survey might be arranged as in Table 2–8. If we were not aware of the small N in this sample, we might jump to the insecure generalization that all non-fat eaters are male. The example may seem frivolous, but scholarly literature abounds with similar if less obviously fallacious conclusions.

2-5 A More Complex Example: Voter Stability

Thus far our examples of tables have been simple ones, fairly easy to read and interpret. Let us examine briefly the rather complicated arrangement of data in Table 2–9 (Relation between Voter Stability, Family Preference, and Social Distance), drawn from a pioneering survey by McClosky and Dahlgren. The title contains two terms which are not immediately clear: "voter stability" and "social distance." From the sequence used in the title to list the three variables, we assume correctly that "voter stability" is the *dependent variable,* and that the authors mean to examine the variables of family party preference and social distance as explanatory or causal *independent variables.* From the tabular arrangement, family preference is actually the *control variable,* though the columns could be shifted easily to set up "social mobility" as the control—from the footnote explanation, apparently the term refers to the same factor as does "social distance."

More light is cast on the term "stability" as we examine the *row captions.* Why have the authors reversed the order of party preference categories in the second section of the table? A moment's reflection yields the answer; the authors are interested in explaining voter stability: it is not simply the catego-ries "Republican" and "Democratic" which are important, but whether or not the voter's present party preference is the same as that of his family background. In each section of the table the first *row* caption lists the same party preference as that which the first *column* caption lists as that of the family. Thus the percentages in the first row of each of the two main parts of the table are comparable: they report the respondents *whose preference is the same as their family's* for the three categories of living environment. We notice that the column captions for the "favorable" and "antagonistic" environmental conditions also reverse the parties in the second part of the table, so that the three columns in each section are sequentially comparable on the variable labelled "social mobility."

With the captions clarified, what can we say about the authors' results? First we should recall the criteria of valid verbal statements about tables listed in Section 2–3, particularly the point that we read the table in the direction in which percentages add to 100 per cent. As you study each of the italicized statements below, refer to the table and try to decide how the data support the statement. Identify a specific comparison of data items which leads to the conclusion. Most of the statements are paraphrased from the authors' text, but one, though true, is an invalid reading of the table because it violates the canon of direction.

1. Social mobility is related to the stability of a voter's party loyalty.

Even lacking a complete explanation of the term "social mobility" we see that the family preference is more likely to be that of the respondent in the "favorable" columns than in the "antagonistic" columns.

2. Family influence increases as members enter other groups with parallel attitudes.

TABLE 2-9. *Relation between Voter Stability, Family Preference, and Social Distance*

Respondent's Preference Is	Family Preference is Republican			Respondent's Preference Is	Family Preference is Democratic		
	Respondent's Social Mobility[a] is				Respondent's Social Mobility[a] is		
	Favorable (Rep)	Neutral	Antagonistic (Dem)		Favorable (Dem)	Neutral	Antagonistic (Rep)
Republican Democratic	84.6% 15.4	60.8% 39.1	42.1% 57.9	Democratic Republican	84.3% 15.5	62.9% 37.0	50.0% 50.0
Sample Size:	39	23	19		32	27	12

[a] "Social Mobility" categories are based on a measure of the environment in which the respondent lives, presumed to reinforce Republican or Democratic affiliation or to be "neutral."
Source: Herbert McClosky and Harold E. Dahlgren, "Primary Group Influence on Party Loyalty," *American Political Science Review,* Vol. 53, September 1959, pp. 757–776.

This statement can be supported by a comparison of the "favorable" and the "neutral" columns in each section of the table. Whether the family was Republican or Democratic, a member in a neutral group (or environment) is less likely to retain the family preference than a member in a favorable group.

3. Family influence decreases as members enter groups with conflicting party attitudes.

The same pattern of reasoning as for Statement 2 applies here. The cross-column comparison is between the "neutral" and "antagonistic" columns.

4. More than 84 per cent of these who remain in a milieu favorable to the politics of the family retain its preference, whereas only about 15 per cent do not.

You should be able to accept this without re-checking the table, since the greatest variation shown is always your first order of business in a preliminary look.

5. Stability declines sharply as one moves from the favorable to the neutral social mobility columns.

Though the wording is different, this statement is a valid rewording of Statements 2 and 3, with the focus on one pair of environmental conditions.

6. In a hostile social environment, the offspring of Democratic families are just as likely to become Republicans as they are to remain Democrats.

Though somewhat surprising, in view of the strong association of favorable environment and party loyalty, this statement is supported by the last column of the table.

7. Offspring of Democratic families are more likely to remain Democrats in a hostile social environment than offspring of Republican families are likely to remain Republicans in a hostile environment.

This calls for another cross-columns comparison—between column three and column six (the two "antagonistic" conditions). The variation is small but supports the statement.

8. Republican voters appear to conform more strongly than Democrats to family influence.

At first glance this statement seems to contradict Statement 7, but if alert you should notice that its structure differs from that of all the previous statements. It is expressed in terms of the *row captions*—Republican and Democratic *voters*—rather than in terms of the column variables—family background and social environment. We do not know from the data in Table 2–9 whether the statement is true or not. Whether it is true or false, we cannot validly accept or reject the statement on the basis of the information before us. The percentages would have to be computed in a different way to permit a valid conclusion on association of voters' party preference with that of family.

Such a recomputation is of course possible and affords an instructive exercise on this problem of the proper direction in which a table must be read. The authors have supplied the necessary breakdown of sample size, but they have not carried the breakdown to the individual cells of the table. Our first step, then, is to *retrieve the frequencies*—the actual number which each percentage entry represents. The procedure of retrieving the frequencies is straightforward: we simply multiply each percentage entry, expressed as a decimal fraction, by the "*N*" at the foot of the column, and substitute the rounded product in the appropriate cell. We round the product because this value represents an *actual number of respondents,* which obviously cannot be fractional. This computation and substitution has been carried out in Table 2–10, but we are not yet through. Statement 8 is saying something about conformity to family influence —this is our new dependent variable. The explanatory variable is present party preference, so we must regroup the data to show a cross-tabulation of the two factors—"conformity" and "present party." Follow the next four steps carefully; the logic behind them will apply to many of your own problems.

1. The six columns are collapsed into two (Family Preference Republican, Family Preference Democratic), yielding Table 2–11 (a).

TABLE 2-10. *Relation between Voter Stability, Family Preference, and Social Distance (Frequencies Only) (Same data as Table 2-9, substituting frequencies for percentages)*

Respondent's Preference Is	Family Preference is Republican			Respondent's Preference Is	Family Preference is Democratic		
	Respondent's Social Mobility is				Respondent's Social Mobility is		
	Favorable (Rep)	Neutral	Antagonistic (Dem)		Favorable (Dem)	Neutral	Antagonistic (Rep)
Republican	33	14	8	Democratic	27	17	6
Democratic	6	9	11	Republican	5	10	6

Source: Table 2-9.

TABLE 2-11(a). *Voter Stability and Family Pre-ference*

Respondent Preference	Family Preference Republican	Respondent Preference	Family Preference Democratic
Republican	55	Democratic	50
Democratic	26	Republican	21

2. The rows of the new Column 2 are switched, so that voters of each party are together. The result is Table 2–11 (b), actually sufficient for our purpose, but we take two more steps for greater clarity in the final table.

TABLE 2-11(b). *Voter Preference in Relation to Family Preference*

Respondent Preference	Family Republican	Family Democratic
Republican	55	21
Democratic	26	50

3. The entries in the new Row 2 are switched to permit new column captions (Conform to Family Party, Do Not Conform to Family Party). Table 2–11 (c) shows the arrangement which fits the new variable of "conformity."

TABLE 2-11(c). *Conformity of Voter Preference to Family Preference*

Respondent Preference	Conform to Family Party	Do Not Conform to Family Party
Republican	55	21
Democratic	50	26

4. Rows and columns are reversed, a step not absolutely necessary but desirable so that the new independent or explanatory variable (voters' party) will appear in the columns adding to 100 per cent. This change is shown in Table 2–11 (d), which also includes recomputed percentages for the two categories of the new independent variable.

On the basis of Table 2–11 (d) we are now able to confirm Statement 8 as true: Republican voters in fact are more likely to conform to the family party than are Democratic voters. An incidental and interesting finding is that the original sample included exactly 76 Democrats and 76 Republicans. Why the apparent contradiction between Statements 7 and 8? Another regrouping, carried out in Table 2–12, is

TABLE 2-11(d). *Conformity to Family Preference, by Party of Respondent*

Conformity of Respondent with Family	Respondent Republican	Respondent Democratic
	Per cent	Per cent
Conforms	72.4	65.8
Does Not Conform	27.6	34.2
Total (*N*)	100.0 (76)	100.0 (76)

Source: Table 2-9.

revealing, and illustrates one facet of the concept of multiple causality.

2-6 Multiple Causality

Table 2–12 (a) shows that Republican voters are slightly less likely to be living in a hostile environment than are Democratic voters, so that loyalty to the family party is perhaps a little easier. On the other

TABLE 2-12(a). *Social Environment as Related to Party Preference*

Respondent's Environment is	Respondent is Republican	Respondent is Democrat
	Per cent	Per cent
Hostile	18.4	22.4
Not Hostile	81.6	77.6
Total	100.0	100.0

hand, respondents *from Republican families* (a different group from the group of *Republican voters*) are slightly less likely to conform to the family party than are respondents from Democratic families. The negligible difference, shown in Table 2–12 (b), is made possible by the fact that the sample of 152

TABLE 2-12(b). *Conformity to Family Preference, by Party of Family*

(This table is exactly the same as Table 2-11(a), with percentages and totals added and new captions for the dependent variable)

Respondent's Conformity	Family Republican	Family Democratic
	Per cent	Per cent
Conforms to Family	67.9	70.4
Does Not Conform	32.1	29.6
Total	100.0	100.0

Source: Table 2-9.

respondents divides equally (76–76) on party preference, but unequally (81–71) on family's party preference. In other words, all three factors—family influence, environment, and voter preference are intermingled. Of the three, clearly family influence came first, so if we use words such as "causal" or "explanatory" for the family preference variable we are on fairly safe ground. Present vote preference and environment are factors occurring simultaneously, however, so it is more difficult to say which is influencing the other, or indeed whether the two may not be separate and related results of family influence. A respondent who has left the family party may have done so partly because of his environment being hostile to it, or having left the family party he may

have sought an environment more congenial to his new beliefs.

It would help if we knew the time sequence of the factors "present party preference" and "environment." Figure 2–1 illustrates six possible patterns of timing and influence for the three variables, all based on the assumption that family party preference is prior in time to one or both of the other two factors, and in some way influential. We might express the six assumptions of Figure 2–1 as follows:

(a) Family preference influences environment, which influences party preference.

(b) Family preference influences party preference, which influences environment.

(c) Family preference influences both environment and party preference, but independently.

(d) Family preference influences environment and party preference, and each of the two latter influences the other.

(e) Family preference and environment each exercise an independent influence on party preference.

(f) Family preference and respondent's party preference each exercise an independent influence on respondent's environment.

We will not continue the discussion of multiple relationships at this point, but the patterns in Figure 2–1 emphasize the complexities of analyzing the relationships of three variables. Rarely in politics is a single explanatory factor enough. Examination of the interaction of several or many causal variables is usually required for even relatively complete understanding.

2-7 Constructing a Table: the Concept of Property Space

Examination and analysis of a table take on added significance if you place yourself in the position of the author as he prepares to organize the data he has gathered into a meaningful array. How are the variables to be arranged? What are the varieties of possible relationships which may help explain a given political attitude, action, or condition? How detailed a breakdown should be shown for such variables as age, income, intensity of attitude, and socioeconomic status?

An introduction to the mechanics of sorting and arranging is given in Chapter 4, where you are asked to prepare your own tables, but a prefatory view from the vantage point of the author at work prepar-

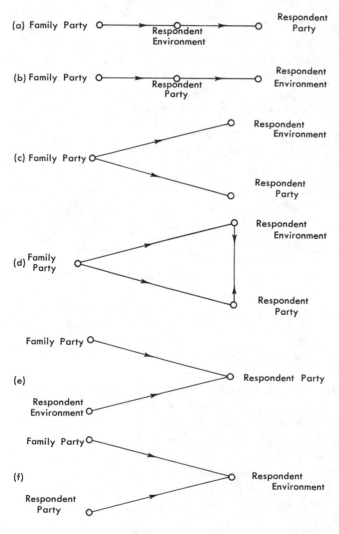

FIGURE 2-1. *Time Sequence and Influence Patterns for Three Variables*

ing his displays will suggest ways to study tables prepared by others as well as ways to handle original data. A useful framework for approaching the task of handling variables is Paul Lazarsfeld's concept of *property space*.* Lazarsfeld asks us to think of the placement of individuals or objects in a table as a process parallel to the location of points in space. Each attribute or property to be tabulated requires a separate "dimension." That is, any variable or property may be considered as one axis of an *n*-dimensional mapping—say the *x*(horizontal) axis of an ordinary two-dimensional graph. The location of the individual or object on this axis is done by placing him in one of the scaled or unscaled categories into which the investigator has divided the data on that variable.

For example, from the data in Exercise 2–4, the respondents might be arranged in a one-dimensional property space by scaling the attribute of intensity of party preference on a seven-point line ranging from "Most Democratic" to "Most Republican," as in Table 2–13.

TABLE 2-13. *Reported Party Preference of Respondents, Scaled by Intensity*

Preference	Per cent	Number
Strong Democrat	18%	123
Moderate Democrat	25	176
Independent Democrat	12	84
Independent	11	76
Independent Republican	6	44
Moderate Republican	17	116
Strong Republican	11	79
Total	100%	698

Source: Exercise 2-4.

The number of categories, or points displayed on such a one-dimensional scale is often up to the investigator, though limited by the raw data available and sometimes by the necessity of adhering to "natural" categories, such as sex. The seven categories above might be rearranged, depending on the particular research design, in a number of different ways:

1. They can be collapsed into a four-category set on a scale of *intensity of party feeling,* ignoring the actual party distinctions—Strongly Partisan, Moderately Partisan, Mildly Partisan, Independent—yielding Table 2–14.

* Paul F. Lazarsfeld and Morris Rosenberg (eds.), *The Language of Social Research* (New York: The Free Press, 1955), pp. 40–62.

TABLE 2-14. *Intensity of Party Feeling*

Intensity	Per cent	Number
Strongly Partisan	29%	202
Moderately Partisan	42	292
Mildly Partisan	18	128
Independent	11	76
Total	100%	698

2. To an investigator interested only in the two-party categories, it might seem useful to collapse the seven groups into three: Democrats, Republicans, and Independents. Again, if interested in the development of independent voting habits, he might choose to combine the original categories, "Independent Democrat," "Independent," and "Independent Republican," into a single group of Independents. These two approaches would yield Tables 2–15 and 2–16.

TABLE 2-15. *Reported Party Preference of Respondents*

Preference	Per cent	Number
Democrat	55%	383
Republican	34	239
Independent	11	76
Total	100%	698

TABLE 2-16. *Reported Party Preference of Respondents*

Preference	Per cent	Number
Democrat	43%	299
Republican	28	195
Independent*	29	204
Total	100%	698

* Includes Independent Democrats and Independent Republicans.

3. Finally, a variety of two-fold tables may be derived from the data, by dichotomizing the results

TABLE 2-17. *Party Preference of Respondents Mentioning a Political Party*

Party	Per cent	Number
Democratic	62%	383
Republican	38	239
Total	100%	622

TABLE 2-18. *Proportion of Partisans and Independents*

Type	Per cent	Number
Partisan	71%	494
Independent	29	204
Total	100%	698

TABLE 2-19. *Strength of Partisanship of Respondents Mentioning a Political Party*

Intensity	Per cent	Number
Strongly Partisan	32%	202
Moderately or Mildly Partisan	68	420
Total	100%	622

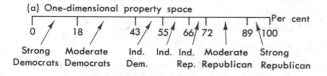

(a) One-dimensional property space

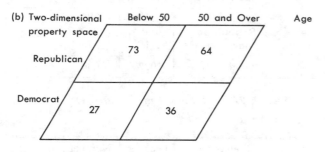

(b) Two-dimensional property space

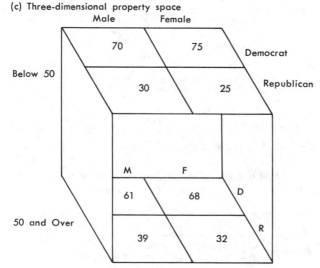

(c) Three-dimensional property space

FIGURE 2-2. *Three Dimensions of Property Space*

into such pairs as Democratic-Republican, Partisan-Independent, or (omitting Independents) Strongly Partisan and Moderately or Mildly Partisan, as in Tables 2–17, 2–18, and 2–19.

2-8 Two Dimensional Property Space

When a second variable is introduced we may conceive of Lazarsfeld's property space as a two-dimensional plane. The raw data used in Table 2–13, for example, may include information on age of respondents and this might be used as a second "axis" to describe each individual's location in such a plane. In Table 2–20, we have collapsed the seven categories of Table 2–13 into five, and have divided our information on the new variable of age into five age brackets, thus yielding a 5 × 5 table of twenty-five cells.

TABLE 2-20. *Intensity of Partisanship by Age*

Party Preference Described as:	Age group				
	21–29	30–39	40–49	50–59	60 & over
Strong Democrat	20%	24%	25%	22%	20%
Moderate Democrat	32	34	38	32	27
Independent	22	23	17	25	19
Moderate Republican	16	11	12	13	20
Strong Republican	10	8	8	8	14
Total	100%	100%	100%	100%	100%
N =	123	140	132	128	178

The variables examined in this table may also be dichotomized either for some theoretical reason connected with the research project or simply for convenience or clarity. Table 2–21 is a result of collapsing the two variables into one of many possible 2 × 2 patterns. Here again, the Independent category of the original data is omitted.

TABLE 2-21. *Party Preference by Age*

Party	Below 50 years old	50 years & over
Democrat	73%	64%
Republican	27	36
Total	100%	100%
N =	313	241

2-9 Property Space of More Than Two Dimensions

With additional variables the "dimensions" of our property space may be increased to three, four, or indeed any number within the limits of available information. Physical parallels to actual space become less meaningful after we pass the third dimension (except in advanced mathematics), but the basic concept of location of individuals or objects by their attributes remains consistent.

TABLE 2-22. *Party Preference by Age and Sex* *(in percentages)*

Party	Below 50 years old		50 years and over	
	Male	Female	Male	Female
Democrat	70	75	61	68
Republican	30	25	39	32
Total	100	100	100	100
$N =$	163	150	151	110

By adding the attribute of sex, for example, to the information displayed in Table 2–21, we obtain the three-dimensional array of Table 2–22. By adding the attribute of income, set up here as a dichotomy,

we have a four-dimensional array. The problem of table format becomes more difficult with the introduction of a fourth variable. It should be solved in accordance with the research design rather than for convenience of presentation, since the arrangement of the variables in the table determines the relationships among them which can be examined. Table 2–23 is one possibility. In general, you will find it more useful to add additional variables *one at a time,* for a series of three-dimensional tables, rather than to introduce a third and fourth simultaneously. By adding each of several possible explanatory factors separately to your tabulations, you will be able to see more clearly the relevance of each to the pattern you are trying to explain. Once you feel that you understand the relationships, you can develop more complicated tables with greater confidence.

In this process, as with all quantitative work, you will quickly learn that examination of the variety of possible relationships among variables is a complex task, to which you must bring all the skill and knowledge you can muster. Tables and statistics do not in themselves lead to substantive political knowledge. Tabulation and analysis of data can be of great assistance, but do not relieve us of the necessity of learning as much as possible about the substance of political science. The more we know about political science generally, the more discerning we will be in our use of numerical data.

TABLE 2-23. *Party Preference by Sex, Controlled for Age and Income (in percentages)*

Party	Below average income				Above average income			
	Below 50 years		50 & above		Below 50 years		50 & above	
	Male	Female	Male	Female	Male	Female	Male	Female
Democrat	75	80	66	73	65	70	56	63
Republican	25	20	34	27	35	30	44	37
Total	100	100	100	100	100	100	100	100
$N =$	83	75	76	60	80	75	75	50

Exercise Set 2. What Do These Tables Say?

2-1. *Party Preference as a Function of Parental Party Preference (in percentages)*

Child's Preference	Both Parents Democrats	Both Parents Republicans	Both Shifted
Democratic	82	22	47
Republican	15	73	37
Other	3	5	16
% of total sample	41	24	6

Note: *Both Shifted* means both parents were inconsistent in their party preferences.
Source: Angus Campbell, Gerald Gurin, and Warren E. Miller, *The Voter Decides* (Evanston, Ill.: Row, Peterson, 1954), p. 99. Reprinted with permission of Harper & Row, Publishers.

1. In which direction will you read this table? Why?

2. What is the dependent variable?

3. What is the independent variable and why was it chosen?

4. Identify the greatest variation between any two entries for the basic comparisons shown in the table (ignoring totals, "other," etc.).

5. What basic hypothesis might the table be intended to test?

6. What causal inferences can you make on the basis of this table?

7. Are there any important omissions?

2-2. *Education and Presidential Vote* (*in percentages*)

Presidential Vote	Education*		
	Elementary	Secondary	College
Goldwater	17	23	43
Johnson	55	57	46
Neither; didn't vote	28	20	11
Total	100	100	100
Number of cases	210	378	114

* Elementary means no more than grade school; secondary means at least some high school and/or vocational school; college means at least some college work.

Source: Leon D. Epstein and Austin Ranney, "Who Voted for Goldwater: The Wisconsin Case," *Political Science Quarterly,* March 1966, Vol. LXXXI, No. 1, p. 90. Reprinted with permission of the publisher and authors.

1. In which direction will you read this table? Why?

2. What is the dependent variable?

3. What is the independent variable and why was it chosen?

4. Identify the greatest variation between any two entries for the basic comparisons shown in the table (ignoring totals, "other," etc.).

5. What basic hypothesis might the table be intended to test?

6. What causal inferences can you make on the basis of this table?

7. Are there any important omissions?

2-3. *Age and Presidential Vote* (*in percentages*)

	Age				
Presidential Vote	21–29	30–39	40–49	50–59	60 and over
Goldwater	26	19	20	21	34
Johnson	52	58	63	54	47
Neither; didn't vote	22	23	17	25	19
Total	100	100	100	100	100
Number of cases	123	140	132	128	178

Source: Leon D. Epstein and Austin Ranney, "Who Voted for Goldwater: the Wisconsin Case," *Political Science Quarterly,* March 1966, Vol. LXXXI, No. 1, p. 91. Reprinted with permission of the publisher and authors.

1. In which direction will you read this table? Why?

2. What is the dependent variable?

3. What is the independent variable and why was it chosen?

4. Identify the greatest variation between any two entries for the basic comparisons shown in the table (ignoring totals, "other," etc.).

5. What basic hypothesis might the table be intended to test?

6. What causal inferences can you make on the basis of this table?

7. Are there any important omissions?

2-4. *Party Activists and Presidential Vote* (*in percentages*)

Presidential Vote	Party Identification*					
	Republicans		Democrats		Independents	
	Activists	Nonactivists	Activists	Nonactivists	Activists	Nonactivists
Goldwater	82	51	2	5	9	12
Johnson	9	21	89	77	64	52
Neither; didn't vote	9	28	9	18	27	36
Total	100	100	100	100	100	100
Number of cases	68	171	81	300	11	65

* Party identification categories have been collapsed so that Republicans include Strong Republicans, Republicans, and Independent Republicans; Democrats include the comparable Democratic categories; and Independents include those with no party leanings.
Source: Leon D. Epstein and Austin Ranney, "Who Voted for Goldwater: The Wisconsin Case," *Political Science Quarterly*, March 1966, Vol. LXXXI, No. 1, p. 92.

1. In which direction will you read this table? Why?

2. What is the dependent variable?

3. What is the independent variable and why was it chosen?

4. If there is a second independent variable used as a control variable, tell what it is and why it was chosen.

5. Identify the greatest variation between any two entries for the basic comparisons shown in the table (ignoring totals, "other," etc.)

6. What basic hypothesis might the table be intended to test?

7. What causal inferences can you make on the basis of this table?

8. Are there any important omissions?

2-5. *Relation of Perceived Closeness of Election and Intensity of Partisan Preference to Voting Turnout, 1956 (in percentages)*

Turnout Status	Election Perceived to Be					
	One sided			Close		
	Intensity of Preference			Intensity of Preference		
	Weak	Medium	Strong	Weak	Medium	Strong
Voted	70	71	73	71	79	89
Did not vote	30	29	27	29	21	11
Total	100	100	100	100	100	100
Number of cases	130	170	88	301	360	226

Source: Angus Campbell, *et al., The American Voter,* abridged ed., 1964. New York: John Wiley & Sons, p. 54. Reprinted with the kind permission of the authors and publishers.

1. In which direction will you read this table? Why?

2. What is the dependent variable?

3. What is the independent variable and why was it chosen?

4. If there is a second independent variable used as a control variable, tell what it is and why it was chosen.

5. Identify the greatest variation between any two entries for the basic comparisons shown in the table (ignoring totals, "other," etc.).

6. What basic hypothesis might the table be intended to test?

7. What causal inferences can you make on the basis of this table?

8. Are there any important omissions?

2-6. *Proportion of Voters in Six Status Groups who are Members of Political Organizations, By Roosevelt and Dewey Voters*

Voters	Low Income			Medium & High Income		
	Catholics	Jews	Protestants	Catholics	Jews	Protestants
Percentage of members	12	8	0	11	3	19
Roosevelt voters	10	8	0	11	3	7
Dewey voters	2	0	0	0	0	12
No. of voters reporting	106	50	32	57	88	57

Source: Gerhart H. Saenger, "Social Status and Political Behavior," *American Journal of Sociology,* September 1945. Reprinted with permission of the publisher and author.

1. In which direction will you read this table? Why?

2. What is the dependent variable?

3. What is the independent variable and why was it chosen?

4. If there is a second independent variable used as a control variable, tell what it is and why it was chosen.

5. Identify the greatest variation between any two entries for the basic comparisons shown in the table (ignoring totals, "other," etc.).

6. What basic hypothesis might the table be intended to test?

7. What causal inferences can you make on the basis of this table?

8. Are there any important omissions?

2-7. *Estimated Degree of Impact of Local Government on Daily Life: by Nation*

Percentage who say local government has	U.S.	U.K.	Germany	Italy	Mexico
Great effect	35	23	33	19	6
Some effect	53	51	41	39	23
No effect	10	23	18	22	67
Other & Don't know	2	3	8	20	3
Total percentage	100	100	100	100	99
Total number	970	963	955	995	1,007

Source: Gabriel A. Almond and Sidney Verba, *The Civic Culture.* Princeton, N.J.: Princeton University Press, p. 81. Reprinted by permission of Princeton University Press. Copyright 1963 by Princeton University Press. All rights reserved.

1. In which direction will you read this table? Why?

2. What is the dependent variable?

3. What is the independent variable and why was it chosen?

4. Identify the greatest variation between any two entries for the basic comparisons shown in the table (ignoring totals, "other," etc.).

5. What basic hypothesis might the table be intended to test?

6. What causal inferences can you make on the basis of this table?

7. Are there any important omissions?

2-8. *Character of Impact of National Government; by Nation* (in per cent)*

Percentage who say:	U.S.	U.K.	Germany	Italy	Mexico
Nat'l. govt. improves conditions	76	77	61	66	58
Sometimes improves conditions, sometimes does not	19	15	30	20	18
Better off without national govt.	3	3	3	5	19
Nat'l. govt. makes no difference	1	1	1	1	2
Other	0	1	0	2	1
Don't know	1	2	4	5	2
Total percentage	100	99	99	99	100
Total number	821	707	676	534	301

* As described by those respondents who attribute some impact to national government.
Source: Almond and Verba, *The Civic Culture*, p. 82.

1. In which direction will you read this table? Why?

2. What is the dependent variable?

3. What is the independent variable and why was it chosen?

4. Identify the greatest variation between any two entries for the basic comparisons shown in the table (ignoring totals, "other," etc.).

5. What basic hypothesis might the table be intended to test?

6. What causal inferences can you make on the basis of this table?

7. Are there any important omissions?

2-9. *Percentage who Discuss Politics; by Sex and Education*

	Total		Primary or less		Secondary or more	
	Male % N	Female % N	Male % N	Female % N	Male % N	Female % N
United States	83 (455)	70 (515)	73 (248)	57 (269)	95 (207)	83 (246)
Great Britain	77 (459)	63 (503)	74 (277)	56 (340)	83 (182)	75 (163)
Germany	77 (442)	46 (499)	74 (352)	42 (440)	88 (90)	74 (59)
Italy	47 (471)	18 (524)	36 (293)	13 (403)	64 (178)	37 (121)
Mexico	55 (355)	29 (652)	49 (285)	26 (592)	77 (67)	56 (60)

Source: Almond and Verba. *The Civic Culture,* p. 390.

1. In which direction will you read this table? Why?

2. What is the dependent variable? (It is not mentioned in the captions.)

3. What is the independent variable and why was it chosen?

4. If there are other independent variables used as control variables, tell what they are and why chosen.

5. Identify the greatest variation between any two entries for the basic comparisons shown in the table (ignoring totals, "other," etc.).

6. What basic hypothesis might the table be intended to test?

7. What causal inferences can you make on the basis of this table?

8. Are there any important omissions?

2-10. *Percentage who Acknowledge Duty to Participate in Local Community; by Sex and Education*

	Total		Primary or less		Secondary or more	
	Male % N	Female % N	Male % N	Female % N	Male % N	Female % N
United States	52 (455)	50 (515)	37 (248)	42 (269)	70 (207)	59 (246)
Great Britain	43 (459)	36 (503)	43 (277)	33 (340)	42 (182)	43 (163)
Germany	31 (442)	16 (499)	29 (352)	16 (440)	40 (90)	22 (59)
Italy	14 (471)	6 (524)	9 (293)	5 (403)	22 (178)	12 (121)
Mexico	31 (355)	24 (652)	29 (285)	22 (592)	39 (67)	36 (60)

Source: Almond and Verba, *The Civic Culture*, p. 390.

1. In which direction will you read this table? Why?

2. What is the dependent variable? (It is not mentioned in the captions.)

3. What is the independent variable and why was it chosen?

4. If there are other independent variables used as control variables, tell what they are and why chosen.

5. Identify the greatest variation between any two entries for the basic comparisons shown in the table (ignoring totals, "other," etc.).

6. What basic hypothesis might the table be intended to test?

7. What causal inferences can you make on the basis of this table?

8. Are there any important omissions?

2-11. *Ideology-pragmatism Orientation of West Berlin Party Officials, by Age Groups, with Party Controlled*
(*In Percentages*)

Ideology-	SPD			CDU		
Pragmatism	Below 40	41–55	55 and Over	Below 40	41–55	55 and Over
Ideological	46	49	63	80	65	80
Pragmatic	54	51	37	20	35	20
Total	100	100	100	100	100	100
(*N*)	(48)	(55)	(27)	(20)	(34)	(20)

Source: William E. Wright, "Ideological-Pragmatic Orientations of West Berlin Local Party Officials," *Midwest Journal of Political Science,* Vol. XI, No. 3 (August 1967), p. 393. Reprinted by permission of Wayne State University Press.

1. In which direction will you read this table? Why?

2. What is the dependent variable?

3. What is the independent variable and why was it chosen?

4. If there is a second independent variable used as a control variable, tell what it is and why chosen.

5. Identify the greatest variation between any two entries for the basic comparisons shown in the table (ignoring totals, "other," etc.).

6. What basic hypothesis might the table be intended to test?

7. What causal inferences can you make on the basis of this table?

8. Are there any important omissions?

2-12. *Favorable Attitudes Toward Religious Belief, Religious Practice, United Nations Forces, and Service in International Forces, by Social Position, Norway, 1966 (in percentages)*[a]

Attitude Toward	Social Position Scale Group[b]								
	1	2	3	4	5	6	7	8	Total
State Church as Institution	42	32	26	23	17	14	13	3	21
State Church as Milieu of Personal Belief and Practice	18	10	13	10	13	6	11	5	11
UN Armed Forces as Institution	9	26	34	43	49	51	66	80	45
Personal Service in UN Forces	3	11	11	14	13	18	28	45	16

a Negative percentages (unfavorable attitudes) and *N*'s not given. Survey conducted in November–December 1966 by Norsk Gallup Institute A.S., with a sample of about 1000.
b Galtung's Social Position Scale is based on eight dichotomized characteristics considered relevant to status: age, sex, income, education, job, work branch, ecology, and geography. For each, one category is scored zero and the other 1:

Characteristic	0	1
Age	young, old	middle age
Sex	women	men
Income	lower half	upper half
Education	lower half	upper half
Job	blue collar	white collar
Branch	primary	secondary, tertiary
Ecology	rural	urban
Geography	periphery	center

Norway has very few 0's or 1's, so these two categories are collapsed in the table. We may interpret the scale groups as meaning—at the extremes—that a middle-aged college graduate (male) working as an executive at company headquarters in Oslo, with above average income, would be scaled at 8, while a young or old scrubwoman cleaning floors at a small village cannery would score zero.
Source: Johan Galtung, in James N. Rosenau (ed.), *Domestic Sources of Foreign Policy* (New York: Free Press, 1967), p. 174. Copyright 1967 by The Free Press, a division of the Macmillan Company. Reprinted with the kind permission of the author and publisher.

1. In which direction will you read this table? Why?

2. What is the dependent variable?

3. What is the independent variable and why was it chosen?

4. Identify the greatest variation between any two entries for the basic comparisons shown in the table (ignoring totals, "other," etc.).

5. What basic hypothesis might the table be intended to test?

6. What causal inferences can you make on the basis of this table?

7. Are there any important omissions?

Reading List

The first two items are included because they contain many examples of tables with political content.

Almond, Gabriel A., and Sidney Verba, *The Civic Culture*. Princeton: Princeton University Press, 1963.*

Campbell, Angus, Philip E. Converse, Warren E. Miller, and Donald E. Stokes, *The American Voter*. New York: John Wiley & Sons, Inc., 1960.*

Lazarsfeld, Paul F., and Morris Rosenberg, eds., *The Language of Social Research*. New York: Free Press, 1955.*

Wallis, W. Allen, and Harry V. Roberts, *Statistics: A New Approach*. Glencoe: Free Press, 1956, especially Chapter 6, "The Art of Organizing Data."

Zeisel, Hans, *Say It With Figures*. New York: Harper and Row, Publishers, 1957.

---

* Paperback edition available.

GRAPHS AND CHARTS:

Mapping Your Data

3

Diagrams are easier to understand than tables of arithmetic. A pattern of comparison buried in the data of a complex table often can be identified only by careful study, but may emerge at a glance from a well-done chart or graph. The appearance of a graph in a book or article signals the reader that the author considers the finding portrayed to be a significant one—important enough to justify the additional time and trouble. And the reader usually responds more quickly to a graph than to a table or a verbal account of the data—he is encouraged to examine the general pattern of a relationship rather than to immerse himself in the details.

3-1 Qualities of a Good Graph

Several features of a good graph are worth stressing, applicable either to the preparation of graphs for your own studies or to the examination of graphs that you come across in your reading.

(1) *A good graph is simple.* It makes a point about the relationships shown in the data without attempting to display all the detail of the source table. The process of creating simplicity may be quite complex; the graph should be thoughtfully planned and carefully executed to show just what the author believes to be the major pattern revealed by his research.

Two exceptions to the principle of simplicity may be allowed. Where the source table itself is relatively simple, it may be possible (and so desirable) to display on the graph all the data the table contains without undue clutter. Figure 3–6 is an example of such a graph, reproducing all the essential data of Table 2–9. Again, where a complex graphic pattern is to be used repeatedly throughout a research study, it may constitute in itself a valuable and worthwhile part of the author's analysis. Figure 3–12 is an example; its complexities require close study, but the authors of the *Atlas of Economic Development* presented a carefully done prefatory explanation of

its detail, and used the design for a series of forty-seven maps displaying world distribution of variables deemed related to development.

(2) *A good graph conforms to the kind of variables displayed.* We should distinguish three kinds of

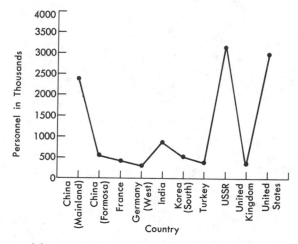

(a) A Bad Graph : Ordered Alphabetically

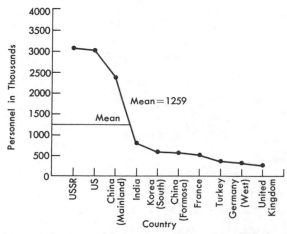

(b) A Better Graph : Ordered by Magnitude, but Horizontal Scale Still Measures Nothing

FIGURE 3-1. *The Ten Largest Military Forces, 1966*

64

variables for this and other quantitative work: nominal, ordinal, and interval. A *nominal* variable is one classified only in terms of unordered names: states, nations, races, cities. An *ordinal* or ordered variable is one susceptible to classification according to a specified order or rank in a numbered series: socioeconomic status may be ranked from "upper upper" to "lower lower," military status from general to private, political parties from left to right, political or personality attributes (hostility, cooperativeness) may be scaled by an index from highest to lowest. Although an ordinal scale sometimes gives the impression of precise measurements, its distinguishing characteristic is that the numbers attached to the ranks are not arithmetic values: an individual in the "middle-middle" socioeconomic status does not have five times as much status as one in the "lower-lower" category, though the two categories may be numbered "5" and "1" for convenience. We might just as well number them "1" and "5." An *interval* scale is used for variables susceptible to meaningful numerical measurement: size, weight, magnitude in numbers or percentages, and time.

It makes little sense to use a coordinate graph to display measurements of an unordered or nominal variable. The *x*-axis of such a graph is designed to show precise measurements on the horizontal coordinate. Figure 3–1(a) is about as bad as a graph can be. Three of its more glaring faults are (1) there

is nothing whatever for the horizontal axis to measure, (2) there are no real intervals on the horizontal axis, though the continuous line suggests them, and (3) there is no ordered relationship of the units on the horizontal axis, which might make the display more reasonable. Figure 3–1(b) displays the same data in a somewhat more sensible format, often used to show patterns of magnitude, location of the mean on a continuum, and proportion of cases in various sectors of the whole. It still violates the principle of not mixing scales, though here we have changed the nominal scale of Figure 3–1(a) to an ordinal scale.

(3) *A good graph accurately reflects the data.* It does not imply the existence of non-existent intervals, or more precise relationships than the data actually possess. A smooth curve should not be displayed without making clear the actual location of the points on which it is based.

Without overburden of detail, a graph should nonetheless specify the essential numerical information. The reader should see without undue effort whether the measurements are proportions of unity (maximum value 1.00), percentages (maximum value 100), absolute numbers, units of time, or divisions of some other scale. The zero should always be shown for an interval scale if the scale contains that value. On the other hand, the zero usually will not appear

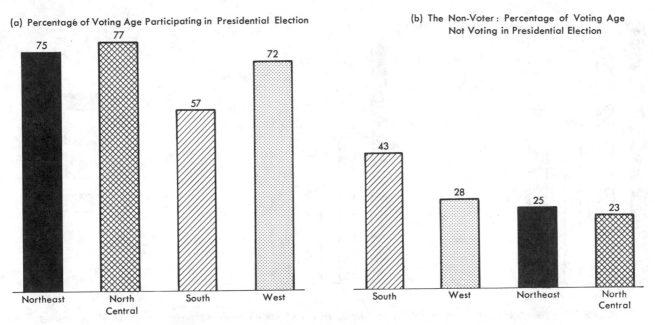

FIGURE 3-2. *Voter Turnout in the United States by Region, 1964*

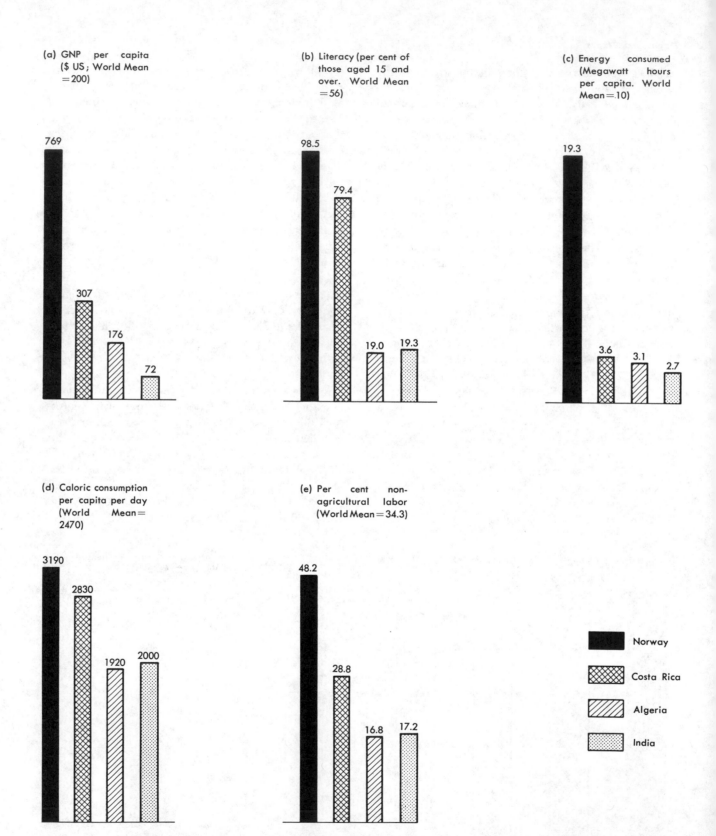

(a) GNP per capita ($ US; World Mean = 200)

769
307
176
72

(b) Literacy (per cent of those aged 15 and over. World Mean = 56)

98.5
79.4
19.0
19.3

(c) Energy consumed (Megawatt hours per capita. World Mean = .10)

19.3
3.6
3.1
2.7

(d) Caloric consumption per capita per day (World Mean = 2470)

3190
2830
1920
2000

(e) Per cent non-agricultural labor (World Mean = 34.3)

48.2
28.8
16.8
17.2

Norway

Costa Rica

Algeria

India

FIGURE 3-3. *Four Standards of Living: Selected Characteristics of Mid-Quartile Countries on a World Ranking by Gross National Product Per Capita*

Source of Data: Norton Ginsburg, *Atlas of Economic Development;* (University of Chicago Press, 1961), and Bruce M. Russett *et al., World Handbook of Political and Social Indicators* (New Haven: Yale University Press, 1964).

on an ordinal scale—technically, there is no such ordinal number as zero.

3-2 Types of Graphs Useful in Political Research

We turn now to a brief discussion of graphs often found in political and social science publications: the bar graph, the coordinate graph, circle and half-circle graphs (sometimes called pie charts and half-pie charts), and a group we call "pure relationship" graphs—used to show non-quantitative patterns of association and partition. We omit the ideograph or pictograph (picture graph), which is common in popular publications and government brochures but rare in academic journals, and the statistical map, valuable in political science but illustrating few additional problems other than skill in draftsmanship.

3-3 The Bar Graph

Display of data for nominal variables is usually best done on a bar graph. The bar graph is more appropriate than a coordinate graph, since we cannot attach numerical values to the nominal categories (Cf. Figure 3–1(a)). For example, in Figure 3–2(a) and 3–2(b) there is no particular logic in the ordering

of the four major regions of the United States for which voter turnout is reported. Northeast, North Central, South and West are simply names, their sequence a matter of arbitrary convention.

Accent the Negative? Notice that the two parts of Figure 3–2 report exactly the same information, since voter turnout is a dichotomous variable (each person of eligible age either voted or did not vote). The decision to focus on complementary percentages in Figure 3–2(b) depends entirely on emphasis. It would be unusual to include both graphs in the same study.

Hatching. For the simple bar graphs of Figure 3–2 there is no special reason, other than artistic, for hatching the bars. If the graphs are to be included in a series which will show the same regions in a variety of relationships, however, use of the same hatching will identify the same region throughout the series. This use of hatching is demonstrated in Figure 3–3, showing a consistent inequality in the distribution of a number of values in four countries chosen as typical of four stages of development (each is a mid-quartile case in a world array based on gross national product per capita).

Horizontal or Vertical? Bar graphs are usually arranged with the bars vertical, especially when a small number of bars are used. The vertical bar seems best for percentage comparisons—the eye is

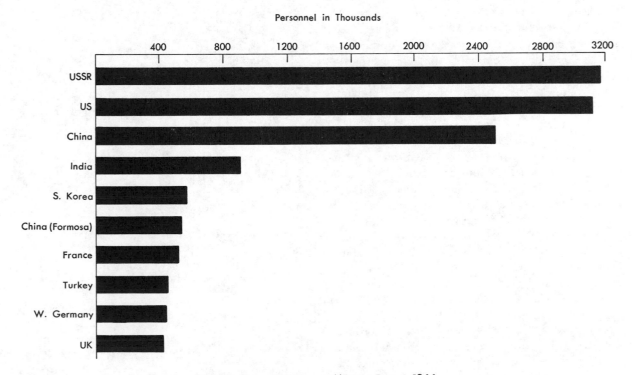

FIGURE 3-4. *Ten Largest Military Forces, 1966*

Infant Mortality per 1000 Live Births   Physicians and Dentists per 100,000 Population

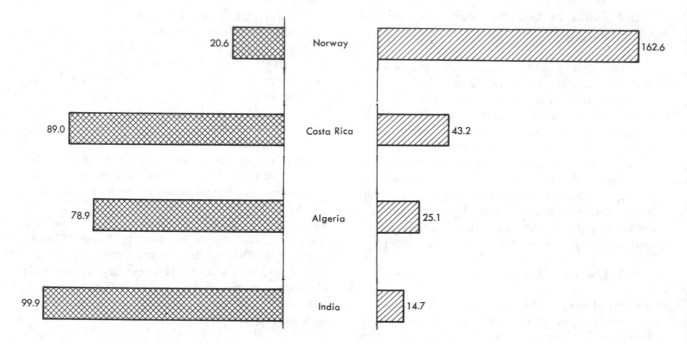

FIGURE 3-5. *Medical Personnel and Infant Mortality in Four Mid-Quartile Countries (on a World Ranking by Gross National Product Per Capita)*

Source of Data: *Atlas of Economic Development.*

more accustomed to seeing 100 per cent as the "highest" value. Horizontal bars are sometimes used in a graph displaying data for a large number of entities (as for all the States in the Union), partly because of the difficulty of lettering so many names in a horizontal line across the page. Where absolute numbers are reported, a horizontal bar seems natural enough, since we are accustomed to counting items (men, ships, aircraft, barrels) on a horizontal line. Figure 3–4, for example, seems a natural way to display the relative size of military forces—the same data in the same sequence as shown in Figure 3–1(b). Horizontal bars are useful where two measurement scales are needed for each unit. Figure 3–5 illustrates this application, the bars to the right measuring medical personnel and the bars to the left infant mortality—the general point of the graph being that countries with a larger percentage of doctors are likely to have relatively lower infant mortality.

Bar Graphs for Ordinal Variables. For an ordinal scale, a series of hatched bar graphs often is more "honest" with the data than a coordinate graph, since most ordinal categories (ranging from low to

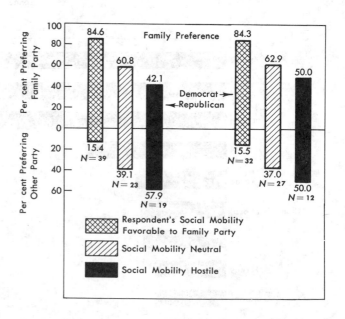

FIGURE 3-6. *Voter Stability, Family Preference, and Social Distance*

Source: Table 2-9.

high) do not fit the precision of measurement which we associate with the division marks of the X and Y axes. Such an ordinal scale (favorable, neutral, hostile) is shown in Figure 3–6, which reproduces the data of Table 2–9. Use of the same hatching for each environmental category permits easy comparison from one group to another, and the horizontal line divides each bar at the breaking point of the dichotomous dependent variable. In interpreting such a graph, the values below the horizontal line are not to be read as negative; the danger that they might be so read probably explains why this pattern is not widely used despite its convenience.

An especially skillful use of bar graphs to show a series of relationships bearing on vote choice and religion is illustrated in Figure 3–7, from the pioneering study of the 1948 election in Elmira, New York. Here the authors combine all three basic kinds of variable—nominal (religion, nativity), ordinal (socioeconomic status index, class identification, the liberal-

conservative spectrum), and interval (age and length of residence)—to drive home a single fundamental finding, as well as to show several variations on it.

Compound Bars. Component portions of an entity may be shown by different hatchings on different portions of a single bar, or on corresponding portions of a series of bars. For example, if our interest is not in the absolute size of the armed forces reported in Figure 3–4, but on their relative proportions of land, sea and air personnel, we use the compound bar device of Figure 3–8. For convenience both in lettering and in making visual comparisons by examining the spaces filled in by like hatchings, vertical bars are preferred for such a series.

Compound bars are also useful for a time series. Figure 3–9(a) shows Space Administration expenditures for a series of years, and demonstrates another problem in construction. In this design, the bar representing expenditures is broken into three areas,

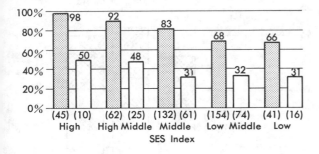 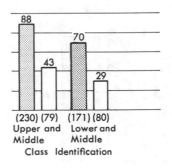 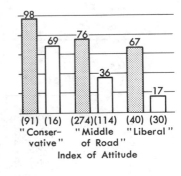

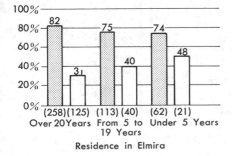 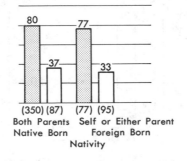 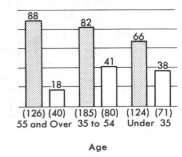

FIGURE 3-7. *Religion in Relation to Party and Other Factors, Elmira, 1948*

Source: Charts XXIV, XXV, XXVI, and XXVIII in Berelson, Lazarsfeld, and McPhee, *Voting.* Chicago: University of Chicago Press, 1954. Reprinted by permission of the University of Chicago Press. Copyright 1954 by the University of Chicago.

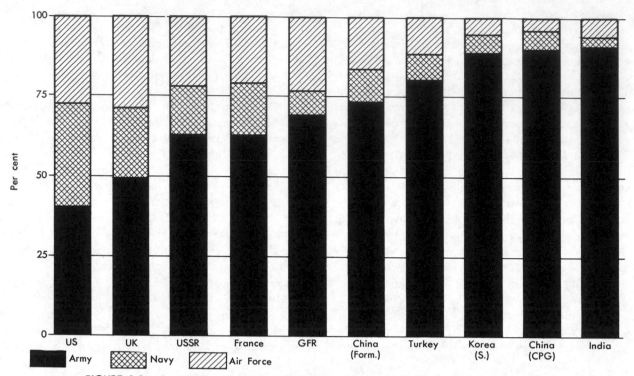

FIGURE 3-8. *Composition of Ten Largest Military Forces, 1966 (Ordered by Increasing Percentage in Army)*

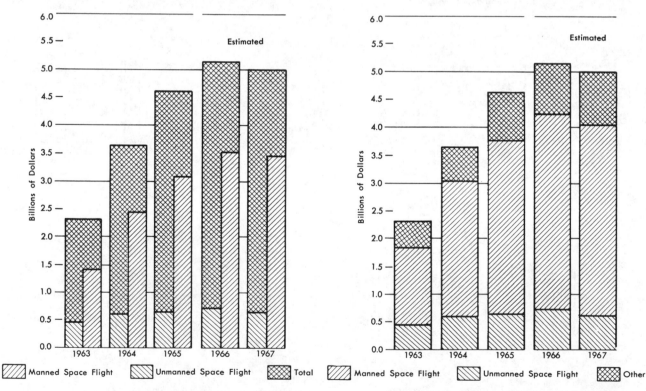

FIGURE 3-9. *(a) A Confusing Graph: Areas not Proportionate to Values (NASA Expenditures for Research and Development: 1962 to 1966)*

Source: Chart prepared by Dept. of Commerce, Bureau of the Census, Data from National Aeronautics and Space Administration.

(b) A Clearer Graph—Areas Proportionate to Subdivisions (NASA Expenditures for Research and Development : 1962–1966)

Source of Data: *Statistical Abstract of the United States, 1967.*

representing research costs of (1) unmanned space flight, (2) manned space flight, and (3) other programs (presumably including administrative overhead). The problem is to decide whether the magnitudes of these three ingredients of the bar are represented by height or by area. If area is the criterion—a reasonable assumption—then the "other" costs are more than the combined costs of the major action programs of the agency—those of the Jet Propulsion Laboratory, Cape Kennedy and Houston. If height is the criterion—a check of the source table reveals that it is—then "other" costs are a relatively minor 20 per cent or so of the total. Figure 3–9(b) is a reconstruction of the graph which makes this clearer. Fallacious area comparisons in bar graphs do not occur frequently, but government brochures are especially guilty of this misleading pattern. The practice is undesirable because there are standard uses (histograms of statistical distributions) in which the width of a bar is a measured element—meaning that the area of the bar is the unit of comparison.

3-4 Coordinate Graphs

You were introduced to the standard coordinate graph of the geometric plane, originated by René Descartes (whence "Cartesian coordinates") in the discussion of the Gini index in Chapter 1. Actually, that discussion did not introduce you to this universally useful model—it merely reminded you of it. You have seen it throughout your school years and in almost every daily newspaper. One of the new mathematics texts for the second grade sets a problem with a bunny rabbit at $(0, 0)$ and a carrot at $(4, 5)$, asking the child to say how many hops the bunny must take to reach the carrot (stipulating of course that the bunny cannot hop diagonally, so making the problem easier at the cost of upsetting the child's sensitivity to nature).* Wall Street market researchers regularly plot the Dow-Jones averages on the Y-axis and the days and years on the X-axis, without a thought as to why they use this design—how else would you do it? Descartes' ingenious device is by now part and parcel of western civilization.

Variations: Use of a Single Quadrant. Political and social science applications of the coordinate graph ordinarily use only a part of the whole Cartesian system. The basic plan permits the location of any point in space by a simple listing of its three coordinates

---

* Answer: 9 hops.

(x, y, z). Each coordinate ranges from zero (the point of origin—of intersection of the three axes) to plus or minus infinity. For points on a plane, the two axes needed (by convention called the X and Y axes) are perpendicular to one another. For points in space, the third axis (by convention, the Z-axis) is perpendicular to the plane defined by the X and Y axes. In the graphs most used in political and social research we rarely see the third-dimensional coordinate. For that matter, most such graphs use only one quadrant of the Cartesian plane—the $(+x, +y)$ quadrant, since negative data are unusual. There are exceptions. Statistical distributions, such as the "normal" bell-shaped curve, are plotted with the mean defined as zero on the X-axis, so that values below the mean fall in the $(-x, +y)$ quadrant. Attitudinal scales (negative for opposition, positive for support, zero for indifferent) also might make appropriate use of the $(-x, +y)$ quadrant. This usage is illustrated in Figure 3–15.

Two Scales. Another important difference between many political and social graphs and the original Cartesian system is the use of *two different scales* on the two axes, each scale measuring one of the two variables compared. Quite commonly our Y-axis is a percentage of a frequency scale, while our X-axis is time, intensity of attitude, score on a questionnaire, or some measure of magnitude. When different scales are used for the two axes, it is important to realize that there is no necessary relation between the physical distances of the two—the length of intervals is a matter of convenience, availability of suitable graph paper, or simply pleasing proportions.

The examples which follow do not exhaust the variety of applications of the coordinate graph to political data, but include those most likely to be found in your reading or to be useful in your own work.

1. *Time Series Relationships.* Time is the unique variable. When paired with another factor on a coordinate graph it almost always is placed on the X-axis, and of course it has no zero value. It is conceivable, though rare in applications that a temporal variable might be measured on both axes (age and tenure of political leaders might be so displayed, and both are measured in terms of time—unlike time itself, both have zero values).

Our first example, Figure 3–10 (a), shows the simple relationship of a highly "visible" election to a less visible one, illustrated in the United States by the well-known impact of presidential contests on

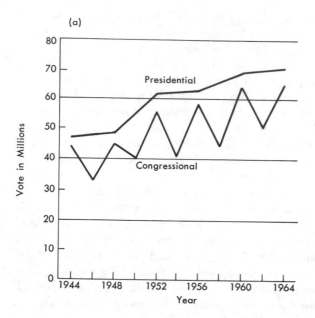

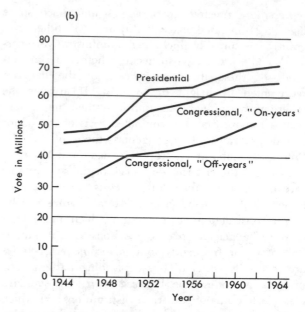

FIGURE 3-10. *Voter Turnout in United States Presidential and Congressional Elections*

turnout in Congressional elections. In the quadrennial years, Congressional voting closely approaches (though never reaches) the presidential turnout. In the off-year (non-presidential) elections, it falls to a consistently lower level. The graph makes its point without labored discussion, and suggests the possible use of two separate "curves," as in Figure 3–10(b), one connecting the Congressional elections in presidential years and another connecting those in off-years, as a clearer portrayal of the impact of the more conspicuous election.

2. *Frequency Polygons.* Coordinate graphs may be usefully combined with bar graphs to bring out relationships not clearly seen if one is used alone. One example is the statistician's histogram—a set of bar graphs indicating frequencies of cases in a given distribution—with a frequency polygon superimposed. The frequency polygon is simply a curve plotted through the midpoints of the top lines of the bars. In such a display, the Y-axis measures the frequencies and the X-axis measures the variation in value for the particular variable whose distribution is being studied. The device is shown in Figure 3–11(a), where we see the theoretical distribution of the values displayed by two dice if thrown thirty-six times (we defer here briefly to the gambler's interest in probability theory in honor of Blaise Pascal, who wrote the first theoretical paper on probability in response to a puzzled inquiry from a noble gambler friend who had been losing consistently and wondered why—as have most of his successors in that role).

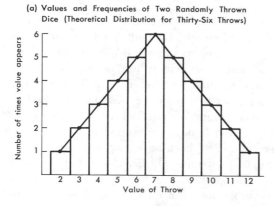

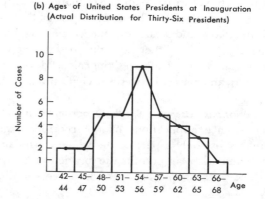

FIGURE 3-11. *Histograms of Frequency Distributions*

If we throw two honest dice many times ("honest" means random throws and an equal chance that any possible pair of the twelve surfaces will come up on any throw), we "expect" the theoretical distribution of Figure 3–11(a) for the eleven possible values. We "expect" this result only in terms of the law of large numbers—we do not really "expect" it on the first thirty-six throws; in fact we should be greatly surprised and probably suspicious if this precise pattern turned up on the first round. But the result is what the experienced gambler knows "in his bones" (pun accidental) to be the average pattern. Snake-eyes (1–1) and boxcars (6–6) are rare, sevens most likely. If a long series of throws fails to turn up a seven, he suspects the dice are loaded.

In Figure 3–11(b) we shift abruptly to a minor political pattern similar to that of the dice. Does the graph imply that the ages of presidents can be predicted by throwing dice? The question is ridiculous, but the patterns share a basic similarity—each reflects a random process. Within the 42–68 age limits, the data reveal the distribution of presidental ages to be very like that of the random dots of the dice. The same is true, of course, of the frequency distributions of a large number of natural characteristics.

More complicated results of random processes lead to the rich lore of inductive statistics. The experienced gambler knows that fifty throws without a seven almost surely means crooked dice (can you compute the probability of a seven? It is 1/6 (50) or 8.3 to 1.). So too, the political scientist knows that if a mean value of ten consistently develops in his data, his testing sample is almost surely not drawn randomly from a universe in which the mean is known to be twenty.

3. *Compound Bars and Curves.* Compound bar graphs may be set parallel to the *X* and *Y* axes of a coordinate graph to show more plainly the patterns of distribution on each. The information-packed graph of Figure 3–12 shows more data in a compact space than any other you are likely to see. Its complexity is justified by the fact that it was planned to be used over and over again as the basic map legend of the *Atlas of Economic Development.* It is so detailed that special explanation is needed:

(a) The curve on the coordinate graph connects 134 points (not shown), each representing the percentage of the population of one country in secondary and higher education in 1954–55. The countries are ranked in order of magnitude on this characteristic—highest at the left

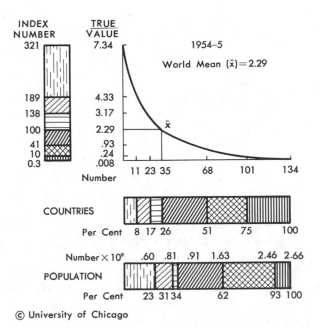

FIGURE 3-12. *Percentage in Secondary and Higher Education: (An Example of a Complex Graphic Display Used by the* Atlas of Economic Development)

Source: Norton Ginsburg, *Atlas of Economic Development.* Copyright 1961 by the University of Chicago. Reprinted by permission of the University of Chicago Press.

and lowest on the right (the *Atlas* gives the complete ranking and values on an opposing page for convenient study). The country ranking highest on the scale is shown to have 7.34 per cent of its population in secondary or higher education (West Germany), the country lowest on the scale (British Somaliland) a miniscule 0.001 per cent.

(b) The world mean $(\bar{x})$ is separately computed by taking the percentage of the world's population in secondary and higher education—it is not a simple unweighted average of values for the 134 countries.

(c) Going next to the horizontal bar graphs below the *X*-axis, the hatchings divide the bar into six segments. On the first bar these correspond to the marks on the *X*-axis itself. The 134 countries are divided into six groups—three equal groups above the world mean and three below the world mean. The number of countries falling in each group is shown on the scale above the bar, with corresponding percentages entered below the bar. The second horizontal bar uses the same hatchings for the same groups of countries, but the scales and the widths of the hatched segments are based on the population of each of the six groups, rather than simply the number of countries.

(d) The vertical bar to the left of the Y-axis uses the same hatchings to identify the range of values included in each of the six groups of countries. The divisions correspond to the marks on the Y-axis. The scale to the right of the bar lists the seven percentages (in secondary or higher education) which divide the world into the six groups. The scale to the left of the bar lists corresponding "Index Numbers" which are calculated simply as percentages of the world mean.

Thus with a little study, one can read from this graph such information as: "Thirty-five countries, or 26 per cent of the 134 countries for which data were available on the characteristic of population percentage in secondary and higher education, were above the world mean of 2.29 per cent. These countries contained about 900,000 people, or 34 per cent of the people in the world. The highest value for any country was 7.34 per cent, or 321 per cent of the world mean."

You will probably not use such a complex display in your own work, but one or more of the devices it employs may suggest a similar combination of a compound bar graph parallel to an axis of a coordinate graph, particularly if a graphic pattern is repeated for several related displays.

4. *Focus on Area.* Use of the area under a plotted curve or between two curves is involved in computation of the Gini index, described in Chapter 1. Area relationships are not often stressed in simple coordinate graphs, and often have no special significance, but sometimes are useful in bringing out patterns not

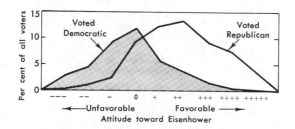

FIGURE 3-13. *Relation of Attitude Toward Eisenhower to Party Vote, 1956*

Source: Angus Campbell *et al., The American Voter* (New York: John Wiley & Sons, Inc.). Reprinted by permission of the publisher.

otherwise apparent. The example of Figure 3–13 uses area to show the relationship of vote choice (Democratic or Republican) to respondent attitude toward the incumbent. The X-axis measures an ordinal scale, based on an index of attitudes toward Eisenhower in the election of 1956. The nine-point scale ranges from most unfavorable (− − −) to most favorable (+ + + + +). The Y-axis shows the percentage of respondents within each of these nine attitude groups who voted Democratic and Republican. In the two-party system, a few adherents of the opposition Democrats were among Eisenhower's strongest supporters but still voted against him, presumably from party loyalty. On the other hand, some Republicans who were most unfavorable to Eisenhower still voted for him, having "nowhere else to go." The great bulk of the sample surveyed mildly approved or mildly disapproved— more the former than the latter, so that a strong voter consensus emerged for his re-election. The central humps of the two party curves are shifted only slightly from the zero point of the X-axis toward the pro-Eisenhower side of the attitude scale, but quite enough for a landslide electoral result.

5. *Conceptual Use of Graphs.* With the precision of scales relaxed or entirely abandoned, the coordinate graph is often used to set forth a verbal proposition in graphic form. The Cartesian pattern is so familiar as to make this a feasible technique of discourse and reasoning. In Robert Dahl's discussion of consensus and disagreement in a democracy, such hypothetical graphs illustrate a variety of patterns of distribution of public opinion on a given issue, showing intensity of feeling about the issue on the X-axis and percentage within each intensity category on the Y-axis. In Figure 3–14 we adapt a few of Dahl's categories, though the original graphs are modified in several ways: (1) an "indifference" category is added to permit use of a zero point on the X-axis, (2) two quadrants are used, the (−x, +y) quadrant being added for the display of opposition attitudes, (3) a short numerical attitude scale is substituted to show more plainly the use of the graph, and (4) hypothetical summary tables are supplied to clarify the distributions.[*]

6. *Graphing a Theory with Generalized Data.* A general theoretical concept not only may be expressed on a graph, but the pattern may be tested with empirical data, at least in a generalized way. An excellent example of such use of non-rigorous data

---

[*] Robert A. Dahl, *A Preface to Democratic Theory.* Chicago: University of Chicago Press, 1956, pp. 93–99.

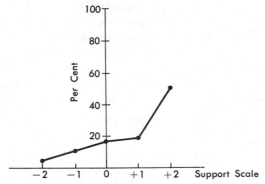

Issue A: Strong Consensus, Strong Preference, Slight Indifference

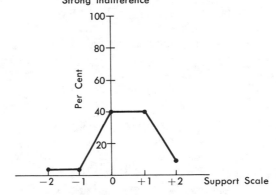

Issue B: Strong Consensus, Weak Preference, Strong Indifference

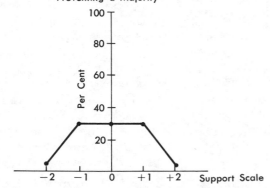

Issue C: Moderate Disagreement, Indifference Preventing a Majority

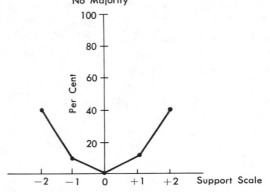

Issue D: Strong Disagreement, No Indifference, No Majority

FIGURE 3-14. *Four Patterns of Consensus and Disagreement*

Hypothetical Opinion Distributions on Four Issues
(in Per Cent)

Attitude	Support Scale Value	Issue A	Issue B	Issue C	Issue D
Strongly For	+2	50	10	5	40
For	+1	20	40	30	10
Indifferent	0	15	40	30	0
Against	−1	10	5	30	10
Strongly Against	−2	5	5	5	40
Total		100	100	100	100
(N)		(?)	(?)	(?)	(?)

is James C. Davies' presentation of his theory of revolution. Davies reasons that:

Revolutions are most likely to occur when a prolonged period of objective economic and social development is followed by a short period of sharp reversal. . . . It is the dissatisfied state of mind rather than the tangible provision of "adequate" or "inade-

quate" supplies of food, equality, or liberty which produces the revolution.*

In other words, it is not sheer economic oppression which leads people to revolt, but the gap between

* James C. Davies, "Need Satisfaction and Revolution." *American Sociological Review*, Vol. 27, No. 1, February 1962, pp. 5–19.

expectation and satisfaction. Expectations rise during a period of improvement in conditions of life, and then are dangerously frustrated when conditions take a turn for the worse. Davies reminds us that Tocqueville adopted a similar thesis in his work on the French Revolution: "Evils which are patiently endured when they seem inevitable become intolerable when once the idea of escape from them is suggested."

In Figure 3–15(a), Davies charts this general theory, bolstering it in his original article with non-rigorous empirically-based time graphs of Dorr's Rebellion of 1842, the Russian Revolution of 1917, and the Egyptian Revolution of 1952. Figure 3–15(b) reproduces his graph of conditions culminating in the Russian Revolution, the time variable on the *X*-axis running from the emancipation of the serfs in 1861 to the disorder following the military disasters of World War I. The inverted *J*-curve of rising expectations followed by their frustration obviously cannot be plotted with precise coordinates, but Davies summons up an impressive quantity of data on agricultural and industrial production, farm and factory pay scales, population increase, and urbanization, combined with historical data on political and economic unrest, in support of the general pattern of the graph in Figure 3–15(b). He does not argue that the theory explains all revolutions, nor that the *J*-curve pattern inevitably results in revolution. His emphasis is rather that some such device is needed for examination of the combination of economic, political, social, and psychological factors which most scholars would agree are involved in violent change.

7. Graphing a Theoretical Relationship with Precise Data. Few political principles have the precision of a mathematical formula, but an apparent exception is the "cube law of representation." According to this "law," the ratio of contested seats won by two parties in a single-member-district electoral system will closely approximate the cube of the ratio of votes. If we let *x* represent the proportion of votes won by a given party (expressed as a decimal fraction of unity or 1.00), then the other party's vote will be 1.00 − *x*. Then if *y* represents the proportion of seats won by the same party, the cube law holds that:

$$y/(1.00 - y) = (x/(1.00 - x))^3$$

This awkward equation has been recast by James G. March into a more convenient formula for *y* (if your algebra is not too rusty, you may enjoy deriving the simpler equation yourself):

$$y = x^3/(3x^2 - 3x + 1.00)$$

The curve of this equation is shown in Figure 3–16 (the cube law makes sense only for positive values of *x* and *y*). Superimposed on the graph are two linear (straight-line) equations derived by Robert Dahl from results of elections for the United States House of Representatives (1928–1954) and Senate (1928–1952). To avoid clutter, the points on which Dahl's lines are based are not shown, but the correlation of actual results with his formulas is extremely high. In his equations, *x* and *y* represent the Democratic party's proportion of votes and seats. You do not need algebra to recognize that the cube law curve approximates a rather steep straight line for values between .3 and .7, and that Dahl's regression lines, based on pure empirical data, fit the slant of the theoretical curve rather well.

(a) The Generalized Concept: Need Satisfaction and Revolution

(b) An Empirical Example: The Russian Revolution

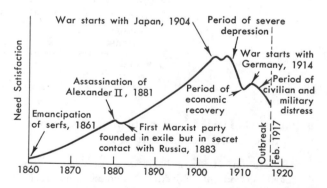

FIGURE 3-15. *The Davies J-Curve of Revolution*

Source: James C. Davies, "Need Satisfaction and Revolution," *American Sociological Review,* Vol. 27, No. 1, February 1962. Reprinted with the kind permission of the author and publisher.

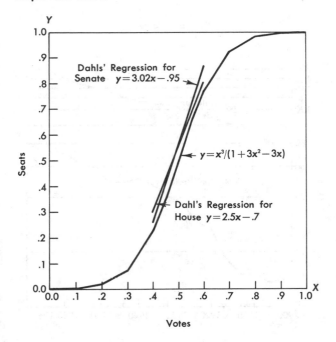

Y
1.0
.9
Dahls' Regression for
Senate $y = 3.02x - .95$
.8
.7
.6
Seats
.5 ← $y = x^3/(1 + 3x^2 - 3x)$
.4
.3 ← Dahl's Regression for
House $y = 2.5x - .7$
.2
.1
0.0
0.0 .1 .2 .3 .4 .5 .6 .7 .8 .9 1.0 X

Votes

FIGURE 3-16. The Cube Law of Representation and Dahl's Regressions for the U.S. Congress

8. *Ratio Graphs and Rates of Change.* Often we are interested not only in comparing change in absolute values of variables, but also in comparing *rates of change*. In a time series we may wish to know whether a value is changing by a constant ratio or whether the rate of change is increasing or decreasing. We may wish to compare rates of change in different time periods for one variable, or to examine the relationship between the rates of change in two or more variables.

The simplest way to make such comparisons is by use of a ratio graph, drawn on a semi-logarithmic graph grid. On semi-logarithmic graph paper (obtainable in almost any college bookstore), one of the two axes is divided into logarithmic values (hence "semi-") rather than arithmetic values. You do not need to understand logarithms to get the idea of a ratio graph, but if you are familiar with the slide rule you will recognize the Y-axis as a slide-rule scale. The key to this scale is simple—all values for equal proportions are measured in equal distances. The measured distance between 200 and 100 is exactly the same as the distances between 100 and 50, 80 and 40, 60 and 30, 40 and 20, 20 and 10—indeed between any pair of values having a 2 to 1 ratio.

The fact that the Y-axis is scaled by ratios means that a plotted curve with a constant *rate* of change

(not a constant change in absolute values) will be a straight line—slanting up if the value is increasing and down if the value is decreasing. On an ordinary graph the fact that one line slants up more steeply than another means merely that it reflects a greater absolute change; a comparison of rates requires a separate computation.

No Zero. Since the ratio of any positive number to zero is infinity, the lowest value shown on semi-logarithmic paper is 1, just as on the slide rule. However, since the scale measures ratios rather than absolute numbers, we can make this 1 as large or as small as we like—it could represent .00001 as easily as 1,000,-000,000, providing only that we keep the other values consistent with it. Two-cycle, three-cycle, and four-cycle grids are available for displaying great ranges of magnitude, each cycle representing values ten times those of the one below.

Comparison of Two Variables. Figure 3–17 shows a comparison of the same data plotted first on an ordinary arithmetic scale and then on a ratio scale. Notice that the curve representing presidential vote appears in the first graph to lag behind the curve representing population, where in the second graph the opposite relationship is shown to exist if ratios are considered. Since 1920 the over-all rate of increase is greater for voting than for population, though this cannot be seen by comparing the absolute increases on the arithmetic scale. The second graph also emphasizes more strongly than the first the abrupt rise in voting in 1920 (women's suffrage) and in 1952, as well as the decline in World War II.

Two Scales for Different Orders of Magnitude. Another advantage of the ratio graph is its usefulness for comparing two variables which have values of a different order of magnitude. Figure 3–18 illustrates this application, comparing rates of increase in the populations of California and Nevada. When plotted as an arithmetic graph the curves are almost impossible to compare because of the great difference in magnitude of the two series. If both curves are placed on the same graph, the Nevada curve is almost a flat line, although—as the ratio graph shows clearly—a population increase of more than 400 per cent occurred during the period. On the ratio graph, the values for California are measured on the left-hand scale and those for Nevada on the right-hand scale. The two scales are possible because the distance between the two curves is of no importance on a ratio graph. Moving a curve up or down on the grid does not change its shape in any way since only ratios are displayed.

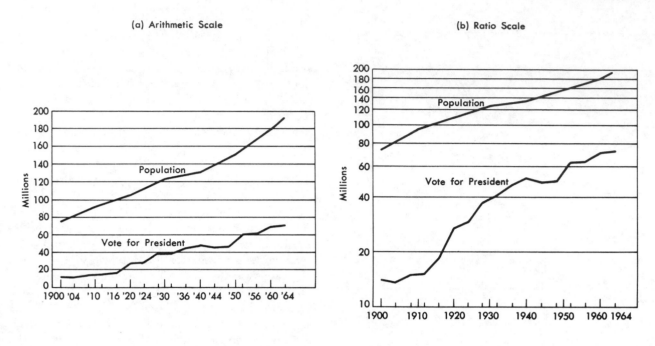

FIGURE 3-17. *Growth in U.S. Population and Popular Vote for President, 1900–1964*

Source: *Statistical Abstract of the United States,* 1966.

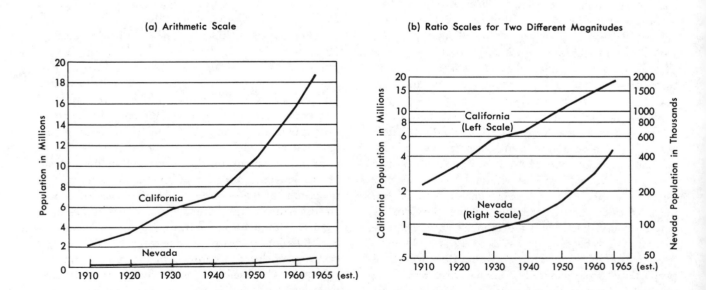

FIGURE 3-18. *Population Growth in California and Nevada, 1910–1965*

Source of Data: *Historical Statistics of the United States.*

Two Scales for Two Units of Measurement. Figure 3–19 shows another advantage of defining two scales on a ratio graph. If we are interested only in comparing rates of change, there is nothing to prevent us from defining the left-hand scale in terms of one kind of unit and the right-hand scale in terms of another. Though we may not be able to add apples and oranges, we can compare their rates of increase or decrease. In Figure 3–19 the left-hand scale measures the gross national product of the United States in billions of dollars and the right-hand scale measures the population of the United States in millions of persons, permitting a comparison otherwise quite difficult to display.

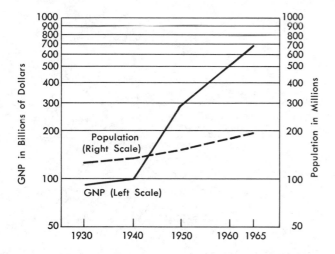

FIGURE 3-19. *Growth in U.S. Population and Gross National Product, 1930–1965 (A Ratio Graph with Scales for Two Different Units)*

Source: *Statistical Abstract of the United States,* 1966.

Ratio graphs are seldom found in political science literature, though used extensively in economics and in the "hard" sciences. As the study of political and social change advances, we may anticipate further experiment with this useful device.

3-5 Circle and Half-Circle Graphs

Commonly called a "pie chart" or a "half-pie," this form of graphic display occurs rarely in technical scholarly work, though it is a favorite for popular presentation of data in newspapers and government publications. Like the compound bar graph, it is convenient for showing the dimensions of component parts for nominal variables; but unlike the bar graph, comparisons between two circle graphs of different sizes are difficult both for the draftsman to design and for the reader to interpret. An advantage is that comparisons between circle graphs of the same size are often more emphatic than those between bar graphs, because of the 360° sweep of the circular "axis" on which the divisions are marked.

Two Political Applications. The circle graph is especially appropriate for budgetary data; its use seems almost inevitable to show how the taxpayer's dollar is sliced up—often the circle graph becomes an actual pictogram of a coin. Figure 3–20 is a standard example, showing the major components of government expenditures at the federal, state, and local levels in the United States. Though exact comparisons are difficult—the circle is not marked as a scale—the relative importance of the principal functions performed by the three levels of government stands out rather clearly.

The half-circle or half-pie graph is well adapted to the display of party distributions, especially in a multiparty system, since it fits easily the left-right political spectrum. Although the half-circle graph is far less used than the circle graph, it is to be recommended for this special purpose in political science. The half-pie is both easier to construct and easier for the reader to study than the full-circle graph—the standard 180° protractor serves nicely to lay out the percentages. Figure 3–21 shows this application for elections in Austria and Britain.

A Note on Mechanics. If you use circle or half-circle graphs in your own work, attention to several special features of this design will help. On a full circle, sectors are usually arranged clockwise by size, beginning with the vertical radius from the center to the "north." This pattern is frequently violated, and in many cases another sequence is more logical, particularly when several circle graphs are used in one display for comparison. If two or more circles are to be compared, it is important that the same sequence and the same radius of origin be used—and the same hatching patterns if hatching is employed. Avoid the temptation to use too many sectors; it is easy to overload the graph with small components. Since there is no marked scale to aid the reader, it is necessary to letter in the names and values for the components. If percentages are not entered on

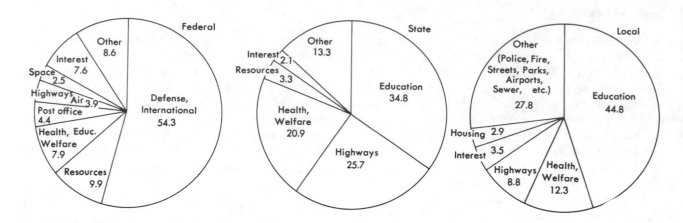

FIGURE 3-20. *General Governmental Expenditure in the United States by Function and Level of Government, 1963*
(in Percentages)

Source: *Statistical Abstract of the United States, 1966,* p. 424.

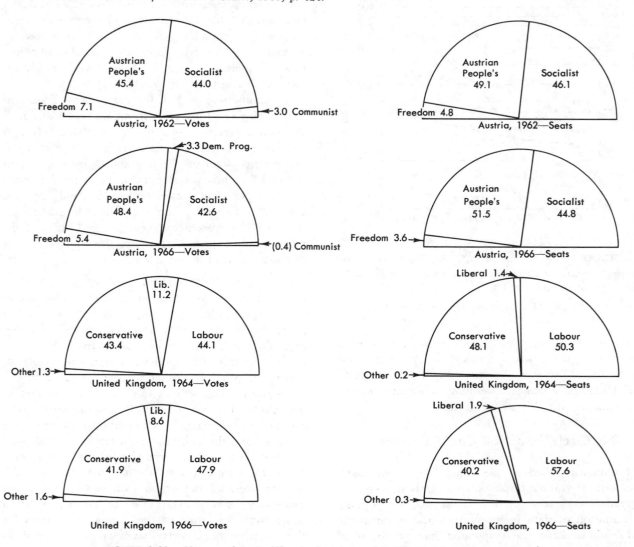

FIGURE 3-21. *Votes and Seats Won in Austrian and British Elections (in percentages)*

Source of Data: *Britannica Book of the Year,* 1967.

80

the graph, it is almost impossible for the reader to estimate them.

For actual construction of a percentage circle or half-circle graph, you will find a conversion table useful, since such mechanical aids as protractors and polar coordinate graph paper are invariably marked off in degrees. (Circular percentage graph paper is in fact manufactured, and can be obtained on special order by your bookstore, though it is not commonly stocked.) Fortunately, conversion of percentages to degrees is a simple procedure, as a little work with Table 3–1 will demonstrate.

TABLE 3-1. *Table for Converting Percentages to Degrees for Circle and Half-Circle Graphs*

Per Cent	Degrees on Half Circle	Degrees on Full Circle
10	18	36
20	36	72
30	54	108
40	72	144
50	90	180
60	108	216
70	126	252
80	144	288
90	162	324

To use the table, add the value in the appropriate column for the even multiple of ten to one-tenth of the value needed for the units place. For example, the values for 47 per cent are obtained by adding:

$$72 + 12.6 = 84.6 \quad \text{(for a half circle)}$$
$$144 + 25.2 = 169.2 \quad \text{(for a full circle)}$$

3-6 Pure Relationship Graphs

From the domains of mathematical graph theory and symbolic logic come two graphic patterns increasingly used in political science—the directed graph and the Venn diagram. Ordinarily without any quantitative reference, they are convenient devices for showing patterns of relationship of persons or units and partitioning of groups or sets. For an adequate grasp of the full possibilities of these graphs you should go to more specialized books. Here we shall look at only a few examples to give you some idea of how they can be used.

Directed Graphs. Relationships among units may be shown by portraying the units as vertices (corners or ends) and the relationships among them as connecting edges (lines), with arrows pointing the directions of the relationships. We distinguish three kinds of relationships which may be so diagrammed: (1) those which are always one-way (dominance, rule, causality), shown with one arrow; (2) those which may be either one-way or two-way (communication, influence, hostility, friendship), shown with either one or two arrows; and (3) those which are always two-way (partnership, mutual defense, social acquaintance, common party membership), shown either with two arrows or with arrows omitted if mutuality of the relationship is well understood. Figure 3–22 shows these usages, the notation style *aRb* meaning that *a* is related to *b*.

In graph theory we focus solely on the linkage relations among units. The general shape of the

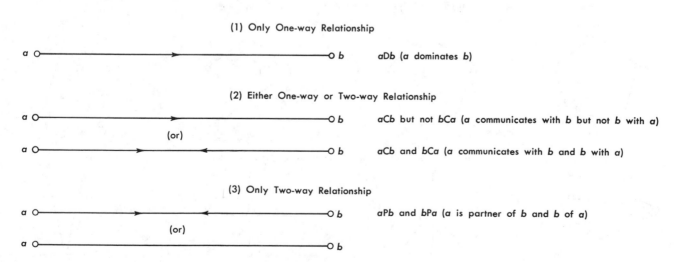

(1) Only One-way Relationship

a ⟶ *b*   *aDb* (*a* dominates *b*)

(2) Either One-way or Two-way Relationship

a ⟶ *b*   *aCb* but not *bCa* (*a* communicates with *b* but not *b* with *a*)

(or)

a ⟶ ⟵ *b*   *aCb* and *bCa* (*a* communicates with *b* and *b* with *a*)

(3) Only Two-way Relationship

a ⟶ ⟵ *b*   *aPb* and *bPa* (*a* is partner of *b* and *b* of *a*)

(or)

a —— *b*

FIGURE 3-22. *Directed Graphs*

diagram is of no importance. The four graphs of Figure 3–23 (a) are all different, representing the four ways in which five units may be associated with the minimum of four linkages. On the other hand, the four diagrams of Figure 3–23 (b) are all identical, all having the same linkage pattern as the fourth graph of Figure 3–23 (a). Some conventions of arrangement are usually followed—left to right, top to bottom, equal lengths for two branching lines— but arrangement is not an essential feature of a directed graph. The tree diagram of Figure 4–3, for example, might have branched up or down or to the left as well as to the right—the layout is planned to suit the use.

Empirical Applications. Directed graphs lend themselves to the study of a wide range of relationships. A complex government or business organization chart is a non-rigorous form of a directed graph. The causal relationships of three variables shown in Figure 2–1 at the end of Chapter 2 is a simple application, as is the logic tree for data sorting in Figure 4–3. Sociologists use a direct adaptation, the *sociogram,* to examine relations in small groups. Sociograms may be used to map relationships such as social friendships, lines of influence, or communications (one-way or two-way), or may be the basis of carefully controlled experiments. A study of informal social relations existing in two groups of five persons each, for example, might reveal the pattern of Figure 3–24, one-way arrows meaning one-way choice of association, and two-way arrows meaning mutual choice. We see clearly that each group is closely knit (except for the isolate case *J,* to which the researcher should

devote special attention). There is little intergroup contact, the only links being *B*'s choice of *F* and *I*'s choice of *C*. In Group 1, *A* seems to be a natural leader; all the other four members choose to associate with him though he extends his choices only to *B* and *E*. The four associates in Group 2, on the other hand, are all equal in this respect.

Experiments with working groups having different linkage patterns have shown that some are more efficient than others in problem solving, that some seem to have higher group morale, and that some are more likely than others to develop leadership. Possible applications to political relationships will occur to you readily. Three examples will suffice. The unidirectional dominance graphs of Figure 3–25 are used to indicate hierarchical, circular, and mixed dominance in a small group. In Figure 3–26 the communication nets display the linkages between the President of the United States and the Chairman of the Council of Ministers of the Soviet Union before and after installation of the "hot line." Notice that the process of sending a message and getting an answer required eight linkage steps before the hot line in comparison with only two afterwards. Figure 3–27 shows two patterns of social control which might represent underground organizations seeking a minimum risk of membership exposure to the police, the first tightly controlled from the center, the second egalitarian. In these graphs, lines alone mean a two-way working relationship, while lines with an arrow mean one-way disciplinary authority.

Quantification. Directed graphs are not merely pictured relationships. They may be used as the basis

(a) Four Different Linkage Patterns for a Group of Five

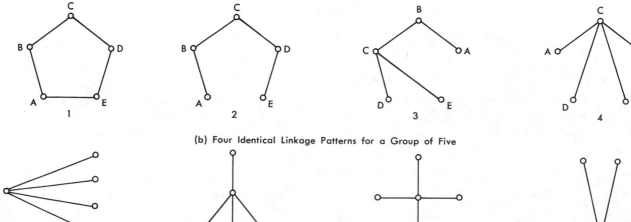

(b) Four Identical Linkage Patterns for a Group of Five

FIGURE 3-23. *Linkage Patterns for a Group of Five*

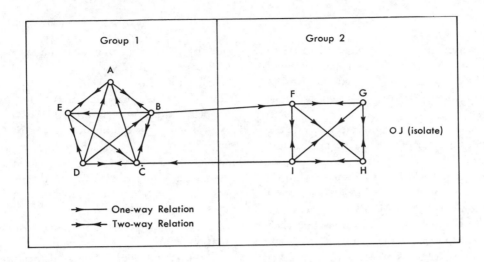

Communication Matrix for Group 1 (M)

	A	B	C	D	E
A	0	1	0	0	1
B	1	0	0	1	0	1
C	1	1	0	1	0
D	1	1	1	0	1
E	1	0	1	1	0

Communication Matrix for Two-Step Message Flow in Group 1 (M^2)

	A	B	C	D	E
A	2	0	2	1	1
B	2	2	1	2	1
C	2	2	2	0	3
D	3	2	2	2	2
E	2	3	1	1	2

Communication Matrix for Three-Step Message Flow in Group 1 (M^3)

	A	B	C	D	E
A	4	5	2	3	3
B	6	5	5	2	6
C	7	4	5	5	4
D	8	7	6	4	7
E	7	4	6	3	6

FIGURE 3-24. *Sociogram of Friendship Relations in Two Groups of Five Persons*

(1) Hierarchy

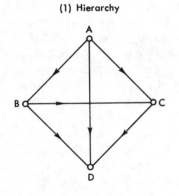

(2) Circular

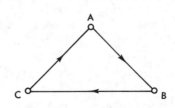

(3) Mixed

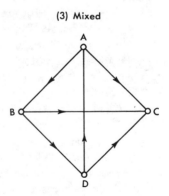

Dominance Matrices

	A	B	C	D
A	0	1	1	1
B	0	0	1	1
C	0	0	0	1
D	0	0	0	0

	A	B	C
A	0	1	0
B	0	0	1
C	1	0	0

	A	B	C	D
A	0	1	1	0
B	0	0	1	1
C	0	0	0	0
D	1	0	1	0

Landau's $H = 1.00$

Landau's $H = 0.00$

Landau's $H = .60$

Landau's Hierarchy Index: $H = \dfrac{12}{n^3 - n} \cdot \sum_{i=1}^{n} \left(V_i - \dfrac{n-1}{2} \right)^2$

(in which V_i's are the row sums in the dominance matrix)

FIGURE 3-25. *Directed Graphs for Three Patterns of Dominance*

for several patterns of quantitative analysis. Detailed discussion of such methods is beyond the scope of this book, but if you work further with graphs of this type you will wish to learn something of these techniques.

1. *Counting Linkages.* The simplest quantitative approach is comparison of the number of linkages between units. For the four patterns of working relationships (all assumed two-way) in Figure 3–23(a), we can count the number of linkages required for any unit to communicate with all the others. We can then add the number of such linkages for each group, arriving at a total—the number of steps required for all units in the system to communicate with all others. The result is shown in Table 3–2.

TABLE 3-2. *Linkages in a Five-Unit System*

System	Linkages Required for All Members To Communicate with All Others	Minimum Linkages Required for Any One Member To Communicate with All Others
1	30	6
2	40	6
3	36	5
4	32	4

2. *Experimental Results.* Actual laboratory experiments have been devised to test the features of these same linkage patterns for groups of five. Among other results was the discovery of a close association between "centrality" of a member in the group and the emergence of a leadership role for the most "central" member in the performance of a work assignment. For Pattern 1 there is no central unit—all five are connected in a circular set of linkages. In Patterns 2, 3, and 4 the degree of centrality of the most central member may be measured by the minimum linkages required to communicate with all other members. These are listed in the last column of Table 3–2, and for all three patterns it is member C who occupies this most central position. In one series of tests it was found that C emerged as leader 67 per cent of the time for Pattern 2, 85 per cent of the time for Pattern 3, and 100 per cent of the time for Pattern 4. Thus the theoretical concept of centrality and empirical findings on leadership were directly correlated.

3. *Matrix Manipulation.* A directed graph may be quantified as an elementary square matrix, with each row and column corresponding to one of the units in the graph. A "1" is entered in a cell if the unit listed in the row has the specified relationship with the unit listed in the column—when rRc (row is Related to

column). A zero is entered in the appropriate cell of the matrix when row does not have the relationship with column. Thus each of the dominance graphs of Figure 3–25 might be set in the matrix form given just below the graph. Landau has developed a Hierarchy Index based on such a matrix, with values ranging from 0.00 if each individual has the same number of dominances as every other, to 1.00 for a system in which maximum hierarchy exists—where every individual i in a group of size N is dominant over $N - i$ others. In Figure 3–25, Landau values for the three systems are given without the computations.

4. *Feedbacks and Cliques.* A matrix may be squared, cubed, and taken to higher powers, by successively multiplying it by itself. The operation of matrix multiplication is laborious but yields several valuable results. The square of a communications matrix will show on the main diagonal (running from upper left to lower right) the number of direct feedbacks to each unit, and in the other cells will show the number of two-step linkages from any unit to any other. The cubed matrix shows on the main diagonal the number of three-step feedbacks to each unit, and elsewhere the number of three-step linkages between all pairs of units. Squared and cubed matrix patterns are shown with Figure 3–24 for the five persons in Group 1. You should check the numbers on the diagonals with feedbacks you can trace on the graph.

If the matrix for a relationship graph showing one-way or two-way choice of friends (or other optional relationships) is simplified by eliminating the entries for one-way choices, we have a symmetrical matrix (for every "1" showing that row chooses column, another "1" shows that column chooses row). If we then define a subgroup or clique as consisting of three or more members, all of whom have a two-way friendship relationship with all others in the subgroup, we can use matrix multiplication to identify the existence, identity, and size of the subgroups. The cubed symmetrical matrix will have a zero on the main diagonal for those units which do not belong to any subgroup so defined, and for those which do belong to such subgroup, the number on the main diagonal helps identify the size of the subgroup involved. For groups of three, this entry will be "2"; for groups of four, it will be "6"; in general, for groups of size n, it will be $(n - 1)(n - 2)$. If the same individual is a member of two such groups, the number on the main diagonal will be twice that which would appear for one group of the same size. We will not carry out any such computations, but you can easily verify the principle by examination of the two graphs in Figure 3–27. The cubed symmetrical matrix of the "disciplined hierarchy" would consist entirely of zeroes—there are no groups of three mutual associates (the system has no feedback). The cubed symmetrical matrix of the conspiracy groups would have a non-zero entry on the main diagonal for each unit—4's for the nine more central members, since each is a member of two subgroups of three, and 2's for the twelve peripheral members, since each is a member of one group of three.

5. *Markov Transition Vectors and Crisis Diplomacy.* John Kemeny, the Dartmouth mathematician who has worked extensively with social science problems, suggests an interesting and useful form of the communications matrix. In his model the row entries for each unit are a listing of the probabilities of the communication process moving from row to column. Putting the "hot line" graphs (Figure 3–26) in the form of such a matrix, we assume that any unit is equally likely to communicate with any other to which it has a direct channel. Entries on each row total 1.00—that is, all of a row unit's one-step communication possibilities are entered, each expressed as a fraction of unity. A matrix constructed in this way (each row adding to 1.00) is called a *stochastic* matrix, and may be used to define a Markov chain (a process moving through a series of states with given probabilities of its moving next to any state in the set). For such a matrix, a "fixed point vector" can often be found: a row of numbers also adding to 1.00, which can be used as a multiplier for the matrix, yielding the very same vector—the very same row of numbers—as a product. Kemeny suggests that this vector, containing a probability listing for each unit in the system, makes an excellent index of importance of units in a communications network (importance only as communication units for the process so described, of course). The probability vectors for the two "hot line" graphs in Figure 3–26 are 1/12 (1, 3, 2, 2, 3, 1)

(a) Before

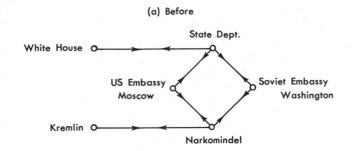

(b) After

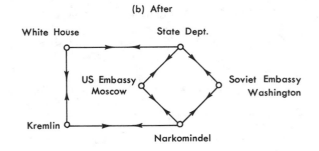

Probability Matrices and Transition Vectors

(a) Before

$$1/12 \ (1, 3, 2, 2, 3, 1) \cdot \begin{array}{c} \\ W \\ S \\ M \\ SE \\ N \\ K \end{array} \begin{array}{cccccc} W & S & M & SE & N & K \\ \left[\begin{array}{cccccc} 0 & 1 & 0 & 0 & 0 & 0 \\ 1/3 & 0 & 1/3 & 1/3 & 0 & 0 \\ 0 & 1/2 & 0 & 0 & 1/2 & 0 \\ 0 & 1/2 & 0 & 0 & 1/2 & 0 \\ 0 & 0 & 1/3 & 1/3 & 0 & 1/3 \\ 0 & 0 & 0 & 0 & 1 & 0 \end{array} \right] \end{array} = 1/12 \ (1, 3, 2, 2, 3, 1)$$

(b) After

$$1/14 \ (2, 3, 2, 2, 3, 2) \cdot \begin{array}{c} \\ W \\ S \\ M \\ SE \\ N \\ K \end{array} \begin{array}{cccccc} W & S & M & SE & N & K \\ \left[\begin{array}{cccccc} 0 & 1/2 & 0 & 0 & 0 & 1/2 \\ 1/3 & 0 & 1/3 & 1/3 & 0 & 0 \\ 0 & 1/2 & 0 & 0 & 1/2 & 0 \\ 0 & 1/2 & 0 & 0 & 1/2 & 0 \\ 0 & 0 & 1/3 & 1/3 & 0 & 1/3 \\ 1/2 & 0 & 0 & 0 & 1/2 & 0 \end{array} \right] \end{array} = 1/14 \ (2, 3, 2, 2, 3, 2)$$

FIGURE 3-26. *Communication Graph of the "Hot Line"*

(a) Disciplined Hierarchy

(b) Egalitarian Conspiracy

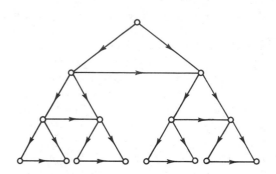

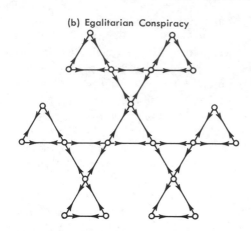

FIGURE 3-27. *Groups of Three in Two Underground Organizations*

and 1/14 (2, 3, 2, 2, 3, 2). If scaled to show the probability that a message is at any given stage in the process at any given time, we obtain the results of Table 3–3.

TABLE 3-3. *Probability of a Message Being at a Given Stage in the Communications Net from White House to Kremlin, Before and After Hot Line*

Unit in Net	Before Hot Line	After Hot Line
White House	.083	.143
State Department	.25	.214
U.S. Embassy, Moscow	.167	.143
Soviet Embassy, Washington	.167	.143
Narkomindel	.25	.214
Kremlin	.083	.143
Total	1.000	1.000

You are not asked to do any problems in quantification of directed graphs, but this short look at their uses may interest you in further exploration. Check the reading list for helpful leads, especially Kemeny's *Mathematical Models in the Social Sciences* and Ore's *Graphs and Their Uses.*

Venn Diagrams. Another form of relationship graph you should know is John Venn's adaptation of Euler's partitioning circles. The standard format of a Venn diagram uses circles within a rectangle to indicate sets or subsets within a universe. Three overlapping circles can be drawn so as to show all possible combinations among them (four or more are possible but confusing and some combinations cannot be shown as single bounded areas). The rectangle representing the universe is called by mathematicians

the *universal set* and by logicians the *universe of discourse*—in either case it is meant to include all possible things being considered.

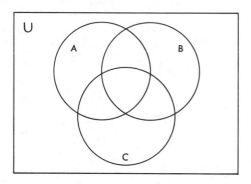

FIGURE 3-28. *Format of a Venn Diagram*

Union, Intersection, and Negation. If a set is defined as all things having a common property, we speak of the *union* of two sets as including all things having *either* property, of the *intersection* of two sets as including all things having *both* properties, and of the *negation* of a set as including all things (in the universe of discourse) *not* having that set's property. The union of Set A and Set B is usually expressed as $A \cup B$, the intersection of Set A and Set B as $A \cap B$, and the negation of Set A as A' or $-A$. Venn diagrams are convenient for displaying these relationships in simple or complex combinations. A few examples appear in Figure 3–29.

Some Political Applications. Logicians use Venn diagrams rigorously to test complicated propositions, syllogisms, and theorems in propositional and class calculus, but like the Cartesian graph grid, the device is becoming a part of standard scholarly exposition for display and discussion of relationships without the logician's precision.

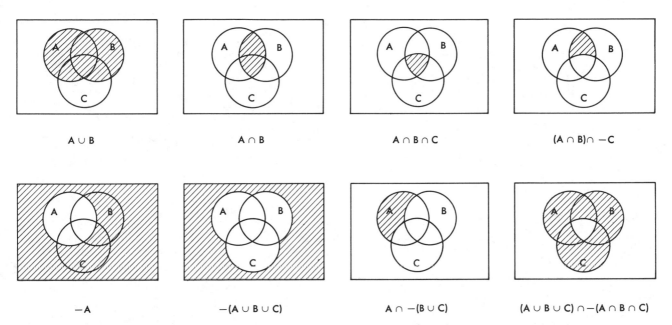

FIGURE 3-29. *Defining Subsets by Venn Diagrams*

1. *Alliances.* We might display the overlapping alliance systems of Figure 3–30 (for convenience we include all original treaty members), as a means of exploring the hypothesis that conflicts within an alliance multiply with broadening commitments of members. The logician usually prefers to retain the full format of circles and intersections, even if some of the subsets are "empty sets," but for less formal use the pattern of Figure 3–30 (c) will seem more natural as a display of interconnections.

2. *Caucusing Groups.* Similarly for the combinations in Figure 3–31 (a), since all Arab states are in either the African caucusing group or the Afro-Asian group, it may seem more informative for the particular purpose to use the diagram of Figure 3–31 (b). Departure from the three-circle convention also will permit a fuller display of all nine UN caucusing groups studied by Vincent in 1961, as in Figure 3–31 (c). In this diagram there are also empty sets (all African members are in the intersection of the

African and Afro-Asian blocs, including the subsets of African states which are also Arab states and those which are also Commonwealth states).

3. *Levels of Government.* The Venn diagram is useful to display relations, functions, expenditures, and inter-level agency organization among the national, state, and local levels of government in the United States or other federal systems. Figure 3–32, on budgets, contains examples of programs actually financed in the several separate and overlapping areas. Other similar uses will occur to you: the three circles might represent functions of the three branches of government (Legislative, Executive, Judicial), or a university's activities (financed from appropriations, endowment, fees, or some combination); two circles could show court jurisdiction (federal, state, with concurrent jurisdiction in the intersection), or the division of constitutional powers in the United States between national and state governments (forbidden powers lying outside the circles).

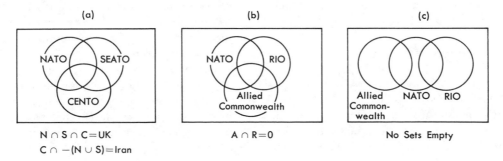

FIGURE 3-30. *Interlocking Alliances Shown by Venn Diagrams*

(a)

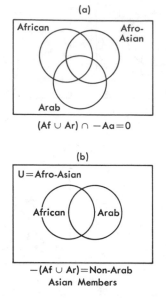

$$(Af \cup Ar) \cap -Aa = 0$$

(b)

U = Afro-Asian

$$-(Af \cup Ar) = \text{Non-Arab}$$
Asian Members

FIGURE 3-31. *UN Caucusing Groups, 1961*

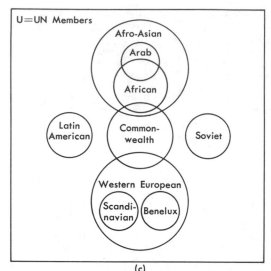

U = UN Members

(c)

Adaptation of Venn Diagram to Show All
Interlocking UN Caucusing Groups in 1961

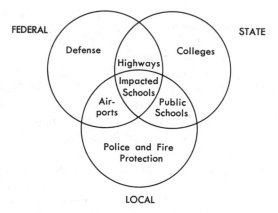

FEDERAL   STATE

Defense   Colleges

Highways

Impacted
Schools

Air-   Public
ports   Schools

Police and Fire
Protection

LOCAL

FIGURE 3-32. *Use of Venn Diagram to Illustrate Source
of Funds for Selected Government Functions*

4. *Elements of a Political Party.* The less formal
pattern of Figure 3–33 is similar in concept to a Venn
diagram and could be redesigned for logical analysis,
but its point is so simple that the formal pattern
would be confusing. The use of concentric circles for
an expanding series of defined groups is a common
method of showing such a relationship.

3-7 A Word on Mechanics

As recently as 1954 the late V.O. Key could
properly deplore the low quality of graphic work
appearing in most social science scholarly journals,
and encourage the amateur draftsman to try his
hand without fear of doing worse. Conditions have

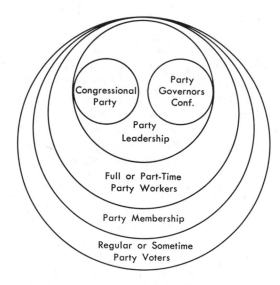

Congressional
Party

Party
Governors
Conf.

Party
Leadership

Full or Part-Time
Party Workers

Party Membership

Regular or Sometime
Party Voters

FIGURE 3-33. *Elements of a Political Party Organization*

improved since then, but you still need not hesitate to
prepare your own graphs, certainly for class reports or
as preliminary drawings for a publisher's art department to perfect. A few suggestions follow for those
who would like to try.

1. Lay in a good supply of graph papers with
various grids, even some you may never use. Since
much of your work with coordinate graphs will
involve percentages, a centimeter scale or a scale in
tenths of an inch will save time and error in plotting
curves.

2. On a finished graph, do not show too many of the scale guidelines; they obscure the main pattern you wish to emphasize. An ideal layout plan is to use "technical paper" (hard erasable translucent sheets obtainable in tablet form with a variety of graph grids for underlay guides) and to draw a preliminary version in pencil. The plotted curve or curves should be the strongest lines on your finished graph, the border lines somewhat lighter, and the small index lines lightest. If two curves on the same graph intertwine to a confusing degree, you will need two kinds of lines, one perhaps broken or lighter than the other.

3. Adhesive hatching tape is available in many different hatching patterns and widths, and saves a great deal of time in the preparation of bar graphs. Adhesive hatched and shaded sheets are also available, which can be cut for hatchings in circle graphs—though the process is rather laborious.

4. Templates for lettering and for drawing circles, squares, rectangles, triangles, and special characters are available to guide your pen or hard pencil accurately. Your results may lack the professional's perfection, but will frequently surprise you by the clarity and neatness these aids help you create.

Exercise Set 3. Now Try Your Hand at Some Graphs

3-1. On the layout provided, prepare bar graphs on the model of Figure 3–6 to show the data of Table 2–2. Mark the bars to show the appropriate percentage cutoff points and hatch by hand, following the hatching patterns of the legend. For Graph A, translate the votes for Johnson and Goldwater into percentages of those voting. For Graph B you can use directly the percentage not voting.

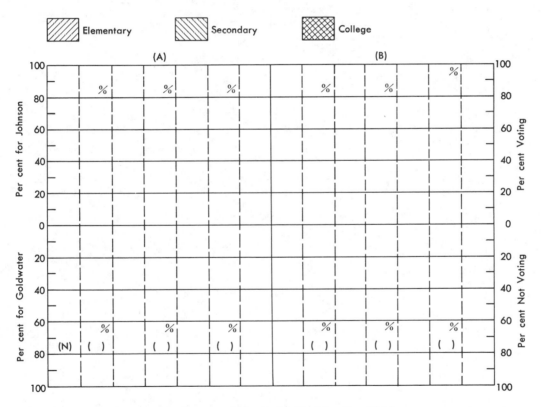

Vote Choice and Non-Voting by Education, 1964

3-2. Prepare a compound bar graph similar to the individual bars in Figure 3–9, showing the components of Goldwater support by the age groups of Table 2–3. The frequencies are retrieved for each age group in the worksheet, but you will need to convert these into percentages of the total *N*. Devise a suitable hatching legend for the five components.

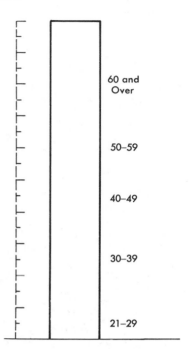

WORKSHEET FOR CONVERTING
FREQUENCIES INTO PERCENTAGES

Age Group	Frequency	Per Cent	(f/N or f/173)
21–29	32	_____	
30–39	27	_____	
40–49	26	_____	
50–59	27	_____	
60 & Over	61	_____	
Total	173	_____	

3–3. Two scales, one at the left and one at the right, may be used on a regular arithmetic graph grid as well as on a ratio graph, as shown in Figure 3–18. This usage is illustrated on the layout form provided, which scales total population by the left scale and voter turnout for presidential elections by the right scale. Plot the two curves from the data given, and from your knowledge of American history, comment on the changing nature of American democracy in this period.

Growth of U.S. Population and Participation in National Elections, 1820-1860

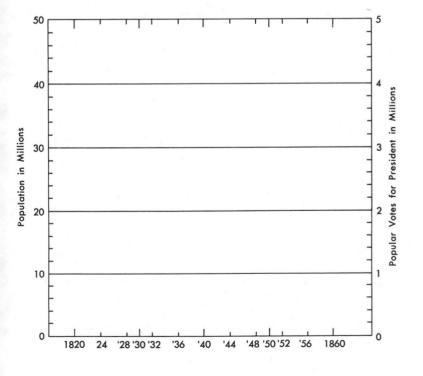

Year	U.S. Population	Popular Votes for President
1820	9,638,453	(no data)
1824		356,038
1828		1,155,350
1830	12,866,020	
1832		1,217,691
1836		1,505,278
1840	17,069,453	2,402,405
1844		2,700,861
1848		2,874,572
1850	23,191,876	
1852		3,142,395
1856		4,044,618
1860	31,443,321	4,689,568

3–4. Prepare a horizontal bar graph scaled with the Gini index curve for voting in the United Nations General Assembly as related to population. Mark the divisions on the bar to show the smallest population commanding a blocking (one-third) vote, the smallest population commanding a majority (use one-half), and the smallest commanding a two-thirds majority. You will need to interpolate the one-third point between .6 and .7, and the two-thirds point between .3 and .4 on the *Y*-axis.

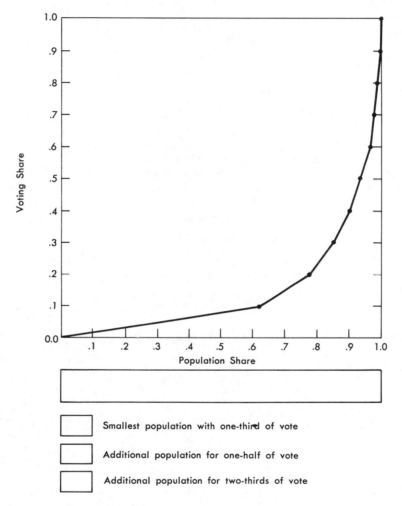

Smallest population with one-third of vote

Additional population for one-half of vote

Additional population for two-thirds of vote

3–5. Sketch a curve on the two grids below to illustrate (a) the general idea that the Gini index of inequality (*Y*-axis) increases steadily as right-wing political influence (*X*-axis) increases; and (b) the modified idea that the curve rises to about the 50 per cent level, but that as right-wing influence exceeds 50 per cent, values must be distributed more evenly to maintain and increase popular support.

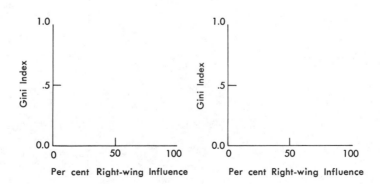

3–6. The cube law curve is reproduced on the layout, with points plotted to show the relation between the Democratic share of the popular vote for president and the Democratic share of the electoral vote in the ten elections from 1928 to 1964. The linear regression formula for these ten elections is computed as $y = 4.44x - 1.683$. Draw the line representing this formula for values of x from .4 to .6, and comment on your results.

WORKSHEET FOR VALUES OF y

If $x = .4$, $4.44x - 1.683 = (4.44 \times .4) - 1.683 = $ _____ $= y$

If $x = .6$, $4.44x - 1.683 = (4.44 \times .6) - 1.683 = $ _____ $= y$

(Place a point at $(.4, y)$ and $(.6, y)$. Draw a straight line between the two points. This is the line of the linear equation which most closely describes the relation between popular votes and electoral votes for the ten elections plotted).

You do not need the data for the ten elections to do this exercise, but they are given here to permit you to plot your own graph more accurately if you wish. You should confirm a few of the points for practice.

Democratic Share of Popular and Electoral Votes, 1928–1964

Year	Share of Popular Vote (x)	Share of Electoral College Vote (y)	Year	Share of Popular Vote (x)	Share of Electoral College Vote (y)
1928	.408	.164	1948	.519	.616
1932	.574	.889	1952	.444	.168
1936	.608	.985	1956	.420	.138
1940	.547	.846	1960	.501	.580
1944	.534	.814	1964	.611	.903

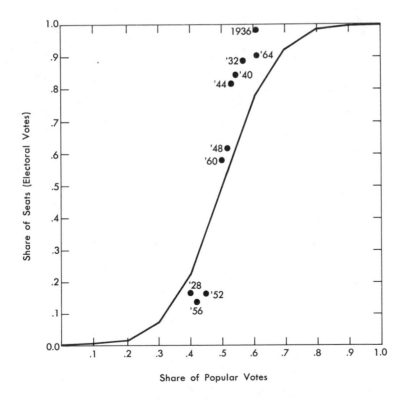

Cube Law Curve and U.S. Presidential Elections

3–7. (a) Use the population and popular vote data of Exercise 3–3 to plot the same two curves called for in that exercise on the ratio graph layout, retaining the same ten-to-one ratio between the left and right scales.

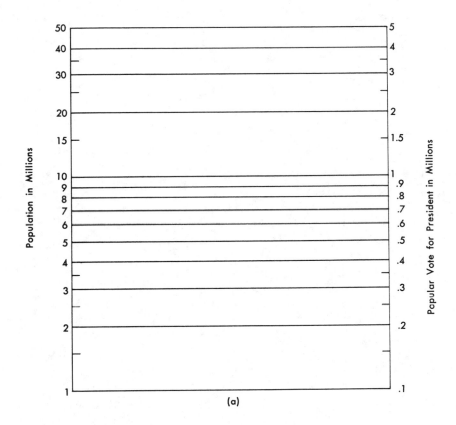

(a)

(b) Plot three curves from the data below on the time series ratio graph of the layout, which is marked with one time series lagging one year after the other, on the assumption that any relation between government funds for university research and production of doctorates would reflect at least a one-year delay. Funding is scaled on the left for years shown at the top; numbers on the right-hand scale are to be used for the two curves indicating number of doctorates in the physical and social sciences for the years shown at the bottom.

Federal Research Funding and Production of Doctorates
in the United States, 1957–1965

Year	Federal Funds for University Research (millions of dollars)	Number of Physical Science Doctorates	Number of Social Science Doctorates
1957	173	—	—
1958	240	2558	1985
1959	256	2846	2063
1960	305	3044	2088
1961	350	3367	2270
1962	442	3890	2325
1963	530	4506	2648
1964	770	4993	2806
1965	—	5704	3023

Source: *Statistical Abstract of the United States, 1967.*

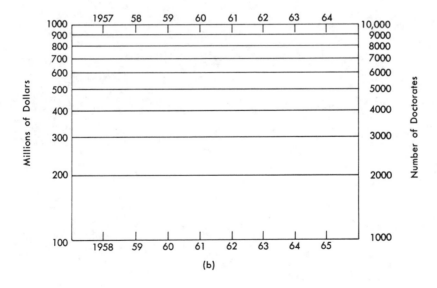

(b)

3–8. (a) Use the circle graph layout to show the source of immigration into the United States for the year ending June 30, 1966, from the data provided. Use a solid-line radius for each major subdivision shown, and a dotted-line radius for each unit within the subdivision. Both the circle and half-circle layouts which follow are marked into arcs, each corresponding to 5 per cent.

Source of Immigration into the United States for the Year Ending June 30, 1966

Source	Number of Immigrants	Per Cent of Total (rounded)
Europe	125,023	39
Italy	(25,154)	(8)
United Kingdom	(21,441)	(7)
North America	127,358	39
Mexico	(45,163)	(14)
Canada	(28,358)	(9)
Asia	39,878	12.5
China & Hong Kong	(17,608)	(5.5)
South America	25,836	8
Africa, Australia, Oceania & Other	4,963	1.5
Total	323,040	100.0

(b) Use the half-circle layouts to show distribution of seats won in the Australian parliamentary elections of 1961 and 1966 by the three major parties. Compute the percentages yourself.

Seats Won in Australian Parliament in Two Elections

Year	Country Party	Liberal Party	Labour Party	Total
1961	17	45	62	124
1966*	21	61	41	123

* One seat of the 124 contested in 1966 was won by "Other." You may ignore it in constructing your graph.

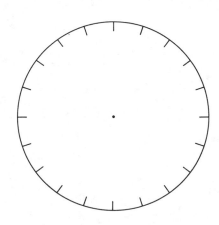
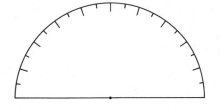
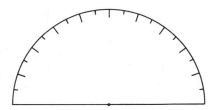

3–9. (a) Label and direct (insert arrows) the graph of the layout as a "dominance" graph, on the (inadequate) assumptions that the "power index" listings really measure national power and that the more powerful country actually dominates all weaker ones. These index numbers represent a composite weighted computation of gross national product, gross national product per capita, total population, military age population, literacy, caloric intake, energy consumption, railroad installation, steel production, and nuclear capability.

Power Index for Five Countries

Country	Index
United States	83
USSR	70
United Kingdom	38
Germany (West)	31
Italy	24

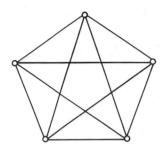

(b) Without any computation, you should be able to use the verbal definition in the text to determine the Landau hierarchy index for this system: H = _____

3–10. Shade the areas on the Venn diagrams described by the union, intersection, and negation combinations below. Since this is not a course in symbolic logic, a verbal translation of each formula is supplied. For all the diagrams, we assume the three subsets listed below.

Subset A	NATO	United States, Canada, United Kingdom, France, West Germany, Italy, Belgium, Netherlands, Luxembourg, Norway, Denmark, Iceland, Portugal, Greece, Turkey
Subset B	SEATO	United States, United Kingdom, France, Australia, New Zealand, Thailand, Pakistan, Philippines
Subset C	Allied Commonwealth	United Kingdom, Canada, Australia, New Zealand, Pakistan

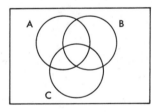

A ∪ B ∪ C

(Those in any of the three groups)

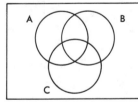

(A ∩ C) ∪ (B ∩ C)

(Commonwealth members of either NATO or SEATO)

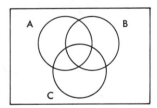

(A ∩ B) ∪ (A ∩ C) ∪ (B ∩ C)

(Those in at least two of the three groups)

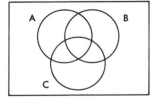

((A ∩ B) ∪ (A ∩ C) ∪ (B ∩ C)) ∩ −(A ∩ B ∩ C)

(Those in two but not all three groups)

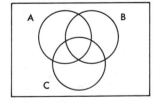

(A ∩ B) ∩ −C

(Members of both NATO and SEATO but not of the Commonwealth)

3–11. (a) Use the general format of a Venn diagram as in Figure 3–32 to illustrate the idea that political science, economics, and sociology are interrelated, and that the following topics fall appropriately in the spaces indicated by the following list. Revise the list if you like.

Political science	Elections
Economics	Trade
Sociology	Family
Political science & economics	Public finance
Political science & sociology	Public opinion
Economics & sociology	Income distribution
All three	Development

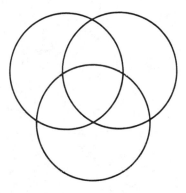

(b) Use the concentric circle device of Figure 3–33 to illustrate the classification of public opinion on foreign policy into three types—that of the "effective public" (opinion leaders), the "articulate public" (those expressing views with some regularity), and the "mass public" (those rarely or never expressing views). Add a fourth and a fifth circle for "decision-makers" and their advisors. Modify or substitute some other classification if you like. The layout has two circles. Add the others and label.

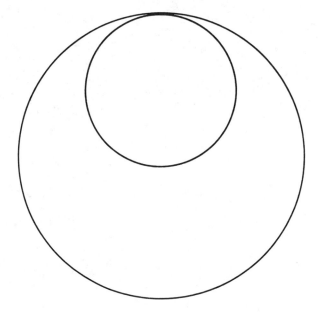

Reading List

Croxton, Frederick E., and Dudley J. Cowden, *Applied General Statistics*. Englewood Cliffs, N. J.: Prentice-Hall, Inc., 1955. Chapters 4, 5, and 6 give a complete exposition of graphic displays, with special attention to ratio graphs.

Dahl, Robert A., *A Preface to Democratic Theory*. Chicago: University of Chicago Press, 1963. Contains several thoughtfully prepared graphs displaying both theories and relevant data.*

Kemeny, John G., J. Laurie Snell, and Gerald L. Thompson, *Introduction to Finite Mathematics*. Englewood Cliffs, N. J.: Prentice-Hall, Inc., 1956.

_____, and J. Laurie Snell, *Mathematical Models in the Social Sciences*. New York: Ginn and Co., 1962.

Ore, Oystein, *Graphs and Their Uses*. New York: Random House, Inc., 1963.*

Schmid, Calvin F., *Handbook of Graphic Presentation*. New York: Ronald Press Co., 1958.

Thomas, Norman L., *Modern Logic*. New York: Barnes and Noble, 1966.*

* Paperback edition available.

4

DATA PROCESSING:

Do Not Fold, Spindle, or Mutilate!

In the exercises of this chapter you will work elementary problems parallel to those of the most ambitious survey projects—coding data, sorting and resorting them into meaningful categories, counting the units in each category, and doing the necessary computations to display the results in tables. Coding, sorting, counting, and computing are the elements of data processing. The exercises in this workbook are prepared on the assumption that mechanical aids are not available to you. Even if they are, there is merit in doing the necessary procedures "by hand" before putting your data through complicated machinery. The logical processes are much the same. Even the most advanced programmer spends far less time at the computer console than at his desk with pen and pad.

Our dedication to handwork is nevertheless limited to its pedagogical value: high-speed data processing equipment and computers make possible many large projects and complex statistical analyses which would be impossible without them. If you have access to such equipment and the skill to use it, you are the better prepared both to engage in significant political research and to understand the scholarly literature resulting from its use. Moreover you will avoid a lot of drudgery and midnight oil. In any event you should be aware of some of the characteristics and powers of data processing hardware, even if you are doing your work by hand. Your worksheets, tally layouts, and computation patterns will be more efficient if they are geared to possible machine use.

In this chapter we touch only briefly on machine methods—good specialized manuals are available and the beginner needs the specialized instruction they supply. One of the best is Kenneth Janda's *Data Processing: Applications to Political Research,* which has the great virtue of emphasizing detailed how-to-do-it instructions for all stages of the versatile punch-card's life—from codebook to FORTRAN IV.

4-1 Coding Your Information

Coding is pretty much a matter of common sense and thinking ahead, although we should distinguish between coding of objective information such as age, party, residence, and other empirical detail, and the more difficult "conceptual" coding of less precisely defined attributes. The authors of *A Cross-Polity Survey* report that they were required to make thousands of sometimes agonizing decisions on border-line or doubtful cases.

Your basic requirements in preparing to code your data are three. First, you need a codebook, which assigns more or less arbitrary meanings to the symbols (usually numbers) listed in it. Second, for orderly compilation of data, you need a coding sheet, on which are entered a set of the preassigned codes describing a corresponding set of characteristics of each unit about which information is being compiled (each respondent in a survey, each legislator in a roll-call analysis, each judge in a scaling study). Finally, you need a set of separate cards, one for each *unit record,* to which the data are transcribed from the coding sheet for convenient sorting. It is sometimes possible to combine coding sheet and unit record.

Codebook. Simple or elaborate, depending on complexity of the project, the codebook must conform to the format of the unit record cards on which the assigned codes will eventually become meaningful descriptions. If machine punchcards are to be used to record a survey, for example, the codebook will identify (1) the specific category of information (the question), (2) the column in which the information is to be entered, and (3) the code number assigned to describe respondent's or investigator's answer to the question.

Example:

Column	Code
4	Question 8. The United States should stop its foreign aid program entirely.

1. Agree strongly
2. Agree, but not very strongly
3. Not sure; it depends
4. Disagree, but not very strongly
5. Disagree strongly

5	Question 9. Race of respondent.

1. White
2. Negro
7. Other

6–7	Question 10. Age of respondent.

Enter present age in a two-digit field (*i.e.,* use two columns)

Quantitative political research involves two basic kinds of numbers—actual numbers (called for in Question 10 of the example) and arbitrary numerical codes representing any agreed meaning we choose. As an actual number, the digit "1" means the quantity "1." For the exercise following this chapter the code digit "1" has the various meanings of "Yes," "Agree strongly," "Connecticut," "Male," "White," "Strong Democrat," "Voted Democratic in 1960," "Barry Goldwater," "Income under $1000," and "Roman Catholic." While there are advantages of convenience and transferability in use of standard coding systems, there is no inherent reason to prevent any digit from representing any meaning you like, providing it is consistent within your project.

The most appropriate standard coding system for political research is that developed by the Survey Research Center of the University of Michigan. It is recommended for your own work unless your special requirements make portions of it inapplicable. In part it conforms to U.S. Census Bureau practice—an exception is its separate code for the politically significant "Border" states. Notice that it permits sorting answers to a "Yes-No" question by the same codes used for "Agree Strongly" and "Disagree Strongly" on a five-point agreement scale. The two-digit field used for states can be processed for region alone by sorting on the first digit only. In an individual project, you might want a simpler code for income or age, for convenience in processing, but it is good practice to retain the actual data. Translation

of age to "Persons of Voting Age," for example, is impossible if only age brackets are recorded, since voting age varies by state.

Survey Research Center Coding Conventions

Code   Content

A. The basic scheme
1   Yes ("good" or most positive)
5   No ("bad" or least positive)
7   Other
8   I don't know
9   Not ascertained
0   Inapplicable (also "none")

B. Agreement
1   Agree strongly
2   Agree, but not very strongly
3   Not sure; it depends
4   Disagree, but not very strongly
5   Disagree strongly

C. State
New England
01   Connecticut
02   Maine
03   Massachusetts
04   New Hampshire
05   Rhode Island
06   Vermont
Middle Atlantic
11   Delaware
12   New Jersey
13   New York
14   Pennsylvania
East North Central
21   Illinois
22   Indiana
23   Michigan
24   Ohio
25   Wisconsin
West North Central
31   Iowa
32   Kansas
33   Minnesota
34   Missouri
35   Nebraska
36   North Dakota
37   South Dakota
Solid South
41   Alabama
42   Arkansas
43   Florida
44   Georgia
45   Louisiana

46   Mississippi
47   North Carolina
48   South Carolina
49   Texas
40   Virginia

Border States
51   Kentucky
52   Maryland
53   Oklahoma
54   Tennessee
55   Washington, D.C.
56   West Virginia

Mountain States
61   Arizona
62   Colorado
63   Idaho
64   Montana
65   Nevada
66   New Mexico
67   Utah
68   Wyoming

Western States
71   California
72   Oregon
73   Washington
81   Alaska
82   Hawaii

D. County. The three-digit codes of the Census, *County and City Data Book.*

E. Congressional District. A two-digit field containing the actual number of the district. At-large districts coded by number of the contest, the first being 98, the second 97, the third 96, etc. 99 reserved for missing data or "Don't know."

F. Age. Code present age in a two-column field. An alternative is to code last two digits of year of birth in a two-column field.

G. Income, net worth, etc. A seven-column field giving actual dollar amount.

H. Number of children, adults, etc. A field wide enough to code highest number in sample.

I. Sex.
   1. Male
   2. Female

J. Race.
   1. White
   2. Negro
   7. Other

Coding Sheet. Format of the coding sheet will depend on the format of unit records to be used in processing the data. For keypunching, horizontal list-

ing is preferable to vertical listing, since the keypunch operator can read it more naturally as the card moves across the punching head. This is especially true if only a portion of the card is required to record the data—the full 80 columns of the coding sheet shown in Figure 4–1 require a somewhat unwieldy fifteen-inch width.

Sometimes a coding sheet may be avoided altogether, if the source data are in sufficiently orderly form to be transferred routinely to unit records. In processing a printed questionnaire (one planned to be marked either by respondent or interviewer), a coding strip can be positioned across the bottom of each page. The device is useful for hand or machine tallying. If a page contains ten questions—responses to be recorded in columns 11–20 of the punchcards, for example—the strip format for the page would be:

11	12	13	14	15	16	17	18	19	20
1	3	5	2	1	8	9	2	1	3

Numbers in the cells represent the coder's takeoff of responses to the questions on the page, and the data are thus available for direct transmission to tally sheet or punchcard. A keypunch operator can work directly from questionnaires so coded with greater accuracy than from a coding sheet with column numbers printed only at the top (as in Figure 4–1), since the column is identified separately for each card.

There follow several specific suggestions about coding, some of them relevant only if machine data cards are to be used as unit records, while others are applicable to any processing system.

1. *Use a "natural" coding scheme.* Digits from 1 to 9 should represent sequences that "make sense" in terms of some familiar ordering, if one is applicable. The Survey Research Center's five-point agreement scale is an example, as are most of the standard conventions. If there is no inherently logical ordering, it is sound practice to use the low digit for the response expected most frequently.

2. *Number questions consistently with data card format.* There is nothing sacred about numerical sequencing of questions. If your first question is to be recorded in column 19, number it 19 on the questionnaire. *Avoid alphabetic sequencing of responses* unless the same letters appear on the data card format (as on some Keysort cards). Errors are multiplied if the coder must translate a sequence of responses listed as "a, b, c, d, e" into the codes "1, 2, 3, 4, 5" or (for age brackets) "21, 30, 45, 55, 65."

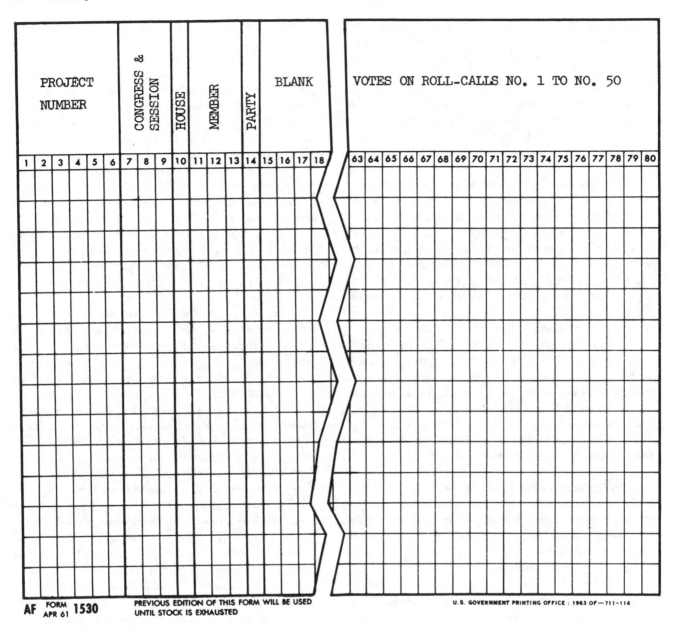

FIGURE 4-1. *Punchcard Transcript Marked Into the Same Fields as the Card Format of Figure 4-4 (B)*

3. *Avoid multiple punching within columns.* The standard punchcard has twelve spaces which may be punched (digits from 0 to 9 and spaces for the "+" and "−" signs; the "+" sometimes appears in codebooks as "&," which some keyboards substitute for it). Since most survey items use fewer categories, there is sometimes a temptation to assign two items to a column (coding, for example, six possible responses to the first question from 0 to 5, and six possible responses to the second question as 6, 7, 8, 9, +, −). This practice results in confusion at the keypunch stage—the cards must be overpunched. It also makes impossible use of the cards for computer processing.

The only multiple punching scheme even to be considered is the alphabetic two-punch-per-column system built into the keypunch machine itself, whereby 26 categories can be designated for the columnar item. It is difficult to think of a listing for which this system would be desirable for any but strictly alphabetic information: simply by using two columns you immediately have 100 categories available (00 to 99).

4. *Avoid the + and −, the blank, and if possible the zero.* Codebooks planned exclusively for processing data on the counter-sorter often assign coded meanings to the "+" and "−" signs, since the machine has sorting bins for these positions. Many large national surveys have used these codes, but the practice has now stopped because of the increasing use of computers in sorting. Few computer programs exist which will process these signs as meaningful codes; indeed many computers will reject them as invalid. The same is true of the rarer practice of using an unpunched field for a code meaning: aside from the inherent confusion of the practice, it too will usually be treated by computers as an invalid signal.

The zero is a valid digit to the computer, and is a standard code for "No Answer," "Not Applicable," and similar meanings, as well as for zero magnitude. The only caution on its use in computer data processing is that many computer programs make use of the "zero test" to terminate a subroutine, as does the IF statement in FORTRAN. It may be used, but with the warning that you should be sure your programmer is aware of the problem.

Unit Records. Selection of the form of unit record for a given project is essentially a decision on whether to do the project by handwork or by automatic data processing equipment. Aside from the question of what is available to you, three general considerations are relevant to the decision.

1. *Size and scope of the project.* For up to 100 cases for an average questionnaire of about 50 items, hand tallying may be faster than putting the project on punchcards and tallying by machine—either counter-sorter or computer. Coding information is essentially a handwork process, whether or not you plan to use data processing equipment. Information from a survey must be hand recorded by interviewer or respondent; it must usually be transcribed by hand to the coding sheet prior to tallying. Only after this labor can the keypunch operator take over. Optical scanners and magnetic sensors transmit information directly from source to processor, but are rarely available in academic research.

2. *The time factor.* In data processing, the word "time" has three distinct meanings: calendar time, real time, and machine time. Calendar time may be

the first consideration if an early deadline must be met—say for your class project as the term nears its end, or the publisher's deadline for your article, typically awaiting final tabulations before the completed manuscript can be sent. Problems of reserving machine time, keypunch errors, mechanical breakdowns, and similar frustrations can play havoc with calendar time. Real time (your own personal hours) more commonly governs the decision as to which type of equipment to use. It includes trips to the computer center, time at the keypunch machine, actually typing in your data on some computers, program writing and debugging time if computer programs are involved, and sheer waiting for people and machines. Machine time itself is very short; even the "slow" equipment is much faster than hand and eye. Sorting is done in hundreds of cards per minute; computations in nanoseconds.

3. *Transferability.* Coordination with other projects and exchange of research results are facilitated by the common language of machine data cards. A set of cards is easily duplicated and with the explanatory codebook will be more universally understood than any other medium.

Whether you plan to work by hand or machine, several general precautions about your unit records will save time and trouble. In data processing, a useful rule is the computerman's satirical "Finagle's First Law: *If anything can go wrong, it will!*"

(1) *Use one card for each case.* Processing can become inordinately difficult or even impossible if several cases are combined on a single card. Cross-tabulation on the two variables of party and religion, for the simplest example of useful manipulation, becomes difficult if one sorted stack contains a mixture of Protestants and Catholics.

(2) *If two cards are needed, repeat identification data.* If data for each case or respondent are so extensive as to require two or more cards, repeat the data likely to be used as explanatory variables in the same columns of each card used for the same case. For example, in a questionnaire the explanatory variables are likely to be of the "identification" type, the dependent variables of the "opinion" or "vote choice" type. Sorting will go more smoothly if the identification questions are recorded on each card, together with as many of the opinion questions as space allows. Even if several additional cards per case are needed, you will still be able to compile your cross-tabulations from sets of single cards. If you anticipate cross-tabulations on two or more opinion questions, one

used as an explanatory factor for the other, these should also be grouped on the same card.

(3) *Reserve enough space.* For any given item, reserve on the card format a "field" sufficiently wide (a space with enough columns) to contain the highest number of digits *possible* (not merely likely) in any answer. If the data are numerical (not code), a safe rule is to allow a field wide enough to contain the total of all your cases, so that the cards could be put on a computer (to compute mean age, for example) without special program provision for a different "Totals" field. As an illustration, if you have 400 cases, the age data should be entered in the last two columns of a five-column field (think of an entry as 00036 for the age 36). Even if you are quite certain the mean age is under 25—so that the 400 cases will sum to less than 10,000—it is better to be safe, and the wider field will allow you to expand the number of cases in a later study.

(4) *Plan some blank space.* Leave space on the unit record cards for afterthoughts, computed indexes, rearrangement of items, or additional information you have gathered but not coded, or which you may decide to gather later.

Failure to follow rules as to card format is, of course, not fatal. Your decisions are not forever binding. Automatic equipment is available (for punchcard processing) to combine variables on a new card format in almost any way you wish.

(5) *Consult the experts.* If there is any chance your data will be used in computer or statistical analysis, consult the programmer or statistician *in advance,* and get all the information you possibly can as to the form in which the data can be most usefully prepared. Computer programs, for example, work with data in defined card fields. A good general rule is to *retain the data in raw form.* The digit "3" in a codebook may mean "Family Income from $5000 to $7500" but to the statistician or computer it is simply the digit "3." There are many sad stories of researchers who have lost valuable time and information by inadequate knowledge of the form in which data must be processed. Members of a field research team once laboriously gathered election data by precincts, laboriously translated all their figures into percentages, threw away the original data, and proudly presented their percentages to a colleague in the statistics department with the suggestion he help them run chi-square values for their study! The chi-square test, as we shall learn, requires the

actual numbers in a distribution; it cannot be performed with percentages. Consultation in advance not only can prevent such a mistake but often will produce ideas for additional data or patterns of analysis valuable to the whole project.

4-2 Sorting Your Data

Attention to a few simple principles will help you in planning an orderly and efficient work schedule for processing your collected unit records into the final product—informative tabular displays. Guides to the logic of cross-tabulating are shown in Figure 4–2, a design for sorting on two variables, and Figure 4–3, which routes you through a four-variable classification. The logic of each is the same: you begin with a unit record and end by locating it in its proper box. Follow for a moment the unit record through the computer flow chart in the first diagram. A flow chart is a complete listing of sequential actions, computations, and decisions on alternatives throughout any process (including a return to the beginning of the process), so designed as to allow for every contingency. The computer programmer uses it to make certain his program leaves nothing to the computer's initiative: the computer has no initiative and will stop or return endlessly to the same routine ("go into a loop") if its program does not make provision for every alternative. Assume you have a stack of 20 unit records showing respondents' answers to two questions (*e.g.,* I = religion: (1) Protestant, (2) Non-Protestant; D = vote: (1) Democrat (2) Republican). The sequence of steps in the flow chart starts with the "Read" instruction, moves through the two branching decisions necessary to identify each card with one of the four tally-boxes corresponding to cells of the eventual table, then returns to read another card until all are tallied. When all are tallied, it concludes with the instruction to total columns and compute percentages. The procedure is the same whether you are tallying by hand or by machine. Figure 4–3 follows the same logic, but is simplified to permit us to follow the additional sorting decisions for a four-variable breakdown, requiring 16 tally-boxes if all four variables are dichotomous. For any variable with more than two categories, you will naturally require more branches than shown—the final set of branches will equal the number of cells called for in the table you plan to construct.

Even a short project will probably involve a number of tables—meaning repeated sorting operations, certainly more variables, and usually more than two

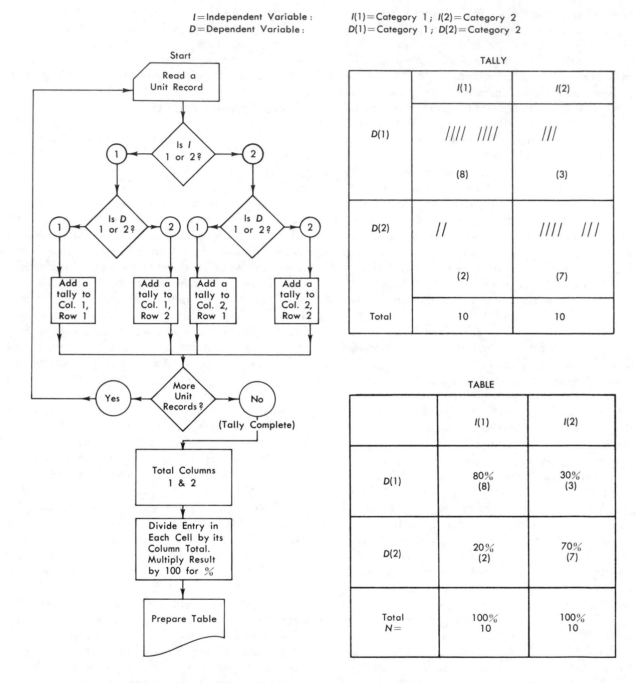

I=Independent Variable: $I(1)$=Category 1; $I(2)$=Category 2
D=Dependent Variable: $D(1)$=Category 1; $D(2)$=Category 2

FIGURE 4-2. *Tally Procedure for a 2 × 2 Table*

categories for each variable. You will avoid confusion and save time by adhering to the few elementary rules listed below. Like the flow chart logic, they apply equally to machine and hand tabulations.

1. *Planning for all the tables you will use.* Proceeding one table at a time results in unnecessary repeat sortings on variables common to more than one table. By anticipating the entire project as one sequence,

you will put first in the sorting process those variables common to all the tables, reserving until last the variables unique to single tables.

This advice is easier to give than to follow: to follow the rule literally requires that you have complete comprehension of your subject and the ability to analyze your research program in depth. Even if these rare conditions are met, usually the results of

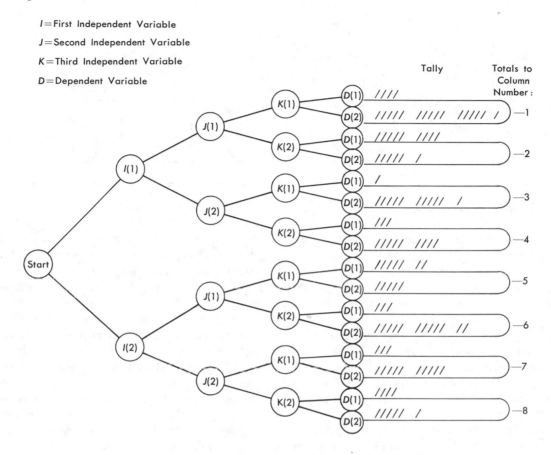

I = First Independent Variable

J = Second Independent Variable

K = Third Independent Variable

D = Dependent Variable

TABLE 4.X. D *by* K, *Controlled for* J *and* I *(in percentages, with N's in parentheses)*

	I(1)				*I*(2)			
D	*J*(1)		*J*(2)		*J*(1)		*J*(2)	
	K(1)	*K*(2)	*K*(1)	*K*(2)	*K*(1)	*K*(2)	*K*(1)	*K*(2)
	Column 1	Col. 2	Col. 3	Col. 4	Col. 5	Col. 6	Col. 7	Col. 8
D(1)	20 (4)	60 (9)	8 (1)	25 (3)	58 (7)	20 (3)	23 (3)	40 (4)
D(2)	80 (16)	40 (6)	92 (11)	75 (9)	42 (5)	80 (12)	77 (10)	60 (6)
Total	100 (20)	100 (15)	100 (12)	100 (12)	100 (12)	100 (15)	100 (13)	100 (10)

FIGURE 4-3. *Simplified Logic Tree for Tallying Four Dichotomous Variables*

some of your tabulations will suggest others you did not originally anticipate. The need for a repeat tabulation should not be considered a failure: often it results from an unexpected finding and shows you are alert to your results as they develop. Don't rely on the data to tell their own story.

2. *Sorting first on the variables with fewest categories.* When consistent with the principle just stated, more efficient sorting results if you sort first the variables with the smallest number of categories,

moving in order to those with larger numbers of categories. For example, you may wish to prepare a table showing distribution of respondents on the four variables of "Response to Opinion Question *X*" (5 categories from "Strongly Agree" to "Strongly Disagree"), "Region" (4 categories), "Sex" (2 categories), and "Party" (3 categories—"Republican," "Democratic," "Independent"). Number of sorting runs and resulting stacks of cards required for the most efficient and the least efficient sequences are

TABLE 4-1. *Sorting Sequence*

Sort No.	Least Efficient Procedure				Most Efficient Procedure			
	Variable	Categories	Sorting Runs	Resulting Stacks	Variable	Categories	Sorting Runs	Resulting Stacks
1.	Opinion	5	1	5	Sex	2	1	2
2.	Region	4	5	20	Party	3	2	6
3.	Party	3	20	60	Region	4	6	24
4.	Sex	2	60	120	Opinion	5	24	120
	Total Runs		86				33	

shown in Table 4–1. The task at the last step can be reduced in complexity by setting the counter-sorter to count only, or in hand sorting by merely tallying without physically separating the stacks resulting from the third sorting.

3. *Collapsing categories.* Assuming that in the above sorting operation you are interested only in a regional breakdown for "South" and "Non-South," though your codebook provides four regional codes, the next step is speeded greatly if you dichotomize as you sort. In hand sorting, simply isolate the "South" cards; all the others are "Non-South." On the counter-sorter, after the machine has arranged the cards into the four regional stacks, assemble the three "Non-South" stacks into a single group for the next sorting operation. By the most efficient sequence of Table 4–1, you enter the last sorting with only 12 stacks instead of 24; by the least efficient sequence, with only 30 instead of 60.

4. *A Sequence for Hand Sorting.* Hand sorting is laborious, but for up to 100 cases not unduly time consuming. As stressed above, accuracy and speed are much greater if each case is recorded on a physically separate card. The coding sheet shown in Figure 4–1, planned for the keypunch operator, is inconvenient for hand sorting, since it is almost impossible to tally cross-tabulations directly from it for more than two or three variables without losing track of the combinations which belong together. With each case on a separate card (sometimes the questionnaires themselves can be used directly), your hand sorting simply duplicates the machine sorting process.

Recalling that your goal is a separate stack of unit records for each cell of the table you plan to prepare, an orderly approach is to clear enough space on your desk to accommodate all these putative stacks, mentally visualizing the space marked off to correspond to the eventual table. If there are to be many cells, it helps to label the spaces destined to contain the stacks. Bookshelves, small cardboard boxes, old envelopes, or file folders are convenient containers if more formal sorting aids are not at hand. The "efficient sequence" for the sorting operation just described would be:

(1) Visualize the eventual table, perhaps as containing 60 cells ("Region" being dichotomized into "South" and "Non-South"). Lay out your sorting workspace accordingly.

(2) Sort the "South" and "Non-South" cards into two stacks. Be sure of course that later tables in your program do not require the whole regional

TABLE 4-2. *Agreement by Party, Sex, and Region*

Opinion	South						Non-South					
	Men			Women			Men			Women		
	Rep	Dem	Ind	Rep	Dem	Ind	Rep	Dem	Ind	Rep	Dem	Ind
Strongly agree												
Agree												
Not sure												
Disagree												
Strongly disagree												

breakdown—if they do, this collapsing is better done at a later stage. On the assumption that this is not so, continue to the next step.

(3) Separate the "South" stack into two: (1) "South, Men"; (2) "South, Women." Do the same for the "Non-South" stack.

(4) The resulting four stacks become twelve at the next sorting pass: each is divided into three—"Republican," "Democratic," "Independent."

(5) For the planned table, you can probably tally the five opinion categories directly on your tally sheet without physically dividing the twelve stacks into sixty. Going through the first stack, tally each card in turn in the space provided on the tally sheet. Keep the stacks separate as you tabulate the other eleven.

(6) You have now done all the tallying needed for the table. Add up the totals in rows and columns, then add up the row totals and column totals to see that they crossfoot and that your grand total corresponds to the number of cases. This check is not an absolute guarantee of accuracy but is usually sufficient.

(7) While your cards are distributed into the twelve stacks, consider whether the same set of independent variables is to be used for other tables on other opinion items in your questionnaire. If so, you can proceed immediately to those tallies, thus saving future sorting time. Or file your cards in twelve identified envelopes for the next phase of your work.

5. *Flexibility of Format.* The sorting sequence has not committed you to a specific table format. For example, with the tabulated data you can rearrange the columns to display six different orderings of the three independent variables ("Region-Sex-Party," "Region-Party-Sex," "Sex-Region-Party," "Sex-Party-Region," "Party-Sex-Region," "and Party-Region-Sex").

6. *Small* N. If you are hand sorting a small sample of 100 or so cases, the sixty-cell breakdown is probably too refined for meaningful analysis. The average cell will contain fewer than two tallies and many cells will contain one or zero. Again, the sorting sequence has not committed you to retention of all sixty cells in your final display. With the results in hand, you can make decisions about collapsing categories or omitting entire rows or columns with considerably more assurance than if the decisions were made in advance. Indeed, this is one of the great advantages of hand sorting: it gives you a "feel" for

the data. In fact, for a very large survey—say of 1500 or more cases—you will find it time well spent to extract a small random sample of the cards and go through the hand sorting sequence before final determination of the sorting routine for machine processing. In almost every instance you will come up with several ideas for new associative combinations, which are often the most valuable features of your final displays.

4-3 Searching for New Variables: A Return to Property Space

This kind of analysis—the testing of new combinations of variables—is the most fundamental you can do. When you hit on a new associative pattern *and recognize it,* you will feel the excitement of discovery. The development of new categories which were not included specifically in the original research design requires careful and informed examination of the results of cross-tabulations arranged in a variety of combinations. An example is the category "Strongly Partisan" of Table 2–14; although not included in the original data, this category might be valuable to a researcher interested in further exploration of political extremism.

In most tabulations you quite naturally set up a group of variables that you consider in advance to be dependent—characteristics or attitudes that you will try to "explain" with another group of naturally independent variables. In survey research, for example, the most "naturally dependent" variables are attitudes, the most "naturally independent" variables are identification characteristics. Returning for a moment to the concept of property space discussed in Chapter 2, we may locate individuals just as easily by cross-tabulating on two attitudes, on a combination of two attitudes with reference to a third, or indeed on any two combinations of attitudes and characteristics, either of which may be as complex as we choose. Lazarsfeld calls this process, when applied to displays of two or more variables, the *reduction* of property space. The survey of attitudes on United States policy in Viet Nam, from which selected data are given below as the basis for Exercise 4–2, includes respondents' answers to two questions, which might be defined as two variables in a table. One of the questions inquired as to the respondent's interest in world affairs; the other asked his opinion about maintenance of United States forces in Viet Nam. A possible display of the results might seek a relationship between these two sets of answers, as in Table 4–3.

TABLE 4-3. *Opinion on U.S. Forces in Viet Nam, Related to Interest in World Affairs*

Forces Should Be:	Interest			
	Exceptional	High	Average	Slight
Increased Reduced Same Don't know				

In examining the results of this table, you might reason somewhat as follows: respondents who are well informed on world affairs and who favor major modification of U.S. policy constitute a distinct group of critics (we will label them "revisionist"); those who criticize on the basis of only average or lower interest are probably motivated by partisanship or have general fault-finding personalities (we will call them "cantankerous"); those who are knowledgeable but favor no change we will term "status quo" supporters; finally, those with only average interest or less who favor no change we will call simply "indifferent." The original 4 × 4 table thus becomes the 2 × 2 display of Table 4–4 through the reduction suggested by the reasoning. Two variables—"Interest" and "Attitude on Forces"—have been reduced to the single one of "Attitude Groups."

TABLE 4-4. *Basic Opinion Groups on U.S. Foreign Policy*

Attitude	Information High	Information Low
Change policy Same or Don't know	Revisionist Status Quo	Cantankerous Indifferent

The four categories resulting from this reduction may of course then be applied in further analysis of the survey results, or in further projects. If found to be useful general types, they might in time find broad application in the whole field of public opinion analysis. It is also possible—indeed it is the usual fate of a new typology on its first trial—that this particular set of labels will prove to have little value. There is a danger in blithely using a label and mistaking it for reality. The semanticist's dictum that "the word is not the thing" is an essential rule in developing any set of analytical concepts.

Substruction of Property Space. In the search for general theoretical typologies, we may find more complicated patterns of relationships among variables than those which can be handled by simple reduction. In the survey on attitudes toward Viet Nam, another question asked for the respondent's opinion as to how the average Vietnamese felt about the presence of United States military forces in his country. This question could be answered: (1) "Resent U.S.," (2) "Neutral," (3) "Welcome U.S.," (4) "Don't Know." Suppose again that we apply some general analytical reasoning to the study of a tabular display of the relationships of this variable with attitude toward maintenance of U.S. forces in Viet Nam. We might come up with something like the following tentative typology:

1. Those favoring expansion of military power, even if those we are protecting object, may be called "aggressive."
2. Those favoring maintenance of existing power, we will call supporters of "containment."
3. Those with an apparent positive desire to keep power within the close proximity of the national territory, we will call "isolationist."
4. Those who would withdraw power even if others desire its expansion on their behalf, we might call "pacifist."
5. Those who are unable to decide even though aware of foreign opinion, we will label "ambivalent."
6. Those who are unable to decide on any change and who also are unaware of foreign opinion, we will call "indifferent."

Applying the definitions of these opinion types to the sixteen cells of the 4 × 4 table which shows relationships between the two variables, we have entered the number of the typology category in the appropriate cells of Table 4–5.

TABLE 4-5. *Foreign Policy Opinion Groups Typed by Attitude toward U.S. Forces in Viet Nam and Opinion of Vietnamese Attitude Toward U.S. Involvement*

U.S. Forces Should Be:	Vietnamese Attitude Is			
	Resentful	Neutral	Welcome U.S.	Don't Know
Increased	1	2	2	1
Reduced	3	3	4	3
Same	2	2	2	6
Don't know	5	5	5	6

It may well turn out that some of the cells in the table are empty or nearly so. An empty or low-entry cell impairs the usefulness of a table, just as a small sample is less significant statistically than a large one. The resulting typology may prove of little use in application. You may well quarrel with some of its assumptions and prefer to write your own definitions and set up your own classifications. The process itself, which Lazarsfeld calls the *substruction* of property space, permits great latitude in redefining categories, in creating new typologies, and in trying them out in other research enterprises. By a grasp of this process, indeed, you often can write your own definitions and set up new categories meaningful in the context of your own research interests. It is the very generality and flexibility of the process which makes it valuable.

4-4 Automatic Data Processing

Our brief attention to the vast world of automated data processing can only introduce you to some of its potential. Even if you never use such equipment yourself, you need to be aware of its advantages, limitations, and a few of the special problems involved in its use. We list here simply a short catalog of the principal devices most commonly available.

The Punchcard. The elementary unit record of all data processing is the standard punchcard shown in Figure 4–4. The card shown is the IBM version, which is the most widely used type. The card contains 80 columns, each of which may be punched in any of twelve positions. The first card in Figure 4–4 has been punched in the standard "Hollerith code," which assigns one punch per column to designate the ten digits and the "+" and "−" signs, two punches per column to designate each of the 26 letters of the alphabet and three special characters, and three punches per column to designate six other special characters.

For a specific project, the card must be divided into *fields* (a field consists of adjacent columns treated in processing as a single unit of information). Specification of field layout is known as the *card format*. The second card in Figure 4–4 has been designed to study roll-calls in the House of Representatives of the United States Congress. The format shown provides for 56 fields:

1. Columns 1–6. Identification data for the project and archive housekeeping.
2. Columns 7–9. Number of the Congress and Session.
3. Column 10. Code for House or Senate.
4. Columns 11–13. Code number for member.
5. Column 14. Code for member's party affiliation.
6. Columns 15–30. Blank (may be used for future additions or processing codes, such as member's state, geographic region, or alphabetic version of his name).
7. Columns 31–80. Fifty fields, each column containing a digit which the codebook identifies as meaning "Yea," "Nay," or "Not Voting" on each of 50 roll-calls

By substituting questionnaire responses for roll-calls and respondents for congressmen, a similar format would be suitable for the results of a survey. Card formats planned for extensive use are often printed on the card itself; you are probably familiar with some used in commercial, banking, and academic record keeping. Special printed formats are used for each of the computer programming systems, or "languages."

The Keypunch Machine. In any project, the source information is almost always first recorded on the punchcards by a keypunch machine. The keypunch has a typewriter-like keyboard, containing keys for all of the Hollerith code characters, used to punch the cards one column at a time. Double-punching of a column (as for the minus sign if needed for numerical data) is possible. Unpunched cards are fed into position, moved automatically across the punching head, and automatically stacked when completed. For a project involving more than a few cards having the same format, the operator usually prepares a special control card. This control card is rolled around a drum contained in the machine, and acts to guide the unpunched cards in the most efficient sequence. To punch a large number of cards having the format of Figure 4–4(b), the operator might prepare the control card to skip automatically the project identification field (which could have been pre-punched by a faster machine) and the blank field.

The machine can also duplicate a previously punched card, or any part of it. If you reach column 80 without error, and then hit the wrong key, the "duplicate" key permits you to transfer the 79 error-free columns to a new card automatically. This feature is especially useful for correcting errors detected in later proofreading, or for replacing mutilated cards.

Keypunch machines are of two kinds—those which print as they punch, and those which do not print.

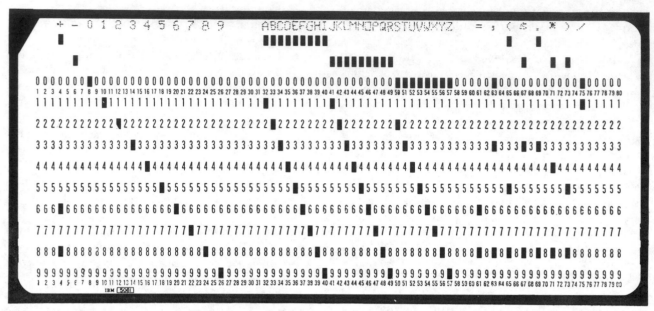

FIGURE 4-4(a). *Hollerith Card Showing Standard Punches for Signs, Digits, Letters of the Alphabet, and Special Characters*

FIGURE 4-4(b). *Hollerith Card Marked into Fields for a Legislative Roll-Call Project*

Unless you are an experienced operator (and so know what you are in for) never sit down at a non-printing keypunch.

Error Detection Devices. Proofreading punched cards for accuracy can be done directly from the printed line at the top if a printing keypunch was used. Other methods of proofreading by eye require special equipment. Unprinted punched cards may be transformed into print by duplicating them on a printing keypunch machine (a slow process, useful only for checking a few cards about which you are suspicious or which have been mutilated); or they may be printed on an *interpreter,* a machine which prints the characters indicated by the punched holes at the top of the card (though in two lines, so that the printed characters are not directly over corresponding columns). Unprinted cards also may be *listed* by a *tabulator,* which prints out the exact contents of each card on a sheet of paper, each line representing the 80 columns of one card.

The most accurate checking is provided by *verifying* the cards. The *verifier* is essentially a simulated keypunch machine which does not punch. Punched cards are fed through it exactly as through the keypunch machine, and the operator presses the keys as if actually punching cards from the source data. If a discrepancy occurs, a red light flashes, and if found to be an actual error, the machine cuts a small notch over the mistake. If no error is found, a notch is cut at the end of the card.

The Reproducer. A set of cards may be duplicated rapidly on this machine (though without any printing, so that care is needed in identification of the new set). The device is useful if the old deck needs replacement because of wear or mutilation, or if several sets of the same data are needed for a class project or shipment to colleagues.

The Counter-Sorter. The machines thus far mentioned are all used in the *preparation* of data cards. Prior to widespread availability of electronic computers, the workhorse of social research data *processing* was the counter-sorter, and it is still a mainstay in many centers even where computers are available. Aside from being more expensive, the use of computers requires considerably more training, and some smaller computers are not well adapted for processing large quantities of card input. A large stockpile of accumulated political and social data is available only on cards whose format was designed for counter-sorter processing.

As its name suggests, the counter-sorter both sorts and counts data cards. It does this at a rate of more than 600 cards per minute, permitting rapid cross-tabulating of typical survey data. Sorters without the counter attachment are used to arrange cards in sequence (numerical, alphabetical, chronological) or to separate cards into different groups for other processing. With the counter attachment, the machine tallies the number of cards in each group.

The machine operates on only one column at a time, placing each card physically in a separate bin, determined by the hole punched in the column for which the sorter is set. There are thirteen bins, one for each of the twelve punch positions and a "reject" bin for cards unpunched in that column. The counter attachment has fourteen tally dials. When set to zero

at the beginning of a sort, these dials record the number of cards placed in each bin, as well as the total number of cards processed. The tally dials can operate independently of the sorting mechanism, a feature useful for the last step of a complex cross-tabulation sequence since it relieves the operator of the task of manually reassembling a large number of small stacks.

The counter-sorter does no computations; tallies must be recorded by hand after each sort. A carefully prepared worksheet is needed, with the desired categories clearly identified. It is easy, too, to use a carbon with your worksheet—the extra copy will be valuable if you must release one to a keypunch operator, a colleague, or a project supervisor.

4-5 The Keysort Card—A Compromise

For many projects based on small samples and short questionnaires, an excellent device midway between handwork and machine data card is the marginal hole punched card, of which the most commonly used type is the Keysort system (patented by the Royal-McBee Company). The card is prepared in a number of sizes and often custom printed for special uses—libraries use it extensively because text may be handwritten or typed on the card, and coding done later for significant items in the written text. A series of round holes are prepunched along the edges of the card, and coding is done by notching a given hole so that it is open to the margin. Sorting is accomplished by inserting a sorter rod (a device resembling an ice-pick) through the entire stack of cards at that hole. Those cards which have been notched at particular holes or combinations of holes can thus be quickly separated from those which have not been notched. Figure 4–5 shows two formats in common library use.

Some of the advantages for small projects:

1. You can type notes on the card; it is even possible to have a questionnaire answered on the card itself.
2. You can work with the cards in your room, not limited by tightly-scheduled machine time.
3. Your library probably has them in stock and may have notch punchers and sorters which you can borrow. On the other hand, you can even make do with an icepick and scissors if need be.
4. Mutilation of cards is rare—a bent or folded card will still smooth out sufficiently to separate from the stack.

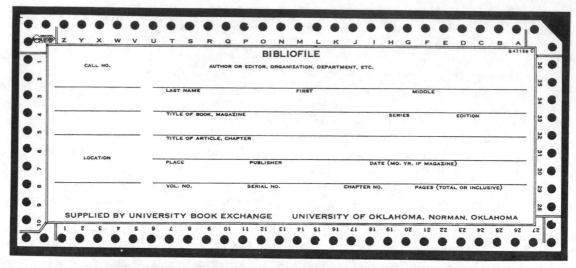

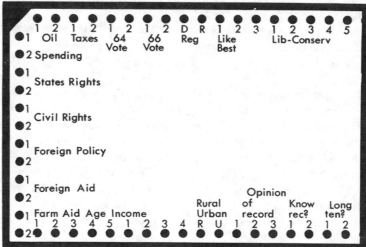

FIGURE 4-5. The *Keysort Card*

5. Changing codes and categories is easier—no computer reprogramming is involved.

Some disadvantages:

1. The total field is limited. The larger card in Figure 4–5 contains 81 holes. Even if these are interpreted as binary bits (each may be either notched or not), the absolute limit of information is 162 bits, as compared with the 800 digital entries of the IBM punchcard.

2. Numerical data are quite difficult to code and even more cumbersome to process. Each digit must be separately entered and separately processed. For a project in which only one or two short numerical items are needed (age, income in thousands of dollars), it is still possible to use the Keysort card. You can compress a two-digit numerical entry into a field of eight

holes if necessary, though the processing is more complicated than if twenty holes (ten for each digit) are available. The scheme depends on multiple punching of a four-hole field for each digit (the four holes may be labelled the "7–4–2–1" holes).

To Code Digit	*Notch Holes*
1	1
2	2
3	1 & 2
4	4
5	1 & 4
6	2 & 4
7	7
8	1 & 7
9	2 & 7
0	1, 2, & 7
	(or leave field blank)

By similar multiple punching, the 26-character alphabet can be compressed into a 5-hole field, though with added difficulty in sorting.

3. The most serious disadvantage is that, if the project is likely to expand, the stack of cards can abruptly become incredibly cumbersome. Special equipment exists for scanning an entire edge of much larger cards than shown in our illustrations, as well as for notching up to 200 cards at once, but these are to be found only in administrative centers which use the system for large managerial operations, such as library acquisition departments, manufacturing and merchandising inventory departments, oil field geological surveys, and similar institutions in which there is a distinct advantage in having written, typed, printed, or graphic information on the card itself.

Keysort in Use: Some Illustrations. The system, when limited to hand notching and sorting with one or two rods, can be effective for recording and cross-tabulating a set of about 25 items of the average questionnaire for something like 100 respondents. Figure 4–5 shows a card code format for a survey questionnaire on voter opinion in a Congressional election, containing the following items:

1. One question on whether respondent knows candidate's voting record.
2. Eight questions testing respondent's information about the candidate's voting record. ("Agreed," "Disagreed," "No opinion"—the third response being coded by leaving the field unnotched).
3. A five-point liberal-conservative scale ranking of the candidate.
4. A four-point item on what respondent liked best about candidate ("Nothing at all" coded as a blank field).
5. A three-point question on respondent's opinion of candidate's record.
6. Respondent's opinion on long congressional tenure.
7. Six identification items on respondent's income bracket, age, residence, party registration, prior vote on candidate, vote intention on candidate (each item coded for one additional response by leaving field blank).

This survey was conducted by personal interview of fifty respondents in selected urban and rural districts; income brackets were determined by class of home, so that some of the items were filled in by the investigator. The fifty cards were prepared directly from the questionnaires, which were planned to facilitate transfer of data by grouping the questions to correspond with the three edges of the card, in the same sequence. To prepare the individual data card, the format card shown in Figure 4–5 was positioned in turn just inside each card's edge as the investigator marked with pencil the holes to be notched on that edge. After the 50 data cards were so marked, the hand notching punch was used to make all the notches called for. The resulting "deck" contained the same information as would a standard machine punchcard deck. For the investigator, the advantages were that he could prepare the "deck" in his hometown over the weekend when the computer center was closed down; he did not need to know how to operate a keypunch machine; he could use a knitting needle to do his sorting; and his tabulations could be completed by Monday morning. Another student with a project of comparable size waited two weeks to gain access to keypunch machine and counter-sorter, besides requiring special supervision by an attendant at each machine. The two projects are typical: the first student completed his term project on time; the second student was probably better trained for larger projects in his future work. The first student's handwork was by no means wasted from this viewpoint, however: the logical processes of coding and sorting were probably more deeply ingrained, and are transferable.

The marginal hole punched card system is especially convenient for coding court cases, propaganda content of broadcasts and other media, political speeches, and other projects in which it is especially convenient to store textual content on the same card with the code (as a dissertation bibliography to be alphabetized). It was used with good success in the content analysis project of Chapter 8 of this workbook. By having each team of judges equipped with notching punch and sorter rod, the code list carefully prepared, and the statements pretyped on the cards, the project was completed in approximately one hour by a group of twelve students acting as three teams of judges.

Exercise Set 4. What Have You Learned?

4-1. Suppose you have conducted a small survey on respondents' attitude toward U.S. policy in Viet Nam and suppose your questionnaire is as follows:

1. Are you a (1) Democrat, or (2) Republican?
2. Do you consider your home to be in the (1) North, or (2) South?
3. Is your family income (1) below, or (2) above the U.S. median?
4. If asked to state your position on U.S. policy in Viet Nam, would you say you are a (1) Dove, or (2) Hawk?

Suppose the coding sheet for ten respondents on this survey is as follows:

Respondent	Party (Question 1)	Region (Question 2)	Income (Question 3)	Dependent Variable (Question 4)
1	1	1	1	1
2	1	1	1	1
3	1	1	1	2
4	1	1	2	2
5	1	2	1	2
6	1	2	2	2
7	2	1	1	1
8	2	1	2	1
9	2	1	2	2
10	2	2	2	2

1. Using these data, set up three 2 × 2 tables showing distribution of Doves and Hawks by (1) Party, (2) Region, and (3) Income. What is your dependent variable and your independent variable in each table?

(1) *Doves and Hawks by Party*

Total N		

Dependent variable: _____

Independent variable: _____

(2)   *Doves and Hawks by Region*

Total *N*		

Dependent variable: _____

Independent variable: _____

(3)   *Doves and Hawks by Income*

Total *N*		

Dependent variable: _____

Independent variable: _____

2. Using Income as a control variable, set up a 2×8 table showing distribution of Doves and Hawks by Party and Region with Income held constant. Ignoring the small *N* (assume that each card represents 1000 respondents), make three valid statements about your results.

Doves and Hawks by Party, Region, and Income

Total *N*								

Statements: (1) _____

(2) _____

(3) _____

3. Reconstruct the table into a 4 × 4 display, in which Dove-Hawk attitude is controlled for Region, and Party is controlled for Income.

Regional Distribution of Doves and Hawks, by Party and Income

Region	Attitude				
Total N					

4–2. The data below represent four items on an actual survey of fifty college freshmen at the University of Oklahoma. Each (unnumbered) row reports the answers to the four questions given by one of the fifty respondents. The verbal meaning of the digital codes is given in the "Code Sheet" which follows the data.

Column 1	Column 2	Column 3	Column 4	Column 1	Column 2	Column 3	Column 4
1	3	1	2	2	3	1	1
1	3	4	3	2	4	4	3
1	4	1	3	2	5	3	3
1	4	2	2	2	3	3	2
1	4	3	2	2	5	3	3
1	4	1	3	2	3	1	3
1	3	4	4	2	3	4	3
1	4	3	3	2	5	3	3
1	4	1	3	2	3	4	3
1	4	3	3	2	4	3	2
1	4	1	2	2	4	4	3
1	3	1	2	2	3	2	2
1	4	2	3	2	3	1	3
1	3	1	4	2	3	4	3
1	3	3	3	2	4	1	3
1	3	3	2	2	3	1	4
1	3	2	3	2	4	1	3
1	3	4	4	2	4	1	3
1	4	2	4	2	4	4	2
1	3	4	3	2	3	4	3
1	4	2	3	2	3	1	1
1	3	4	3	2	4	4	1
1	3	4	2	2	3	2	2
1	4	4	3	2	3	4	1
1	4	1	2	2	3	4	2

CODE SHEET

Column 1: Are you in ROTC?
　　1. Yes
　　2. No

Column 2: How would you describe your interest in world affairs?
　　1. Not interested
　　2. Slight interest
　　3. Average
　　4. Above average
　　5. Exceptional interest

Column 3: How do the average Vietnamese regard U.S. involvement in their country?
　　1. Resent the U.S.
　　2. Have neutral attitude
　　3. Welcome the U.S.
　　4. I don't know

Column 4: U.S. military forces in Vietnam should:
　　1. Be reduced
　　2. Remain at current strength
　　3. Be increased
　　4. I don't know

1. Treating *ROTC Status* (Question 1) as the independent variable, set up a table showing *Interest in World Affairs* (Question 2) as the dependent variable. (This will be a 5 × 2 table; that is, one with five rows and two columns in the basic display.)

Interest in World Affairs, by ROTC Status

Interest in World Affairs	ROTC	Non-ROTC
None	0%	0%
Slight		
Average		
Above average		
Exceptional		
Total	100%	100%
N		

2. Treating *Attitude toward U.S. Forces* (Question 4) as the dependent variable, *ROTC Status* (Question 1) as the first independent variable, and *Interest in World Affairs* (Question 2) as a dichotomous control (second independent) variable, set up a table displaying your results. Dichotomize *Interest in World Affairs* into the two categories: (1) Slight and Average, (2) Above and Exceptional. The result will be a 4 × 4 table, organized as follows:

Attitude toward U.S. Forces in Viet Nam, by ROTC Status and Degree of Interest in World Affairs

U.S. Forces Should Be:	Interest Slight or Average		Interest Above & Exceptional	
	ROTC	Non-ROTC	ROTC	Non-ROTC
Reduced	%	%	%	%
Same				
Increased				
Don't know				
Total	100%	100%	100%	100%
N				

3. *Reduction.* Carry out the reduction suggested in Tables 4–3 and 4–4 of this chapter. Then use the resulting categories as a dependent variable for a new table, in which *ROTC Status* is the independent variable.

Basic Opinion Groups, by ROTC Status

Group	ROTC	Non-ROTC
Revisionist	%	%
Cantankerous		
Status quo		
Indifferent		
Total	100%	100%
N		

4. *Substruction.* Carry out the substruction suggested in Table 4–5 of this chapter. Then use the resulting categories as a dependent variable for a new table, in which ROTC Status is the independent variable.

Foreign Policy Opinion Groups, by ROTC Status

Group	ROTC	Non-ROTC
Aggressive	%	%
Containment		
Isolationist		
Pacifist		
Ambivalent		
Indifferent		
Total	100%	100%
N		

4–3. *Now Do Some Coding and Tabulating.*

1. The basic coding scheme of the Survey Research Center is given in this chapter. Other coding conventions for this exercise, including a few substitutions for the standard codes, are given below. Using these as your codebook, prepare the coding sheets for keypunching the thirty-four unit records listed. These unit records are drawn from a much larger sample: they actually represent only the respondents who favored Goldwater

as the Republican nominee prior to the 1964 convention, and are further limited to certain regions of the country. Other respondents are omitted from our listing.

In preparing the coding sheet, be sure to enter only one digit in each square. Where the data consist of two or more digits, provision is made for the necessary number of columns (for example, a two-column "field" is provided for age of respondent.) The coding sheet must correspond exactly to the card format specifications.

Card Format

Columns 1–2	Identification: Survey Number (in this case, 11 on each card)
Columns 3–4	Identification: Respondent Number (from 01 to 34: enter zeroes)
Column 5	Blank
Column 6	Party preference
Column 7	How voted in 1960
Column 8	Republican Presidential choice for 1964
Columns 9–10	Home state
Columns 11–12	Age
Column 13	Income
Column 14	Sex
Column 15	Race
Column 16	Religion
Columns 17–18	Blank
Columns 19–20	Coder's Identification (use last two digits of your Student ID)

Other Coding Conventions for Use in this Exercise:

Column 6. Party preference

1. Strong Democrat
4. Independent
7. Strong Republican

Column 7. How voted in 1960

1. Voted—Democratic
2. Voted—Republican
7. Did not vote

Column 8. Republican Presidential choice for 1964

1. Barry Goldwater
2. Henry Cabot Lodge
3. Richard Nixon
4. Nelson Rockefeller
5. George Romney
6. William Scranton
7. Margaret Chase Smith
8. Harold Stassen

Column 13. Income (yourself and immediate family)

0. Under $1000
1. $1000—$1999
2. $2000—$2999
3. $3000—$3999
4. $4000—$4999
5. $5000—$5999
6. $6000—$7499
7. $7500—$9999
8. $10,000—$14,999
9. $15,000 and over

Column 16. Religion

1. Roman Catholic
2. Orthodox Catholic
3. Jewish
4. Protestant
9. Don't know; no answer; no preference

Card No.	Party Preference	1960 Vote	1964 Rep. Choice	Home	Age	Income ($1000's)	Sex	Race	Religion
01	Strong Dem.	D	G	New Orleans	21	5	M	White	Catholic
02	Strong Rep.	R	G	Houston	35	9	F	White	Prot.
03	Indep.	None	G	Atlanta	25	6	M	White	Prot.
04	Strong Dem.	None	G	Miami	40	15	F	White	Prot.
05	Strong Dem.	None	G	Little Rock	45	20	M	White	Prot.
06	Strong Dem.	D	G	Richmond	28	5	F	White	Prot.
07	Indep.	D	G	Austin	32	7	M	White	Prot.
08	Strong Rep.	R	G	Dallas	48	8	F	White	Prot.
09	Strong Dem.	R	G	Fort Smith	54	17	M	White	Prot.
10	Strong Dem.	D	G	Mobile	71	5	F	White	Prot.
11	Strong Dem.	D	G	Tampa	59	19	M	White	Prot.
12	Indep.	R	G	Savannah	22	7	F	White	Prot.
13	Strong Rep.	R	G	Charlotte	44	9	M	White	Prot.
14	Indep.	D	G	Raleigh	35	4	F	White	Prot.
15	Strong Dem.	D	G	Natchez	33	6	M	White	Prot.
16	Indep.	R	G	Shreveport	53	8	F	White	Prot.
17	Strong Dem.	R	G	Norfolk	43	12	M	White	Prot.
18	Strong Dem.	D	G	San Antonio	29	25	F	White	Prot.
19	Strong Dem.	D	G	Baton Rouge	64	14	M	White	Prot.
20	Strong Dem.	R	G	Montgomery	37	19	F	White	Prot.
21	Strong Dem.	R	G	Tallahassee	78	8	F	White	Prot.
22	Strong Rep.	D	G	Jackson	38	6	F	White	Catholic
23	Strong Dem.	D	G	Topeka	28	5	M	White	Prot.
24	Indep.	R	G	Chicago	36	13	F	White	Prot.
25	Strong Dem.	R	G	St. Paul	29	8	M	White	Catholic
26	Strong Dem	D	G	Detroit	48	16	F	White	Prot.
27	Strong Dem.	R	G	Cleveland	56	12	M	White	Prot.
28	Indep.	R	G	Des Moines	67	6	F	White	Prot.
29	Indep.	D	G	Indianapolis	53	20	M	White	Prot.
30	Strong Dem.	R	G	Madison	24	4	F	White	Prot.
31	Strong Dem.	R	G	St. Louis	39	9	F	White	Catholic
32	Strong Dem.	None	G	Lincoln	28	10	F	White	Prot.
33	Strong Dem.	None	G	Fargo	66	7	M	White	Prot.
34	Indep.	None	G	Omaha	45	14	M	White	Prot.

CODING SHEET No. _____

Survey Number _____   Coder _____   Coder No. _____

1	2	3	4	5	6	7	8	9	10	11	12	13	14	15	16	17	18	19	20

CODING SHEET No. _____

Survey Number ____   Coder _____   Coder No. _____

1	2	3	4	5	6	7	8	9	10	11	12	13	14	15	16	17	18	19	20

2. Prepare a table showing distribution of Goldwater preference by Religion, controlling for Region. Information on total number of respondents is entered in the table format and from this you can compute the necessary data for "Other" preferences. Note that the table collapses the two Midwest Regions of the SRC code into one.

Pre-Convention Goldwater Strength, by Religion and Region

Preference	South		Midwest	
	Protestant	Catholic	Protestant	Catholic
Goldwater				
Other				
Total				
N	91	11	83	25

4–4. Devise a system for use of Keysort for coding a project involving twenty-five Supreme Court cases, votes and opinions of nine judges on each, providing for five categories of cases and prior and subsequent history of each case.

Reading List

By far the most useful introduction to data processing for political scientists is the handbook by Janda. The books on computer programming, not dealt with in this chapter, are included because it is at this point in the exercises that the value of computer processing becomes clear. Those who wish to examine the subject will find helpful the sample Fortran programs in Appendix C.

Backstrom, Charles H., and Gerald D. Hursh, *Survey Research*. Evanston: Northwestern University Press, 1963. This is one of the volumes in Northwestern's excellent series of handbooks for research in political behavior, and contains good illustrations of tabulating forms.*

Harris, L. Dale, *Fortran Programming*. Columbus: Charles E. Merrill Publishing Co., 1965.*

Hartkemeier, Harry P., *Fortran Programming of Electronic Computers*. Columbus: Charles E. Merrill Publishing Co., 1966. A workbook, with exercises.*

Hyman, Herbert, *Survey Design and Analysis*. New York: Free Press, 1965. The logic of cross-tabulation is made clear, with notes on use of the counter-sorter.

Janda, Kenneth, *Data Processing: Applications to Political Research*. Evanston: Northwestern University Press, 1965. Deals exhaustively with punchcard processing and kinds of hardware, and describes in detail several computer programs developed at Northwestern for special use in political research.*

Kent, Allen, *Textbook on Mechanized Information Retrieval*. New York: John Wiley and Sons, Inc., 1962. A thorough exposition of varieties of marginal-hole punched cards, as well as other equipment.

Miller, Delbert C., *Handbook of Research Design and Social Measurement*. New York: David McKay Co., Inc., 1964. Good examples of worksheet layouts.*

Shao, Stephen P., *Statistics for Business and Economics*. Columbus: Charles E. Merrill Publishing Co., 1967. Chapter 3 discusses processing methods, including the use of Keysort.

---

* Paperback edition available.

STATISTICS

A Little Dab'll Do You

This limited exposure to three elementary statistical tests is planned to show you the meaning of statistical inference and to enable you to apply the tests to the problems in the remaining exercises of the workbook. It will not, of course, make you a statistician—the jocular subtitle above implies only that with relatively little effort you can acquire a general knowledge of what statisticians do. You can also learn to apply simple forms of the tests to a variety of political data distributions. Hopefully the exercises of this chapter will encourage you to learn more by emphasizing the relevance of statistics to political analysis. The political scientist need not be a statistician, but he needs to know enough about statistics to communicate meaningfully with the statistician—to obtain and apply the expert's advice in his own research.

5-1 Inference

Statistical inference is the drawing of conclusions about a population[1] on the basis of the characteristics of a sample. From the sample, we *infer* that something is probably true or not true about the population from which it is drawn. *Inferential statistics* derives such conclusions by analyzing the findings of *descriptive statistics*. In descriptive statistics we learn to compute measures of a collection of cases arranged according to some sort of scaled variable. A collection of ten persons, for example, usually displays a variation in income from one person to another. Income is thus a

variable. If the ten persons are listed according to magnitude of income, we have an ordered *distribution* or array of this variable, from which may be computed such measures as the median, mode, mean, range, quartiles, deciles, interquartile range, variance, and standard deviation.[2] By examining such measures we obtain a fairly accurate idea of the characteristics of our group of ten persons on the income variable.

By comparing one of these measures (for example, the mean or variance) with what is known of a given population, we can *infer* that the particular collection of cases in our distribution is or is not reasonably representative of that population. If our income distribution had a mean of $1,000,000, for example, we could reasonably doubt that it was representative of the population of incomes in the United States.

By applying a precise inferential test we would be able to define this reasonable doubt in more exact terms: we might be able to say, for example, that the chances are at least a thousand to one against our sample of ten incomes having been drawn randomly from the general population of United States incomes. The statistician would say that the *null hypothesis* (that the sample is drawn randomly) is rejected at the .001 significance level. By this he would mean that

---

[1] In statistics, "population" means the whole collection of cases of a given attribute or group of attributes. Typical "populations," in this meaning, are *all* persons, *all* Republicans, *all* Democrats, *all* party members, *all* voters, *all* incomes, *all* opinions on a particular public question, *all* congressmen, *all* countries, *all* Protestants, *all* Protestant Republicans who voted in 1964, *all* Democratic blue-collar workers in the South, *all* students aged 18, or *all* roll-calls in the U.S. Senate on Administration-supported measures. Mathematical statistics distinguishes between finite populations and infinite populations, though some obviously finite populations like those just listed may be treated as infinite by deeming them to include all past, present, future, and possible cases of the defined group.

[2] Brief definitions of these terms:

Mean: the arithmetic average of the individual observations in the distribution.

Median: the midpoint of a distribution arrayed in order of magnitude.

Mode: the value in a distribution which occurs with the greatest frequency.

Range: the difference between the highest and lowest values in a distribution.

Quartile: a value which occurs at one of the division points when the distribution is divided into equal quarters.

Decile: a value which occurs at one of the division points when the distribution is divided into equal tenths.

Interquartile range: the difference in magnitude between the values which fall at the 75% quartile and the 25% quartile.

Variance: the average of the squared differences between the observations and the mean (sometimes called the "mean squared deviation").

Standard deviation: the square root of the variance (sometimes called the "root square mean").

his test indicates that such a sample would be drawn from the population of United States incomes *by pure chance* in no more than one case out of a thousand. A *probability* is a number that lies on the interval from zero to 1, including the end points of the interval—that is, it can range from zero probability ($p = 0.00$) to complete certainty ($p = 1.00$). It may be thought of as the frequency of occurrence of an event in a large number—actually an infinite number—of trials. Thus an equal chance is described as having probability of .50, one chance in a hundred as having probability of .01, and one chance in a thousand as having probability of .001. Conversely, of course, the probability in our example is .999 or more that the sample was *not* drawn randomly from the population of United States incomes.

Notice that the test has not led the statistician to absolute certainty. So long as there are at least ten incomes in the United States which average $1,000,000, there is a chance, no matter how small, that a random sample might turn them up. Though the chance would be extremely remote, we ordinarily use an inferential test to reach conclusions which are much less certain. It is important to keep in mind that some degree of uncertainty remains even with the most rigorous test.

5-2 Sample and Population : Statistic and Parameter

In all work with statistics, we need to be alert to a basic distinction between two kinds of tests—parametric and nonparametric. To the statistician any measure of a sample (such as the mean, the variance, or the standard deviation) is a *statistic;* the corresponding measure for the population is a *parameter*. A parametric test consists of using a given statistic to estimate the parameter to which it corresponds, as a

basis for deciding (within given probability limits) whether the sample is or is not drawn from that population. The use of parametric tests depends on the mathematical theory of the law of large numbers and the central limit theorem. The law of large numbers is that the larger the sample, the closer the sample statistic is to the population parameter. The central limit theorem, even more fundamental to the theory of statistical inference, is that the *sampling distribution* of a statistic (for example, the distribution of sample means for repeated random samples drawn from the sample's parent population) approaches the normal ("bell-shaped curve") distribution as sample size increases, even if the population itself does not have a normal distribution.

Thus if you make a decision about a hypothesis on the basis of a parametric test, you must be sure that one of two conditions is met. You must be sure that either (1) your random sample is from a population having a normal distribution, or (2) your sample is large enough. Some parametric tests require the first of these conditions, some the second. Some require even more restrictive conditions. The widely used test known as Student's *t* (from the pseudonym of its originator, W. S. Gosset), on which much of modern sampling theory is based, was designed to test whether a sample with a given mean could have come from a population with a given mean. Its use is valid only for a variable measured by the standard number system—an equal-interval scale with a zero point (such as age, income, height, weight, or test scores of ability or achievement). It is often used improperly for orders or scaled attitudes, such as party preference, social status, and test scores on opinion or attitude questionnaires. For most political research based on samples, you are unlikely to know whether the population is statistically normal. If you know anything about it—and often you do not—what you do know will fre-

the small society

OF COURSE WE'RE GLAD YOU'RE ABOVE AVERAGE BUT JUST BEAR IN MIND THAT NOWADAYS THAT'S BELOW AVERAGE —

Nonparametric Tests Make no Assumptions about the Population from which the Sample Is Drawn.

quently suggest that it is not normal. For this reason you will usually be safer with *nonparametric* tests, which make no assumptions about the population from which the sample is drawn. The three test statistics described in this chapter are nonparametric, chosen deliberately to help you avoid the most common beginner's error of using an improper test.

An important point about any statistical sample is that it must be truly random. The entire theory of statistical inference is based on this assumption, and does not apply if the assumption is not met. Two serious research problems result from this requirement. First, there is the obvious problem of achieving randomness. Quota sampling as used by some polling organizations, in which the field interviewer is left free to choose his sample within defined categories, may yield reasonably accurate results, but the nonrandom feature (interviewer selection of cases) makes it impossible to say exactly how much statistical error may be involved. The second research problem resulting from the requirement of randomness is that of defining clearly the population from which the sample is taken. A sample drawn with the most carefully designed random method from the telephone book can be used only for inferences about the population of telephone subscribers. A sample randomly drawn from the entire population of the United States does not tell us anything (statistically speaking) about the population of voters. Even more caution in defining the statistical population is necessary when your sample is not random, but consists of some convenient "captive" group such as a class of college students. The group may be representative of a number of larger ones—of various populations—but you cannot safely assume this to be true without some verification.

5-3 Testing of Hypotheses

In setting up a statistical test it is conventional to word the proposition we are testing so as to assert that no *significant difference* exists between the sample and the population, or between two samples if the test is for their independence, or that no significant association exists between two variables.

Null hypothesis. Since the test is designed so as to determine the probable truth or falsity of a proposition which states that no significant discovery will result—that the status is *quo ante*—the proposition is called the *null hypothesis* (H_0).

The null hypothesis is the hypothesis that the observed difference between the population parameter and the sample statistic is due to random sampling variability. All statistical models that use probability distributions of sample statistics (the normal distribution, the binomial, the *t,* or the chi-square distribution) assume that the sample is random. If the event is statistically rare (for example, if it would occur at random only five times in a hundred or less) we *reject* the null hypothesis. Rejection of the null hypothesis often implies acceptance of an alternative hypothesis, although great care is required on this point. Ordinarily there are a considerable number, even an infinity, of alternative hypotheses, and the inexperienced analyst is sometimes tempted to assert the validity of one to which he has some prior subjective commitment. Typically, you will word your null hypothesis deliberately with the expectation (and hope) that it will be proved false—that the test will justify its rejection.

Significance level. Once the null hypothesis is set up, the researcher must determine the significance limit at which he is prepared to accept or reject it: in other words, how sure he feels he must be of his results. In practical work, this choice is restricted to the significance levels (probability values) for which standard tables have been computed and published. (Probabilities of .10, .05, .02, and .01 are commonly used). He must then determine which *statistic* to use in his test. He then computes that statistic and compares his result with the theoretical distribution of the statistic, ordinarily by consulting a published table showing its value for various probabilities and for distributions of various sizes. If his result equals or exceeds the value shown in the table for a given probability, he rejects the null hypothesis.

The significance level—for example, $p = .05$, should be selected before the test is performed. This avoids the temptation to alter the level in order to confirm one's hopes or expectations.

The testing procedure may be illustrated by recalling our sample of ten incomes. If we draw ten samples of ten incomes from the population of the United States, each sample will have its own small distribution—its mean, variance, standard deviation, range, and other statistical descriptors. By the central limit theorem, the *means* of the samples (as well as the other sample statistics) will tend to cluster about the mean (or other corresponding parameters) of the parent population. While the mean of one small sample may be as remote from the true population mean as was our million-dollar average income from the true mean income of the United States population, the *mean of the sample means* approaches more and more closely to the true population mean as sample size or number of samples increases. For an infinite number of samples, the mean of sample means is exactly equal to the population mean. The mean of all possible samples in a complete permutation of cases in the population for the given sample size also is exactly equal to the population mean (as with cointosses or throws of dice). In the process of drawing your samples, you will obtain successively better estimates of the population mean, always with a known probability of error. (In the gambling model, the more you play—if randomly—the more nearly you will break even). The range of this error for a given probability is called the *confidence interval,* and the end-points of the range are the *confidence limits.* The procedure is analogous to estimating the true time by averaging from several inaccurate clocks, except that the distributions of sampling statistics for samples of various sizes have been worked out with precise mathematical methods. We can say, for example, from a sampling estimate of population income, that the true mean income is about $4800 (*estimate of parameter*) with a 95 per cent chance (*significance level,* or probability of .95) that it lies within the range $4700-$4900 (*confidence interval*). In this example, $4700 is the lower confidence limit and $4900 the upper confidence limit. Of course you must remain cautiously aware that the conclusion just reached implies a 5 per cent probability ($p = .05$) that the true mean does *not* fall in the confidence interval. Confidence is not assurance.

The combination of precision and vagueness involved in probability statements is intuitively unsatisfying to some and occasionally is a target of scornful comment about all statistical analysis in contrast with the greater precision claimed for the physical sciences. Perhaps it will help to recall—if you have qualms—that the very same procedure is used in every physics laboratory when a value is fixed by averaging a series of readings from a measuring instrument. The careful delineation of probable error in a statistical test corresponds exactly to the similarly well defined range of error in statistical mechanics—error dramatized whenever a carefully engineered bridge unexpectedly collapses or a space vehicle blows up on its pad.

5-4 Errors

Whether the hypothesis is accepted or rejected, there is always a possibility that the test has resulted in an error. The table below shows the possible combinations of outcomes of a statistical test, and the terms commonly used to identify the two major areas of possible error. For each result, we have added a descriptive phrase to aid your memory.

	H_0 Accepted	H_0 Rejected
H_0 True (No Association)	Correct Conclusion "Nothing there" effect	Type I Error "Seller's risk" "I went out on a limb and it broke" effect
H_0 False (Association)	Type II Error "Buyer's risk" "It was there, but I didn't see it" effect	Correct Conclusion "Eureka!" effect

5-5 Yule's Q Test for Two Dichotomous Variables

The first test we will learn is easily and quickly computed and has many uses in the preliminary analysis of data. It is a rough and practical guide to (1) *the approximate degree* of association of two variable attributes, and (2) *the direction* of the association.

It was designed for purely practical work and lacks the precision of more refined tests. It is limited in that it can be applied in its original form only to a 2×2 table (one displaying two dichotomous variables), and in that it is not possible to attach a fixed probability to any given value of the statistic. On the other hand, many political arrays are in dichotomous form, or can easily be reduced to a dichotomous table for quick inspection of the general pattern of relationships. Moreover, the Q test is *margin-free:* it tests proportions as well as numerical frequencies, and so may be used for a 2×2 table which shows only percentages. As a coefficient should, it ranges in values from -1.00 to $+1.00$, with the 0.00 value interpreted to mean that there is no association at all between the two variables in the table.

Q is defined as the quotient of the *difference* between the cross-products of a 2×2 table divided by their *sum.* If we label the four cells of a table showing the cross-tabulation of two variables as in the diagram below, then the formula will yield the Q value, whether the cells contain frequencies or percentages.

First Variable	Second Variable	
	$+$	$-$
$+$	a	b
$-$	c	d

$$Q = \frac{ad - bc}{ad + bc}$$

Use of Q in Scaling. The Q test has many applications. One of the most useful to political analysis is the preliminary sorting of legislative roll-calls for scaling a cluster of legislators or a cluster of bills having a common attribute. Roll-calls thought to represent a given general pattern may be compared pairwise as follows:

TABLE 5-1.

Vote 1	Vote 2 +	−	Vote 3 +	−	Vote 4 +	−
+	8	4	6	6	2	10
−	2	10	4	8	8	4
	$Q = .82$		$Q = .33$		$Q = -.82$	

The first display shows that 18 of the 24 voting members voted the same way on both roll-calls (8 for and 10 against), while only six voted "inconsistently" (in terms of scale analysis). The high Q value means that the pair of roll-calls will probably "scale" as part of a group indicating similar voting blocs. The low Q value for the comparison of Votes 1 and 3, on the other hand, indicates the larger number of such "inconsistencies" (actually 10 in this case), so the researcher would probably drop the third roll-call from his scaled group. In scaling, a high negative value, as in the third display, shows both that the two roll-calls are similar and also that in his eventual scale group, the analyst should reverse the plus and minus signs (that is, the "Yes" on Vote 1 and the "No" on Vote 4 reflect the same basic attitude, as anti-Administration or pro-Labor).

Limitations. Unfortunately, quite different distributions may yield the same value. Some of the limitations of the Q test are illustrated by the following examples of individual roll-calls, vote choice being one variable and party affiliation the other.

TABLE 5-2. *Perfect Positive Association*

	Rep	Dem	Rep	Dem	Rep	Dem
Yes	25	0	25	20	12	0
No	0	40	0	20	13	40
	$Q = +1.00$		$Q = +1.00$		$Q = +1.00$	

With a "Yes" vote identified as the + portion of the dependent variable and "Republican" as the + portion of the independent variable, the Q test yields a perfect positive value of $+1.00$ for either perfect *one-way* or perfect *two-way* association. Two-way

association is illustrated in the first display (*all* Republicans voted "Yes," *all* Democrats "No"). But if all Republicans voted "Yes," the value comes out the same no matter how the Democrats divide (with the sole exception of the case of all Democrats also voting "Yes"). The second display shows an example of such *one-way* association. Similarly, if all Democrats voted "No," as in our third display, the value comes out the same, no matter how the Republicans divide, again with the sole exception of the case of all Republicans also voting "No."

TABLE 5-3. *Complete Absence of Association*

	Rep	Dem	Rep	Dem	Rep	Dem
Yes	25	40	0	0	5	8
No	0	0	25	40	20	32
	$Q = 0.00$		$Q = 0.00$		$Q = (160 - 160)/320$ $= 0.00$	

These tables demonstrate that the Q value is zero when the *proportions* are the same. If the above tables were translated into percentages, each column summing to 100 per cent, the percentages would be the same for the two columns of each table.

5-6 Spearman's Rho (ρ): A Coefficient of Rank Correlation

In political and social research some of the most useful statistical tests are those which may be applied to distributions based on rankings, as compared with those based on specific quantitative values. We are often uncertain of the accuracy of specific measurements but more nearly certain of rank order. For scaled attributes, rankings are often all we have to work with.

Spearman's ρ (lower-case Greek rho) is a correlation coefficient related to the more complicated product-moment coefficient of correlation, but is far easier to compute. At some advanced political statistical research centers, it is considered more useful for many of the imprecise associations studied in their work. Like the Q statistic and other coefficients it ranges from -1.00 (perfect negative correlation) to $+1.00$ (perfect positive correlation), with the 0.00 value indicating no association at all. Unlike the Q test, however, precise probabilities may be attached to its values for specified numbers of ranked pairs. The computational pattern essentially consists of attaching a rank number to each item in each of two paired distributions, squaring the difference between each of the paired ranks, and applying the formula to the sum of these squared differences.

Example: A left-wing group and a right-wing group have ranked five senators on a scale meant to measure the quality of "most valuable statesman."

TABLE 5-4. *Coefficient of Rank Correlation*

	Left-Wing List	Right-Wing List	Difference	D^2
Senator V	1	5	4	16
Senator W	2	4	2	4
Senator X	3	3	0	0
Senator Y	4	2	2	4
Senator Z	5	1	4	16
			Sum D^2 = 40	
			$N = 5$	

$$\rho = 1.00 - \frac{6 \text{ Sum } D^2}{N(N^2 - 1)} = 1.00 - 240/120$$
$$= 1.00 - 2.00 = -1.00$$

As we would have assumed from the original tabulation, the judges' rankings were exactly opposite: we have a perfect negative correlation. If our political information about the two groups of judges is sufficient, we would be safe in rejecting a null hypothesis that they are essentially similar in their opinions of the value of senators.

In the example just given we had information only about the ranks. The statistic may be applied as well to a pair of distributions involving variable data of any kind, by ranking the items in each in order of

TABLE 5-5. *Rank Correlation with Tied Ranks*

Country	(1) GNP per cap ($U.S.)	(2) Energy per cap (Megawatts)	Rank 1	Rank 2	D	D^2
Colombia	330	3.8	1	2	1	1
Malaya	298	3.1	2	3	1	1
Turkey	276	1.8	3	5	2	4
Brazil	262	2.9	4	4	0	0
Mexico	197	5.7	5	1	4	16
Ghana	135	1.0	6	7.5	1.5	2.25
Indonesia	127	0.8	7	9	2	4
India	72	1.0	8	7.5	.5	.25
China	56	1.3	9	6	3	9
Burma	52	0.2	10	10	0	0
				Sum D^2 = 37.5		
				$N = 10$		

$$\rho = 1.00 - (6 \times 37.5)/10(100 - 1)$$
$$= 1.00 - 225/990 = +.77$$

magnitude. Table 5-5 illustrates the procedure, as well as the standard method for dealing with tied rankings.

Significance of the value obtained for the coefficient of rank correlation is tabulated in Appendix F for up to thirty paired rankings. You can see the general pattern of the significance table by thinking of it as a display of the probability that the ranking represented by the coefficient might be obtained by a random process such as throwing dice. For two paired rankings, the coefficient must be either +1.00 or −1.00, since there is no possible order of judging except perfect agreement or perfect disagreement. Each of the two outcomes being equally likely by a random process, no probability higher than .5 can be established. For three paired rankings there are six possible random (and equally likely) outcomes, shown in Table 5-6 with the corresponding coefficients.

TABLE 5-6. *Possible Orderings for Three Paired Rankings by Two Judges*

Rank 1	Possible Orderings for Rank 2					
1	1	1	2	2	3	3
2	2	3	1	3	1	2
3	3	2	3	1	2	1
$\rho =$	+1.00	+0.5	+0.5	−0.5	−0.5	−1.00

Clearly the coefficient will be +1.00 one-sixth of the time ($p = .167$), and +0.5 *or higher* one-half of the time ($p = .5$). When we compare our actual value for ρ with those in the table, we may consider our actual value a "sample" statistic and the value in the table a "population" parameter—the population being the theoretically infinite number of trials postulated by the concept of a random process. It may occur to you that a larger number of judgings even of a sample so small as two persons should yield greater assurance than if only two judges' rankings are used. Of course this is true, and an extension of the statistic to one of multiple rank correlation is possible. For example, if two students are ranked identically by two teachers (by grades of A and C), we cannot say that the rank correlation coefficient of +1.00 connotes any significant probability beyond .5, but if ten teachers are consistent in ranking the same two students, there is a very small chance that the result would occur by a random process (note, however, that it still *could* happen: the student with the ten low grades may take some comfort from the slight probability of about .001).

5-7 The Chi-Square (χ^2) Test

The chi-square test (χ is the lower-case Greek chi) is one of the most useful and versatile of all statistical tests, and may be applied to a great variety of political research problems. Essentially it is based on a comparison of the *sum* of squared deviations from the mean in a given sample with the *variance* of the theoretical or assumed population. The basic statistical formula for this ratio is:

$$\chi^2 = SS/\sigma^2$$

in which

SS = sum of squared deviations from the mean in the sample, and

σ^2 = variance of the population (variance is the average squared deviation; σ is the lower-case Greek sigma). This basic formula becomes, by algebraic manipulation for the applications used in the exercises of this section:

$$\chi^2 = \Sigma\,(O - E)^2/E$$

in which Σ (capital Greek sigma) is the summation sign, meaning that we add a series of values, each of which is determined by the expression which follows the Σ, or in this case the series of values defined by $(O - E)^2/E$,

O = an *observed* value in the sample distribution being tested,

E = an expected value corresponding to the observed value.

An example will clarify these terms and illustrate the summation process in the computation of χ^2 for a 2×2 table. Using the data given in Chapter 1 for literacy rates of polities which were formerly colonies of Britain and France, we use the same table format as for Yule's Q, adding both row and column totals:

	Former British	Former French	Total
High Literacy	15	7	22
Low Literacy	4	13	17
Total	19	20	39

The four cell entries of the basic table are our "Observed" values (15, 7, 4, and 13), and we use the marginal totals to arrive at the corresponding "Expected" values. We are testing a hypothesis that literacy and former colonial ruler are not associated variables; in other words we need a table which divides up the marginal totals among the four cells so as to show no association—to produce a Q value

of zero. The layout below shows how we obtain this "Expected" table (forget for the moment that we cannot have "fractional" countries!):

	Former British	Former French	Total
High Literacy	(19)(22/39) = 10.72	(20)(22/39) = 11.28	22
Low Literacy	(19)(17/39) = 8.28	(20)(17/39) = 8.72	17
Total	19	20	39

This new table supplies all the additional values needed to apply our formula and to find χ^2. For convenience, we will use the same type table as for Yule's Q, adding extra letters for the marginal totals and the grand total:

TABLE 5-7. *Computation of Chi-Square*

a	b	e
c	d	f
g	h	T

Cell	O	E	$O - E$ (or D)	D^2	D^2/E
a	15	$ge/T = 10.72$	4.28	18.32	1.71
b	7	$he/T = 11.28$	−4.28	18.32	1.62
c	4	$gf/T = 8.28$	−4.28	18.32	2.21
d	13	$hf/T = 8.72$	4.28	18.32	2.10

$$\chi^2 = \Sigma\,(D^2/E) = 7.64$$
$$df = 1$$
$$p < .01$$

In applying the information that the χ^2 value for our table is 7.64, we make use of the χ^2 table in Appendix G. There we find that for one "degree of freedom" the value 6.635 is entered in the column headed "$p = .01$" and the value 7.879 in the column "$p = .005$." Since our computed value for this test lies between those two, we conclude that the probability (that the association shown between literacy and former colonial ruler could arise by a random process) is somewhat less than one chance in a hundred and somewhat more than five chances in a thousand. We therefore enter on the last line the conclusion that the probability is less than .01.

The number of degrees of freedom is a major consideration in almost all statistical tests. Briefly, it is the number of entries in a distribution of a given size which are "free" to vary randomly in magnitude if the total of all entries is fixed. In a distribution of ten entries, nine entries may vary freely, but once these nine values are determined, the tenth is not "free" but results automatically from the constraint of the known total for all ten values. A 2×2 table of the format of Table 5-7 has only *one* degree of freedom, since (given the row and column totals) the entry in any one cell determines the entries in the other three. A detailed example of the 2×2 table is given in Appendix G. The general rule for determining degrees of freedom in a table of R rows and C columns, with both R and C greater than one, is:

$$df = (R - 1)(C - 1)$$

The formulas in the worksheet for the "Expected" values result from the definition of "Expected"—given the marginal totals, we "expect" from the null hypothesis that the entries will show no association between the two variables. The two entries on the first row should represent the same ratio as the two entries on the second row $(a/b = c/d)$; the two entries in the first column should represent the same ratio as the two entries in the second column $(a/c = b/d)$. For any cell, the expected value which fits these ratios is calculated by dividing the product of its two marginal totals by the grand total.

Without going into the mathematics of the χ^2 distribution, we can get an intuitive idea of its power by considering some of its characteristics:

1. Since the ingredient of the basic formula, SS/σ^2, representing the sample, is SS, or sum of squared deviations from the sample mean, the numerator in the χ^2 statistic is (a) never negative—a squared negative number becomes positive, and (b) not limited in magnitude by averaging: it is not the sample variance, but the *total* of squared deviations. In fact, χ^2 can range in value from zero to infinity.

2. For the same reason, χ^2 will have a different distribution for each value of N; that is, for each sample size. If the *proportions* of two frequency distributions are the same, the ratio of the two χ^2 values is exactly equal to the ratio of the two N's. In our example of former British and French colonies, if each entry in the table were exactly doubled, the value for χ^2 would be twice as great.

3. The χ^2 statistic is thus extremely sensitive both to sample size and to the difference between sample variance and population variance. The variance, as noted in Section 5-1, is the *average* squared deviation from the mean in any distribution, so the comparison is essentially between total variation in the sample (Sum of Squares, abbreviated SS) and mean variation in the population. A related statistical distribution (that of the phi-coefficient—ø), which can vary only from zero to 1.00, has been expanded into a distribu-

tion which can vary for large samples from zero to infinity, with a precise value assigned for any combination of sample sizes, sample variances, population variances, and probability of the value being exceeded by chance. This remarkable result permits us to assign an exact probability to the chance that a given value of χ^2 may be exceeded for any given sample size when compared to any given population variance.

Applications. We will use the χ^2 test for two general purposes: as a test of the probability that two variables in a table are associated (H_0: they are not), and as a test of "fit"—that is, of the probability that a given distribution is drawn from some population having a known or theoretical distribution. For both applications we compare the frequencies in our table with those which "ought to be" there: "ought to be" there on the assumption that the two variables are not associated, or "ought to be" there on the assumption that the population has some known distribution. We compare, in other words, the observed frequencies with the expected frequencies.

In our worksheets for the computation, the E values, for "expected" frequencies, are obtained in two ways:

1. For tests of association of two variables, the "expected" frequencies are those which would appear in the table on the null hypothesis of no association of the two variables. The computational pattern used in our example of former French and British colonies is repeated on the worksheet of Table 5-8. In checking the worksheet for 2×2 tables, you will notice that each D (or $O - E$) value comes out the same, except that were we to use $O - E$ instead of the absolute difference, two of the values would be positive and two negative. For this reason, a simpler formula is sometimes used for a 2×2 table, but here we have retained the more general formula, since it is equally adaptable to larger tables. A worksheet for the simpler formula is supplied in Exercise Set 8.

2. For tests of "fit" with a population distribution, the "expected" frequencies are those which would appear in the table if the sample frequencies were distributed exactly according to the known breakdown of the population. The population distribution to be "expected" may be, for example, the known voting data; it may be some theoretical statistical distribution —the normal, the binomial, the Poisson or other; or it may be set arbitrarily in the null hypothesis to test whether the true proportions of the population are of a certain magnitude (the test then determines the probability that this is so).

TABLE 5-8. *Worksheets for Computation of* χ^2

(a) *The 1 × 2 table*

	Observed (in Sample)	Expected (U.S. Census Averages)	Difference	D^2	D^2/E
Voters	180	.70(320) = 224	44	1936	8.6
Non-Voters	140	.30(320) = 96	44	1936	20.3
Total	320	$\chi^2 = \text{Sum} \quad (D^2/E) = 28.9$ For 1 Degree of freedom, $p < .001$			

(b) *The 1 × n table*

Region	Regional Sample Total	Observed Voters	Expected Voters	Difference	D^2	D^2/E
Northeast	130	100	.74(130) = 96.2	3.8	14.44	.15
North Central	140	95	.76(140) = 106.4	11.4	129.96	1.22
South	150	90	.57(150) = 85.5	4.5	20.25	.24
West	80	60	.72(80) = 57.6	2.4	5.76	.1
Total	500	$\chi^2 = \text{Sum} \ (D^2/E) = 1.71$ For 3 degrees of freedom, $p > .50$				

(c) *The 2 × 2 table*

Type table

	+	−	Totals
+	a	b	e
−	c	d	f
Totals	g	h	T

Frequency distribution in sample

	South	Northeast	Totals
Voters	90	100	190
Non-Voters	60	30	90
Totals	150	130	280

Cell	O	E	D	D^2	D^2/E
a	90	ge/T = 101.8	11.8	139.24	1.37
b	100	he/T = 88.2	11.8	139.24	1.58
c	60	gf/T = 48.2	11.8	139.24	2.89
d	30	hf/T = 41.8	11.8	139.24	3.33
		$\chi^2 = \text{Sum } D^2/E = 9.17 \quad df = 1 \quad p < .005$			

Explanation of Worksheets in Table 5-8

(a) *The 1 × 2 table*

The problem: You have drawn a sample of 320 respondents, 180 of whom report that they voted in 1964, and 140 of whom report they did not vote. You wish to test the sample's conformity to the national voting turnout pattern. The null hypothesis

might be: The sample does not differ significantly from the national population of voting age persons as to turnout.

Observed: This column lists the sample distribution on the turnout variable.

Expected: This column lists the frequency distribution which would result if the null hypothesis were true. You obtain the U.S. Census averages (70 per cent and 30 per cent) from the best available source—here the percentages are rounded from Table 2-2.

Difference: These values are the absolute difference between the Observed and the Expected values. In these worksheets we have ignored the + and − signs.

Degrees of Freedom: There is one degree of freedom because only one of the cells of a 1 ×2 table may be filled in "freely." Once the value of one cell is fixed, the value of the other cell results automatically, given the total number of cases in the sample.

Probability: Entering the chi-square table (Appendix G contains an abridged table sufficient for the exercises, together with an explanation of how to use it) with one degree of freedom, we find that our result, 28.9, is greater than the entry in the .001 column, meaning that there is less than one chance in a thousand that our sample of voters and non-voters was drawn randomly from the U.S. population of persons of voting age.

(b) *The 1 × n table*

The problem: You have drawn a sample of 500 respondents, strictly pre-stratified to conform to the regional distribution of U.S. voting-age population. In other words, the frequencies in the "Regional Sample Total" column are already known to be an accurate representation of the population on the *regional* variable. You wish to test the turnout variable in the distribution for each region. Does your sample also represent with reasonable accuracy the voting turnout patterns of the four regions? The null hypothesis might be: Regional turnout in the sample does not differ significantly from actual regional turnout of U.S. voting-age population.

Observed: These frequencies are obtained from your sample. Each cell contains the number of voters found in the sample for that region. Non-voters are not recorded.

Expected: The multipliers are obtained from the U.S. Census voting percentages for each of the four regions (Table 2-2), and applied to the sample regional totals. The resulting values represent the regional distribution of voters which the sample would have disclosed if the null hypothesis were true.

Degrees of Freedom: There are three degrees of freedom because values for three of the four cells may

be determined freely before the value in the last cell can be established.

Probability: Entering the chi-square table with three degrees of freedom, we find our result, 1.71, to be smaller than the entry in the .50 column, meaning that there is a greater than even chance that our sample of voters and non-voters in each region was drawn randomly from the actual regional populations of voting age.

(c) *The 2 × 2 table*

The problem: To determine whether turnout in the South differed significantly from that in the Northeast, using the data from the same sample for these two regions. The null hypothesis might be: Turnout does not differ significantly in the two regions.

Observed: The first two entries represent the number of voters in the sample for the two regions, the last two the number of non-voters.

Expected: On the null hypothesis of *no association* between the regional variable and the turnout variable, the expected values are calculated from the marginal totals and the grand total so as to yield a 2 × 2 table with a Q value of zero. The resulting "Expected" table is:

101.8	88.2	190
48.2	41.8	90
150	130	280

Difference: In a 2 × 2 table, these values are all equal, though two would be positive and two negative if absolute values were not used in the worksheets.

Degrees of Freedom: Given all four totals, only one cell may be determined "freely." For example, given the marginal totals, once the number of voters in the South is fixed at 90, those in the Northeast must be 100, or 190 − 90; non-voters in the Northeast must then be 30, or 130 − 100; and non-voters in the South must be 60, or 150 − 90.

Probability: Entering the chi-square table with one degree of freedom, we find our result, 9.17, to be greater than that in the .005 column, meaning that there is less than that probability that the association shown on the table would arise by chance in a sample of 280.

Three warnings concerning use of the test are in order:

1. For its application, you must use the *numbers* or frequencies of the distribution or table, not the percentages. Sometimes it is possible to retrieve these frequencies from a table of percentages, or from the text which accompanies it, or even from the source data from which the table was prepared. But you *must* have the frequencies or you cannot apply the test.

2. The test is invalid if the expected value for any cell is less than 5. If a cell frequency is less than five, cells may sometimes be combined (in $1 \times n$ or $m \times n$ tables). If the resulting combination would be meaningless, a larger sample should be obtained.

3. The χ^2 distribution is a *continuous* distribution, but any table of frequencies is *discontinuous*. For this reason, it is recommended that tables or distributions involving small numbers be subjected to a correction factor. This correction (known for its originator as "Yates' correction") is quite simple. It consists of subtracting $1/2$ or $.5$ from each value in the D column of the worksheets. We have not introduced this correction factor in the exercises; significance sought in these problems is not seriously affected. For tables involving large numbers, the correction is hardly necessary and will affect the final value very little. For precise work the correction should always be made in 2×2 tables, especially for small expected frequencies. A simple formula for 2×2 tables, with the correction, is given at the end of Chapter 8. You can get an idea of the reasoning behind the correction by comparing the proportionate difference between say the values 362 and 361.5 on the one hand, and the values 6 and 5.5 on the other. Impact of the correction is negligible in the first case, but in the second case it amounts to more than 8 per cent.

5-8 Other Statistics

The three tests described in this chapter are among the simpler used in political and social research. You should find them useful tools, but in your future projects you will encounter situations in which they offer little or no help—in which some other test is needed or is better suited to your data. If you work further with statistics you will often find that a new statistical test is closely related to one you have already learned —there is a basic unity derived from the underlying concept of random processes and, for sampling statistics, the necessity for correcting for sample size.

The formula for Yule's Q, for example, can be converted into a more useful test of two-way associa-

tion which uses the same numerator but a different denominator (the square root of the product of the four marginal totals). This is the statistic called the phi-coefficient ($\emptyset$), which like χ^2 requires use of actual frequencies, not percentages, but unlike χ^2 varies from -1.00 to $+1.00$. The phi-coefficient in turn is derived from χ^2—it is the square root of χ^2/N (though when computed this way it cannot have a minus sign). The value $\emptyset^2$ may be considered the average amount of χ^2 contributed by each observation in a 2×2 contingency table.

Generalized versions of Yule's Q have been developed by Goodman and Kruskal for testing association in tables larger than 2×2. Known as lambda and gamma, (λ and γ), they are relatively new (1954), but already are increasingly used in political research.

To determine whether the means of several groups differ significantly, you will need to master the testing procedure known as *analysis of variance*. Simple analysis of variance (ANOVA is a commonly used abbreviation) results in the test statistic called F, or the variance ratio. The basic question asked in ANOVA is easily grasped: is the variation *between groups* enough greater than the variation *within groups* to show that the groups probably represent different parent populations? The computation consists of two steps. First, we find the mean for each group, and considering this set of means a distribution, we find the *variance of the means*. This value is called the *between-group variance*. We then take the variance of each group, and considering this set of variances another distribution, we find the *mean of the variances*. This value is the *within-group variance*. The ratio *Between/Within* is the F ratio, values for which are tabulated in the most general distribution used in statistical inference.

For the two-group case, an analysis of variance may be applied in the shorter form of the *t*-test, referred to in Section 5.2. The value for t is also a ratio—the difference of the two means divided by the estimated standard deviation of the difference between the means. The t value may be used to test whether a sample mean differs significantly from a given population mean (if known), or whether the means of two groups differ significantly from one another. To use either analysis of variance or the *t*-test you must be sure that your data meet the conditions required by the theory from which they were developed, a grasp of which will come only with more study and experience.

Indeed, this briefest of all introductions to statistics should be followed by a good deal more study and experience if your work with it is not to be lost. Two words of advice are in order:

1. *Try to learn more.* To develop your skills further, there is really no substitute for a good statistics course (or even two, since a first course is often limited to descriptive statistics). Programmed texts are now available and can be valuable alternatives to formal courses if you have the diligence to work through to the end. Of the books in the reading list at the end of the chapter, three deserve special note: Amos, Brown, and Mink's *Statistical Concepts* is a good programmed introduction without computational detail, planned as a preview to more complete study. Zelditch's *A Basic Course in Sociological Statistics* is designed for the beginner and is well suited to home study. Blalock's *Social Statistics* is the best introduction for social scientists, though some portions will be tough going for those to whom mathematics is a foreign field. Both Zelditch and Blalock include many political examples. The best book is usually one you have studied before, although it is also true that the nonparametric tests of greatest use in social research often are omitted from a general introductory text, since they derive from more specialized statistical theory and are not typical of the tests on which the fundamental concepts of inference are based. For this reason, you will find special incentive and aid in books which emphasize the relevance of statistics to political analysis—the volumes by V.O. Key and Hayward R. Alker, Jr., and *Legislative Roll-Call Analysis,* by Anderson, Watts, and Wilcox.

2. *Practice what you have learned.* Review and use the simple tests we have presented in your own projects. When you encounter a table in your reading, check its approximate significance by Yule's Q—you will usually need to dichotomize it first, or by the χ^2 test. Work up simple tables from news stories containing numerical comparisons, and test them in the same way. From data in commonly available references, from time to time run a rank correlation, keeping the paired groups small enough to make the computation simple. Without use, these tests will be quickly forgotten, but with even occasional practice they will become a permanent part of your analytical toolkit.

Exercise Set 5. Now Test These Hypotheses

5–1. *The Q test of association in a 2 × 2 contingency table.*

Notation for cross-products computations:

First Variable	Second Variable	
	+	−
+	a	b
−	c	d

Formula: $Q = (ad - bc)/(ad + bc)$

(1)

TABLE 5-A. *U.S. Senate Vote on Dirksen Amendment to Permit School Prayers*

Vote	Republican	Democrat
Yea	27	22
Nay	3	34

Source: *Congressional Record.* September 21, 1966.

$H_0: Q = 0.00$ (Verbally: Vote is not associated with party affiliation)

WORKSHEET FOR COMPUTATION OF Q

$ad = 27 \times 34 =$ _____

$bc = 22 \times 3 =$ _____

$ad - bc =$ _____

$ad + bc =$ _____

$Q = (ad - bc)/(ad + bc) =$ _____

1. Is the null hypothesis accepted or rejected? _____
2. Is Republican membership associated with support or opposition? _____
3. What is there in the Q value to determine your answer to Question 2? _____
4. Is the association, if any, a strong one? _____

(2)

TABLE 5-B. *Political Activity in a Japanese Community, by Sex*

	Men	Women
Active	57	28
Inactive	81	100

Source: Yasumasa Kuroda, "Political Role Attributions and Dynamics in a Japanese Community," *Public Opinion Quarterly,* Vol. XXIX, No. 4, Winter 1965–66, pp. 602–613.

$H_0: Q = 0.00$ (Verbally: Political activity is not associated with sex)

WORKSHEET FOR COMPUTATION OF Q

$ad = 57 \times 100 =$ _____

$bc = 28 \times 81 =$ _____

$ad - bc =$ _____

$ad + bc =$ _____

$Q = (ad - bc)/(ad + bc) =$ _____

1. Is the null hypothesis accepted or rejected? _____
2. Is political activity more associated with men or with women? _____
3. How is your answer to Question 2 determined by the Q value? _____
4. Is the association, if any, a strong one? _____
5. In the source article the author states as one of his major conclusions that "Japanese women are politically inactive." Is this justified by the results of your test? _____
6. If your answer to Question 5 is "Yes," explain below. If your answer is "No," reword the author's conclusion to accord with your results.

(3) **TABLE 5-C.** *Party Preference of Leaders and Advisors in a Japanese Community*

Party Preference	Leaders	Advisors
Conservative	20	3
Socialist	1	6

Source: Kuroda, *op. cit.,* p. 606.

$H_0: Q = 0.00$ (Verbally: Party preference is not associated with role)

WORKSHEET FOR COMPUTATION OF Q

$ad = 20 \times 6 =$ _____

$bc = 3 \times 1 =$ _____

$ad - bc =$ _____

$ad + bc =$ _____

$Q = (ad - bc)/(ad + bc) =$ _____

1. Is the null hypothesis accepted or rejected? _____
2. In the article cited under Table 5-B, Kuroda concludes that there is a potential conflict between the leaders and their advisors, based on their differences in party preference. Do you agree or disagree? _____
3. Using Kuroda's data, the following table was constructed, controlling the variables of Table 5-C for age:

(4) **TABLE 5-D.** *Party Preference in a Japanese Community, by Role and Age*

Party Preference	Over 45		Under 45	
	Leaders	Advisors	Leaders	Advisors
Conservative	20	3	0	0
Socialist	0	0	1	6

1. Run the Q test for each section of the new table, to see what has happened to the relationship found in Table 5-C.

For Over 45, $Q = (ad - bc)/(ad + bc) =$ _____ = _____

For Under 45, $Q = (ad - bc)/(ad + bc) =$ _____ = _____

2. Notice what happens if we combine the two sub-tables of Table 5-D differently:

Party Preference by Age

Party	Over 45	Under 45
Conservative	23	0
Socialist	0	7

$Q = $ _____

Political Role by Age

Role	Over 45	Under 45
Leaders	20	1
Advisors	3	6

$Q = $ _____

3. Which is the more important influence on party preference, role or age? _____
4. Of the two strong associations, Role-Preference and Role-Age, which is stronger? _____
5. Is the inference justified by the data? _____
    5.1. The Socialists will increase in power as the older conservative leadership dies out. _____
    5.2. Japanese politicians become more conservative with age. _____
    5.3. Practically all Japanese leaders in the group surveyed are old and conservative. _____
    5.4. Japanese political leaders and their advisors appear to differ significantly in party preference, judging by this survey sample. _____

(5)   **TABLE 5-E.** *Pre-Convention Goldwater Support, by Region and Religion, 1964*

	National		Midwest		East		South		West	
	Prot.	Cath.	Prot.	Cath.	Prot.	Cath.	Prot.	Cath.	Prot.	Cath.
Goldwater	15%	10%	12%	8%	8%	8%	22%	18%	16%	15%
Other	85	90	88	92	92	92	78	82	84	85

Source: Irving Crespi, "Right-Wing Conservatism: The Goldwater Case," *Public Opinion Quarterly*, Winter 1966, p. 528.

1. In the source article, the author states: "Nationally, Protestants favored Goldwater to a statistically significant degree more than did Catholics, but this is in part due to the disproportionate representation of Protestants in the South and Midwest. When region is controlled, only in the Midwest is there a statistically significant difference between Protestants and Catholics in the level of Goldwater support." Though we do not have exact "statistical significance" levels for the Q test, you can use it for a rough guide in verifying such a statement. Run the test for the five sub-tables of Table 5-E:

WORKSHEET FOR COMPUTATION OF Q

	National	Midwest	East	South	West
$ad =$	_____	_____	_____	_____	_____
$bc =$	_____	_____	_____	_____	_____
$ad - bc =$	_____	_____	_____	_____	_____
$ad + bc =$	_____	_____	_____	_____	_____
$Q =$	_____	_____	_____	_____	_____

2. In which region is there no apparent relation at all between Goldwater support and Protestantism? _____
3. If the author's statement is assumed to be valid on the basis of more advanced statistical tests, about what Q value would correspond to the "statistically significant" level? _____

(6) **TABLE 5-F.** *Effect of Education Campaign on Attitude toward U.S. Loan for Britain as Related to Respondents' Trust in England's Cooperation*

Attitude to Loan	Experimental Group (Subjected to Educational Campaign)		Control Group (Not Subjected to Campaign)	
	Trust England	Do Not Trust England	Trust England	Do Not Trust England
Approve	70%	18%	45%	17%
Do Not Approve	30	82	55	83

Source: H. H. Hyman and P. B. Sheatsley, "Some Reasons Why Information Campaigns Fail," *Public Opinion Quarterly,* Vol. **XI** (1947), pp. 413–423.

1. For the Experimental Group, $Q = $ _____
2. For the Control Group, $Q = $ _____

WORKSHEET FOR COMPUTATION OF Q

$ad = $ _____ _____

$bc = $ _____ _____

$ad - bc = $ _____ _____

$ad + bc = $ _____ _____

$Q = $ _____ _____

3. Is approval of the loan positively associated with trust in England in the experimental group? _____

   In the control group? _____

4. Does it appear that the "education campaign" strengthened public approval of the loan? Give reason for your answer:

5. Without reference to the Q values, but referring only to the original table, does the education campaign appear to have had any significant effect on those who do not trust England? _____

6. Verify your answer to Question 5 by running Q tests on the table in the rearranged form below:

	Trust England		Do Not Trust England	
	Experimental	Control	Experimental	Control
Approve	70%	45%	18%	17%
Disapprove	30%	55%	82%	83%
	$Q = $ _____		$Q = $ _____	

(7) **TABLE 5-G.** *Respondent's Vote Intention by Usual Vote of Father, and for Usual Vote of Father Controlled for Spouse's Vote Intention, Elmira, 1948*

Respondent	Father Rep.	Father Dem.	Spouse Rep. Father R	Spouse Rep. Father D	Spouse Dem. Father R	Spouse Dem. Father D
Republican	83%	46%	95%	94%	32%	11%
Democratic	17	54	5	6	68	89

Source: Berelson, Lazarsfeld, and McPhee, *Voting*, 1954, pp. 89 and 135. Reprinted by permission of The University of Chicago Press.

From the data of the original tables, which are translated into percentages above, the two additional tables following were constructed:

Respondents and Spouses

	Spouse R	Spouse D
Respondent R	95%	18%
Respondent D	5	82

Spouses and Fathers

	Father R	Father D
Spouse R	88%	48%
Spouse D	12	52

1. Run the Q test for the five contingency tables:

WORKSHEET FOR COMPUTATION OF Q

	Respondent & Father	R & F (Spouse R)	R & F (Spouse D)	Respondent & Spouse	Spouse & Father
$ad =$					
$bc =$					
$ad - bc =$					
$ad + bc =$					
$Q =$					

2. Based on your results, are people likely to vote the same as their fathers? _____

3. Are they likely to vote the same as their spouses? _____

4. Which is the stronger relationship, that with fathers or that with spouses? _____

5. When the association of respondent's vote intention with usual vote of father is controlled for spouse's vote intention, it essentially disappears when spouse's vote intention is _____

But it remains substantial when spouse's vote intention is _____

6. Are Republicans more likely to marry within the party than Democrats? _____

(8) **TABLE 5-H.** *Voting, Governmental Expenditures, and Level of Economic Development (by number of countries, N = 26)*

	Voting High	Voting Low	Development High Voting Hi	Development High Voting Lo	Development Low Voting Hi	Development Low Voting Lo
Expenditures High	10	6	8	3	2	3
Expenditures Low	2	8	2	1	0	7

Source: Hayward R. Alker, Jr., *Mathematics and Politics*. New York: The Macmillan Company, 1965, pp. 90–92. Reprinted with the kind permission of the author and the publisher. Copyright 1965 by Hayward R. Alker, Jr.

In the above example, Alker explores the notion that a high level of voting results in a high level of governmental expenditures. By controlling for the level of economic development, he shows how a new variable may help explain an apparent relationship more fully. The two sub-tables to the right of Table 5-H are the result of this control, and are known as "partials" of the table on the left. Notice that the partials "add up" to

the original table: that is cell *a* of the original table is the sum of the corresponding cells *a* of the two partials, etc. By adding the partials differently, we can obtain two new tables:

Expenditures and Development

	Development High	Development Low
Expenditures High	11	5
Expenditures Low	3	7

Voting and Development

	Development High	Development Low
Voting High	10	2
Voting Low	4	10

1. Run the Q test for the five 2×2 tables of this example:

WORKSHEET FOR COMPUTATION OF Q

	Exp-Vote	Exp-Vote Dev. Hi	Exp-Vote Dev. Lo	Exp-Dev	Vote-Dev
$ad =$	_____	_____	_____	_____	_____
$bc =$	_____	_____	_____	_____	_____
$ad - bc =$	_____	_____	_____	_____	_____
$ad + bc =$	_____	_____	_____	_____	_____
$Q =$	_____	_____	_____	_____	_____

2. Does the first table seem to show a strong relationship between government expenditures and high voting level?   _____

3. When controlled for development, does this relationship remain strong in highly developed countries?   _____

4. Does it remain strong in countries of a low level of development?   _____

5. When the new variable (development) is separately associated with expenditures and with voting, in the last two tables, is the strength of these two associations about the same as that between voting and expenditures in the original table?   _____

(9)   **TABLE 5-I.** *Goals of Peace Corps Volunteers Before and After Service*

Goals	Pre-Peace Corps N	Pre-Peace Corps %	Post-Peace Corps N	Post-Peace Corps %
Career Goals Not Defined	732	34	261	12
Government	231	11	424	20
Other	1163	55	1441	68
Total	2126	100	2126	100

Source: Robert Calvert, Jr., "The Returning Volunteer," *Annals of the American Academy of Political and Social Science,* May, 1966, p. 111.

1. There are two ways in which we might dichotomize the above table for use of the *Q* test to measure association of Peace Corps service with choice of government careers. Each yields a different result:

Career Goal & Peace Corps Service

	After Service		Before Service	
	N	%	*N*	%
Government	424	20	231	11
Other & None	1702	80	1895	89
Total	2126	100	2126	100

Career Goal & Peace Corps Service
(for those with goal defined)

	After Service		Before Service	
	N	%	*N*	%
Government	424	23	231	17
Other	1441	77	1163	83
Total	1865	100	1394	100

Run the *Q* test for each of these tables:

WORKSHEET FOR COMPUTATION OF *Q*

	Goal & Service	Career Goal & Peace Corps Service (for those with goal defined)
$ad =$	$(20 \times 89) =$ _____	$(23 \times 83) =$ _____
$bc =$	$11 \times 80 =$ _____	$17 \times 77 =$ _____
$ad - bc =$	_____	_____
$ad + bc =$	_____	_____
$Q =$	_____	_____

2. In which table does the association, if any, appear stronger?   _____

3. What basic difference in the way the tables were constructed accounts for this?

4. Which of the two *Q* values gives the more accurate measure of the influence of Peace Corps service on choice of a career in government?

5–2 *Testing for Rank Correlation.*

(1) **TABLE 5-J.** *Pride in Governmental System and Confidence in Redress of Grievance*

Country	(A) Proud of System	(B) Feel They Can Do Something About Unjust Regulation	WORKSHEET			
			Rank A	Rank B	Rank Difference	D^2
USA	92%	75%				
Britain	90	62				
Germany	9	38				
Italy	3	28				
Mexico	38	38				

Sum D^2 _____

Source: *Civic Culture,* pp. 142, 199.

$$N \text{ (number of pairs)} = \underline{\hspace{3cm}}$$

$$\rho = 1.00 - \frac{6 \times \text{Sum } D^2}{N(N^2 - 1)} = 1.00 - \frac{\underline{\hspace{1.5cm}}}{120} = \underline{\hspace{2cm}}$$

H_0: Pride in Government and Confidence are not significantly related.

Alternate hypothesis: the two attributes are significantly related.

Significance level: .05 (Note: this means we have decided to reject the null hypothesis only if we find the relationship so high that it would be equalled or exceeded by chance only 5% of the time or less).

Statistic: Spearman's ρ

Value of ρ required to reject H_0: 0.9

On the basis of your computation, is the null hypothesis rejected? _____

(2) **TABLE 5-K.** *Pride in Governmental System and Lack of Interest in Election*

Country	(A) Proud of System	(B) No Feeling About Election	WORKSHEET			
			Rank A	Rank B	Difference	D^2
USA	92%	9%				
Britain	90	20				
Germany	9	24				
Italy	3	46				
Mexico	38	30				

Sum D^2 _____

Source: *Civic Culture,* pp. 199, 132.

$$N \text{ (number of pairs)} = \underline{\hspace{3cm}}$$

$$\rho = 1.00 - (6 \text{ Sum } D^2/(N^3 - N) = 1.00 - \frac{\underline{\hspace{2cm}}}{120} = \underline{\hspace{2.5cm}}$$

H_0: Pride and Interest are not significantly related.

Alternative hypothesis: the two attributes are significantly related.

Significance level: .05

Statistic: Spearman's ρ

Value of ρ required to reject H_0: .9 (Note: either a positive or a negative value of .9 or higher is significant, though of course the relation tested must be defined accordingly).

On the basis of your computation, is the null hypothesis rejected? _____

(3) **TABLE 5-L.** *Does a Strong Socialist Party Tend To Weaken the Appeal of Communism? (Communist and Socialist Percentage of Total Vote in Recent Years)*

Country	(A) Communist Vote	(B) Socialist Vote	WORKSHEET			
			Rank A	Rank B	D	D^2
Italy	24.0%	17.5%				
Finland	22.7	24.5				
France	21.0	15.2				
Indonesia	17.0	26.0				
Iceland	15.7	18.7				
Chile	12.0	17.8				
India	10.1	10.0				
Luxembourg	7.1	32.6				
Sweden	4.0	47.7				
Japan	2.8	34.7				
Australia	.5	51.9				
Britain	.1	45.0				

Sum D^2 _____

Source: *World Handbook of Political and Social Indicators,* pp. 89, 93.

N (number of pairs) = _____ . $\qquad \rho = 1.00 - \dfrac{6 \text{ Sum } D^2}{1716} =$ _____

H_0: Communist and Socialist Vote are not significantly related.

Alternative hypothesis: the two factors are significantly related.

Significance level: .05

Statistic: Spearman's ρ

Value of ρ required to reject H_0: .5. (Note: a value of $+.5$ would tend to support a hypothesis that Communism and Socialism are mutually reinforcing; a value of $-.5$ would tend to support a hypothesis that strength of one party is associated with weakness of the other).

On the basis of your computation, is the null hypothesis rejected? _____

If rejected, what is your tentative answer to the question in the table title? _____

Would it be equally valid to reverse the names of the parties in this question? _____

(4) **TABLE 5-M.** *Communist Electoral Success and Strength of Catholicism*

Country	(A) Communist Vote	(B) Catholics in Total Population	WORKSHEET			
			Rank A	Rank B	D	D²
Italy	24.0%	99.5%				
Belgium	2.5	96.8				
Luxembourg	7.1	96.7				
France	21.0	83.0				
Germany	2.2	48.4				
Netherlands	3.9	40.4				
Britain	.1	8.0				
Denmark	2.2	.6				
Iceland	15.7	.4				
Norway	3.2	.2				

Sum D² _____

Source: *World Handbook of Political and Social Indicators*, pp. 89, 249.

$$\rho = 1.00 - (\underline{\hspace{2cm}}/990) = \underline{\hspace{2cm}}$$

H_0: Communist Success and Catholicism not significantly related.
Significance level: .05
Statistic: Spearman's ρ
Value of ρ required to reject: _____
On the basis of your computation is the hypothesis rejected? _____

(5) **TABLE 5-N.** *Does a Close Runoff Primary Hurt the Party in the General Election?*

Oklahoma Gubernatorial Runoff (Dem.)	Winning Candidate	Losing Candidate	(A) Margin	(B) Dem. % General Election	WORKSHEET			
					Rank A	Rank B	D	D²
1930	63.6%	36.3%	27.3%	59.1%				
1946	53.4	46.5	6.9	53.2				
1950	50.1	49.8	.3	51.2				
1954	51.9	48.0	3.9	58.6				
1958	69.6	30.3	39.3	78.7				
1962	50.1	49.9	.2	44.5				

Sum D² _____

Source: *Oklahoma Votes, 1907–1962*, p. 55.

$N = \underline{\hspace{2cm}}.\quad \rho = 1.00 - (6 \text{ Sum } D^2/210) = 1.00 - \underline{\hspace{2cm}} = \underline{\hspace{2cm}}$

H_0: Close runoff primaries are not related to the party's success in the general election.
Alternative hypothesis: (1) Close runoffs help the party; (2) Close runoffs hurt the party.

Significance level: .05

Statistic: Spearman's ρ

Value of ρ required to reject H_0: _____

On the basis of your computation, is the null hypothesis rejected? _____

If rejected, which alternative hypothesis does your result support? _____

(6) **TABLE 5-O.** *Relation of Type of Agriculture to Normal Party Preference. (In* Southern Politics, *V. O. Key suggests that historic party loyalties are reinforced by continuing patterns of cotton farming in the South and wheat agriculture in the Midwest. This table tests the idea by a comparison of the six Oklahoma Congressional Districts.)*

District	Cotton Farms	Grain Farms	(A) Cotton/ Wheat Ratio	(B) Dem. Vote Pres. Av. 1952–64	WORKSHEET Rank A	Rank B	D	D^2
1	46	6210	.0074	37.4%				
2	492	831	.59	48.7				
3	431	149	2.89	63.3				
4	118	417	.28	49.8				
5	141	689	.20	44.7				
6	4151	6520	.64	50.1				

Sum D^2 _____

Source: *U.S. Census, Congressional District Data Book.*

$N =$ _____. $\rho = 1.00 - (6 \text{ Sum } D^2/210) =$ _____

H_0: V. O. Key is wrong: there is no such relationship.

Alternatives: (1) V. O. Key is right: there is a significant positive relationship, (2) V. O. Key is wrong: there is a significant negative relationship.

Significance level: .05

Statistic: Spearman's ρ

Value of ρ required to reject in favor of Alternative (1) _____

Value of ρ required to reject in favor of Alternative (2) _____

On the basis of your computation, is V. O. Key right? _____

(7) **TABLE 5-P.** *Exposure to Political Communications and Community Activity*

Country	(A) Reporting High Exposure	(B) Believe One Should Be Active in Local Community	WORKSHEET Rank A	Rank B	D	D^2
USA	59%	51%				
Britain	36	39				
Germany	57	22				
Italy	26	10				
Mexico	39	26				

Sum D^2 _____

Source: *Civic Culture,* pp. 189, 133.

$$N = \underline{\hspace{2cm}} . \quad \rho = 1.00 - (6 \text{ Sum } D^2/120) = \underline{\hspace{2cm}}$$

H_0: There is no significant relationship between the extent of high exposure to political communications and the proportion of citizens who feel a sense of responsibility to be active in their local communities.

Alternative hypothesis: There is a significant relationship between the two factors.

Significance level: .05

Statistic: Spearman's ρ

Value of ρ required to reject H_0: \underline{\hspace{2cm}}

On the basis of your computation, is the null hypothesis rejected? \underline{\hspace{2cm}}

If not, at what level could you reject it? \underline{\hspace{2cm}}

(8) **TABLE 5-Q.** *Tests of Marxist Theory I: Industrial Labor Force and Unemployment*

Country	(A) Employment in Industry*	(B) Unemployed*	WORKSHEET			
			Rank A	Rank B	D	D^2
Britain	35.2%	1.2%				
Germany	31.9	2.5				
Austria	27.5	4.9				
Denmark	24.2	4.2				
Norway	23.7	1.7	7.5	2.5	6.25	
France	23.4	.6				
Finland	22.2	1.7	7.5	.5	.25	
New Zealand	21.8	.04				
Japan	20.4	2.8				
United States	19.2	7.0				
Israel	18.0	1.3				
Italy	17.8	6.3				

Sum D^2 \underline{\hspace{2cm}}

* Employment is percentage of working-age population; unemployment is percentage of wage & salary earners.
Source: *World Handbook of Political and Social Indicators*, pp. 185, 191.

$$\rho = 1.00 - (6 \text{ Sum } D^2/1716) = \underline{\hspace{2cm}}$$

H_0: There is no significant relationship between relative size of industrial labor force and relative amount of unemployment.

Alternatives: (1) Marx's contention that advancing industrialization under capitalism is accompanied by advancing unemployment, thus sharpening the class struggle. (2) That advancing industrialization creates more jobs and thus lowers unemployment.

Significance level: .05

Statistic: Spearman's ρ

Value of ρ required to reject H_0: \underline{\hspace{2cm}}

On the basis of your computation, is the null hypothesis rejected? \underline{\hspace{2cm}}

Does your result support either of the alternative hypotheses? \underline{\hspace{2cm}}

(9) **TABLE 5-R.** *Tests of Marxist Theory II: Industrialization and Working-Class Awareness*

Country	(A) Employment in Industry	(B) Communist Vote	(C) Socialist Vote
Britain	35.2%	.1%	45.0%
Switzerland	35.1	2.6	29.2
Germany	31.9	2.2	34.0
Luxembourg	29.4	7.1	32.6
Sweden	28.1	4.0	47.4
Austria	27.5	3.0	45.0
Belgium	26.1	2.5	36.3
Australia	25.2	.5	51.9
Denmark	24.2	2.2	43.7
Norway	23.7	3.2	48.8
France	23.4	21.0	15.2
Finland	22.2	22.7	24.5
New Zealand	21.8	.1	45.9
Iceland	21.3	15.7	18.8
Japan	20.4	2.8	34.7
Netherlands	20.3	3.9	31.6
Canada	20.0	.0	11.4
United States	19.2	.0	.0
Israel	18.0	3.5	13.6
Italy	17.8	24.0	17.5

Source: *World Handbook of Political and Social Indicators*, pp. 185, 89, 93.

WORKSHEET						
Rank A	Rank B	Rank C	Diff. (A − B)	D^2	Diff. (A − C)	D^2
1	17.5	5.5	16.5	272.25	4.5	20.25
2						
3	14.5		11.5	132.25		
4						
5						
6		5.5			.5	.25
7						
8						
9	14.5		5.5	30.25		
10						
11						
12						
13	17.5		4.5	20.25		
14						
15						
16						
17	19.5		2.5	6.25		
18	19.5		1.5	2.25		
19						
20						

Sum D^2 = _____ Sum D^2 = _____

For Communist Vote and Industrial Labor: $\rho = 1 - ($ _____ $/7980) =$ _____

For Socialist Vote and Industrial Labor: $\rho = 1 - ($ _____ $/7980) =$ _____

H_0: Ratio of Industrial Labor Force is not significantly related to "working-class awareness" as such awareness is manifested in Communist and Socialist voting strength.

Alternatives: (1) Industrial Labor Force is significantly related to Communist vote. (2) Industrial Labor Force is significantly related to Socialist vote. (3) Industrial Labor Force is significantly related to both Communist and Socialist vote.

Significance level: .05

Statistic: Spearman's ρ

Value of ρ required to reject H_0: _____ . Is H_0 rejected? _____

Which, if any, of the alternative hypotheses is supported by your results?

5–3   *The Chi-Square Test: Does the Distribution Fit?*

To simplify computations, most of the source data used in this section have been rounded, with proportions of the original data retained so that approximately the same confidence levels will hold. Though the chi-square test can be used on tables of any size, the exercises are limited to three types: (1) 1×2 table, (2) the $1 \times n$ table, and (3) the 2×2 table.

The 1 × 2 Table

(1) We have drawn a random sample of 80 respondents, and it tests out at 60 Democrats and 20 Republicans. Registrations in the county from which the sample was drawn are known to include 80% Democrats and 20% Republicans. Is the sample significantly different at the 5% level from what is known of the population from which it is drawn?

Discussion: The chi-square test is based on comparisons of the sample frequencies with the "expected" frequencies—"expected" meaning those we would "expect" to find if the sample exactly represents the population from which it is drawn. In this case, since our sample contains a total of 80 respondents and the population from which it is drawn is known to consist of 80% Democrats and 20% Republicans, we should "expect" the 80 respondents to consist of:

Democrats: 80% of 80, or 64

Republicans: 20% of 80, or 16

On the basis of this information about the "expected" frequencies, we can complete the computation of the chi-square "goodness of fit" test by filling in the worksheet.

WORKSHEET FOR COMPUTATION OF χ^2

Party	Observed in Sample	Expected in Sample	Difference	D^2	D^2/E
Democrat	60	64	4	16	.25
Republican	20	16	4	16	1.00

Degrees of freedom: 1 $\qquad\qquad\qquad\qquad\qquad$ $\chi^2 = 1.25$

H_0: The sample is not significantly different from the population of registrations.

Alternative: The sample is significantly different.

Significance level: .05

Statistic: χ^2

Value of χ^2 required to reject H_0: 3.841

Is the null hypothesis rejected? _____

Would you reject at the 10% level? _____

(2) *Information Campaign for the British Loan.* In the example of Table 5-F, the experimental group of persons who had been subjected to an information campaign on behalf of a U.S. loan to Britain were found to favor the loan in the ratio of about 200/190, whereas the "control" group not so indoctrinated opposed it in the ratio of about 400/200 (that is, two-thirds of the control group opposed the loan). For a chi-square test on effectiveness of the information campaign, we may deem the control group to represent the "population" and the experimental group to represent the sample. We obtain the "expected" frequencies by applying the "population" percentages to the total number of cases in the sample:

For the loan: 1/3 of 390, or 130

Against the loan: 2/3 of 390, or 260

WORKSHEET FOR COMPUTATION OF χ^2

Attitude	Observed in Sample	Expected	Difference	D^2	D^2/E
For Loan	200	130	70	4900	
Against Loan	190	260	70	4900	

Degrees of freedom: 1 $\qquad\qquad\qquad\qquad\qquad$ $\chi^2 = $ _____

H_0: The information campaign had no significant effect on attitudes toward the loan.

Alternative: The campaign significantly changed attitudes toward the loan.

Significance level: .05

Statistic: χ^2

Value of χ^2 required to reject H_0: 3.841

Is the null hypothesis rejected?_____

Discussion: This may seem a complicated way to show something which was obvious at the start, but the method will enable us to test other hypotheses for which the decision to reject is much closer.

The 1 × n Table

(3) *Goldwater Support by Regions.*

WORKSHEET FOR COMPUTATION OF χ^2

(1) Region	(2) Percentage of National Sample in Region	(3) Number for Goldwater in Poll	(4) Expected for Goldwater Col. 2 × Total	(5) D	(6) D^2	(7) D^2/E
East	30%	200	360	160	25,600	
Midwest	30	300	360	60	3,600	
South	25	500	300	200	40,000	
West	15	200	180	20	400	

Total = 1200

Degrees of freedom: 3

$\chi^2 =$ _____

H_0: There was no significant regional difference in Goldwater's pre-convention support.

Significance level: .001 (that is, we reject only on odds of 1000 to 1).

Statistic: χ^2

Value of χ^2 required to reject H_0: 16.268

Is the null hypothesis rejected? _____

(4) *Lack of Pride in Nation for Respondents of Low Civic Competence.* The *Civic Culture* survey scaled respondents by "civic competence" roughly according to their feelings about their effectiveness and involvement in national or local government. The (rounded) results below permit application of the chi-square test for a cross-national comparison of those falling in the lower end of the scale.

WORKSHEET FOR COMPUTATION OF χ^2

Country	Low Competence N	% of total	Number Who Expressed no Pride in Nation	Expected % × total	D	D^2	D^2/E
U.S.	200	11	27	53	26	676	
Britain	200	11	42	53	11	121	
Germany	400	22	96	106	10	100	
Italy	500	28	185	134	51	2601	
Mexico	500	28	130	134	4	16	

Total = 480

Degrees of freedom: 4

$\chi^2 =$ _____

H_0: Among those rating low in civic competence there is no significant difference among national groups on the attribute of lack of national pride.

Alternative: Even those who do not feel much involved in the political system of their country differ significantly from one country to another on the attribute of national pride.

Significance level: .001

Statistic: χ^2

Value of χ^2 required to reject H_0: 18.465

Is the null hypothesis rejected? _____

The 2 × 2 Table

(5) *Religion as a Factor in Pre-Convention Goldwater Support: The South.*

	Protestants	Catholics	Total
Goldwater	440	45	485
Others	1560	205	1765
Total	2000	250	2250

WORKSHEET FOR COMPUTATION OF χ^2

Cell	Observed	Expected	Difference	D^2	D^2/E
Goldwater-Prot.	440	$(2000/2250) \times 485 =$			
Goldwater-Cath.	45	$(250/2250) \times 485 =$			
Others-Prot.	1560	$(2000/2250) \times 1765 =$			
Others-Cath.	205	$(250/2250) \times 1765 =$			

Degrees of freedom: 1 $\chi^2 =$ _____

H_0: Protestants and Catholics in the South did not differ significantly in pre-convention Goldwater support.

Significance level: .05

Statistic: χ^2

Value of χ^2 required to reject H_0: 3.841

Is the null hypothesis rejected? _____

(6) *Religion as a Factor in Pre-Convention Goldwater Support: The Midwest.*

	Protestants	Catholics	Total
Goldwater	250	50	300
Others	1750	550	2300
Total	2000	600	2600

WORKSHEET FOR COMPUTATION OF χ^2

Cell	Observed	Expected	Difference	D^2	D^2/E
Goldwater-Prot.	250	$(2000/2600) \times 300 =$			
Goldwater-Cath.	50	$(600/2600) \times 300 =$			
Others-Prot.	1750	$(2000/2600) \times 2300 =$			
Others-Cath.	550	$(600/2600) \times 2300 =$			

Degrees of freedom: 1 $\chi^2 =$ _____

H_0: Protestants and Catholics in the Midwest did not differ significantly in pre-convention Goldwater support.

Significance level: .05

Statistic: χ^2

Value of χ^2 required to reject H_0: 3.841

Is the null hypothesis rejected? _____

(7) *Freshmen Democratic Congressmen and Support of President Johnson.* "Democratic House freshmen are giving President Johnson's legislative program less support this year than in 1965, according to a *Congressional Quarterly* study of roll call votes," states a *CQ* release from Washington on October 1, 1966. By running percentages on bills on which Johnson is reported to have taken a stand, we are able to reconstruct the following table of voting by 76 Democratic "freshmen."

	1965	1966	Total
Bills Supported	92	37	129
Bills Opposed	20	11	31
Total	112	48	160

WORKSHEET FOR COMPUTATION OF χ^2

Cell	Observed	Expected	Difference	D^2	D^2/E
Supported 1965	92	$(112/160) \times 129 =$			
Supported 1966	37	$(48/160) \times 129 =$			
Opposed 1965	20	$(112/160) \times 31 =$			
Opposed 1966	11	$(48/160) \times 31 =$			

Degrees of freedom: 1 $\qquad\qquad$ $\chi^2 =$ _____

H_0: There is no significant difference in Democratic freshman congressmen's support of Johnson's legislative program from 1965 to 1966.

Significance level: .05

Statistic: χ^2

Value of χ^2 required to reject H_0: 3.841

Is the null hypothesis rejected? _____

Reading List

Alker, Hayward R., Jr., *Mathematics and Politics*. New York: The Macmillan Co., 1965. Demonstrates the underlying relationship of a number of bivariate and multivariate tests, simplified by use of dichotomous cases.*

Amos, Jimmy R., Foster L. Brown, and Oscar G. Mink, *Statistical Concepts*. New York: Harper and Row, Publishers, 1965. A programmed overview for beginners, planned to accompany study of a fuller text.*

Anderson, Lee F., Meredith W. Watts, Jr., and Allen R. Wilcox, *Legislative Roll-Call Analysis*. Evanston: Northwestern University Press, 1966. Clear explanations of several statistical tests useful in the study of legislative behavior.*

Blalock, Hubert M., *Social Statistics*. New York: McGraw-Hill Book Co., Inc., 1960. The standard text for social scientists, and the single volume most useful in political research.

Chernoff, Herman, and Lincoln E. Moses, *Elementary Decision Theory*. New York: John Wiley and Sons, Inc., 1959. Both descriptive and inferential statistics presented in terms of modern decision theory. Planned for a beginning course but not for the non-mathematical militant.

Croxton, Frederick E., and Dudley J. Cowden, *Applied General Statistics*. Englewood Cliffs, N. J.: Prentice-Hall, Inc., 1955.

Diamond, Solomon, *Information and Error*. New York: Basic Books, Inc., 1959. An entertaining introduction to inference for the beginner, with examples from psychology.

Gorow, Frank F., *Statistical Measures*. San Francisco: Chandler Publishing Co., 1962. An elementary introduction, assuming additional study.*

Kaplan, Abraham, *The Conduct of Inquiry*. San Francisco: Chandler Publishing Co., 1964. Part VI (Chapters 25–29) is an insightful discussion of the role of statistical hypotheses and tests in behavioral science.

Key, V. O., Jr., *A Primer of Statistics for Political Scientists*. New York: Thomas Y. Crowell Co., 1954. Deals chiefly with descriptive statistics and correlation methods. Valuable for its complete bibliography of political science research using statistics up to the time of publication.*

Moroney, M. J., *Facts from Figures*. Baltimore: Penguin Books, Inc., 3rd ed., 1956. A popular treatment of probability and statistical inference, including non-mathematical introductions to statistical quality control and the analysis of variance and co-variance.*

Shao, Stephen P., *Statistics for Business and Economics*. Columbus: Charles E. Merrill Publishing Co., 1967. Includes useful chapters on the assembly and processing of data.

Wallis, W. Allen, and Harry V. Roberts, *Statistics: A New Approach*. Glencoe: Free Press of Glencoe, 1956. With an emphasis on social research, the authors present a large number of cautionary examples of misuses of statistics.

Zelditch, Morris, Jr., *A Basic Course in Sociological Statistics*. New York: Holt, Rinehart and Winston, Inc., 1959. A combined textbook and workbook "designed with the specific and pleasant intention of attracting the student who is frightened of mathematics." Many of the examples use data of interest to political scientists.

---

* Paperback edition available.

SURVEY RESEARCH:

How to Ask Questions

In the modern study of political behavior, a great contribution has been made by political survey research. Most of the major surveys have been large-scale enterprises, requiring the cooperation of teams of investigators and analysts, besides considerable funding. Our introductory look at the field of survey work, though cursory, should prepare you to engage in a team project with somewhat more knowledge of what is involved than if you were a complete novice, and furnish some guidelines for conducting a small survey of your own as a learning exercise.

6-1 The Sample

In preparing to conduct a survey, an important part of the technical advance planning is the drawing of the sample. Practical considerations will always limit the adequacy of the sample, even in the most ambitious and costly project, but a few precautions will help avoid serious error.

Simple Random Sample. As the brief look at statistical tests in the last topic emphasizes, it is not so much the sheer size of the sample which is important, but whether it is actually representative of the population it is supposed to represent. The famous *Literary Digest* poll of 1936 was based on a sample of millions but was so biased that it lives in history for its egregious miscalling of the greatest presidential landslide on record. On the other hand, scientifically selected samples of from 1500 to 3000 are now commonly used to obtain fairly reliable data on the entire population of the United States. The basic principle of scientific sampling is that the sample be truly random: that all persons in the population it is supposed to represent have an equal statistical chance of being included in it.

A purely random sample of the whole population is often less economical than one chosen on some selective principle related to the purpose of the survey. The smaller the subpopulation you want to study, the more waste there will be in a sample of the whole. In a project on attitudes of new students, you would

not draw a random sample of all students (though a smaller group of upperclassmen might well be included in a separate sample for comparison). Similarly a survey of all adults of voting age in a community is uneconomic if the survey is concerned only with the attitudes of labor union members. Sometimes the subpopulation cannot be identified in advance, so that the sample must be drawn from a larger group; in a survey to test views of voters in a city election, for example, it is usually not possible to identify those most likely to vote, though it is almost certain that there will be fewer voters than would turn out in elections for governor or president.

Stratified Sample. An important criterion of sample size is *homogeneity* of the population with respect to the attribute you are testing. If there is only one party on the ballot, or if the population is 100 per cent conformist, a sample of 1 is adequate. If there are six candidates in a primary race, or if opinion is split among several policy alternatives, each supported—or thought to be—by a distinct socioeconomic substratum, the sample must be large enough to tap each significant group. Homogeneity affects sampling error in terms both of number of subgroups and evenness of division among the subgroups. A landslide election is fairly easy to predict (that is, a small sample is adequate), but for one so nearly even as the Kennedy-Nixon contest of 1960, no sample could provide a safe prediction—though the polls could tell us that it would be close.

By careful identification of significant subgroups, each then sampled on a random selection basis, the sampling error may be reduced. This is the theory behind the stratified sample, which permits a better estimate for the whole population than does a purely random sample of the same size. Just how much better will depend again on homogeneity of the subgroups. If each subgroup were perfectly homogenous —if all Northerners, all women, all Catholics, all urbanites, or all blue-collar workers thought exactly alike—life would be easier for the pollsters.

In the stratified sample, a certain proportion of the total sample is required to be from each stratum. The national Gallup sample, used in 1964 to survey the pre-convention support of Goldwater, on which exercises 5-1 (Table 5-E), 5-3(3), 5-3(5) and 5-3(6) were based, uses a stratification on size-of-community (seven groups ranging from central cities of 1,000,000 and over to rural areas) and geographic regions. A minimum of 1500 individuals are interviewed, distributed among 150 randomly chosen sampling points. Only within the sampling point (blocks in cities) does the sample depart from the random probability principle, and even there, the interviewer is not left free to pick his respondents—he must follow a precisely set procedure planned to minimize error. Interviewers are notoriously likely to omit people who are hard to find—those who are not at home because both husband and wife are at work, those who live in walk-up apartments or in garage apartments at the rear of a lot, and those who harbor barking dogs. The Gallup organization, for example, stipulates the simple but useful rule that its interviewers conduct only one interview at each household, and for an equal number of men and women.

If you wish your sample to reflect the composition of the voting-age population of the United States on one or more stratifications, Table 6-1 will be helpful. It was developed from the large sample used by the Bureau of the Census as the basis for our table on voter turnout in Chapter 2, supplemented by approximations on religion and party preference from the Gallup data. Another possible use for Table 6-1 is to compare your own sample with the Census estimate for a given variable. The pattern used in Exercise

TABLE 6-1. *Stratification of United States Voting-Age Population by Eleven Variables (in percentages)*

By Region		By Religion		
Northeast	26.3	Protestant	67	
North Central	28.1	Catholic	25	
South	29.3	Jewish	4	
West	16.3	Other	4	
By Sex		**By Turnout**		
Men	47	Voted (1964)	70	
Women	53	Did Not Vote	30	
By Race		**By Politics**		
White	90	Democrat	50	
Nonwhite	10	Republican	27	
(Negro)	(9.4)	Independent	23	
By Age		**By Education**		
21–24	9	8 years or less	29	
25–44	41	9–11 years	18	
45–64	34	12 years	33	
65 and over	16	Over 12 years	20	
By Ecology		**By Employment**		
Metropolitan	65	Employed		58
Non-metropolitan	35	Agricultural	4	
		Non-agricultural	54	
		Unemployed		2
By Income		Not in Labor Force		40
Under $3000	18	Alternative Employment Groups, by Race[a]		
$3000–$4999	20		White	Nonwhite
$5000–$7499	28	White collar	47.5	19.5
$7500–$9999	16	Blue collar	36.2	40.7
$10,000 and over	18	Service	10.7	31.7
		Farm	5.6	8.1

a For entire labor force over 14, excluding unemployed.

Source: Retrieved from *Statistical Abstract of the United States* (Washington: Bureau of the Census, 1967), Tables 322 and 530. Percentages rounded and cases not reported omitted. Estimates for religion and political preference approximated from data of the Gallup Organization.

5-3(1) for the chi-square test, for example, could be used to show whether your sample is reasonably representative of the age stratification of the United States voting-age population. It is also possible to weight the identified subgroups in your sample in accordance with the known national percentages, and then to use the weighted results to project your own sample into one presumably more representative of the whole nation ("stratification after selection"). If your survey is planned to test attitudes for a regional or local group, similar stratifications can be derived from more detailed data in the Census Bureau's *Statistical Abstract of the United States* or *County and City Data Book*.

Two points about a national stratified sample require further attention. (1) It does not include a state-by-state breakdown, and since state electoral votes are counted as entities in the electoral college results, the sample would need to be reorganized to take this into account in an election which appeared fairly close—not necessarily by a fifty-state breakdown, but by a somewhat more detailed regional division. (2) Special treatment will often be needed for groups representing high homogeneity or low total percentages. In the use of its similar sample to test pre-convention Goldwater support, the Gallup organization found so high a negative correlation between race and preference for Goldwater that Crespi retabulated the results with Negroes excluded, feeling that this strong association might mask possible correlations among whites, for example, between region and preference.* This result demonstrates the general difficulty with a completely random sample if an investigator is interested in some particular group which is not large enough to show up in significant numbers. If interested in wealthy Negroes, the investigator would need to develop a special sample for the purpose: he would have to go out and find them. The same is true for many other groups which might be politically significant though numerically few: county central committee members, Southern district attorneys, or such influential professional categories as lawyers, doctors, and ministers.

Since the design of a large sample for a comprehensive survey is a highly technical procedure, requiring well organized group activity with adequate financing, we shall not attempt to deal with it here.

---

* This aspect of his article is explained in a letter to the author from Irving Crespi, Vice-President of the Gallup Organization, April 26, 1967.

The interested student is referred to the excellent manual by Backstrom and Hursh, *Survey Research,* which is both a complete introduction to the subject and a guide to further technical literature.

6-2 The Questionnaire

Writing a good questionnaire requires experience. Many mistakes will creep into the first draft even if it is prepared by experts. For this reason, it is always necessary to *pre-test* a questionnaire to discover as many such errors as possible: unintentionally misleading questions, unintentionally "loaded" phrases, words familiar to the investigator but likely to be beyond the everyday vocabulary of many respondents, and questions which appear clear enough but turn out to convey an incomplete or ambiguous meaning.

In writing a questionnaire you should have clearly in mind the purpose of the survey. Prepare by reading relevant reports of similar surveys, noting as many facets of the subject as you can think of. The actual questions may be of several types. With your survey topic in mind, as well as the broader field in which it falls, you should practice drafting questions under some of the categories noted below.

Questions to Identify the Respondent. Reviewing the discussion in Chapters 1 and 2 about the several kinds of variables and how they are used to locate the respondent in property-space, you will usually be interested in a variety of respondent-identification items.

Simple Factual Identification. These questions will elicit basic "census" data, such as age, sex, race, income, occupation, residence, voter status, and the like, and usually represent no difficulty except on touchy or prestige-involved categories. Some respondents will resent a question on income, for example; identification of race is usually best done by the investigator himself. Obviously you should avoid such terms as "blue-collar," "white-collar," "manual laborer," and "unskilled laborer," which are either meaningless to the respondent or may seem to reflect on his status.

Identification of Respondent's Information. These questions are framed to find out what the respondent knows about the subject of the survey. If he has never heard of the subject, it is useless to ask what he thinks of it. On the other hand, a few "filter" questions may remind him of things which otherwise he would not recall.

Identification of the Respondent's Role. These questions are meant to place the respondent in his social and political context. Is he a leader or politically inactive? Does he commonly talk politics with his friends? What sources of political influence is he subject to, and what influences does he exert himself? Club memberships, church-going habits, even ordinary social visits, help place the respondent in the politically interacting public. The alert investigator often can discover useful leads on respondent's role by direct observation.

Decision Questions. These are the crucial items concerned with the substantive content of the survey, on which the respondent is asked to make some sort of choice. Though there is no clear-cut dividing line, two broad categories of decision questions will usually be included—those seeking specific choices and those meant to discover underlying motivations.

Specific choices. Respondent is asked, for example, whether he intends to vote for Candidate A or Candidate B in a forthcoming election, whether he is for or against the upcoming bond issue, whether he thinks something is good or bad, or whether his attitude is one of strong support, support, neutrality, opposition, or strong opposition.

Motivation. The investigator is usually interested not only in the respondent's specific choices, but also in the reasons for them. Why is he for Candidate A? Why does he "strongly support" or "strongly oppose"

the administration policy in Viet Nam? Why is he for or against open housing, school integration, federal aid to education, medicare, legislative reapportionment, or prayers in school? Questions to discover underlying factors which influence decisions are the most difficult to prepare. Thorough probing of motivation requires skilled depth interviewing. Information on motivation which can be obtained by standardized questions is especially valuable, however, since it often helps to identify broadly based and lasting opinion categories significant beyond the range of the sample in terms of persons surveyed, specific topics covered, and the time of the survey.

Clues for motivational questions may emerge in a carefully planned pre-test. Two techniques are commonly used: an open-ended question and a standardized list of alternative "reasons." In an open-ended question, the respondent is asked to state in his own words (for example) why he thinks Candidate A is a better choice than Candidate B, or what aspect of medicare is especially appealing or objectionable. The open-ended question lends to the standardized questionnaire an element of depth interviewing, but has the disadvantages of being quite time consuming and difficult to code. The standardized list of alternatives, on the other hand, is no more complicated than any multiple-choice question. The respondent is simply asked to mark one of several "reasons." For example, if he has indicated a preference for Jones over Smith in a gubernatorial race, the next item might be:

The Alert Investigator Often Can Discover Useful Leads on Respondent's Role by Direct Observation

"Good afternoon, sir, we're taking a public-opinion poll on Vietnam. There are a few questions..."

"Could you possibly hold on a minute, please? I'll be right back."

"O.K., pencil-pusher, fire away!"

Drawing by W. Miller; © 1966 The New Yorker Magazine, Inc.

If asked to pick one reason for supporting this candidate, which would you select?

I have always voted the party ticket.
He has experience in public office.
He is an honest man.
All the newspapers I read are for him.
None of the above.

A good compromise between the open-ended question and the standardized list is to include some open-ended questions at the time of the pre-test. You can then try to word the most frequent answers in standard versions for the actual survey.

6-3 Structure of Questions

While structured questions are in form either dichotomous (yes-no, true-false, good-bad, for-against) or multiple choice, several techniques have been developed for scaling responses into more meaningful categories than would be possible by either type.

1. One method is to attach a numerical weight (not disclosed to respondent) to each response in a multiple choice listing:

Do you think the President's trip to the Far East is important to our foreign policy? Would you call it:

		Weight
1_____	Very important	(8)
2_____	Important	(7)
3_____	Unimportant	(3)
4_____	Very unimportant	(2)

2. Another method, adapted from a form used by Osgood, is called the "semantic differential." It consists of placing a pair of responses at opposite ends of a line, the respondent being asked to mark the point on the line which most nearly represents his answer. The line may be broken into parts (usually seven) to force a specific weighting, or it may be continuous, and the response later weighted by use of an overlaid transparency. In neither case does the weighting scale appear on the printed questionnaire.

Do you think NATO is important to our foreign policy? Mark the place on the line which most closely represents your opinion.

Important__ __ __ __ __ __ __Unimportant
Important_____Unimportant

3. A combination of the semantic differential and scaled response techniques, especially useful in detecting motivation factors, is illustrated below:

The President's trip to the Far East will probably have the effect of:

	Agree		Disagree		
	1	2	3	4	5
Helping allied cooperation					
Increasing danger of war					
Helping promote peace					
Helping Democrats in the election					
Improving allied morale					

4. Another form of dichotomous question used to examine basic attitudes asks for a simple "agree-disagree" response to several related statements, each presumed to be characteristic of some basic attitude like conservatism, isolationism, liberalism, or aggressiveness. An example, designed to test the isolationism-cooperation continuum, might be:

The UN is in general
a good thing   Agree_____   Disagree_____
We should strengthen
NATO   Agree_____   Disagree_____
Foreign trade is good
for the country   Agree_____   Disagree_____
The Peace Corps is a
constructive
program   Agree_____   Disagree_____
We need to keep our
foreign aid program
going, perhaps with
better supervision   Agree_____   Disagree_____

In this pattern, respondent is given a score based on the number of agreements to the entire set of questions: "5" would represent "most internationalist," "0" would represent "most isolationist."

5. More difficult to validate is a variation of the above example, in which each successive statement is "stronger" or "weaker" than the one before it, so that the respondent would be expected to give the same answer to all questions above (or below) it in the list:

Do you agree or disagree with the following statements about the UN?

                                        Agree   Disagree

The UN is in general a good
  thing and should be
  strengthened into a world
  government.   _____ _____

The UN should have a
  permanent military force
  strong enough to enforce
  peace.   _____ _____

The United States should cooperate with the UN in our own foreign policy programs. _____ _____

The United States should remain in the UN even though it is often ineffective. _____ _____

The UN should not be abolished even though it is rather useless. _____ _____

If the statements actually constitute a scale ranging from strongest to weakest, the number of agreements immediately locates the respondent in a ranking of all respondents. Theoretically, a respondent replying "Agree" to the first question on the above list should also reply "Agree" to all the others. A respondent replying "Agree" to the last question, on the other hand, might well reply "Disagree" to all four of the others. The result will be that respondents will be categorized into six groups: those making scores of 5, 4, 3, 2, 1, and 0. Scaled sets are discussed more fully in Chapter 7, to which you should refer if you plan to use this device in your own work.

6. *Item Ranking Methods.* Especially useful in a primary election survey is the technique of asking the respondent to rank a list of items (in this case candidates) in order of his preference, rather than simply to select the one he favors. The method is adaptable as well to the ranking of groups or officials according to the respondent's opinion of their importance, influence, or other attribute. When the number of items to be ranked is large, they should be subdivided into several manageable short lists.

Paired rankings are often used in "trial heats" to determine how various combinations of party candidates would probably compare in an actual election:

If the two parties were to nominate the following persons for president, for which would you probably vote?

Vote for		Vote for
_____ Johnson	or	Goldwater _____
_____ Kennedy	or	Romney _____
_____ Johnson	or	Hatfield _____

The use of paired rankings becomes impractical for a long list, because of the large number of possible permutations. It requires six pairs to rank four items as shown in the boxed display at the foot of the page.

6-4 To Structure or Not To Structure?

Even if the survey instrument is to be a completely written questionnaire to be filled in by the respondent, it is useful to think of each question as though you plan to use it in an oral interview. To what extent is the question *structured*? How much does it restrict or guide the respondent's thinking or the form of his response? The investigator must achieve a nice balance between the one extreme of over-structured questions, which may inhibit the respondent or bias his answers, and the other extreme of overly open-ended questions, which may have the virtue of not influencing the answers but also the disadvantage of not conveying enough information to elicit any answer at all. Aside from coding difficulties, the under-structured question may actually misdirect the respondent, so that his answer is off the subject. In an oral interview, these complications are detected by a skilled investigator as the interview proceeds. In a written questionnaire, however, they must be anticipated.

A helpful model for structuring questions is the familiar Stimulus-Response paradigm, which forces the investigator to keep constantly in mind the respondent's possible range of reactions to the question. Think of each question as having two functions: (1) providing an appropriate *stimulus* to the respondent, and (2) evoking a *response* useful to the purpose of the survey. Either of these two functions may be *structured* or *free*. We thus have a four-fold typology of questions:

Stimulus	Response	
	Free	Structured
Free	SF-RF	SF-RS
Structured	SS-RF	SS-RS

Which of the following organizations would you say is most influential in state politics, comparing them two at a time?

	Most influential		*Most influential*	
_____	Labor unions	or	Chamber of Commerce	_____
_____	League of Women Voters	or	County commissioners	_____
_____	Labor unions	or	League of Women Voters	_____
_____	Chamber of Commerce	or	County commissioners	_____
_____	County commissioners	or	Labor unions	_____
_____	League of Women Voters	or	Chamber of Commerce	_____

Examples of each type:

Stimulus Free, Response Free:	Thinking now about American foreign policy, do you have any particular opinions you would like to mention?
Stimulus Structured, Response Free:	What is your reaction to the bombing of targets in North Viet Nam?
Stimulus Free, Response Structured:	There has been quite a bit of news recently about the possibility of peace talks on Viet Nam. Do you feel anything that has happened makes a settlement: (1) Likely? (2) Unlikely?
Stimulus Structured, Response Structured:	About the bombing of targets in North Viet Nam—do you think we should: (1) Stop it? (2) Keep it up? (3) Expand it?

6-5 Bad Questions

Many of the mistakes the inexperienced question-writer can make are outlined by Backstrom and Hursh. Their categories are listed below, with some of the illustrations drawn from recent events.

Errors of Ambiguity. The question may be:
1. *Incomplete.* "Did you vote in the last election?" (Respondent often does not recall any election since the last one in which he did vote.)
2. *Imprecise.* "Do you think the government's policies are responsible for the market being so low?" (What government? What policies? What market? How low?)
3. *Indefinite in time.* "The Demonstration Cities Bill provides for future spending of about $100 billion. Are you for or against this program?" (How many years in the future? Spending for what and when?)
4. *Indefinite in comparisons.* "Do you think Oklahoma spends too much for welfare?" (More than other states? More than for other functions? What kind of welfare?)
5. *Too simple.* "Do you see many public officials?" (See in person? See on TV? National, state, or local officials? How many is many?)
6. *Too complicated.* "The Demonstration Cities Bill is intended to dramatize some potential solutions to urban problems. Do you favor or oppose it?"

("Dramatize" by action, or by stage, screen and TV? What solutions? What does "potential" mean?)
7. *Too general.* "Do you think most people take politics seriously?" (Does "most" mean a majority or almost all? Does "people" mean all humans, all Americans, all adults, all citizens of the state, all residents of the city? Does "politics" mean national, state, local, or private? How serious is serious?)

Errors of Misunderstanding. The question may be:
1. *Outside the experience of respondent.* "Some people say President Johnson is egocentric. Do you agree or disagree?" So obvious an error would be rare, but respondent may be equally unaware of other terms which the investigator takes for granted.
2. *Too technical.* "Do you favor judicial review of legislation?" Many errors of misperception may be avoided by a brief explanation included as part of the question: "Under our system of government, the courts can rule that a law passed by Congress or a state legislature or even a city or town, is unconstitutional and cannot be enforced. Do you think the courts should have this power?"
3. *A violation of idiom.* "In the national highway program, the federal government must often take interstate right-of-ways. Do you think it should be able to do this?" Many respondents will hear "take States' rights away."

Errors of Intentional or Unintentional Loading. The question may:
1. *Present unfair alternatives.* "The Demonstration Cities Bill will result in the national debt going up more than $100 billion and probably won't accomplish much at that. Won't you sign this petition against it?"
2. *Malign the opposition.* "Those opposing the Demonstration Cities Bill are worried that Secretary Weaver, a Negro, will have charge of the program. Don't you think this is a prejudiced point of view?"
3. *Damn with faint praise.* "Some think the Demonstration Cities plan will do practically nothing to solve the big cities' problems. Others think it may do a little good. Do you think we ought to adopt it?"
4. *Omit alternatives.* "The experts who have studied big city problems have worked out a

program to solve some of them. Do you think we ought to make a start on such a program?"

5. *Use emotionally charged language.* "The communists have always said that our American system of free government and free enterprise will be driven into bankruptcy and destroyed by all the big spending we are doing. The Demonstration Cities Bill will drive us another $100 billion into debt. Aren't you against this?"

6. *Use prestige names and words.* "The President, Vice-President, all the Cabinet members, the mayors of New York, Chicago, and almost all other big cities, and most members of both Houses of Congress, are in favor of this program to improve our cities. Do you agree with them?"

Miscellaneous Errors. The question may be:

1. *Too short—deficient in needed information.* "Do you think the Geneva Agreements of 1954 are a reasonable basis for settling the Viet Nam war?"

2. *Too long—overabundant in unneeded information.* "A bill now before Congress would provide federal money for a number of existing grant-in-aid programs, most of which are related to cities, including slum clearance projects, metropolitan improvement projects, city and regional planning, urban renewal programs, and the like. It also contains provisions for low interest rate financing of housing for low-income families, expansion of Federal Housing Administration mortgage insurance to completely new towns, authority for FHA mortgage insurance to include building of group medical installations, grants to local governments for preservation of historic structures, and assistance to farm families in the purchase of new homes by rural housing loans. It appropriates $24 millions the first year for planning, $250 millions for urban renewal projects over a two-year period beginning July 1, 1967, and $900 millions for the other projects over the same two-year period. Do you favor or oppose this bill?"

3. *Argumentative—also usually too long.* "Since our big cities have over half of the population and contribute about 75% of the taxes, and have been having such serious problems—like the riots in Los Angeles, and all these demonstrations—it has been proposed that a federal program be started which would involve a study project this next year, and after that a start on slum clearance, more funds for housing loans,

and a number of other projects. Over a ten-year period the total cost of all these projects would be only about one and a half percent of the national income. Are you for or against this bill?"

4. *Impossible to answer because in two parts.* "Do you favor the Demonstration Cities Bill or should we expand the Federal Housing Act? (1) Agree (2) Disagree"

5. *Over-folksy.* "Don't you think it's about time to get with the mess in the big cities and put this bill over?"

6. *Confused by double negatives.* "Would you say you are not opposed to this bill?"

7. *Too stilted.* "Many eminent authorities feel that the contemporary urban culture presents many problems of social disorganization and individual alienation of the utmost urgency, compelling appropriate remedial action on the part of the governmental sector of our society. Would you feel that such remedial activity is (1) proper, or (2) improper?"

6-6 Planning Your Own Survey: An Adventure in Discovery

When you undertake a survey of your own, you will realize almost at once that you are engaged in a "do-it-yourself" project.* You must select your own survey topic, prepare the survey instrument yourself, and refine it by pre-testing. Only general guidelines can be supplied.

Select Your Subject. Your topic should be selected from a field in political science of special interest to you and in which you have already acquired some knowledge of the substantive background and recent research. Your work is more likely to be well planned and to make a relevant empirical contribution than if done in a field new to you. As you develop plans for your survey, try to add to your background in

---

* In the experimental use of this workbook with the author's classes, each student prepared, administered, and reported on a survey as his major term project. The assignment was found to give valuable experience with a number of quantitative methods, but additional specific preparation included readings in Herbert Hyman, *Survey Design and Analysis* (New York: Free Press, 1955), Charles H. Backstrom and Gerald D. Hursh, *Survey Research* (Evanston: Northwestern University Press, 1963), and Delbert C. Miller, *Handbook of Research Design and Social Measurement* (New York: David McKay Co., Inc., 1964).

both the theoretical work relevant to your subject and in the continuing process of empirical testing of accepted political lore.

Start by searching the literature, both for suggestions and—once you have landed on a topic—for detailed information on what others have done. Immerse yourself in the subject; learn thoroughly the "state of the art." Then work out specific wording of a few hypotheses gathered from your reading and try them on your teachers and fellow-students. A few suggestions in several fields follow, but these are far from complete, intended only to trigger your own search. The works mentioned, as well as other sources of ideas for survey topics, are cited in a special section of the reading list at the end of the chapter.

Political Socialization. If you are interested in the processes whereby an individual becomes a "political man," and the influences which determine what kind of political man he becomes, examine such classic works as the "authoritarian personality" studies, Almond and Coleman's *Politics of the Developing Areas,* Hyman's *Political Socialization,* and Greenstein's *Children and Politics.* A few hypotheses you might glean from these are:

That childhood experiences exercise a strong influence on an individual's future political behavior.

That family authority patterns are reflected in the authority patterns of the political system.

That individuals whose parents were inconsistent in political party preference will be less intense in their own party preference than individuals whose parents were consistent.

Political Opinion and Reference Groups. Political group theory, important in political science since Bentley and sharpened greatly by David Truman, has profited from the sociological study of reference groups—groups with which an individual identifies strongly enough that he draws his own values from them.

Possible hypotheses to explore:

That membership in groups with conflicting values is associated with weaker support of related political issues, whereas membership in groups which share values tends to reinforce support of related political issues.

That the impact of a reference group on a member's political behavior is related to the member's view of how important the group is to his non-political interests.

That political persuasiveness of a communication to an individual from a reference group varies with salience of the group to the individual, in part determined by content and channel of the communication.

Political Ideology. Empirical study of political values is in its infancy but is a field of great promise. Impact of ideology on different classes of society, influences on the development of belief systems, and public acceptance of specific concepts of classical political theory are aspects from which an unlimited number of useful survey topics could be devised. Some possible hypotheses suitable for testing are:

That a moral or ethical principle will find greater support if expressed as an ideal than if expressed as a rule of action.

That support for a traditional principle of a given group's belief system is strongly correlated with education of respondents.

That recognition of the logical association or consistency of two or more principles packaged in a traditional belief system ("If you believe thus, you will believe so") is spotty among the mass public.

That consensus on basic democratic principles is greater among political "influentials" than among members of the general electorate.

Political Culture Norms. Cross-national cultural studies are related to ideology but are more broadly concerned with the total societal complex. They are also difficult to organize, expensive to conduct, and so are relatively rare. Their findings are also likely to be controversial. For the student of comparative politics or international relations, however, they offer a fascinating field of survey research. UNESCO has sponsored a number of such studies, including *National Stereotypes and International Understanding,* one of a series on international tensions. Buchanan and Cantril's *How Nations See Each Other* summarizes some of the UNESCO data for nine countries. Most relevant to political science is the 1965 study by Cantril, *The Pattern of Human Concerns,* reporting on interviews conducted with some 20,000 respondents in fourteen countries—including several developing nations and communist countries never surveyed before. Another outstanding project is the five-nation survey reported by Almond and Verba in *The Civic Culture,* particularly in its emphasis on the concept of "civic competence," from which additional survey topics can readily be developed. You may not be able to conduct your survey in foreign countries (see Exercise Set 10 for two small individual projects which did use international samples), but you can adapt some of the themes used in the larger surveys to your own community.

International Politics. Most surveys in international

relations will be concerned with opinions on foreign policy, on the United Nations, or on specific international crises. Useful ideas for projects will emerge from Rosenau's provocative study *Public Opinion and Foreign Policy* and from his two Free Press readers, *International Politics and Foreign Policy* and *Domestic Sources of Foreign Policy*. The 1967 volume of the International Yearbook of Political Behavior Research, *Quantitative International Politics: Insights and Evidence,* edited by David Singer, should also supply a number of valuable leads.

Possible hypotheses in foreign policy:

That a person's interests in foreign policy express the interests of his more important group associations.

That limited formal education makes for simple solutions in foreign policy.

That support of international institutions such as the UN is greater in the abstract than in specific action situations.

That the range of alternatives finding substantial public support is sharply reduced in high tension situations as compared with low tension situations.

If your interest is in *judicial behavior* you might explore the hypothesis that support is greater for some leading judicial doctrine if identified with the authority of the U.S. Supreme Court than if the ruling is merely described as a principle. In the field of *legislative behavior* the work of Wahlke and Eulau is especially useful as idea sources. One of their surveys is the source of Tables 6-E and 6-F in the Exercise Set: you might turn the approach around and try to see if public views of the proper role of a legislator vary in the same way as those of the legislators themselves.

Incomplete as it is, this selection indicates the variety and scope of sources for your survey topic. Other ideas will occur to you from the survey briefs which accompany the exercises for this chapter, other tables in the workbook, and the reading list discussion below. In particular you should examine the professional political science journals, not neglecting the *Public Opinion Quarterly.*

Identify Your Variables. Having made a tentative decision on the general theme of your survey, think ahead to the tables you would like to present in your final written report. As you set up your tentative hypotheses, rough out a series of blank table formats and fill in the captions. Start with a few simple two-dimensional formats, each planned to examine the association between one behavior or attitude variable and one explanatory or causal variable. The process will force you to sharpen and clarify your plans in preparation for writing the specific questions needed to locate each respondent precisely in the "property space" defined by the variables.

Explanatory variables. For most projects, the independent (and control) variables will be respondent identification categories. Recall the three types of identification questions mentioned in Section 2—simple factual identification, identification of respondent's information, and identification of respondent's role. An interesting cross-tabulation in *The Civic Culture* survey examined the association between respondents' willingness to express opinions and the level of respondents' political information. McClosky's "leaders and followers" study, briefed in the exercises of this chapter, is an excellent example of use of role variables. Use your originality in developing information and role categories so that you can examine association patterns besides those of the elementary "census data" variety.

Attitude variables. The political opinions or attitudes you seek to explain—your dependent variables—will include specific choice items and motivation items, the latter requiring more thought and care in formulation. The beginner should avoid unusually complex motivational categories, but it is good experience to include at least one such variable planned to tap reasons for respondent choice. Your results may not satisfy you, but it is worthwhile to make the effort to explore some of these more fundamental and lasting political factors.

Write Your Questions. Attention to the list of variables you intend to identify will serve as a useful guide to the kind of questions you will need. Try to anticipate categories which may turn out to be useful, remembering that it will be too late to obtain any additional information once the survey is completed. It is much better to collect data which in the end you may not use than to omit an item which may turn out to be needed for a crucial cross-tabulation or control. Be on guard, of course, against the hazards involved in field use of a lengthy questionnaire. An unnecessarily long set of questions is costly in both time and respondent attention.

It is good practice to include several different wordings of the more important attitudinal items—to ask the same questions in different ways. This is a good safeguard against unintended bias or ambiguity. Of course, the different versions should be scattered throughout the questionnaire rather than grouped together. By comparing responses for consistency, you may find one version more satisfactory for the final tabulations.

In preparing the preliminary list do not hesitate to include any questions which come to mind. Plan to discard items rather than to expand. If you have not discarded a good many items by the time your final questionnaire is completed, you probably have some faulty questions in it.

Try your hand at one or more scaled set of questions or a grouping to which an index value can be attached. The experience is valuable even if your results turn out not to be actually scalable. The elementary three-point index used in the McClosky survey described in the exercises is one which requires relatively little special computation, and adds to the clarity of the tabular displays.

Pre-test Your Survey. The most experienced experts in survey research never trust their own questions, and neither should you. The pre-testing procedure is as essential a part of preparing a satisfactory instrument as the original drafting of the questionnaire. Ideally the pre-test should be administered to a small sample drawn from the same group who will constitute the total sample for the final survey. It should be administered in the same manner, and by the same interviewers. In your own project, you are probably your own interviewer, which is actually an advantage—you are the person most familiar with your questions and can judge most accurately whether you are getting useful responses from the pre-test respondents.

A check list of flaws to watch for at the pre-test stage includes the variety of "bad question" categories described in Section 6–5. Look especially for awkward wording, ambiguities, questions which the respondent obviously does not understand or misinterprets, and for items which elicit a high percentage of "Don't Know's." For attitude items repeated in more than one wording, check for consistency of responses.

The pre-test is also a useful check on the time required for administration of the finished questionnaire. If you have the common experience of finding that the average respondent requires thirty minutes to complete what you envisaged as a five-minute questionnaire, consider ways and means of cutting down the length. The average mail questionnaire, for example, should not require more than ten minutes to complete.

With the pre-test results in, do preliminary computations for some or all of the tables you plan to include in your final report. You may discover useless items, categories not likely to be filled, and confusing identification groupings, as well as items inadvertently omitted but needed for one of the tabulations you had intended to include.

6-7 A Note on the Exercises

For preliminary practice in literature searching and "hypothesis brainstorming," a selection of tables from major political surveys is given in the exercise set following this chapter, together with brief descriptions of the original projects from which they are drawn.

As you examine each, identify the variables displayed and jot down a few questions which the investigators might have used to elicit the tabulated responses. Some of the variables are simple identification items; others are diffuse attitudinal categories. Think of the table in terms of your own project. Does it suggest any pattern which might be useful either in writing your questionnaire or in analyzing your expected results?

Work out a formal *null hypothesis* for the table (a briefly worded statement that there is no association between or among the variables). Without testing for statistical significance, decide tentatively what the table seems to show. Is the null hypothesis likely to be rejected? Phrase a short sentence in non-statistical language which you think the investigator might have used in his written account of the results shown in the table. Finally, if the source article or book is available, go to the original report and read what the authors actually said. Do your conclusions agree? If not, recheck the table and find what led you astray—or whether you can challenge the author's own statement. Satisfying (when you are right) or sobering (when you are wrong), the experience is invaluable in planning your own work. It furnishes a sort of acid test of your ability to read and discuss a table.

Relevance. As your survey project unfolds, constantly keep in mind the principle of relevance—the relationship between theory and fact. Knowledge grows by the interaction of ideas and empirical investigation, of conceptualization and the testing of concepts. This is especially evident in the contributions of survey research to political science. If you can develop your project as such a link between theoretical propositions about politics and objective findings about political reality, you are well on the road to becoming a competent research scholar.

Exercise Set 6. Do It Yourself

Part 1. Write Some Questions.

1. Prepare four questions on a topic of your own to illustrate the four variations of the Stimulus-Response model (Section 6-4).

(a) SF-RF _____

(b) SF-RS _____

(c) SS-RF _____

(d) SS-RS _____

2. Prepare a scaled set of five questions of increasing or decreasing intensity, of the type illustrated in Section 6-3, part 5. Select your own topic.

Intensity Level

(a) _____

(b) _____

(c) _____

(d) _____

(e) _____

3. On a separate sheet, prepare your own list of "bad questions" to illustrate each of the 23 types of standard errors listed. After each question, rewrite it so as to eliminate the objectionable feature.

Part 2. How Would You Word the Hypothesis?

On the pages following, you will find 13 tables, with a brief account of the major surveys from which they were selected. For each table listed below, state the null hypothesis verbally. For uniformity, mention the dependent variable first, the independent variable next, and the control variable, if any, last.

Example: The first table of Exercise Set 2, "Party Preference as a Function of Parental Party Preference."

H_0: Party preference of children does not differ significantly for children of Democratic parents as compared with children of Republican parents or with children of parents whose party preferences shifted.

1. Leaders and Followers, Table 6-A

H_0: _____

_____

2. Leaders and Followers, Table 6-B

H_0: _____

_____

3. Consensus in the Affluent Society, Table 6-C

H_0: _____

_____

4. Consensus in the Affluent Society, Table 6-D

H_0: _____

_____

5. Burke's Theory of Representation, Table 6-E

H_0: _____

_____

6. Burke's Theory of Representation, Table 6-F

H_0: _____

_____

7. Children and Politics, Table 6-G

H_0: _____

_____

8. Children and Politics, Table 6-H

H_0: _____

_____

9. Attitudes of Panamanian Students, Table 6-I

H_0: _____

_____

10. Voting Behavior of London Students, Table 6-J

H_0: _____

_____

11. Women in Politics, Table 6-K

H_0: _____

_____

12. The Non-Voter, Table 6-L

H_0: _____

_____

13. The Non-Voter, Table 6-M

H_0: _____

_____

Survey Briefs

1. Leaders and Followers   218
2. Consensus in the Affluent Society   220
3. Burke's Theory of Representation   220
4. Children and Politics   222
5. Views of British and Panamanian Students   224
6. Women in Politics   224
7. The Non-Voter   226

1. *Leaders and Followers.* The historic survey on which Tables 6-A and 6-B are based was first reported in the *American Political Science Review* in 1960. It supplied an intensive investigation of the familiar notion that the American two-party system tends to result in non-ideological parties, agreeing on most important issues since to win they must appeal to approximately the same elements of the electorate. The questionnaire was self-administered, consisting of 390 scale items, including respondent's attitudes on twenty-four major national issues then considered important. The "leaders" sample consisted of 3020 delegates to the national party conventions of 1956 (1788 Democrats and 1232 Republicans), including high-ranking party leaders—state governors, senators, national committeemen, as well as lesser officials—precinct workers, and block captains. The "followers" sample was essentially the Gallup sample. Gallup interviewers distributed the questionnaires, and 1484 usable ones were returned, closely matching chief characteristics of the United States voting population.

The "support ratio" entries in the tables represent the average response of respondents in the columnar groups to questions regarding support of the issues listed, with the value 1.00 assigned to the response "increase," .50 to the response "same," and 0.0 assigned to the response "decrease." Thus they permit comparisons between columnar categories by supplying a single index, ranging from zero to 1.00, describing, for example, the average attitude of Democratic leaders on foreign aid, and another describing the average attitude of Republican leaders on the same question. The most general finding of the study was that Republican and Democratic leaders were more widely separated (by a difference of .21 in support ratios) than were Republican and Democratic followers (whose support ratios differed by only .04).

TABLE 6-A. *Comparison of Party Leaders and Followers on Reliance on the United Nations, by Percentages and Ratios of Support*

Reliance on United Nations		Leaders		Followers	
		Dem. $N = 1,788$	Repub. $N = 1,232$	Dem. $N = 821$	Repub. $N = 623$
			(%'s down)		
% favoring:	Increase	48.9	24.4	34.7	33.4
	Decrease	17.6	34.8	17.3	19.3
	Same, n.c.	33.5	40.7	48.0	47.3
Support Ratio		.66	.45	.59	.57

Source: Herbert McClosky, Paul J. Hoffmann, and Rosemary O'Hara, "Issue Conflict and Consensus among Party Leaders and Followers," *American Political Science Review,* Vol. 54 (1960), pp. 406–427.

TABLE 6-B. *Comparison of Party Leaders and Followers on Public Control of Atomic Energy, by Percentages and Ratios of Support*

Public Control		Leaders		Followers	
		Dem. $N = 1,788$	Repub. $N = 1,232$	Dem. $N = 821$	Repub. $N = 623$
			(%'s down)		
% favoring:	Increase	73.2	45.0	64.2	59.4
	Decrease	7.2	15.3	7.1	10.0
	Same, n.c.	19.6	39.7	28.7	30.6
Support Ratio		.83	.65	.79	.75

Source: Same as Table 6-A.

2. *Consensus in the Affluent Society.* One interesting use of survey data accumulated over the years is illustrated by Robert E. Lane's far-ranging examination of American opinion trends, "The Politics of Consensus in an Age of Affluence," (*American Political Science Review,* Vol. 59, No. 4, December 1965, pp. 874–895). By comparing polls and surveys taken at different points in time, but asking identical or essentially similar questions, Lane attempts a non-rigorous test of the generalization that economic conditions in a society have broad political consequences. Tables 6-C and 6-D represent two of the time-trend patterns studied: a general level of optimism, and the more specific attitude toward racial integration in schools.

Comparing polls taken at different times presents certain statistical problems; the sampling error may diverge in two successive polls so that an invalid conclusion seems supported. Unlike the panel survey, in which the same respondents are interviewed at two or more times (before and after an election), each successive poll has its own randomly drawn sample. The usual published poll (including those of the American Institute of Public Opinion used here) does not include information on the size of the sample, although it is available— usually about 1600. Lane recognizes these and other difficulties in using survey data for comparing opinion in times of economic insecurity and economic security. He calls his article "a speculative historical study making use of such data as come to hand."

3. *Burke's Theory of Representation.* Should the elected representative consider himself responsible to his constituents or to his own conscience? Edmund Burke's dictum, that "not local purposes, not local prejudices ought to guide, but the general good," is the classic statement of the "trustee" theory of representation. To examine this doctrine's acceptance by actual legislators, Eulau and associates interviewed almost all members of four state legislatures during the 1957 sessions—in all, 474 interviews of about two hours duration were conducted. The states—California, New Jersey, Ohio, and Tennessee—represent different regions, different party divisions, and different degrees of urbanization, so that we might expect the results to be typical of state legislatures in general.

The authors distinguish two concepts in Burke's theory: the *focus* of representation (which interests come first—those of the local district or of the state as a whole?), and the *style* of representation (how does the legislator view his own role—as a delegate, expressing his constituents' views, or as a Burkean trustee, following his own best judgment?). From the results, three categories emerged for both the areal-focal and the role variables—a more or less pure Burkean type (state-oriented, trustee), its opposite (district-oriented, delegate), and a group between those two poles (state-district-oriented, politico). Legislators in the third group typically felt they could represent both state and district interests without serious conflict, and that they could represent their constituents' views and their own at the same time.

Tables 6-E and 6-F display some of the results of the study, examining the possible effect of party competitiveness on areal orientation, and the degree of association of the two basic Burkean concepts—areal focus and role.

If at all possible you should read the entire source article. It is recommended as a model of empirical research, in which the methods of modern political science are used to examine a long-standing issue of democratic theory.

TABLE 6-C. *Perceptions of Life Now, Earlier, and Later*

"Ten years from now, do you believe Americans will generally be happier than they are today?" (AIPO, May 18, 1939). "As you look to the future, do you think life for people generally will get better—or will it get worse?" (AIPO, March 15, 1952; Aug. 29, 1962)

	1939	1952	1962
	(%)	(%)	(%)
Better (happier)	42	42	55
Worse (not happier)	35	34	23
No difference		13	12
No opinion	23	11	10

Source: Robert E. Lane, "The Politics of Consensus in an Age of Affluence," *American Political Science Review,* Vol. 59 (1965), pp. 874–895.

TABLE 6-D. *Changing Attitudes Toward Integration*

"Would you, yourself, have any objection to sending your children to a school where a few of the children are colored? Where half of the children are colored?" (AIPO)

	Per Cent "Yes"			
	Where a Few Children Are Colored		Where Half of Children Are Colored	
	Outside South	South	Outside South	South
	(%)	(%)	(%)	(%)
1958	13	72	39	81
1959	7	72	34	83
1963 (June)	10	61	33	78
1965 (May)	7	37	28	68

Source: Same as Table 6-C.

TABLE 6-E. *Political Character of Electoral Districts and Areal Role Orientations in Three States**

	Political Character of District		
Areal Role Orientation	Competitive ($N = 72$)	Semi-competitive ($N = 77$)	One-party ($N = 96$)
District	53%	48%	33%
District-and-State	28	34	33
State	19	18	34
Total	100%	100%	100%

* California, New Jersey and Ohio. "Non-respondents" on the areal dimension have been omitted.
Source: Heinz Eulau, John C. Wahlke, William Buchanan, and LeRoy C. Ferguson, "The Role of the Representative: Some Empirical Observations on the Theory of Edmund Burke," *American Political Science Review,* Vol. 53 (1959), pp. 742–756.

TABLE 6-F. *Areal-Focal and Representational Role Orientations in Four States*

Representational Role Orientation	District-oriented ($N = 89$)	State-District-oriented ($N = 64$)	State-oriented ($N = 44$)
Trustee	37%	55%	84%
Delegate	36	8	—
Politico	27	37	16
Total	100%	100%	100%

Source: Same as Table 6-E.

4. *Children and Politics.* When in life do people acquire basic political ideas? Considering the importance which psychologists attach to childhood influences, it is remarkable how little political research has been directed to the formative years. Greenstein's survey of 659 New Haven children, necessarily conducted by individual interviews, is a landmark in the investigation of the roots of political socialization. Tables 6-G and 6-H report some comparisons between children and adults and among children of different ages.

Striking differences between children and adults are brought out, suggesting further study of the transitional adolescent years, during which the characteristic adult cynicism about politics apparently is formed. The most familiar political leaders are perceived far more favorably by the child than by the adult—mayor and president are benevolent figures, the mayor providing parks and swings, snow removal, and schools at the local level, while the president assures freedom, peace, and safety for the people at the national level.

Greenstein reports that the child's benevolent image persists under questioning aimed at identifying both the office and individual political leaders. Moreover, it seemed impossible to evoke cynicism even by questions structured deliberately to do so—children simply did not respond to such references. There may be implications in these findings for study of lifelong respect for authority and attachment to the political system of the country, even after adulthood brings a decreasingly favorable image of particular political leaders and offices.

In the footnote cited for Table 6-G, the author points out that the column reporting adult opinion of the president is not strictly comparable—the wording and the alternatives were different and the sample was national. Approval of President Eisenhower was probably higher in the East than in the South. Similar polls controlled for region indicate the "approval" entry might have been about 65 per cent, still lower than that for the children.

TABLE 6-G. *Children's Evaluations of Three Political Executives Contrasted with Adult Evaluations of President Eisenhower During the Same Time Period*

| | Children | | | | Adults[a] |
	Mayor	Governor	President		President
Very good	62%	40%	71%	Approve	58%
Fairly good	27	28	21		
Not very good	4	2	4	Disapprove	27
Bad	1	—[b]	1		
Don't know	6	30	4	No opinion	15
Number of cases	651[c]	643[c]	649[c]		

a February 1958 AIPO findings, reported in March 1958 release. These findings are based on a national sample. On their comparability with the New Haven data, see footnote 11 in source.

b Less than 1 per cent.

c Number of cases does not equal complete sample due to invalid responses.

Source: Fred I. Greenstein, *Children and Politics* (New Haven: Yale University Press, 1965).

TABLE 6-H. *Children's Images of the Mayor and President, by School Year**

| | School Year | | | | |
	4th	5th	6th	7th	8th
Mayor					
Benevolence: "helps us" "gives us freedom"	20%	16%	9%	3%	4%
Normative role: "does good things" "tells what is right or wrong"	7	12	13	8	12
Services to children: "makes parks and swings"	15	14	1	11	15
Number of cases	55	82	98	115	151
President					
Benevolence	26%	11%	5%	5%	4%
Normative	5	9	11	3	7
Number of cases	62	80	95	112	160

* Percentages are based on those children who were able to produce a description of the executive role, whether or not the description was "reasonably accurate" (excluding grossly inaccurate or vague statements).

Source: Same as Table 6-G.

5. *Views of British and Panamanian Students.* Further data on political socialization are shown in Table 6-I and 6-J, from two surveys of selected student groups. Both studies were made in 1960, though the respondent samples were widely separated both geographically and culturally. However, both studies have the common feature of distinguishing for social class in groups from which a considerable number of future political leaders are likely to come.

The Panamanian sample consisted of 91 eleventh-grade students from two large secondary schools in Panama City. The private school, one operated by a Catholic order, is a prestige institution, attended by children of the social elite, including those of many government officials. The public school is the largest in the city, with a reputation for political activism by students and a democratic, anti-clerical tradition. Thus the two groups are categorized by the authors as "Upper Class" and "Middle and Lower Class." The questionnaire for the Panama survey, incidentally, included a number of items from Greenstein's study of New Haven children.

The London study is based on a larger sample—respondents were 740 third-year students of British nationality at four London colleges. The author points out that in the context of British society, all the respondents may be considered middle class because of the jobs they will enter after graduation, so that those who report they have working-class parents are themselves upwardly mobile in the social scale. Table 6-J unfortunately does not include N's, but the author tells us that the group with working-class parents is 23 per cent of the total. (From other information in the source article, it appears that N's for the six columns of the table are approximately: 275, 88, 27, 44, 60, 6, with "Don't Know's" omitted).

These two surveys, with the Greenstein study, afford a few glimpses of three distinct stages in the process of personal and political maturation—childhood, late adolescence, and young adulthood. If political socialization continues throughout life—as it undoubtedly does—each phase is nonetheless a partial product of what has gone before.

6. *Women in Politics.* Another little-studied aspect of political socialization is the participation of women in both formal and unofficial political organizations. Since the enactment of women's suffrage in the United States in 1920, both major political parties have provided for equal representation of women on their national committees—a principle adopted as well by many state party organizations. Thus the number of women party officials tends towards equality with men, though there is some doubt that they exercise an equivalent influence. The authors of Table 6-K became interested in the political role of women as a result of a larger intensive study of political socialization in the United States and Canada, finding that women constituted almost one-third of the party officials interviewed in Minneapolis and Seattle. The data reported are based on interviews with 98 women in Democratic party positions and 110 women in Republican party positions, together with a mail questionnaire covering the same items addressed to members of the League of Women Voters in the two cities. The League is the leading nonpartisan voluntary association of women interested in public affairs; it never endorses candidates, but has a well-deserved reputation for consistent support of governmental and social reforms. The groups compared in Table 6-K are both politically active, then, but differ in that one group consists of partisan activists while the other consists of nonpartisan activists.

TABLE 6-I. *Attitudes of Panamanian Students toward Cubans, North Americans, and Russians*

		Private School Per Cent	Public School Per Cent
Cubans			
	Like	23	51
	Indifferent	56	47
	Don't like	21	2
	Total	100	100
	N	(34)	(43)
North Americans			
	Like	21	32
	Indifferent	61	39
	Don't like	18	29
	Total	100	100
	N	(33)	(44)
Russians			
	Like	18	26
	Indifferent	43	36
	Don't like	39	38
	Total	100	100
	N	(33)	(42)

Source: Daniel Goldrich and Edward W. Scott, "Developing Political Orientations of Panamanian Students," *The Journal of Politics*, Vol. 23, No. 1, February 1961, pp. 84–107.

TABLE 6-J. *Social Class and Inter-Generation Voting Behavior: London University Students*

Students' Party Ties	Students With Middle-Class Parents Who Vote:			Students With Working-Class Parents Who Vote:		
	Conservative %	Labour %	Liberal %	Conservative %	Labour %	Liberal %
Conservative	52	16	18	43	20	33
Labour	15	54	22	5	43	17
Liberal	15	12	60	32	10	50
Other and D.K.	18	18	—	20	27	—
Total	100	100	100	100	100	100

Source: Mark Abrams, "Social Trends and Electoral Behaviour," *The British Journal of Sociology*, Vol. 13, No. 3 (1962), pp. 228–42.

TABLE 6-K. *Relation of Age of First Party Identification to Parental Agreement in Political Party Support for Women Party Officials and League of Women Voter Members*

Age of First Identification	Women Party Officials		League of Women Voter Members	
	Parents for Same Party	Parents not for Same Party	Parents for Same Party	Parents not for Same Party
6 years & under	29%	22%	4%	3%
7–9 years	30	17	13	12
10–12 years	28	24	26	25
13–15 years	6	27	25	15
16–18 years	8	10	32	45
(N)	(130)	(41)	(267)	(155)

Source: "Variable Partisan Commitment among Politically Active Women," by David Bromley, Allan Kornberg, and Joel Smith, a paper presented at the Midwest Conference of Political Scientists, May 1968, Chicago. Reprinted with the kind permission of the authors.

7. *The Non-Voter.* In the United States, with so high a democratic tradition, so much value placed on the vote, and regular saturation campaigns by all the media to get out the vote in national presidential elections, why does turnout remain disappointingly low? Aside from those legally or extra-legally barred from the ballot, what kind of person is the non-voter?

The most extensive scientific studies of the American electorate are those conducted by the Survey Research Center of the University of Michigan, going back to the 1948 election. Data from surveys in the three elections of 1948, 1952, and 1956 were drawn on by the authors of *The American Voter,* a work which the late V.O. Key called "a monumental performance...in the adaptation of survey analysis to the study of problems that really bear on the political system." Tables 6-L and 6-M, from the chapter on voting turnout, concentrate attention on two aspects of the problem—concern of respondent about the outcome, and party preference of the non-voter. Other relationships studied include respondent perception of closeness of the election, interest in the campaign, sense of political efficacy, and sense of citizen duty.

Association between turnout and concern over outcome (Table 6-L) is a simple and expected pattern, but the time trend figures of Table 6-M are more difficult to interpret. The authors report that of all the statistical relationships in all of the Center's surveys, few have shown so violent a change over time as this one. Earlier opinion polling in the 1930's had seemed to establish a fairly firm principle that most non-voters were Democratic—a behavior pattern apparently related to the fact that low-income people tended to be both non-voters and Democrats. The sequence of data in Table 6-M seems to explode this legend, but what does the table actually say? Try your hand at interpreting it before turning to the next exercise for an additional analysis.

TABLE 6-L. *Relation of Degree of Concern About Election Outcome to Voting Turnout, 1956*

	Degree of Concern Over Election Outcome			
	Don't Care at All	Don't Care Very Much	Care Somewhat	Care Very Much
Voted	52%	69%	76%	84%
Did not vote	48	31	24	16
	100%	100%	100%	100%
Number of cases	230	367	627	459

Source: Angus Campbell, Phillip E. Converse, Warren E. Miller, and Donald E. Stokes, *The American Voter: An Abridgment* (New York: John Wiley and Sons, Inc., 1964).

TABLE 6-M. *Postelection Preference of Nonvoter, 1948 to 1956[a]*

	1948	1952	1956
Would have voted Democratic	82%	52%	28%
Would have voted Republican	18	48	72
Total	100%	100%	100%
Number of cases	192	417	429

[a] Among nonvoters giving a preference between major-party candidates.

Source: Same as Table 6-L.

Part 3. Review Your Statistics

1. The last table examined (Table 4-7 in *The American Voter*) is an excellent example of a deceptively simple array which is difficult to interpret. If we apply the Q test to the percentages by pairs, we find a relatively high coefficient for the 1948–1952 pair, almost as high a coefficient for the 1952–1956 pair, and a very high coefficient for the 1948–1956 pair.

Compute the Q values for the three pairs:

Clearly the table is showing something, but just what? We might have said after 1952 that "most non-voters are Democrats," but the 1956 result makes this highly improbable. We might say "in two elections out of three the non-voters preferred the winner," but two out of three is not a very significant result. We might reason that the entire period covered was one of Democratic decline, and a rank correlation on the three elections, comparing actual Democratic election strength with Democratic strength among non-voters does yield a correlation of $+1.00$, but for $N = 3$ no very significant conclusion is possible.

Falling back on your general knowledge of political science and of American politics, you will recall the frequent emphasis on the strength of incumbency. Identifying the three elections by this variable, we have something like the following scale:

(1) In 1948: Democratic candidate was incumbent, and won.

(2) In 1952: Neither candidate was incumbent, but Democratic incumbent gave strong support to the non-incumbent Democratic candidate.

(3) In 1956: Republican candidate was incumbent, and won.

With this scale in mind we are in a position to test the proposition that incumbency is a more influential factor with the disinterested non-voters than with those who vote, perhaps because of the greater visibility and more familiar name of the person who is actually president. The following exercise leads to one method of testing the idea.

Step 1. Retrieve the frequencies:

	1948	1952	1956
D	157	217	120
R	35	200	309

Step 2. Determine "expected" values from the actual two-party election results in per cent:

	1948	1952	1956		1948	1952	1956
D	52%	45%	42%		100	188	180
R	48	55	58		92	229	249

Step 3. Reconstruct the table to show actual and expected frequencies on the incumbency variable for each party:

	1948	O	E	D	D^2	D^2/E
	Democratic incumbent	157	100	57		
	Republican non-incumbent	35	92	57		

$$\chi^2 =$$

	1956	O	E	D	D^2	D^2/E
	Republican incumbent	309	249	60		
	Democratic non-incumbent	120	180	60		

$$\chi^2 =$$

H_0: Non-voter preference for incumbent not significantly greater than that of voters.
Significance level: .05
Statistic: χ^2
df = 1.
χ^2 value needed to reject: _____
Is H_0 rejected for Democrats _____ for Republicans? _____

2. Obtain the Q value for each of the two tables below as a preliminary test of significance of association. Then compute the chi-square value to test the null hypothesis at the .05 level.

TABLE 6-N. *Interest in World Affairs by ROTC Status* (from Chapter 4)

Interest Level	ROTC	non-ROTC	Total
Average & Lower	12	14	26
Above Average	13	11	24
Total	25	25	50

$Q = (ad - bc)/(ad + bc) =$ _____

Chi-square worksheet

O	E	D	D^2	D^2/E
12	$(1/2)\,26 =$			
13	$(1/2)\,24 =$			
14	$(1/2)\,26 =$			
11	$(1/2)\,24 =$			

df = 1 $\chi^2 =$

H_0: Interest not significantly related to ROTC status.
Significance level: .05

Is H_0 rejected? _____

TABLE 6-O. *Voter Turnout by Education* (Revised from Chapter 2).

	Per cent and (N)		
	College	Non-college	Total N
Did not vote	11 (12)	23 (136)	148
Voted	89 (102)	77 (452)	554
Total	100 (114)	100 (588)	702

$Q =$ _____

Chi-square worksheet

O	E	D	D^2	D^2/E
12	$(114 \times 148)/702 =$			
102	$(114 \times 554)/702 =$			
136	$(588 \times 148)/702 =$			
452	$(588 \times 554)/702 =$			

$\chi^2 =$

H_0: Voter turnout not related to education.
Significance level: .05

Is H_0 rejected? _____

Reading List

Part 2 of this list is added to supply a source of hypotheses about politics for those in search of ideas for a survey of their own. It is, of course, far from complete, and could be expanded almost indefinitely. In addition to the books listed, which include both survey reports and theoretical studies, you will find help in the many journal articles reporting on survey research. A list of the principal journals which frequently publish such articles is given in the reading list for Chapter 10.

1. *Books About Survey Research*

Backstrom, Charles H., and Gerald D. Hursh, *Survey Research*. Evanston: Northwestern University Press, 1963.*

Hyman, Herbert, *Survey Design and Analysis*. New York: Free Press, 1955.

Lazarsfeld, Paul F., and Morris Rosenberg (Eds.), *The Language of Social Research*. New York: Free Press, 1955.*

Merton, Robert K., Marjorie Fiske, and Patricia L. Kendall, *The Focused Interview*. New York: Free Press, 1956.

Miller, Delbert C., *Handbook of Research Design and Social Measurement*. New York: David McKay Co., Inc., 1964.*

2. *Sources of Hypotheses for an Original Survey*

Almond, Gabriel A., and Sidney Verba, *The Civic Culture: Political Attitudes and Democracy in Five Nations*. Princeton: Princeton University Press, 1963.

_____, and James S., Coleman (Eds.), *Politics of the Developing Areas*. Princeton, N. J.: Princeton University Press, 1960.

Apter, David E. (Ed.), *Ideology and Discontent*. New York: Free Press, 1964; Vol. V of the *International Yearbook of Political Behavior Research*.

Bailey, Harry A., Jr. (Ed.), *Negro Politics in America*. Columbus: Charles E. Merrill Publishing Co., 1967.

Berelson, B. R., P. F. Lazarsfeld, and W. N. McPhee, *Voting*. Chicago: University of Chicago Press, 1954.

Buchanan, William, and Hadley Cantril, *How Nations See Each Other*. Urbana: University of Illinois Press, 1953.

Campbell, Angus, Philip E. Converse, Warren E. Miller, and Donald E. Stokes, *The American Voter*. New York: John Wiley and Sons, Inc., 1960.

_____, *Elections and the Political Order*. New York: John Wiley and Sons, Inc., 1966.

_____, Gerald Gurin, and Warren E. Miller, *The Voter Decides*. Evanston: Row, Peterson, 1954.

Cantril, Hadley, *The Pattern of Human Concerns*. New Brunswick, N.J.: Rutgers University Press, 1965.

Dahl, Robert A., *Who Governs? Democracy and Power in an American City*. New Haven: Yale University Press, 1961.

Eulau, Heinz, Samuel J. Eldersveld, and Morris Janowitz (Eds.), *Political Behavior: A Reader in Theory and Research*. New York: Free Press, 1956.

_____, (Ed.), *Political Behavior in America: New Directions*. New York: Random House, Inc., 1966.

Farrell, R. Barry (Ed.), *Approaches to Comparative and International Politics*. Evanston: Northwestern University Press, 1966.

Free, Lloyd A., and Hadley Cantril, *The Political Beliefs of Americans: a study of public opinion*. New Brunswick, N.J.: Rutgers University Press, 1967.

Greenstein, Fred I., *Children and Politics*. New Haven: Yale University Press, 1965.

Huntington, Samuel P. (Ed.), *Changing Patterns of Military Politics*. New York: Free Press, 1962; Vol. III of the *International Yearbook of Political Behavior Research*.

Hyman, Herbert H., *Political Socialization, a study in the psychology of political behavior*. Glencoe, Ill.: The Free Press, 1959.

Janowitz, Morris (Ed.), *Community Political Systems*. New York: Free Press, 1960; Vol. I of the *International Yearbook of Political Behavior Research*.

Katz, Daniel, Dorwin Cartwright, Samuel Eldersveld, and Alfred McClung Lee (Eds.), *Public Opinion and Propaganda*. New York: Holt, Rinehart and Winston, 1954.

Key, V. O., Jr., *Southern Politics in State and Nation*. New York: Alfred A. Knopf, Inc., 1949.

Lane, Robert E., *Political Ideology: Why the American Common Man Believes What He Does*. New York: Free Press, 1962.*

Lazarsfeld, Paul F., Bernard Berelson, and Hazel Gaudet, *The People's Choice*. New York: Duell, Sloan and Pearce, Inc., 1944.

Marvick, Dwaine (Ed.), *Political Decision-Makers*. New York: Free Press, 1961; Vol. II of the *International Yearbook of Political Behavior Research*.

Rose, Richard (Ed.), *Studies in British Politics: A Reader in Political Sociology*. London: Macmillan Co., 1966.

_____
* Paperback edition available.

Rosenau, James N. (Ed.), *Domestic Sources of Foreign Policy*. New York: Free Press, 1967

_____, (Ed.), *International Politics and Foreign Policy: A Reader in Research and Theory*. New York: Free Press, 1961.

_____, (Ed.), *National Leadership and Foreign Policy: A Case Study in the Mobilization of Public Support*. Princeton: Princeton University Press, 1963.

_____, *Public Opinion and Foreign Policy, an operational formulation*. New York: Random House, 1961.

Ross, H. Laurence (Ed.), *Perspectives on the Social Order*. New York: McGraw-Hill Book Co., Inc., 1963.*

Schubert, Glendon (Ed.), *Judicial Decision-Making*. New York: Free Press, 1963; Vol. IV of the *International Yearbook of Political Behavior Research*.

Singer, J. David (Ed.), *Quantitative International Politics: Insights and Evidence*. New York: Free Press, 1967; Vol. VI of the *International Yearbook of Political Behavior Research*.

Truman, David B., *The Governmental Process*. New York: Alfred A. Knopf, Inc., 1951.

Wahlke, John C., and Heinz Eulau (Eds.), *Legislative Behavior: A Reader in Research and Theory*. New York: Free Press, 1959.

_____, Heinz Eulau, William Buchanan, and Leroy C. Ferguson, *The Legislative System: Explorations in Legislative Behavior*. New York: John Wiley and Sons, Inc., 1962.

7

INDEXES AND SCALING:

Light from the Political Spectrum

With the results of a survey or other quantitative study in hand, we are confronted with the problem of organizing the data in some meaningful way. Tabular presentation may suffice, but in preparing a table we are usually trying to identify or to learn more about some political or social characteristic by examining how it varies in relation to other factors. For this kind of examination you will often need an index or scale—a special measuring instrument with which to measure variation in your data. The survey questionnaire itself may incorporate a scale, but advance planning is necessary.

Indexes and scales abound in modern society. Labor and management dispute over the relation between the cost-of-living index and the index of average wages. Government gears farm price supports to the parity scale. Stock market and commodity prices are reported daily by more than a dozen indexes ranging from the simple to the esoteric. Baseball batting averages, intensity of earthquakes (on the Richter scale), the Weather Bureau's "comfort index" for combined temperature and humidity—these are a few samples of relationship measures which have become a part of daily life.

You have already learned about a few indexes used or suggested for political research. In Chapter 1 we explored the Gini Index of Inequality. In Chapter 2, McClosky's use of a Social Mobility Index was needed for Table 2–9. In Chapter 3 we looked briefly at Landau's Hierarchy Index and Kemeny's Index of a Communicator's Importance. The simple but effective "Support Ratio," used by McClosky in Tables 6–A and 6–B, can be applied to a wide range of attitude questions for which only three answers are suitable (Yes-No-Indifferent; More-Less-Same; Support-Oppose-Neutral). Though not usually so considered, two of the statistics studied in Chapter 5 can be used as indexes—Yule's Q as an index of association and Spearman's rho as an index of rank relationship or of consistency in judging.

7-1 Qualities of a Good Index

A good index should be *valid, reliable, simple,* and *useful.* Of these desirable qualities, the first two relate to the scientific soundness of the index and the others to practical convenience.

By *valid* we mean that the index really measures what it is supposed to measure. Validity is a two-part problem—definition and calibration. "Definition" consists of carefully specifying just what it is we are trying to measure. This is sometimes a simple task. McClosky's Support Ratio, with its three-point scale, was designed to measure the range of respondent attitudes (support, opposition, or neutrality) toward a long list of government policies, so that the problem of definition could be completely solved. More complex properties like political development, authoritarianism, political tolerance, social status, and leadership present correspondingly complex problems of definition rarely solved to everyone's satisfaction. "Calibration"—the second part of the problem of validity—consists of checking the measuring rod for accuracy. Do the marks on its scale really correspond to the variations of the property to which we apply it? It is not often that a completely satisfactory test of validity can be found for a scale of a political or social attribute. Rarely can we correlate changes in the index value with independently measured changes in the attribute. Statements describing validity of a new scale often include such modest phrases as "correspondence with considered judgments of experienced observers," "correlation with well established scales for similar or related characteristics," "known-group method," or simply "face validity." For some factors so general a term as "face validity" is sufficient: the Support Ratio is an example, carrying enough built-in plausibility to convey assurance that it is indeed an accurate instrument for the elementary property being measured.

By *reliable,* we mean that the measuring instrument will produce the same results (the same numbers) when used to measure like variations of the same property over and over again at different times and places. Lack of reliability leads to different results on different runs, as if we had an elastic yardstick, shorter at times and longer at times. Reliability can be tested only by repeated use under the same conditions. Even when this is possible complete confidence rarely can be established for the ordinal scales and indexes most used in political and social research. As with "validity," we must usually be content with less rigorous tests of reliability: the test-retest method for the same group of respondents, or split-half or odd-even correlation of responses to items on one survey.

Simplicity and *usefulness,* the practical qualities of an index, are related. Simplicity usually refers to ease of computation and understanding. To be useful an index must be understandable, yet a complex composite device like the cost-of-living index or farm parity may be readily grasped by a wide public. Over-simplicity in such indexes would impair validity, reliability, and usefulness: if essential items were omitted, they would not measure accurately what it costs the worker to support his family or what the farmer must pay for the things he must buy.

7-2 Kinds of Index Values

Numerical values used for an index are related to the kind of variable being measured. Here you should review the types of data described at the beginning of Chapter 3. As one criterion of a suitable graph you learned to identify *nominal, ordinal,* and *interval* scales. Most sociopolitical indexes and scales are ordinal, often with contrived intervals based on percentage or number of responses of a given type. For such scales we are usually satisfied if a few broad groupings can be distinguished. Use of percentages, ratios, or scores measured in standard deviations may produce an illusion of precision—to the layman, of pointless precision—but such refined measurements are only preliminary devices for establishing broader categories. Just as a teacher may examine and grade his students on several hundred items to produce an eventual sorting into letter grades from A to F, so you may test a respondent's attitude on a hundred public policy items as a basis for classifying him on a three-point scale as Conservative, Moderate, or Liberal.

For the many interval variables relevant to political research—variables which in principle if not always in fact can be counted or measured with fair precision—an index is usually made by translating the raw data into an average or some ratio of unity: of 100 per cent or of 1.00. Literacy is most naturally measured by setting 100 per cent equal to the whole of the population of a given attained age. Time series indexes are usually set with 100 per cent equal to values in a base year—the "last normal year" or a year for which reasonably complete data were first available. Gross national product as an indicator of comparative national economic strength must first be translated into a common unit—usually United States dollars—and then could be indexed as a percentage of the world mean for comparisons among countries. GNP as an indicator of comparative economic development, on the other hand, is best expressed as an average—*GNP per capita* (in turn for international comparisons indexed as a percentage of the world mean). The *per capita* principle is modified for events of rarer occurrence: births and deaths per 1000, students per 100,000, or deaths from domestic violence per 1,000,000.

Weighting. For either interval or ordinal scales, a composite index is usually constructed by weighting its several ingredients according to a judgment of their relative importance. For some composite economic indexes, weighting can be reasonably precise—an ingredient of the cost of living index would be obtained by multiplying the average price of a needed commodity by the average quantity of it purchased or deemed necessary. Weighting of social and political scales is a less certain operation—sometimes done merely to create a significant spread for sorting classes, though usually with some plausible rationale. Such reasonable if admittedly arbitrary weighting of ordinal classes is included in the "Social Participation Scale" developed by F. Stuart Chapin to measure participation in community groups and institutions. A respondent's total score is computed by counting each membership in an organization as 1, attendance at meetings as 2 for each organization attended, financial contributions as 3, each committee membership as 4, and each office held as 5.

7-3 A Simple, Untested Index : Citizen Political Action

The best way to assess general concepts about indexes and scales is to examine a few. We shall look briefly at three scaling instruments, each illustrating a different method of index construction. Our first example is the "Score Card for Citizen Political

Action" used by the League of Women Voters of Pennsylvania. Easy to administer and score, it does not purport to be highly "scientific" in terms of statistical standards of validity and reliability, but it includes most kinds of behavior usually associated with political involvement by citizens not in party leadership positions.

SCORE CARD FOR CITIZEN POLITICAL ACTION

League of Women Voters of Pennsylvania
(*Score one point for each "yes")

VOTING—Did you vote

Once in the last four years? _____
Two to five times? _____
Six or more times? _____

PUBLIC ISSUES—Do you

Inform yourself from more than one source
on public issues? _____
Discuss public issues frequently with more than
one person? _____

INDIVIDUAL ACTION ON PUBLIC ISSUES—Did you

Write or talk to your Congressman or any
other public official—local, state, or national—
to express your views once in the past year? _____
Two or more times? _____

GROUP ACTION ON PUBLIC ISSUES—Do you

Belong to one or more organizations that take
stands on public issues? _____

PRIMARY ELECTION ACTIVITY—Did you

Discuss the qualifications needed for the offices
on the ballot? _____
Work for the nomination of a candidate before
the primary election once in the last four
years? _____

GENERAL OR MUNICIPAL ELECTION ACTIVITY
Did you

Work for the election of a candidate once in
the last four years? _____

FINANCIAL SUPPORT—Did you

Contribute money to a party or candidate once
in the last four years? _____

TOTAL SCORE _____

    * 10–12 points—An outstanding citizen!
       6–9 points—An average citizen.
       5–0 points—A citizen?

Though not formally tested for reliability, the index has considerable built-in "face validity." It reflects knowledgeable definition of the attribute to be measured and supplies an informed calibration device in its unweighted twelve-point scale. The categories established by the specified cutting points are reasonably described, though the scores defining them are arbitrary and technical survey use might result in minor modification. Research with the "Score Card" relating its results to other sociopolitical and demographic variables could well prove valuable.

7-4 A Racial Conservatism Scale

A more refined scaling method is used in Bennett's racial conservatism questionnaire, part of a study of independent voting in Carrolton, Georgia. The five-alternative response pattern is weighted from 1 to 5, but in one direction for "liberal" statements and in the other for "conservative" statements. Thus the racial conservatism score for a respondent is easily obtained by adding the numbers assigned in advance to each response. In the original questionnaire, these items were mixed with forty-two others aimed at testing "general conservatism," so that the respondent would not identify them so clearly as a measure of his racial attitudes.

The scale was developed for a class project, and so had no established validity or reliability except by test-retest results (which were good). It contains several items special to the time and locale of the Carrolton sample, which would be modified in a more general test of racial attitudes (the references to Robert Kennedy, Martin Luther King, Vietnam, Julian Bond*).

RACIAL CONSERVATISM SCALE

THE WEAKEST POINT OF AMERICAN DEMOCRACY IS THE UNJUST TREATMENT OF NEGROES.
Strongly Agree 1 Agree 2 Undecided 3 Disagree 4 Strongly Disagree 5
_____

FEDERAL HOUSING PROJECTS SHOULD BE AVAILABLE TO PERSONS SOLELY ON THE BASIS OF NEED WITHOUT DISCRIMINATION ACCORDING TO RACE.
Strongly Agree 1 Agree 2 Undecided 3 Disagree 4 Strongly Disagree 5
_____

THE BEST WAY TO SOLVE RACIAL PROBLEMS IS TO STICK CLOSE TO THE MIDDLE OF THE ROAD, TO MOVE SLOWLY, AND TO AVOID EXTREMES.
Strongly Agree 5 Agree 4 Undecided 3 Disagree 2 Strongly Disagree 1
_____

WHETHER WE AGREE WITH THEM OR NOT WE MUST ADMIRE PERSONS WHO STAND UP FOR

---

* Julian Bond (a Negro elected to the Georgia legislature and an outspoken critic of the Vietnam policy) was denied his seat and subsequently reinstated by order of the United States Supreme Court. The controversy was current at the time of the survey.

WHAT THEY BELIEVE, SUCH AS GENERAL MAC-ARTHUR, ROBERT KENNEDY, AND DR. MARTIN LUTHER KING.

Strongly Agree 1   Agree 2   Undecided 3   Disagree 4   Strongly Disagree 5

_____

PEACE PICKETS AND RACIAL DEMONSTRATORS SHOULD BE DRAFTED AND SENT TO THE FRONT IN VIETNAM.

Strongly Agree 5   Agree 4   Undecided 3   Disagree 2   Strongly Disagree 1

_____

PERSONS WHO ARE VOCAL IN THEIR VIEWS, SUCH AS JULIAN BOND, SHOULD NOT BE ALLOWED A SEAT IN THE STATE LEGISLATURE.

Strongly Agree 5   Agree 4   Undecided 3   Disagree 2   Strongly Disagree 1

_____

A BUSINESSMAN SHOULD HAVE A RIGHT TO SERVE ONLY THOSE PERSONS HE PLEASES, JUST AS A MANUFACTURER SHOULD BE ALLOWED TO HIRE ONLY THOSE HE CHOOSES.

Strongly Agree 5   Agree 4   Undecided 3   Disagree 2   Strongly Disagree 1

_____

INDIVIDUALS SHOULD BE ELECTED AND APPOINTED TO PUBLIC OFFICE SOLELY ON THE BASIS OF PERSONAL QUALIFICATIONS WITHOUT REGARD TO RACE.

Strongly Agree 1   Agree 2   Undecided 3   Disagree 4   Strongly Disagree 5

_____

FEDERAL AID TO EDUCATION SHOULD BE USED AS A TOOL TO SPEED UP SCHOOL INTEGRATION ON THE LOCAL LEVEL.

Strongly Agree 1   Agree 2   Undecided 3   Disagree 4   Strongly Disagree 5

_____

_____   TOTAL SCORE

The most "liberal" possible score of 9 represents a response weighted 1 on all items; the most "conservative" score of 45 results from a response weighted 5 on all items. Within the maximum range of 37 points, the completely undecided respondent would score 3 on each item for a total of 27, the theoretical mean. How should the 37-point scale provided by this questionnaire be divided into broader categories for tabulation and analysis? Several methods can be used, the choice depending partly on the size of the sample—the problem of empty cells—and partly on how you decide to define "liberal" and "conservative." You could adopt one of three reasonable methods, any of which would serve in a particular project.

(1) You may force a distribution from the actual scores of respondents. Thus, the scale could be dichotomized at the mean score into two equal groups (racial liberals and racial conservatives) or divided by percentiles into any desired number of equal groups. By a more complicated forced distribution you might divide respondents by a rough approximation of statistical normality, in the manner of teachers who "grade on the curve." Thus five groups might be distinguished (Most Liberal, Liberal, Moderate, Conservative, Most Conservative) at the 10, 30, 70, and 90 percentiles of the actual scores arrayed by magnitude. The obvious disadvantage of this method is that it tells you nothing about how your sample compares with the greater universe; it only serves to classify the members of the test group itself.

(2) You may work out your group divisions from the logic of the test instrument. Since the completely undecided respondent would score 27, it is plausible to reason that all scores higher than 27 indicate some degree of racial conservatism and all scores lower some degree of racial liberalism. Other cutting points could be established arbitrarily—in the manner of teachers who have a standard expected performance for a given grade. A more refined approach, corresponding (for a distribution of possible scores rather than actual ones) to grades "on the curve," would be to divide the scale according to random expectation. Instead of dividing your respondents into five groups from "Most Liberal" to "Most Conservative" by their own scores, you would compute random probabilities for each category—as by throwing pentahedronal dice nine times. If you decide on this approach you should consult a statistician to help fix the division points.

(3) You may have available or develop empirically for yourself a standard set of scores. If the test instrument is identical or similar to one which has been used before, previous results will indicate the approximate spread to be expected. Long-established scales (the College Boards, the Minnesota Multiphasic Personality Inventory, the IQ) supply precise measurements which allow you not only to set reasonable groupings for your respondents but also to check their standings against a larger universe.

Short of a standardized pattern, you can approach the same effect by an adequate pre-test of your instrument. Rather than allowing your respondents to fix their own scale (Method 1), or depending entirely on your own best judgment (Method 2), you can estimate the expected distribution by giving the test to a small sample in advance. You can then establish approximate dividing points on the basis of this smaller but actual set of answers. If the pre-test is given to even as few as ten persons you will still obtain some idea of how the categories may divide.

In practice, you may hit on some combination of the three approaches. For his racial conservatism scale, Bennett's pre-test indicated that his items and scoring system would probably result in a reasonable spread above and below the theoretical mean, and so he decided to fix 27 as the tentative dividing point. For his sample of Carroltonians the range was from 13 to 40 and the actual mean turned out to be 27.3. Wishing only a simple breakdown, he classified those with scores over 27 as "conservative," and those with scores under 27 as "liberal," retaining in the "moderate" group only the small number of respondents who scored exactly 27.

7-5 A Social Distance Scale

A third technique of scaling is illustrated by the widely used Social Distance Scale developed by Bogardus to measure degree of social acceptance between persons or groups.* With variations it has been used in research on political attitudes in England, Russia, and the Philippines; on social distance between China and Japan, Latin America and the United States, Negroes and whites, Hindus and Moslems, lawyers and doctors; and for the study of

---

* Emory S. Bogardus, *Social Distance* (Yellow Springs, Ohio: Antioch Press, 1959).

conflict and acceptance in a great variety of other national ethnic, occupational, religious, and political groups. Deceptively simple, easy to administer and score, it is a highly refined and strongly validated instrument for the investigation of many patterns of conflict and cooperation, readily modified for a specific study.

Only one form of the Bogardus scale and one scoring method are shown here: an application to measurements of "racial distance." The respondent is asked to check each "race" or ethnic group in as many of the seven rows as his feelings dictate. A check in any of the first six rows indicates that he would accept members of that group in the role specified. The negatively stated seventh item, "would exclude from my country," is checked only if the respondent rejects the first six relationships and so has made no other marks in the column.

The last line, for entering the respondent's scores, does not appear on the printed form given the respondent; it is added here to show the simplest scoring method, found as reliable as any. From the scores entered by a group of respondents for a given ethnic group, a Racial Distance Quotient is computed as the arithmetic mean of the lowest numbers marked. If from a sample of 100 Americans, 77 indicated acceptance of the English to close kinship by marriage, the scorer would enter a "1" for each at the bottom of the column headed "English." If the remaining 23 did not indicate acceptance of the English to kinship by marriage, but did mark the second category,

BOGARDUS RACIAL DISTANCE SCALE

Category (Acceptance)	English	Swedes	Poles	Koreans	Etc.
1. To close kinship by marriage					
2. To my club as personal chums					
3. To my street as neighbors					
4. To employment in my occupation					
5. To citizenship in my country					
6. As visitors only to my country					
7. Would exclude from my country					
Lowest Number Marked					

acceptance "to my club as personal chums," the scorer would enter a "2." The Racial Distance Quotient for this sample's acceptance of the English would be:

$$RDQ = \big((1 \times 77) + (2 \times 23)\big)/100$$
$$= (77 + 46)/100 = 1.23$$

The value 1.23 for racial distance between Americans and English is the actual value resulting from a broad sample of Americans ($N = 2053$) in 1956.

Another form of the Racial Distance Quotient measures the respondents themselves. When a respondent scores the English, Swedes, Poles, and Koreans, he is also scoring himself. By taking the arithmetic mean of his scores for all the groups, we obtain his personal Racial Distance Quotient as a measure of his overall racial position. The mean of personal quotients for a sample of 100 measures the position of the sample. A quotient based on a listing of all significant subgroups could then be used as a sort of tension index for the whole society. The 1956 survey of 2053 Americans included a listing of 30 ethnic groups, the mean of all reactions (61,590 scores) being 2.08. This value, then, is a Racial Distance Quotient for the generalized American attitude toward ethnic groups. On the average, Americans would accept foreigners as neighbors, but would (barely) draw the line at accepting them as personal friends.

7-6 Guttman Scaling

The underlying principle of the Bogardus scale was developed by Louis Guttman, and scales incorporating this pattern of sequential increase in intensity of an attitude are called Guttman scales. They have many applications in social and political research. Guttman's basic idea is that for any single attitude pattern which varies in intensity, it should be possible to establish an ordered series of verbal statements ranging from the weakest to the strongest expression of the attitude. Agreement with the strongest statement in such a series should imply agreement with all the weaker statements; agreement with any statement should imply agreement with any others of less intensity. In the Bogardus social distance scale, the assumption is that acceptance to close kinship by marriage represents the "closest" social distance. If a respondent checks this item, he would presumably be willing to accept the same persons in the less intimate relationships of his club, his neighborhood, his occupation, and his country. Willingness to accept a foreigner to citizenship, on the other hand, would not imply acceptance to the closer relationships listed above Item 5, though it should imply acceptance of the same foreigner as a visitor to the country.

An important condition of a satisfactory Guttman scale is that the attitude being measured must truly be a single factor. If it is a composite of inconsistent and sometimes conflicting factors, a scaled set of questions to measure it will probably fail. Adequate validation of a Guttman scale includes a major test for *unidimensionality,* the term describing this condition. As with other "failures" in quantitative research, the failure of a Guttman scale may provide important information—that an attitude pattern previously thought to be a single identifiable factor is not that simple, but a complex combination of several interacting variables.

A physical parallel to Guttman scaling often used to illuminate the basic principle will be helpful here. If you have a handful of rods of different lengths and no measuring instrument you cannot say how long any rod actually is in any metric scale, but you can say that any one of them is longer or shorter than any other. You can go further—you can arrange the rods in an ordered array by length and then use this array to classify other rods. Any new rod will fall into one of the previously scaled classes. Thus without knowing anything about absolute metric values of length you still have a useful sorting device—an ordinal scale for ranking the length of rods. With rods, you can visually sort, and the scale based on the array carries its "face validity" without inconsistency. With abstract behavior qualities you cannot be so sure, but Guttman also provides the built-in reliability test of unidimensionality. If the scaled set of items does not elicit an ordered set of responses, you know that the measuring instrument is not measuring—that the attitude or other variable under examination is not what you thought it was. It is as if you were using your scaled set of rods to measure the age of your friends: a rough relationship will prevail for ages 1 to 20, but it will be clear with a large sample that other factors are at work. So too an attitudinal scale of questions meant to measure aggressiveness, cooperation, conservatism, authoritarianism, or hostility will probably turn up a considerable number of "inconsistencies," or responses not in logical order, indicating that more than one influence is affecting the answers.

If the inconsistencies are not too numerous, if your scaled set of questions or statements seems to prove out for several runs, you may cautiously begin to believe that it indeed taps a basic identifiable variable of human behavior. If with careful checking of validity and reliability it remains consistent for many groups of respondents in many times and places, as does the Bogardus scale, you may safely shout a soft "Eureka!" You have discovered a way to measure something hitherto unmeasureable. Guttman's powerful technique, when it works, answers the social scientist's persistent problem of the unmarked yardstick.

7-7 Scaling Roll-Calls

Although originally designed for questionnaires in psychological testing, the Guttman scaling technique has been successfully applied to a variety of political research projects involving the analysis of roll-calls in legislative bodies, sets of judicial decisions by plural member courts, and votes in international assemblies (particularly the United Nations). When used for such analyses, the original psychologist's technique is "turned around." Instead of writing and testing a set of questions as a measuring instrument, the political analyst considers the bills, cases, or resolutions to constitute a set of questions to which the congressmen, judges, or UN delegates have been asked to respond. He seeks to determine from the actual recorded responses whether a scaled grouping of the members or issues exists.

Guttman Criteria. Although the original criteria of scalability outlined by Guttman were intended as standards for a scale designed by the psychological researcher himself, they are commonly applied to roll-call analysis as well, though sometimes less rigorous standards are considered reasonable, as still yielding meaningful results. In part they are arbitrary, in part basic.

1. *Unidimensionality, or consistency of the scale.* If the set of scaled questions (or votes) yields too many inconsistencies or "errors," the scale is useless. The difficulty arises in deciding how many is "too many." Guttman felt it permissible to allow one "error" in ten responses, and the usual measure of acceptability of the entire scaled set is called the *Coefficient of Reproducibility:*

$$\text{CR} = 1.00 - (e/r)$$

Where: e = errors

r = responses

By this standard, the scale would be deemed unsatisfactory if the value of the coefficient of reproducibility falls below .90. Values of the coefficient range from zero to $+1.00$; it cannot be negative. A minimally acceptable scaled set of ten questions put to 100 respondents would elicit 1000 responses, of which no more than 100 should be "errors":

$$\text{CR} = 1.00 - (100/1000) = 1.00 - .10 = .90$$

2. *One-sidedness.* A set of scaled responses must not be too one-sided. It is usual to omit roll-calls, for example, unless at least 20 per cent voted against the majority. A set of scaled roll-call votes should also include some on which the split was close to 50–50. A minimal standard is that there should be no items on the scale to which responses are unanimous. The reason for this standard is inherent in the concept of the Guttman scale as a measuring device. If respondents are unanimous on an item, we have no information as to how they are divided, so the item is meaningless. A parallel example for an identification item would be "Are you a human being?" Aside from the omission of unanimous response items, the cutting point depends on the investigator, who may wish as detailed a scale as the data permit or who may be satisfied with fairly broad groupings.

The principle of including some items on which the split is close to 50–50 is also an aspect of the scale's usefulness as a measuring instrument. The more clearly identifiable distinct "steps" or cutting points in the scale, the more completely the scale measures the attitudinal universe involved. The concept is similar to that of having enough marked subdivisions on a yardstick or other metric instrument to make it useful.

3. *Error Distribution.* Within the 10 per cent tolerance of error, the errors should not be concentrated on one item, or even a small number of items. Such concentration suggests the item (the question or roll-call) should be omitted—it is probably not measuring the attitude the scale is meant to measure. In the selection of roll-calls, court cases, or United Nations votes, for a scaled set, some analysts have found it useful to apply Yule's Q test to successive pairs of votes, in the pattern described in Chapter 5, Section 5-5. Though the Q test is deficient as a statistical test in that no precise probability can be attached to its value, it has several features which make it useful for identifying scalable items: (1) a value of $+1.00$ indicates a perfectly scalable pair of items; (2) a value of -1.00 also indicates a perfectly scalable pair of items and shows by the negative sign that a "No" vote on Item 2 is associated with a "Yes" vote on Item 1; (3) some idea of the proportion of

inconsistencies or "errors" is yielded by the extent to which the Q value falls below its maximum.

Duncan MacRae has used the Q statistic to scale roll-calls in Congress and finds on the basis of empirical work that a Q value of about .80 will yield scalable sets of roll-calls even without preliminary identification of issue groupings by the investigator. The procedure consists of computing the Q value of *all pairs* of roll-calls, and arbitrarily including as scalable the set of roll-calls in which all possible pairs have a Q value of .8 or higher.

4. *Number of Scaled Items.* The larger the number of items in a scaled set of questions or roll-calls, the more satisfactory the resulting scale. Guttman fixed a minimum of ten items, but this standard applied to the construction of psychological test questions. In analysis of court decisions and roll-calls the investigator may often have a scalable set of fewer items which nevertheless is consistent with his other information as well as with the other Guttman criteria, and the result of his research may still be useful.

5. *Items with Identical Response Patterns.* If the group of respondents is large, it is unlikely that response patterns will be identical for any pair of questions, but this may very well occur for small groups—for example in a scaled set of Supreme

Court decisions. While a display of these identical responses may be desirable in a particular research report, it should be clear that the two items represent a single step on the scaled set. Retaining such a pair of items is comparable to placing two marks on a yardstick at the very same place.

7-8 An Example from Senate Roll-Calls

Some of the procedural problems encountered in scaling a set of roll-calls may be demonstrated by using a small sample, since any large number of scaled items or respondents requires repeated computations best handled by a computer. From the U.S. Senate roll-calls in the 1965 session, the *Congressional Quarterly* identified six key votes on Medicare, Voting Rights, and Education, and we shall use these with a selected sample of ten senators.

Each of these six roll-calls might fit into a variety of attitudinal scales, but all six may be identified as belonging to a common universe—pro-administration or anti-administration—since the President took a position on all of them. The votes and the translation into administration support are given in Table 7-1.

To this point we have simply assembled the raw data on the six roll-calls, without knowing whether

TABLE 7-1. *Administration Support-Record of Ten Senators, 1965.*

Votes of Ten Selected Senators							Same Votes as Pro- or Anti-President						
	1	2	3	4	5	6	1	2	3	4	5	6	Total
Sparkman (Ala.)	Y	N	Y	N	N	N	+	+	+	+	−	−	4
Murphy (Calif.)	N	Y	N	N	N	Y	−	−	−	+	−	+	2
Talmadge (Ga.)	Y	N	Y	N	N	N	+	+	+	+	−	−	4
Fong (Hawaii)	Y	N	Y	Y	Y	Y	+	+	+	−	+	+	5
Tydings (Md.)	Y	N	Y	Y	Y	Y	+	+	+	−	+	+	5
Kennedy (Mass.)	Y	N	Y	Y	Y	Y	+	+	+	−	+	+	5
Montoya (N.M.)	Y	N	Y	N	Y	Y	+	+	+	+	+	+	6
Morse (Ore.)	Y	N	Y	Y	Y	Y	+	+	+	−	+	+	5
Pastore (R.I.)	Y	N	Y	Y	Y	Y	+	+	+	−	+	+	5
Tower (Tex.)	N	Y	N	N	N	N	−	−	−	+	−	−	1
Total +							8	8	8	5	6	7	

Roll-Call	President's Position
1. Education Act of 1965	Yea
2. Curtis Amendment to make Medicare optional	Nay
3. Medicare	Yea
4. Kennedy Amendment to abolish poll tax in Voting Rights Act	Nay
5. Cloture of debate on Voting Rights Act	Yea
6. Voting Rights Act of 1965	Yea

they will scale. For our next step we have two choices: (1) We can reorganize the order of both roll-calls and senators on the assumption that a scaled set is involved, or (2) we can use MacRae's device of Q testing all pairs of roll-calls to determine which items will scale. The Q test procedure would be required for any considerable number of roll-calls about which we had no special information. In this case we have the single point of information on presidential support. We will therefore illustrate the first process, and then use the Q test procedure as confirmation.

Step 1. Reorder the Array. If the items indeed scale, it is a good working hypothesis that both roll-calls and senators will be ordered according to their marginal totals of support. These are entered in the right-hand portion of the table. The roll-calls range from Number 3, which "carried" by 8 to 2, to roll-call 4, on which our sample of ten senators was divided 5 to 5. The senators range from Montoya, who supported the President's position on all six items (6–0), to Tower, whose record is 1–5. Carrying out the rearrangement called for, we obtain the array of Table 7–2.

Alternative Procedure: Compute the Q-Matrix. Since this set of "responses" contains 6×10 entries, or 60 in all, and has only five "errors" in the Guttman sense of inconsistent responses, the coef-

TABLE 7-2. *Senators and Roll-Calls Arrayed by Support Totals ("errors" shown in parentheses)*

	1	2	3	6	5	4
Montoya	+	+	+	+	+	+
Morse	+	+	+	+	+	−
Fong	+	+	+	+	+	−
Tydings	+	+	+	+	+	−
Pastore	+	+	+	+	+	−
Kennedy	+	+	+	+	+	−
Sparkman	+	+	+	−	−	(+)
Talmadge	+	+	+	−	−	(+)
Murphy	−	−	−	(+)	−	(+)
Tower	−	−	−	−	−	(+)

ficient of reproducibility meets the minimum standard (CR = $1.00 - 5/60$ = .92). However, we note that almost all the errors are concentrated on a single item, roll-call 4. We could simply eliminate this item and retain the others, but to illustrate the more complete procedure suggested by MacRae, we compute the Q value for each pair of roll-calls in Table 7–3.

The Q values computed in this way tell us several things. First, there is a cluster of five roll-calls (Nos. 1, 2, 3, 5, and 4) on which the voting was perfectly associated—these roll-calls will scale without error. MacRae permits a Q minimum of .80 for analysis

TABLE 7-3. *Worksheet for Computation of Q Values for Paired Roll-Calls*

	Roll-call 2 + −	Roll-call 3 + −	Roll-call 6 + −	Roll-call 5 + −	Roll-call 4 + −
Roll-call 1 +	8 0	8 0	6 2	6 2	3 5
−	0 2	0 2	1 1	0 2	2 0
Q =	1.00	1.00	.50	1.00	−1.00
Roll-call 2 +		8 0	6 2	6 2	3 5
−		0 2	1 1	0 2	2 0
Q =		1.00	.50	1.00	−1.00
Roll-call 3 +			6 2	6 2	3 5
−			1 1	0 2	2 0
Q =			.50	1.00	−1.00
Roll-call 6 +				6 1	2 5
−				0 3	3 0
Q =				1.00	−1.00
Roll-call 5 +					1 5
−					4 0
Q =					−1.00

of large numbers of roll-calls. Second, on roll-call 4 the association was negative: those supporting the President on other issues opposed him on this one. In our final array we should reverse the signs for this roll-call. Third, roll-call 6 is not sufficiently associated with the others to be included with them in a scaled set. Fourth, roll-call 6 is, however, perfectly associated with roll-calls 5 and 4: these three constitute a second, partly overlapping cluster. We realize the great power of MacRae's method when we reflect that all these conclusions are drawn from the raw data alone, without any political information about the roll-calls. Although we knew the President's position on each, we did not use this knowledge in the derivation of the Q values.

Results of the computations should be summarized for convenience in a matrix of Q values, which will serve to identify issue-clusters (issues on which the voting pattern was very nearly the same). In our example, we reverse the sign for roll-call 4, and display the results in Table 7–4.

TABLE 7-4. *Matrix of Q Values for Six Senate Roll-Calls*

Roll-Call	2	3	6	5	4
1	100	100	50	100	100
2		100	50	100	100
3			50	100	100
6				100	100
5					100

Step 2. Voting Array Based on the Q-Matrix. After identifying probable issue-clusters, it is time to take stock of any political information we have about the roll-calls. The first cluster we have identified (roll-calls 1, 2, 3, 5, and 4) includes votes on the Education Act, Medicare, Cloture of the Voting Rights debate, and the Kennedy Poll Tax Amendment. The second cluster includes the Voting Rights Act itself, Cloture of debate on it, and the Kennedy Poll Tax Amendment. The reason we found perfect but negative association of the other items with roll-call 4 (the Kennedy Amendment) is that liberals generally supported it, southerners and conservatives generally opposed it, while the President's position was determined by organizational considerations—his opposition was a maneuver calculated to build consensus sufficiently to obtain cloture of debate (which was invoked May 25, by a vote of 70–30, with all 100 senators present and 67 "yea" votes needed).

Using this added information, we can reconstruct our original array with some hope that meaningful voting blocs of senators will emerge. Actually, there are only two changes: the reversal of signs for the Kennedy Amendment, and a shift in position for Montoya, who supported the President's organizational maneuver on the Kennedy Amendment and so had a perfect 6–0 record on the presidential support array. We might consider the revised array to constitute a "pure" liberal-conservative scale, and tentatively classify the senators in the groups listed at the right in Table 7–5.

In the final revision of our scale, the only inconsistency is Senator Murphy's vote for final passage of the Voting Rights Act (roll-call 6). We also see more clearly why this roll-call did not have a high Q value with the "liberal" cluster, inconsistencies

TABLE 7-5. *A Tentative Liberal-Conservative Scale*

	1	2	3	6	5	4	Bloc
Morse	+	+	+	+	+	+	
Fong	+	+	+	+	+	+	
Tydings	+	+	+	+	+	+	Northern Liberals
Pastore	+	+	+	+	+	+	
Kennedy	+	+	+	+	+	+	
Montoya	+	+	+	+	+	−	Administration Liberals
Sparkman	+	+	+	−	−	−	Southern Democrats (Liberal on Welfare, Conservative on Race)
Talmadge	+	+	+	−	−	−	
Murphy	−	−		−	(+)	−	−	Northern Conservatives (Sometimes Liberal on Race)
Tower	−	−		−	−	−	−	Southern Conservatives (Liberal on Nothing)

arising from the regional-directed votes of Senators Sparkman and Talmadge as well as from Murphy's single "liberal" vote.

7-9 Cluster Analysis and Scale Analysis

The use of the Q-matrix has actually served three purposes: identification of issue-clusters, identification of voting-bloc clusters of senators, and identification of a scale of items which will roughly measure the conservative-liberal continuum. At this point we should recall the Guttman scaling principle regarding items with identical response patterns. In our final array, the first three roll-calls may as well be collapsed into one, if our only objective is to find a scale: all ten senators voted consistently for or against all three issues. There is some variation on all the other items. For use as a scale, the array could be abbreviated by using only the portion to the right of the vertical line: the scaled steps which are the basis of the bloc classifications all appear in this portion of the table.

On the other hand, if we are primarily interested in measurement of closeness of association within voting blocs, we will retain all the roll-calls. The Q test having resulted in sorting out the major groupings, we can proceed readily with the construction of a matrix of all voting pairs, entering in each cell the percentage of times the two members voted together (Table 7-6).

Index of Interagreement. The decision is up to the researcher as to how much agreement should exist among members of a group to justify calling it a voting bloc. One simple measure on which to base the decision is the Index of Interagreement, which is the arithmetic average of the agreement percentages of all pairs of voters in the bloc. In our example, the index is obviously 100 for two blocs: (1) the "Northern Liberals"—Morse, Fong, Tydings, Pastore, and Kennedy; and (2) the "Southern Democrats"—Sparkman and Talmadge. If we add Montoya to the "Northern Liberals," the index works out as 94.3, still a high degree of agreement:

$$\text{Index of Interagreement} = 1415/15 = 94.3$$

If we place Montoya instead with the Sparkman-Talmadge bloc, we obtain an index of 234/3 or 78.0. The usual standard is to insist on an index of 80 both for the group as a whole and for all pairs within it. On this basis we would include Montoya with the liberals, and could also consider that Murphy and Tower (as well as Sparkman and Talmadge) constituted a bloc of two.

Index of Cohesion. A second measure of agreement within a voting bloc is Rice's Index of Cohesion, which is based on the extent to which the bloc's voting deviates from a 50–50 split. Its value varies from zero at the 50 per cent level (the assumption being that a 50–50 division is the most probable random voting result) to 1.00 if all in the bloc vote together ("Yea" or "Nay"). For example, if the votes of a given group are either 30 or 70 per cent "Yea," the Index of Cohesion is .40, since both 30 and 70 percent are 20 percentage points away from 50 per cent. In the group of ten senators of our example, cohesion of the entire group on the six roll-calls is shown in Table 7–7.

TABLE 7-7. *Cohesion of Ten Senators on Six Roll-Calls*

Roll-call	1	2	3	4	5	6	All
Per cent "Yea"	80	80	80	70	60	50	70
Index of Cohesion	.60	.60	.60	.40	.20	0.0	.40

TABLE 7-6. *Matrix of Voting Pairs*

	Fong	Tydings	Pastore	Kennedy	Montoya	Sparkman	Talmadge	Murphy	Tower
Morse	100	100	100	100	83	50	50	17	0
Fong		100	100	100	83	50	50	17	0
Tydings			100	100	83	50	50	17	0
Pastore				100	83	50	50	17	0
Kennedy					83	50	50	17	0
Montoya						67	67	33	17
Sparkman							100	33	50
Talmadge								33	50
Murphy									83

Index of Likeness. To compare two groups, Rice proposes the Index of Likeness, which has a maximum value of 1.00 if the two groups vote exactly alike, and is zero if they vote exactly opposite. Ranges between these extremes are computed by taking the difference between the two blocs' affirmative voting percentages and subtracting this difference from 1.00. In our example, the Sparkman-Talmadge bloc had a presidential support score of 67 per cent, the Murphy-Tower bloc a score of 25 per cent, so the Index of Likeness for these two blocs is:

$$\text{Index of Likeness} = 1.00 - (.67 - .25) = .58$$

7-10 Other Applications

Extensive use has been made of scaling and cluster bloc analysis for judicial decisions and international bodies. The exhibits in Tables 7–8 and 7–9 illustrate

TABLE 7-8. *Scalogram Analysis of Non-Unanimous Civil Liberties Cases, U.S. Supreme Court, 1959 Term*

Cases \ Justices	Douglas	Black	Warren	Brennan	Stewart	Frankfurter	Harlan	Whittaker	Clark	Vote +	Vote −
Smith *v.* California	+	+	+	+	+	+	−	+	+	8	1
Kinsella *v.* United States	+	+	+	+	+	−	−	+	+	7	2
Henry *v.* United States	+	+	−	+	+	+	+	+	−	6	3
Hudson *v.* North Carolina	+	+	+	+	+	+	+	−	−	7	2
Grisham *v.* Hagen	+	+	+	+	−	+	+	−	+	7	2
Mackey *v.* Mendoza	+	+	+	+	+	+	−	−	−	6	3
Talley *v.* California	+	+	+	+	+	−	+	−	−	6	3
Rios *v.* United States	+	+	+	+	+	−	−	−	−	5	4
Elkins *v.* United States	+	+	+	+	+	−	−	−	−	5	4
Ohio *v.* Price	+	+	+	+	np	−	−	−	−	4	4
McElroy *v.* United States	+	+	+	+	−	−	−	−	+	5	4
Abel *v.* United States	+	+	+	+	−	−	−	−	−	4	5
Niukkanen *v.* McAlexander	+	+	+	+	−	−	−	−	−	4	5
Parker *v.* Ellis	+	+	+	+	−	−	−	−	−	4	5
Flemming *v.* Nestor	+	+	+	+	−	−	−	−	−	4	5
Wolfe *v.* North Carolina	+	+	+	+	−	−	−	−	−	4	5
Gonzales *v.* United States	+	+	+	+	−	−	−	−	−	4	5
Nelson *v.* Los Angeles	+	+	np	+	−	−	−	−	−	3	5
Kimm *v.* Rosenberg	+	+	+	+	−	−	−	−	−	4	5
Levine *v.* United States	+	+	+	+	−	−	−	−	−	4	5
Wyatt *v.* United States	+	+	+	−	−	−	−	−	−	3	6
Nostrand *v.* Little	+	+	−	−	−	−	−	−	−	2	7
Hannah *v.* Larche	+	+	−	−	−	−	−	−	−	2	7
McGann *v.* United States	+	−	−	−	−	−	−	−	−	1	8

	Douglas	Black	Warren	Brennan	Stewart	Frankfurter	Harlan	Whittaker	Clark	Total
Participations	24	24	23	24	23	24	24	24	24	214
Inconsistencies			1		1	1	3		2	8
Scale Score	24	23	21	20	9	6	5	3	2	
Scale Score as % of first	100	96	87.5	83.5	37.5	25	20.4	12.5	8.3	

Coefficient of Reproducibility $= 1 - 8/214 = .963$

Legend:

    + = for the civil liberty claim

    − = against the civil liberty claim

    np = non-participation

Source: S. Sidney Ulmer, "Scaling Judicial Cases: A Methodological Note," *American Behavioral Scientist,* Vol. 4, No. 8, April 1961, page 32. Reprinted with the kind permission of the author and publisher.

TABLE 7-9. *Scalogram of Colonial Questions in General Assembly, 1956–1957*

	1	2	3	4	5	6	7	8
Italy	+	+	+	+	A	+	+	+
S. Africa				+		+	+	+
UK-Fr-Aus-B-L-P*	+	+	+	+	+	+	+	A
Neth-NZ	+	+	+	+		+	A	A
Dom Rep	+	+	+	+	A	+	A	A
Finland	+	+	+	A	A	+	A	A
Turkey	+	+	+	A	A	A	A	A
Nor-Den-Swdn	+	+	+	+	+	+	−	−
Israel-China	+	+	+	+	A	+	−	−
Iceland	+	+		+		+	−	−
Chile	+	+	(−)	A	A	+	−	−
Canada	+	+	+	+	+	A	−	−
US	+	+	+	A	+	A	−	−
Hond-Nicaragua	+	A	+	+	A	A	−	−
Peru-Austria	+	+	+	+	A	A	−	−
Ireland	+	+	+	+	+		−	−
Cuba	+	+	+	+	A		−	−
Brazil	+	+	+	+	A	A	−	−
Colombia	+	+	+	A		A	A	−
Spain	+	+	+	A	A	−	A	A
Paraguay	+	+	+	A	−	A	−	−
Argentina-Venezuela	+	+	A	A	−	−	−	−
Ecuador		+	+	−	−	−	−	
Pakistan	+	+	+	−	−	−	−	
Philippines	+	+	+	−	−	−	−	
Ceylon	+	(−)	+	−	−	−	−	
Thailand	+	+	A	−	−	−	−	
Cambodia	+	A	A	A	−	−	−	
Panama	+		A	−	−	−		
Uruguay-Bolivia	+	A	−	−	−	−	−	
Costa Rica	+	A	−	−	−	A		
Liberia	+	−	−	−	−	A		
Ethiopia-Tunisia	+	−	−	−				
Laos	+	−	−	−				
Mexico	+	−	−	A				
El Sal-Gua-H-G**	+	−	−	−	−	−	−	
Lebanon	A	A	A	A	A	−	−	−
Burma-I-I-N#	A	−	−	−	−	−	−	
Morocco	A	−	−		−	−	−	
Afghanistan	A	−	−		−	−	−	
Hungary						−	−	−
Jordan	−				−	−	−	−
Arab-Sov##	−	−	−	−	−	−	−	

+ = procolonial, − = anticolonial, A = abstention, no entry = no vote, ( ) = inconsistency.

* UK, France, Australia, Belgium, Luxembourg, and Portugal.

** El Salvador, Guatemala, Haiti, Greece.

Burma, India, Indonesia, Nepal.

Egypt, Iran, Iraq, Libya, Saudi Arabia, Sudan, Syria, Yeman, Albania, Bulgaria, Byelorussia, Czechoslovakia, Poland, Rumania, Ukraine, USSR, Yugoslavia.

Source: Adapted from Leroy N. Rieselbach, "Quantitative Techniques for Studying Voting Behavior in the UN General Assembly," *International Organization,* Spring 1960, pp. 300–301, with the kind permission of the author and publisher.

TABLE 7-10. *Voting Agreement Matrix for Sixteen Selected States on Colonial Issues in the United Nations General Assembly, 1956–1957*

	It	Fr	NZ	Sw	Can	Pe	Br	Vn	Th	Bo	Mx	Lbn	Mo	Eg	Su	USSR
Italy	—	75	62	62	50	62	62	25	25	12	12	12	0	0	0	0
France	75	—	75	75	62	50	50	25	25	12	12	0	0	0	0	0
New Z.	62	75	—	62	50	50	50	25	25	12	12	0	0	0	0	0
Sweden	62	75	62	—	87	75	75	50	50	37	37	25	25	25	25	25
Canada	50	62	50	87	—	87	87	50	50	37	37	25	25	25	25	25
Peru	62	50	50	75	87	—	100	50	50	37	37	37	25	25	25	25
Brazil	62	50	50	75	87	100	—	50	50	37	37	37	25	25	25	25
Venezuela	25	25	25	50	50	50	50	—	87	62	75	62	37	50	50	50
Thailand	25	25	25	50	50	50	50	87	—	75	62	50	50	62	62	62
Bolivia	25	25	25	37	37	37	37	62	75	—	75	50	62	75	75	75
Mexico	25	25	25	37	37	37	37	75	62	75	—	50	62	75	75	75
Lebanon	25	0	0	25	25	37	37	62	50	50	50	—	50	37	37	37
Morocco	0	0	0	25	25	25	25	37	62	50	50	50	—	75	75	75
Egypt	0	0	0	25	25	25	25	50	62	75	75	37	75	—	100	100
Sudan	0	0	0	25	25	25	25	50	62	75	75	37	75	100	—	100
USSR	0	0	0	25	25	25	25	50	62	75	75	37	75	100	100	—

only two of the numerous research studies of this type. The scalogram of Supreme Court civil liberties cases is by Sidney Ulmer, and the study of General Assembly colonial issues is by L.N. Rieselbach.

Ulmer's scale ranges from "most liberal" to "least liberal," and as with our example of senators on the administration support scale, the array which results serves to identify both justices and cases as occupying some determinable position on the scale. In Table 7–8, Ulmer has computed a scale score for the justices —they range from Justice Douglas (100 per cent "liberal") to Justice Clark (8.3 per cent). He also supplies the vote division for each case, with which we could classify the cases into groups ranging from those in which the civil liberty claim is least likely to be rejected (Smith *v.* California) to those in which the civil liberty claim would be defended only by the most liberal justice (McGann *v.* United States). Notice the large group of thirteen cases—more than half the total—decided by a vote of 5–4, 4–4, or 5–3.

Rieselbach's scale in Table 7–9 ranges from "most colonial" to "most anti-colonial," and is based on the eight colonial issues which came to a vote in the General Assembly in the 1957–1958 session. The numbers at the top of each column refer to these eight issues:

1. Approval of French accomplishments in Togoland.
2. Resolution to define a request for information on non-self-governing territories as an "important question" requiring a two-thirds vote.

3. Creation of an ad hoc committee to examine information on non-self-governing territories.
4. Maintenance of the status quo in West Irian pending a Dutch-Indonesian agreement.
5. Request that trust powers submit estimates of time required for their trust territories to become independent.
6. Resolution to place the West Irian dispute on the agenda.
7. Race conflict in South Africa.
8. Treatment of Indians in South Africa.

The idea of the Guttman scale as applied to these eight votes is that only the most die-hard colonial power (or South Africa, of course, when present) would vote against consideration of Item 8, while only the most doctrinaire anti-colonialists would be unwilling to give France some credit for trying to do well in Togoland.

Rieselbach's scalogram is also the basis for the voting agreement matrix in Table 7–10, constructed in the same manner as the one for our ten senators in Table 7–6. The sixteen states were selected at random from the list of United Nations members, but Italy and the USSR were included deliberately to represent the two extremes identified by Rieselbach. Boxes have been drawn on the matrix to show clusters with a high index of likeness and a very low index of likeness.

In this chapter we have explored scaling from two contrasting viewpoints—as a technique in questionnaire construction and as a method for roll-call analysis. The research task is quite different in the two approaches. In working out a scaled set of questions, the emphasis is on conceptualization in the substantive theory of the subject *before* you write the questions. In roll-call analysis, the need for grounding in theory is no less, but arises at a later stage in the project—*after* you have identified scaled groupings by mechanical sorting of the data. The original Guttman technique has been reversed. Instead of putting questions to the legislators or justices, we consider the bills or cases on which they have made decisions to constitute the scaled questionnaire, and our job is to discover which set of bills or cases actually fit the concept. Once a scaled set has been identified, its usefulness in political theory will depend largely on sophisticated interpretation of the political processes at work.

Exercise Set 7. Can You Find a Scaled Set?

7-1 The roll-calls for this exercise are drawn from a group selected by the Congressional Quarterly Staff and the League of Women Voters of the United States as "strategic votes on key issues" in the first session of the 90th Congress (January 10 to August 10, 1967, prior to the late summer recess). A random sample of 32 members of the House of Representatives was drawn, and the votes of each on the six roll-calls are given in the table. The Administration had a position on all six issues, so that an "Administration Support Score" can be calculated for each congressman. You are asked to:

(1) Translate the votes into +'s and −'s, to indicate support for or opposition to the Administration position, following the pattern of Table 7–1.

(2) After summing the rows and columns for support totals, rearrange the congressmen and the roll-calls in a scalogram array similar to that of Table 7–2. This work will be simplified by grouping the fourteen congressmen with support scores of 6 and the seven with support scores of zero. Of the eleven remaining congressmen, six have "consistent" voting patterns and five have "inconsistent" patterns. We define a "consistent" pattern by the criterion of Guttman unidimensionality as one of the following:

	Support Score
+ + + + + +	6
+ + + + + −	5
+ + + + − −	4
+ + + − − −	3
+ + − − − −	2
+ − − − − −	1
− − − − − −	0

Scale errors will be minimized by grouping congressmen with the same support score and working toward the "middle" of the scale (the "+++−−−" pattern for this array) *from each end*. For each group with the same support score, list first those with "inconsistent" voting patterns, then those with consistent patterns. Thus in this exercise if you find two congressmen with a support score of 4, you would list first the inconsistent

Number	Roll-Call	Administration Position	Vote in House of Representatives	
			Yea	Nay
1	Appropriation for Department of Housing and Urban Development (delete rent supplements)	Nay	233	171
2	Same (delete urban renewal in model cities projects)	Nay	193	213
3	Food Stamp Program (amendment requiring states to pay 20 per cent of cost)	Nay	173	191
4	Teacher Corps (recommit and strike)	Nay	146	257
5	Rat Control Act (rule for floor consideration)	Yea	176	207
6	Inter-American Development Bank (increase in funds)	Yea	275	122

pattern "$+++-+-$", then the consistent pattern "$++++--$" as you move from the upper end of the array. Moving from the lower end, for support scores below 3, you may find two congressmen with support scores of 1: the inconsistent pattern "$---+--$" should be listed below the consistent pattern "$+-----$" to reduce errors.

Identification of the six roll-calls, with the Administration position on each, is given above, with the results for the whole House of Representatives added to permit you to check reliability of the sample.

(3) Compute the Coefficient of Reproducibility for the resulting Scalogram:

$$CR = 1.00 - \text{Errors/Responses} = 1.00 - \underline{\hspace{1cm}}/192 = \underline{\hspace{2cm}}$$

(4) Compute Yule's Q for a comparison of the sample of 32 congressmen with the whole House of Representatives, using only the Yea and Nay totals on all six roll-calls for each.

	Total Yea's on six roll-calls	Total Nay's on six roll-calls
Sample		
Whole House		

$$Q = (ad - bc)/(ad + bc) = (\underline{\hspace{0.5cm}} - \underline{\hspace{0.5cm}})/(\underline{\hspace{0.5cm}} + \underline{\hspace{0.5cm}}) = \underline{\hspace{2cm}}$$

(5) Draw a broken line on your scalogram, similar to that of Table 7–2, to divide the congressmen into groups with similar voting patterns. On the basis of what you know about the issues involved, discuss briefly your results as to:

1. Republicans with a strong pro-administration score

_____

2. Democrats with a strong anti-administration score

_____

3. Two pairs of inconsistent responses:

Bevill and Waggonner _____

Walker and Zwach _____

WORKSHEET FOR EXERCISE 7–1. ADMINISTRATION SUPPORT RECORD OF THIRTY-TWO CONGRESSMEN ON SIX KEY ROLL-CALLS, 1967

Congressman	Party	State	Votes						Same Votes as Pro- or Anti-Administration (+ or −)						Support Score (Total +)
			1	2	3	4	5	6	1	2	3	4	5	6	
Bevill	D	Ala.	Y	Y	N	Y	N	Y							
Dickinson	R	Ala.	Y	Y	Y	Y	N	N							
Leggett	D	Cal.	N	N	N	N	Y	Y							
Van Deerlin	D	Cal.	N	N	N	N	Y	Y							
Holifield	D	Cal.	N	N	N	N	Y	Y							
Bell	R	Cal.	Y	N	Y	N	N	Y							
Monagan	D	Conn.	N	N	N	N	Y	Y							
Fuqua	D	Fla.	Y	Y	Y	Y	N	Y							
O'Neal	D	Ga.	Y	Y	Y	Y	N	N							
Matsunaga	D	Hawaii	N	N	N	N	Y	Y							
Reid	R	Ill.	Y	Y	Y	Y	N	N							
O'Hara	D	Ill.	N	N	N	N	Y	Y							
Halleck	R	Ind.	Y	Y	Y	Y	N	N							
Kyl	R	Iowa	Y	Y	Y	Y	N	N							
Watts	D	Ky.	Y	N	N	N	N	Y							
Waggonner	D	La.	Y	Y	N	Y	N	N							
Mathias	R	Md.	N	N	N	N	Y	Y							
Harvey	R	Mich.	N	N	Y	N	N	Y							
Zwach	R	Minn.	Y	Y	N	N	N	Y							
Martin	R	Neb.	Y	Y	Y	Y	N	N							
Helstoski	D	N.J.	N	N	N	N	Y	Y							
Walker	D	N. Mex.	N	Y	N	N	Y	Y							
Robison	R	N.Y.	Y	N	Y	N	N	Y							
Halpern	R	N.Y.	N	N	N	N	Y	Y							
Vanik	D	Ohio	N	N	N	N	Y	Y							
Albert	D	Okla.	N	N	N	N	Y	Y							
Corbett	R	Penna.	Y	N	N	N	N	Y							
Ashmore	D	S. Car.	Y	Y	Y	Y	N	N							
Gonzalez	D	Texas	N	N	N	N	Y	Y							
Lloyd	R	Utah	Y	Y	Y	Y	N	Y							
Kee	D	W. Va.	N	N	N	N	Y	Y							
Zablocki	D	Wisc.	N	N	N	N	Y	Y							
				Total											

WORKSHEET FOR EXERCISE 7–1. SCALOGRAM OF CONGRESSMEN AND ROLL-CALLS ARRAYED BY SUPPORT SCORES

Congressman	Votes						Support Score (Total +)
	1	2	3	4	5	6	
							6
							6
							6
							6
							6
							6
							6
							6
							6
							6
							6
							6
							6
							6
							5
							4
							4
							4
							3
							3
							3
							2
							1
							1
							1
							0
							0
							0
							0
							0
							0
							0
Total +	24	21	19	20	16	15	

7–2. For the more complete analysis called for in this exercise, we supply data for a small congressional delegation, but suggest that you substitute a group of roll-calls of special interest to you, following the same worksheets. The most complete source of readily available data is the Congressional Quarterly's *Congress and the Nation,* which presents selected key roll-calls from 1945 to 1964.

In the 1962 session of the 87th Congress, six votes were reported by the *Congressional Quarterly* as being "key" votes. These were, with the administration position on each:

Roll-Call	Administration Position
1. Creation of a Department of Urban Affairs (recommit)	Nay
2. Revenue Act of 1962	Yea
3. Food & Agriculture Act of 1962 (recommit)	Nay
4. Trade Expansion Act of 1962 (recommit)	Nay
5. Foreign Aid Act of 1962	Yea
6. Approval of U.S. purchase of $100 millions in UN bonds	Yea

On these roll-calls the Oklahoma members of the House of Representatives voted as follows:

	1	2	3	4	5	6
Albert	N	Y	N	N	Y	Y
Edmondson	N	Y	N	N	Y	Y
Jarman	Y	Y	Y	Y	N	N
Steed	Y	Y	Y	Y	N	Y
Wickersham	Y	Y	N	N	N	Y
Belcher	Y	N	Y	Y	N	N

Step 1. Translate these votes into pro-administration (+) and anti-administration (−), and add up the marginal totals.

	1	2	3	4	5	6	Total
Albert							
Edmondson							
Jarman							
Steed							
Wickersham							
Belcher							
Total							

Step 2. Rearrange both roll-calls and Congressmen into as completely scaled an array as possible, by moving roll-calls with highest number of +'s to the left and Congressmen with highest numbers of +'s to the top. Draw a step-line to divide the resulting array.

Roll-Call ___ ___ ___ ___ ___ ___

Congressman

Coefficient of Reproducibility $= 1.00 - e/r = 1.00 -$ _____ $=$ _____.

Step 3. Following the alternative procedure for computation of a Q-value matrix, compare the six roll-calls, using the worksheet below.

WORKSHEET FOR COMPUTATION OF Q VALUES FOR PAIRED ROLL-CALLS

	Roll-call 2 + −	Roll-call 3 + −	Roll-call 4 + −	Roll-call 5 + −	Roll-call 6 + −
Roll-call 1 + −					
$Q =$					
Roll-call 2 + −					
$Q =$					
Roll-call 3 + −					
$Q =$					
Roll-call 4 + −					
$Q =$					
Roll-call 5 + −					
$Q =$					

MATRIX OF *Q* VALUES FOR SIX KEY ROLL-CALLS, OKLAHOMA CONGRESSIONAL DELEGATION

Roll-call	2	3	4	5	6
1	___	___	___	___	___
2		___	___	___	___
3			___	___	___
4				___	___
5					___

Step 4. Try your skill in developing an "internationalism" scale for these six congressmen, using only roll-calls 4, 5, and 6. Check their paired *Q* values to determine whether the votes on them will scale.

Congressmen	Roll-calls 6	4	5
	_____
	_____
	_____
	_____
	_____
	_____

Step 5. Prepare a matrix showing percentage of agreement among the pairs of congressmen.

	Edmondson	Wickersham	Steed	Jarman	Belcher
Albert	___	___	___	___	___
Edmondson		___	___	___	___
Wickersham			___	___	___
Steed				___	___
Jarman					___

Step 6. Compute the Index of Interagreement for the following groups:

Albert-Edmondson   _____

Albert-Edmondson-Wickersham   _____

Jarman-Belcher   _____

Five Democrats
(all but Belcher)   _____

Entire Delegation   _____

Step 7. Using your results on the internationalism scale for three bills only, compute the Index of Likeness as a measure of the comparison between the three congressmen who ranked highest on the scale and the three congressmen who ranked lowest.

Index of Likeness =_____

7–3. Compute the Index of Reproducibility for the Colonial Vote scalogram, being certain to count as separate votes those shown by groups of states whose votes were identical. Omit abstentions and blank entries: that is, include only $+$ and $-$ entries.

Index of Reproducibility = _____

7–4. In the Supreme Court scalogram, considering Douglas-Black as a voting bloc and Whittaker-Clark as another, compute the Index of Likeness of the two groups.

Index of Likeness =_____

7–5. For the states identified on the Colonial Issues voting agreement matrix, compute the Index of Interagreement for:

1. Sweden-Canada-Brazil-Peru: _____

2. Morocco-Egypt-Sudan-USSR: _____

What is the Index of Likeness for the two groups? _____

Reading List

Alker, Hayward R., Jr., and Bruce M. Russett, *World Politics in the General Assembly.* New Haven: Yale University Press, 1965. The advanced technique of factor analysis, not discussed in this chapter, is used to study clusters of issues and states in the United Nations.

Anderson, Lee F., Meredith W. Watts, Jr., and Allen R. Wilcox. *Legislative Roll-Call Analysis.* Evanston: Northwestern University Press, 1966.*

Beyle, Herman C., *Identification and Analysis of Attribute-Cluster Blocs.* Chicago: University of Chicago Press, 1931.

Congressional Quarterly, *Congress and the Nation: 1945–1964.* Washington, D.C.: Congressional Quarterly, Inc., 1965.

MacRae, Duncan, Jr., *Dimensions of Congressional Voting.* Berkeley: University of California Press, 1958.*

Rice, Stuart A., *Quantitative Methods in Politics.* New York: Alfred A. Knopf, Inc., 1928.

Schubert, Glendon, *Quantitative Analysis of Judicial Behavior.* New York: Free Press, 1959.

Truman, David B., *The Congressional Party: A Case Study.* New York: John Wiley and Sons, Inc., 1959.

Wahlke, John C., and Heinz Eulau (Eds.), *Legislative Behavior: A Reader in Research and Theory.* New York: Free Press, 1959.

---

* Paperback edition available.

CONTENT ANALYSIS:

Who Said What, When, and How?

Language is the principal tool of politics. The spoken or written word expresses our political philosophy, appeals for voter or follower support, directs the details of workaday public administration and heroic military campaigns, delicately probes nuances of diplomatic negotiations, broadcasts outrageous propaganda, and firmly states the commandments and guarantees of our law.

Words and phrases are the symbols by which people communicate, the basis of civilization itself. Communication assumes that the semantic value of a verbal message is the same for the sender as for the receiver. Communication may break down if the parties to a dialogue cannot establish identity of meaning. Different cultural backgrounds, different contexts and references, different times, and different languages are among the factors which create "noise" in the communications network. You may feel that these sources of noise are so serious an obstacle to ordinary understanding as to make futile any effort at quantification of the meaning of verbal messages. Nevertheless, scientific study of words in context, frequency of use of particular words and sequences, typical sentence length, and other language patterns has practical applications in a wide range of fields, from psychotherapy to communications engineering. It has helped establish authorship of literary works and spuriousness of legal documents. In recent years political scientists have turned their attention to the examination of patterns in significant political messages.

8-1 Political Uses of Content Analysis

Systematic study of verbal symbols is the task of the relatively new and complex field known as content analysis. Its application to political science stems largely from the pioneering work of Harold Lasswell in the 1930's and 1940's, and from the important methodological advances made in two major research enterprises at Stanford University—the RADIR project (on Revolution and the Development of International Relations) under the direction of Ithiel de Sola Pool in the 1950's, and the projects on the origins of World War I and the Sino-Soviet split sponsored under the Studies in International Conflict and Integration program under the supervision of Robert North in the 1960's.[1]

Among political themes which these and other scholars have examined with the tools of content analysis are such topics as Nazi propaganda in World War II, the use of political symbols in the leading "prestige" newspapers of Britain, France, Germany, Russia, and the United States from 1890 to 1949, key symbols in Soviet and Chinese communist propaganda to the United States, Politburo images of Stalin, the Goebbels diaries, a number of political biographies (including several studies of Woodrow Wilson), American presidential campaign speeches, and various serial radio and television programs.

Methods used in content analysis have developed as research applications have broadened to encompass such ambitious projects as the Stanford group's investigation of the whole corpus of diplomatic texts on the origins of World War I. Appropriate methodology depends in part on the field of research. Take, for example, the first methodological problem in any content study—you must decide on the *unit of analysis*. What portion of any given message will you fix as the basic building block? The linguist may break verbal patterns into individual phonemes; the psychiatrist may look for speech interruptions ("uhs," "ahs," and silences); the lexicographer will identify individual words; the cultural anthropologist or folklorist may be interested in an entire thought pattern represented by a story plot. Most political research entails the identification of key words or phrases

---

[1] The first Stanford project is outlined in Lasswell, Lerner, and Pool, *The Comparative Study of Symbols: An Introduction* (Stanford: Stanford University Press, 1952). A valuable methodological guide resulting from the second project is North, Holsti, Zaninovich, and Zinnes, *Content Analysis: A Handbook with Applications for the Study of International Crisis* (Evanston: Northwestern University Press, 1963).

representing major political "symbols" or of units of meaning—"unit perceptions," a concept described more fully in Section 8–3. As content analysis has evolved into a major research field during the past three decades, we can distinguish five distinct patterns of study, all of them still useful approaches to various kinds of research problems.

1. Qualitative Analysis. Most "practical" day-to-day propaganda analysis carried on by government agencies is essentially non-quantitative. The informed expert—the Kremlinologist or China-watcher—searches the message output of a given source for clues to policy shifts, attitudes of key political leaders or groups, or military decisions. Often this kind of educated detective work will turn up a significant finding which would have been obscured or ignored by the most sophisticated statistical analysis. The first isolated reference to China's nuclear experiments, for example, is readily identified as significant by the informed expert or the journalist, but a word or phrase count would either omit it as not included in the pre-established categories or at best lump it with "miscellaneous policy themes." This important field of applied content analysis is less concerned with theoretical development of the field than with immediate practical problems. It does not differ essentially from good political intelligence work or intellectual analysis in general. Current usage tends to exclude it from the basic field of content analysis, which is usually defined as the use of quantitative techniques to study verbal messages—retaining, however, appropriate emphasis on the importance of the meaning of the message.

2. Frequency Counts. The first quantitative method used in modern content analysis was the frequency count. Comparing the frequency of occurrence of words or themes, column inches of newspaper space, minutes of radio time, and similar sorting-and-counting operations were used to identify political support or opposition, concern with particular topics, or level of abstraction. One of the more advanced techniques of the frequency-count type is a statistical measure of relative spread of vocabulary in a given text, developed by G. Udney Yule (the British statistician who originated Yule's Q, which you learned in Chapter 5). This measure, known as Yule's K, has a high value for low vocabulary and a low value for high vocabulary, and is designed to measure the "slopes" of the normal distribution curve rather than the entire distribution, so that it is relatively independent of sample size. Ithiel de Sola Pool used Yule's K effectively in his study *The Prestige Papers* (part

of the Stanford RADIR project) to show that the newspaper editorials of the leading journals studied became more stereotyped in wartime and under totalitarian control, and showed greater variation in peacetime and under democratic regimes, as well as varying greatly by time, authorship, and language.[2]

3. Contingency Analysis. A step forward from sheer counting is the identification of two or more verbal patterns ("symbolic units") which often appear together. As Pool puts it, contingency analysis "asks not how often a given symbolic form appears in each of several bodies of text, but how often it appears in conjunction with other symbolic units."[3] Pool's own study of democratic symbols, for example, explores the association of words and phrases connoting democracy with terms suggesting the three principal varieties of the democratic tradition—the Anglo-American concept of representative government, the European continental concept of participation of the common people (the "fourth estate"), and the concept of human freedom. The approach affords a telling application of word-counts to political problems by encouraging the maximum use of traditional political theory in the construction of associational categories, but with the added value of empirical tests for the traditional concepts.

4. Valence. The existence and strength of linkages between a verbal symbol and its context are crucial aspects of its role in a message. At an elementary level, the "valence" of a word or phrase is gauged roughly by use of such categories as pro and con, favorable and unfavorable, friendly and hostile. An important advance in measuring valence is the work of Charles E. Osgood, a psychologist who has worked effectively with political material. Osgood's method is called "evaluative assertion analysis," and builds on his work with the "semantic differential," a device briefly mentioned in Chapter 6. We shall not detail these sophisticated techniques here, but the process entails an evaluative scaling of "attitude objects" referred to in a source text, resulting in an ordering of attitudes and associations characteristic of the author or authors. In an analysis of the Goebbels diaries, for example, Osgood found the concept "Hitler" closely associated with the concept of "Self

---

[2] G. U. Yule, *The Statistical Study of Literary Vocabulary* (Cambridge: The University Press, 1944). Pool's empirical work with the statistic in reported in his *The Prestige Papers: A Survey of Their Editorials* (Stanford: Stanford University Press, 1952), pp. 25–36.
[3] Pool (Ed.), *Trends in Content Analysis* (Urbana: University of Illinois Press, 1959), p. 196.

Praise," and separately associated with the concepts "German Generals," "Bad Morale," and "Internal Frictions." The two latter concepts in turn were associated most closely with "German Public." By constructing such associational patterns, significant variations over time and among sources can be detected.[4]

5. Intensity. Measurement of the intensity of an attitude is often implicit in the quantitative methods listed above. Frequency counts assume that strength of an attitude will be shown by the relative frequency of its mention in a source text—for example, that partisan support will be revealed by column inches of favorable newspaper comment. Contingency frequency counts of associated concepts suggest approximate intensity of concern with particular associations. Osgood's evaluative assertion techniques entail explicit measures of strength of the associated meaning patterns detected. Robert North's projects for the Stanford Studies in International Conflict and Integration have involved experimentation with several scaling devices for measurement of intensity of a verbal symbol—intensity of hostility, friendship, power, and other perception concepts relevant to political research. Methods such as Guttman scaling, pair-comparisons, and Osgood's evaluative assertion technique have been found to yield reliable results. The psychologist's "Q-sort" technique, based on a forced distribution of unit statements into ranked categories by teams of trained judges, is one such scaling device used by the Stanford projects, and is explained in more detail in Section 8–5 as the basis for the group problem in content analysis which you are asked to carry out in Exercise Set 8. We have chosen this method for detailed explanation because its use involves almost all of the basic processes in content analysis without overtaxing the modest statistical knowledge assumed in this workbook.

Before turning to the mechanics of the Q-sort intensity scale we must first examine briefly several steps essential to any actual research project in quantitative content analysis: category identification, coding of content themes, and the separation of "affect" and "action" statements. These topics are not treated exhaustively, but in brief "cookbook" style, essentially as a set of instructions for the exercise which follows.

If you are suspicious of the general approach used in quantitative content analysis, or of the validity of

the research operations involved in the exercise which follows, you may find one reassurance in the principle of redundancy.

Redundancy is defined in information theory as the quantity of information contained in a message above the minimum required to convey the desired meaning. Enough redundancy can make up for considerable semantic noise. Our exercise in content analysis is based on Communist propaganda broadcasts, a source unusually rich in redundancy.

8-2 Category Identification

In the examination of verbal messages, we are usually interested in some clearly defined *range of content*. The following set of categories, used by the Stanford International Conflict and Integration Studies Center in the project dealing with the Sino-Soviet split, will illustrate the concept of defining our range.

1. Perceptions of Policy Conditions: goals, aims, preferences, choices, means to achieve goals.
2. Perceptions of Resolution of Conflict: means of resolution, expected results of resolution.
3. Perceptions of Capability: numerical (not qualitative) estimates of state capability.
4. Perceptions of Power: qualitative and relative estimates of state capability.
5. Perceptions of Friendship: approval, cooperation, support.
6. Perceptions of Hostility: enmity, obstructionism.
7. Perceptions of Satisfaction: success, contentment, confidence.
8. Perceptions of Frustration: failure, disappointment, anxiety about goals.

The same collection of source material might be used to study several or all of the above categories. The same statement, for example, might say something about policy, about conflict resolution, about capability, about power, etc. An orderly approach to analysis requires that we identify clearly just what category we are going to study in one specific part of our research.

8-3 Coding

The first step in coding is to define our unit of analysis. As we have seen, much content analysis has been done with frequency counts of key words or phrases (how often per page the phrase "American imperialists" occurs in Hanoi broadcast intercepts). The device described here is that used by the Stanford group to code *themes*, rather than words alone.

---

[4] Charles E. Osgood, George J. Suci, and Percy H. Tannenbaum, *The Measurement of Meaning* (Urbana: University of Illinois Press, 1957), and Osgood's chapter in Pool, *Trends in Content Analysis,* pp. 33–38.

1. The Atomic Theme or Unit-Perception. The source statement is broken down into a group of single basic unit statements. An example of this process is drawn from Khrushchev's press conference of May 19, 1960, commenting on the American U-2 flights over Soviet territory:[5]

Source: *Pravda*, May 19, 1960
Perceiver: Khrushchev
Perceived: Khrushchev
Target: U.S.

Source statement:
Of course it is for President Eisenhower to decide whether to send or not to send his planes. It is another question whether they will be able to fly over our territory. This is decided by us, and very definitely for that matter. We shall shoot these planes down: we shall administer shattering blows at the bases whence they came and at those who have set up these bases and actually dispose of them.

Capsule statements:
1. This (whether or not U.S. will be able to fly over the USSR) is DECIDED by us....
2. We (USSR) SHALL SHOOT these planes (U.S.) down....
3. ...we (USSR) SHALL ADMINISTER shattering blows at the bases whence they (U.S. planes) came....
4. ...we (USSR) SHALL ADMINISTER shattering blows...at those who have set up these bases and actually dispose of them (bases).

2. Identification of the Unit Statement. The elements which make up a unit statement are:
1. The *perceiver* (Khrushchev in the example).
2. The actor whose action is *perceived* (also Khrushchev, since he is talking about what "we" will do).
3. The *target,* or recipient of the action (the United States).
4. The *descriptive-connective,* or the action or attitude expressed which relates or connects the actors ("is decided," "shall administer shattering blows," "shall shoot down"). It is this element of the unit statement which is the focus of our attention in coding the statement as a whole, since it is the only element which can vary in intensity or type on any scale we set up to describe the category we are investigating.

A unit statement must not contain more than *one* perceiver, *one* perceived, *one* target, or *one* descriptive-connective, though the "perceived" and the "target" may be missing from some statements. Compound sentences, with two or more targets (or other elements), are broken down into two or more unit statements. Exceptions are permitted for collective nouns and inseparable pairs used as perceiver, perceived, or target ("U.S. aggressors," "Soviet revisionist group," "Vietnamese people," "United States and its henchmen") but in no case may a unit statement contain more than a single descriptive-connective.

3. Masking the Unit Statements. In preparing a set of unit statements for coding and scaling, it is convenient to put each on a separate card in masked form, so that the identity of the actors will not influence the opinion of the judges who do the scaling. The following example will illustrate the method:
1. *Source statement*: "The treacherous Chinese have sent military forces into Korea in order to exterminate the Korean people."
2. Unit statements drawn from source statement:
   a. "The Chinese are treacherous."
   b. "The Chinese have sent military forces into Korea."
   c. "The Chinese intend to exterminate the Koreans."
3. Masked form of the unit statements:
   a. X is treacherous.
   b. X has sent military forces into Y.
   c. X intends to exterminate Y.

Each card containing a masked statement should be marked with an appropriate identification code, so that it can always be matched with the original.

4. Partial Masking. Depending on the purpose of the analysis, it may not be necessary or desirable to mask both actors. If we are studying the range of Soviet attitudes toward different countries, for example, we should mask the targets but would not need to mask the perceiver, USSR. In contrast, if we are studying the attitudes of various countries to the United States, we should mask the perceivers but would not need to mask the "perceived" or "target" actor, United States.

8-4 Affect and Action Statements Separated

All unit statements will be found to fall into two distinct groups—those which express an attitude or evaluation, and those which describe an action. Statements a and c from the list above are of the "affect" type, statement b of the "action" type. It is not pos-

---

[5] These examples of capsule statements are drawn from the excellent handbook by Robert C. North and associates, *Content Analysis* (Evanston: Northwestern University Press, 1963), with the kind permission of the publisher.

sible to scale a set of statements consistently if the set includes statements from both types. A scale of "hostility," for example, might use statements a and c; but statement b would not fall into such a scale very reasonably. On the other hand, it would fit well into a scale of belligerence or aggressiveness. Before undertaking an actual scaling operation it is necessary to separate the unit statements into *Affect* and *Action* groups.

8-5 Scaling: The Q-Sort Scale

A number of effective scaling systems have been developed. The *Q*-sort was originally devised for clinical psychological research but is adaptable to content analysis if the universe of statements is not too great. It has the virtue of forcing the judges to evaluate the entire group of statements and to rank them by a predetermined rank-order. The procedure reduces the influence of individual personality differences in judges (and sometimes leads to loud arguments).

1. Values on the Scale. The *Q*-sort assigns a value from 1 to 9 to each statement, according to the judge's opinion of its intensity level. As an illustration, assume we have 100 masked statements about the United States, 50 obtained from Russian broadcasts and 50 obtained from Peking broadcasts during the Viet Nam "bombing pause." The sources are, of course, masked, but can later be identified by suitable codes. Judges are asked to *Q*-sort the entire mix of 100 statements according to a scale of hostility ranging from 1 (least hostile) to 9 (most hostile). However, the judges do not merely assign these values subjectively; they are required to discriminate among the statements carefully, and to arrange them in the nine categories in exactly fixed proportions. These proportions are given in Table 8-1 and approximate the normal distribution or "normal curve."

2. Q-Sort is a Forced Array. The reason for this forced distribution is to avoid "bunching" of relatively similar statements into a high or low category. In our illustrative universe of Soviet and Chinese statements, for example, the judges might well put almost all of them in category 9, indicating highest hostility. We wish more discrimination in our sorting, to make subsequent comparisons more meaningful. The *Q*-sort forces the judges to put only five statements of 100 in category 9, and to put the largest number of statements, 18 in the example, in category 5, as "average" in hostility. In other words, we are not actually assign-

ing values which represent absolute measures of hostility. We are seeking instead values which represent the *relative* position of each statement in the entire collection of hostile statements.

3. The Q-Sort Distribution. Table 8-1 displays the *Q*-sort distribution according to intensity categories (1 to 9), and the percentage of statements which must be assigned to each category by the judges. In addition, it shows the actual number of statements which must be assigned to each category from universes of 25, 50, and 140 statements.

TABLE 8-1. *The Q-Sort Distribution*

Intensity Category	Percentage of Statements Required by Q-Sort Array	Number of Statements from Sample of:		
		25	50	140
1	5	1	3*	7
2	8	2	4	11
3	12	3	6	17
4	16	4	8	22
5	18	5	9	26
6	16	4	8	22
7	12	3	6	17
8	8	2	4	11
9	5	1	2*	7

* Actually 2.5, so quotas for categories 1 and 9 are interchangeable.

4. Analyzing the Results. A simple method of computing the resulting values is to prepare a worksheet on which the coded identification of each statement is entered. Once the judges have assigned intensity values (a convenient method is for the judges to place the cards in nine numbered boxes), these values can be written on the worksheet without marking the cards. The cards can then be shuffled and used again for other judges or another project. From the worksheet we can easily compute the average intensity level for any identified variable. In our illustration of the Russian and Chinese broadcasts, we add the intensity values assigned the Russian statements, and divide the sum by the number of statements, obtaining an average intensity for Russia. We then do the same for the Chinese statements, and so have a basis for comparing the two. The formula for computing the average intensities might be described as follows:

$$\text{Intensity Index} = \frac{\text{Sum of intensity values}}{\text{Number of statements}}$$

If in our sample of 100 capsule statements, the 50 from Chinese sources had a combined intensity value of 282, the formula would yield an index of 282/50 = 5.6; if the 50 from Russian sources had a combined value of 218, the index would be 218/50 = 4.4.

The Q-sort method is also valuable in making comparisons across time. To pursue our illustration, we might compare the intensity values of a selection of statements from Soviet sources during the Stalin, Khrushchev, and Kosygin periods. The Stanford group has used the Q-sort to quantify the development of hostility in the spiraling war crisis of 1914.

5. Limitations of the Q-Sort. It must be clearly understood that the Q-sort technique does not result in a scale of absolute intensities. Consequently, values of two sets of statements previously scaled separately cannot be compared with one another (each would have an average intensity of exactly 5.0).

Proper judging requires that the judges understand clearly the attribute they are judging, such as hostility. It is good practice for them to discuss this aspect of their work with a number of illustrative statements in a pre-test session. Elaborate statistical methods have been developed to determine reliability of judging, but we will not detail them here.

You should realize, however, that measuring the reliability of judging or of coding text into categories of any kind is an essential part of the research design in all content analysis work. Low levels of agreement by judges or coders on an item suggest that it is probably too complex or vague a term to be useful in the analysis, or perhaps that the judges or coders need more training in what it means. A high index of agreement is desirable, but undue emphasis on a fixed standard of reliability may well make the coders over-cautious and inclined to omit items on which they feel the slightest uncertainty. Tests of reliability should be made without the judges' knowing that their work is being subjected to such tests.[6]

Finally, Q-sort is impractical for too large a set

---

[6] For the Q-sort, Spearman's coefficient of rank correlation, which you learned in Chapter 5, is one possible test for consistency of two judges. Another with wider application for both coding and judging is a simple ratio of agreements to total items judged or coded ($R = A/N$). Thus if two judges or coders, working separately on 50 items, assign the same category to 40 of them but differ on the remaining 10, the formula yields $R = 40/50$, or .80 as the index of reliability. The advantage of this simpler test is that it can be applied to the coding of unranked categories as well as to a ranked scale such as the Q-sort. A disadvantage is that there is no way to assign statistical significance to the value except in comparison with a group of such ratios computed for a number of pairs of judges.

of statements. Discrimination capacity of judges breaks down at some point as a result of the necessity of making pair-wise comparisons among all possible pairs of statements. Once valid judging is established on the basis of a series of consistent results, however, it is possible to develop a nine-statement pattern scale for a particular perception category. The nine "pattern statements" represent characteristic descriptive-connectives for the nine intensity levels, and can be used as a sort of nine-point yardstick with which to measure other statements.

8-6 A Content Analysis Project Using Q-Sort

Our previous exercises have dealt with known data and known results. The project outlined in Exercise Set 8 is based on raw source material, as an actual experiment in content analysis, and requires some advance planning. Judging teams should be selected and the judging procedure discussed in a pre-judging session. Typed cards containing the statements to be sorted and numbered boxes or other suitable containers for the nine intensity categories must be prepared in advance—Keysort marginal punchcards have been used successfully. Though designed as a class experiment, the project can easily be adapted to a homework exercise, but ideally you should enlist three friends who have not seen the original identification of the coded statements to serve as judges under your instruction.

A note on the source of the statements used in the exercise is in order. A source citation is sometimes difficult. These propaganda excerpts are from translations of foreign radio broadcasts made daily by a United States government agency which requests that quotations from its formidable output not be attributed to it, although quotations and use of the contents are authorized. The reason for this self-imposed anonymity is perfectly valid—the work is done under extreme pressure of time and serious political consequences might ensue from publicized errors. The extracts used here are now sufficiently dated that the danger no longer exists, but the request for non-attribution must still be honored.

Unlike the other exercises, this project will lead to answers which will depend entirely on the work of the judges in your own content analysis operation. There is no "answer in the back of the book."

Exercise Set 8. Who Is Most Hostile?

The project involves classification of seventy-five unit statements into categories which represent a scale of increasing intensity of hostility. Of these, 35 are extracted from radio intercepts of Moscow, Peking, and Hanoi broadcasts about the Honolulu conference (U.S.-South Vietnam) in February 1966, and 40 are from the same sources after the Manila conference in October 1966. Following the listing of the source statements, the work-sheets list the descriptive-connectives, with space for entering the intensity value which the judges assign each statement. For your class project these statements should be pre-typed on a card deck, with masked codes so that source and time can be determined after the sorting is completed.

The procedure is as follows:

1. Sort the entire universe of 75 statements into nine intensity categories, adhering to the Q-sort forced distribution as follows:

Intensity category (1 is weakest, 9 is strongest)	1	2	3	4	5	6	7	8	9
Number from sample of 75 statements	4	6	9	12	13	12	9	6	4

2. Record the intensity category of each statement on the worksheets; sum them for each source and time group. Compute the average intensity for each group and for the entire array of 75 (note: the last computation is merely a check; if the Q-sort is properly carried out, the average intensity will always be 5.00).

3. Tabulate the results in the display format of Exercise 8–1.

4. Enter the actual count of statements in each intensity category for the five subgroups (all Moscow, all Peking, all Hanoi, all Honolulu, and all Manila) in the worksheet of Exercise 8–2. Multiply each frequency by four as explained there, retaining the actual frequency counts as well.

5. Do the five chi-square computations called for in Exercise 8–2, using the frequency values resulting from the multiplication by four.

6. Do the chi-square tests called for in Exercise 8–3 (the 2×2 tables), using the actual frequencies collapsed into two dichotomous cells for each group.

The coded reference numbers (1.01 to 6.13) which appear with the raw source statements are not simply statement numbers; they are keyed to the list of *descriptive-connectives* extracted from the source statements for use in the exercise. Thus some of the source statements have no reference number, meaning that no suitable descriptive-connective was extracted. Others have several reference numbers, corresponding to the number of descriptive-connectives used. Following the judging, the cards may be sorted on the first digit of the reference number to re-create the original six groups.

Moscow in English to the United Kingdom, 9 February 1966.

1.01.   (Mention of negotiations in Honolulu communique) was merely intended to mislead the public.

1.02.   The Honolulu conference shows that talk about Washington's desire for a peaceful settlement of the Vietnam conflict was mere hypocrisy.

America's leaders have again shown the world that they are determined to crush the Vietnamese people's heroic struggle for their freedom and independence.

Moscow in Italian to Italy, 10 February 1966.

1.03   (The Honolulu documents) are the specter of acts of brigandage and further escalation of the dirty
1.04.   war.

1.05.   (The Honolulu plan for social reforms) not only represents a grotesque monstrosity but also a proof
1.06.   of unprecedented impudence and vile falsehood.
1.07.

1.08. The monstrous falsehood and unheard-of hypocrisy of the documents approved at Honolulu fully corresponds to the dishonest policy of brigandage which Washington pursues in Indochina.

1.09. The question is what purpose, insofar as Washington is concerned, was served by the Honolulu spectacle from which there has emerged such a pernicious smell?

1.10. (Resumption of bombing) brought to light the complete hypocrisy and propaganda character of
1.11. the so-called U.S. peace offensive.

1.12. Washington is not even thinking about any attempt to find a peaceful solution for the Vietnamese problem.

Peking International Service in English, 9 February 1966.

2.01. (Honolulu conference was held) to discuss the ways and means of intensifying the war of aggression in Vietnam.

2.02. The result of the conference indicated that the Johnson administration would continue its double-
2.03. faced tactics of war escalation and peace hoax for the purpose of oppressing and enslaving the South
2.04. Vietnamese people.

2.05. (Honolulu social reform plans) mean the adoption of certain deceitful measures.

2.06. The declaration and the communique have made it clear that while widening its war the Johnson administration will go on with its "peace talk" fraud.

2.07. U.S. aggressor will not lay down his butcher knife.

2.08. The war launched by U.S. imperialism in South Vietnam is an aggressive and unjust one.
2.09.

Peking International Service in English, 10 February 1966.

2.10. (Honolulu conference) plotted to expand the U.S. war of aggression against Vietnam.

2.11. The Honolulu declarations and speeches are nothing but a large volume of new-look poison gas.

Hanoi in Vietnamese to South Vietnam, 11 February 1966.
(From text of statement by DRV Foreign Ministry)

3.01. (Honolulu conference was to discuss) intensifying and expanding the war of aggression in Vietnam.

3.02. In essence the so-called U.S. "economic, social, welfare, and democracy program" consists merely in extremely barbarous maneuvers to step up the war of aggression.

3.03. (U.S. reference to commitments) is a trick which cannot conceal the blatant U.S. aggression in Vietnam.

3.04. (Honolulu conference) is also a new gross encroachment of the U.S. imperialists on the sacred inde-
3.05. pendence and sovereignty of the Vietnamese people, a blatant flouting of the 1956 Geneva agreements on Vietnam and international law.

3.06. The DRV Government declares: In face of the U.S. imperialists' schemes to step up and expand the aggressive war...the Vietnamese people are determined...to smash all military schemes and deceptive tricks of the U.S. imperialists.

Hanoi International Service in English, 10 February 1966.

3.07. (Honolulu statements) smell of colonialism and betrayal....
3.08.

3.09. U.S. imperialists committed themselves to continue their policy of aggression and enslavement....

3.10. ...the U.S. imperialists have revealed their true colors as an impudent and cruel imperialist aggressor.
3.11.
3.12.

Moscow TASS International Service in Russian, 25 October 1966.

4.01. The communique repeats slanderous assertions about "aggression and infiltration from the north."

4.02. Besides this, two other documents were approved which have the pretentious captions "Aims of Freedom" and "Declaration on Peace and Progress in Asia and the Pacific Basin," which announce the intention to "fight aggression, hunger, poverty and disease" and to "create a region of security, order, and progress" in southeast Asia.

4.03. The abundance of wide-ranging appeals for peace and progress cannot conceal the fact that the real aim of the countries taking part in the conference is to continue and extend their aggression in Vietnam.

Moscow in Serbo-Croatian to Yugoslavia, 25 October 1966.

4.04. The proceedings at the Manila conference convincingly show that its participants were not in the least concerned with peace in Vietnam.

4.05. During the Manila conference, the United States was in fact forced to abandon the camouflage cover of deceitful phrases about its aspirations for peace in Vietnam with which it had tried to disguise the war conference.

4.06. Its aim is to secure the support of the South Vietnamese village population for the Saigon puppet clique or, should this fail, to intimidate the former and break its will to struggle for freedom and independence.

4.07. At the Manila conference, U.S. diplomacy did its best to create this false impression that the aggression in Vietnam was not a U.S. war alone.

4.08. Washington was waging a war of its own in the interest of its own egoist aims.

4.09. In the communique to the Manila conference, despite the hypocritical phrases on the need to seek peace in Vietnam.

4.10. ...there is a direct indication that the United States intends, as before, to pursue a policy of escalating its aggression in southeast Asia.

4.11. The whole question then is one of giving shape to a new organization in the area of the Pacific and southeast Asia, an organization which will be a pliable instrument in the struggle to establish U.S. imperalist domination in the area.

4.12. The conference of the countries which are taking part in the Vietnam war, which ended in Manila today, adopted plans pregnant with new threats to the security and freedom of the Asian peoples.

4.13. (plans are threat) to peace throughout the world.

Peking NCNA International Service in English, 27 October 1966.

5.01. While U.S. imperialism is fraternizing with the Soviet revisionist leading group to make a dirty deal over the Vietnam question. . . .

5.02. In line with the gangster logic of the U.S. aggressors, Johnson, at the conference, continued to harp

5.03. on the shopworn theme that North Vietnam had "invaded" South Vietnam.

5.04. The joint communique adopted by the conference which smacked of gunpowder stated that U.S. imperialism and its henchmen would never allow South Vietnam to be "conquered."

5.05. To coordinate the U.S. imperialist trick of "forcing peace talks through war."

5.06. This is out-and-out blackmail and shameless humbug with the aim of pushing the scheme of holding

5.07. "peace talks by inducement" and asking the Vietnamese people to surrender to the U.S. aggressors outright.

5.08. In order to continue its war of aggression in Vietnam and to occupy South Vietnam permanently,

5.09. U.S. imperialism, taking the Honolulu conference of last February as a model, has drawn up a military "pacification" plan for suppressing the South Vietnamese people and a series of measures for political deception.

5.10. The conference has also revealed the U.S. imperialists' designs to plot a new anti-China alliance and to enslave the peoples of Asia permanently.

5.11. In other words, this vast area of Asia and the Pacific, including China, is to be placed under the

5.12. domination and enslavement of U.S. imperialism.

5.13. The paper tiger, U.S. imperialism, has all along been employing alternately the counterrevolutionary two-way tactics of war and "peace"—when it fails to win in war, it uses deception; when its deception fails, it resorts again to war.

5.14. However, no matter what "peace" tricks it may play or what military adventure it may embark upon, U.S. imperialism is doomed to final defeat.

Hanoi VNA International Service in English, 27 October 1966.

6.01. These documents adopted by the United States and its henchmen at the conference have pointed to the following four points in the U.S. scheme against Vietnam: To step up and expand the aggressive war against Vietnam;...

6.02. To urge the Vietnamese people to accept their insolent conditions for a peaceful settlement.

6.03. The Manila conference's documents and the statements made by Johnson and his stooges at the summit are all characterized by cynicism.

6.04. But right in the first part of their joint communique they stressed that their basic policy was to abide by their commitments to the Saigon traitors.

6.05. The conference was part of the U.S. scheme to intensify and expand its aggressive war in Vietnam.

6.06. The peaceful solution proposed by the United States at the Manila conference is still more cynical and insolent than the conditions which the United States had earlier put to the Vietnamese people and had been categorically rejected by the latter.

6.07. He (Johnson) pretended to ignore the object of protest of the Philippine and world's people, which is the U.S. unjust aggressive war in Vietnam.

6.08. But the Johnson clique's perfidious allegations can deceive nobody.

6.09. These maneuvers could in no way hide the truth and, in the eyes of the world's people, the Manila conference remains an insipid farce.

6.10. The Manila conference has once again laid bare the U.S. imperialist's policy of intensifying and
6.11. broadening their war of aggression in Vietnam, and their peace hoax.

6.12 The cynical and deceitful allegations of the United States and its quislings at the Manila conference were an insolent challenge to world public opinion.

6.13. The world's people see still more clearly the utterly reactionary nature of the Johnson clique.

WORKSHEET FOR CODING INTENSITY VALUES:

Descriptive Connectives from Communist Broadcasts on the Honolulu Conference, February 1966.

Moscow, February 1966.   Value Assigned

1.01. merely intended to mislead public   _____

1.02. mere hypocrisy   _____

1.03. acts of brigandage   _____

1.04. escalation of the war   _____

1.05. grotesque monstrosity   _____

1.06. unprecedented impudence   _____

1.07. vile falsehood   _____

1.08. unheard-of-hypocrisy   _____

1.09. pernicious smell emerges   _____

1.10. complete hypocrisy   _____

1.11. has propaganda character   _____

1.12. not even thinking of peaceful solution   _____

                                          Total value   _____

                                          Total$/N = T/12$ _____

Peking, February 1966.

2.01. intensify war of agression   _____

2.02. double-faced tactics of war escalation & peace hoax   _____

2.03. oppressing people of X   _____

2.04. enslaving people of X   _____

2.05. deceitful measures   _____

2.06. peace talk fraud   _____

2.07. not lay down butcher knife   _____

2.08. aggressive   _____

2.09. unjust   _____

2.10. plotted to expand war of aggression   _____

2.11. large volume of new-look poison gas   _____

                                          Total value   _____

                                          Total$/N = T/11$ _____

Hanoi, February 1966. Value Assigned

3.01. intensify and expand war of aggression _____

3.02. barbarous maneuvers to step up war of aggression _____

3.03. trick to conceal blatant war of aggression _____

3.04. gross encroachment on sovereignty and independence _____

3.05. blatant flouting of agreements _____

3.06. deceptive trick _____

3.07. smell of colonialism _____

3.08. smell of betrayal _____

3.09. aggression and enslavement _____

3.10. impudent _____

3.11. cruel _____

3.12. imperialist aggressor _____

Total value _____

Total/$N = T/12$ _____

Total Honolulu _____

Total/$N = T/35$ _____

Descriptive Connectives from Communist Broadcasts on the Manila Conference, October 1966.

Moscow, October 1966.

4.01. repeats slanderous assertions _____

4.02. approved documents with pretentious captions _____

4.03. real aim is to continue and extend aggression _____

4.04. not in the least concerned with peace _____

4.05. camouflage cover of deceitful phrases _____

4.06. aims to intimidate village population _____

4.07. did its best to create false impression _____

4.08. aims are egoist _____

4.09. used hypocritical phrases on seeking peace _____

4.10. intends to pursue policy of escalating aggression _____

4.11. aims to establish imperialist domination _____

4.12. plans are pregnant with new threats to security and freedom _____

4.13. plans are threat to peace throughout the world _____

Total Value _____

Total/$N = T/13$ _____

Peking, October 1966. Value Assigned

5.01. (U.S. and Soviet Union) fraternizing to make dirty deal _____

5.02. use gangster logic _____

5.03. aggressors _____

5.04. statements smacked of gunpowder _____

5.05. use imperialist trick _____

5.06. (offer to withdraw) is out-and-out blackmail _____

5.07. (offer to withdraw) is shameless humbug _____

5.08. (pacification plan) is to suppress the V. people _____

5.09. (pacification plan) is political deception _____

5.10. aim is to enslave the peoples of Asia permanently _____

5.11. imperialist aim of domination _____

5.12. imperialist aim of enslavement _____

5.13. uses counterrevolutionary deception _____

5.14. uses "peace tricks" _____

Total value _____

Total/$N = T/14$ _____

Hanoi, October 1966.

6.01. plan to step up and expand the aggressive war _____

6.02. (conditions for settlement) are insolent _____

6.03. (conference documents) are all characterized by cynicism _____

6.04. policy is to abide by commitments to Saigon traitors _____

6.05. scheme to intensify and expand aggressive war _____

6.06. solution proposed is cynical and insolent _____

6.07. unjust aggressive war _____

6.08. perfidious allegations _____

6.09. conference is an insipid farce _____

6.10. policy is intensifying and broadening war of aggression _____

6.11. policy is peace hoax _____

6.12. statements are cynical and deceitful allegations _____

6.13. (Johnson clique) is utterly reactionary _____

Total value _____

Total/$N = T/13$ _____

Total Manila _____

Total/$N = T/40$ _____

Summary Values

Total both Moscow groups (1 & 4) =   _____

$T/25 =$ _____

Total both Peking groups (2 & 5) =   _____

$T/25 =$ _____

Total both Hanoi groups (3 & 6) =   _____

$T/25 =$ _____

Grand Total (all (75 statements) =   _____

$T/75 =$ _____

8-1. Using your results from the judging of the 75 statements, fill in the following table:

Hostility Values of Communist Broadcasts About the United States, by Source and Time*

Source	February 1966 (Honolulu Conference)	October 1966 (Manila Conference)	Mean Value
Moscow			
Peking			
Hanoi			
Mean value			5.00

* Based on 75 source statements, 25 from each source, distributed by Q-sort array into nine intensity categories, the number in each category approximating the normal distribution.

8-2. Review your Statistics

One use of the chi-square test is to determine whether an observed distribution varies significantly from a theoretical distribution of observations. Since the Q-sort procedure begins by forcing the observations into a distribution approximating the normal, we can test each of the subgroupings by comparing the actual array for the subgroup with the theoretical distribution for the same number of observations—the "expected" frequencies. For our exercise we are handicapped in that the expected values for several of the intensity categories would be less than five. By standard chi-square principles, we would combine categories so that our smallest contained at least five in the "expected" column. To simplify these exercises, however, we are assuming that we had four times as many source statements as we actually had—an assumption which by strict standards invalidates our results. However, the actual broadcasts from which the source statements were taken in fact continued at some length in the same vein, and the assumption is therefore less dangerous to accuracy than would be true if the "N" were the number of respondents in a survey sample.

In preparation for the following chi-square computations, therefore, our first step is to recount the number of statements falling into each intensity category for each of the subgroups above, and then to multiply these "observed" frequencies by four in order to implement the assumption of a larger universe:

Intensity category	Q-Sort Per cent	Expected for 100 Statements (4 × 25)	Observed Moscow (× 4)	Observed Peking (× 4)	Observed Hanoi (× 4)
1	5	5			
2	8	8			
3	12	12			
4	16	16			
5	18	18			
6	16	16			
7	12	12			
8	8	8			
9	5	5			

Intensity Category	Q-Sort Expected for 140 statements	Observed Honolulu (× 4)	Q-Sort Expected for 160 statements	Observed Manila (× 4)
1	7		8	
2	11		13	
3	17		19	
4	22		26	
5	26		28	
6	22		26	
7	17		19	
8	11		13	
9	7		8	

WORKSHEET FOR COMPUTATION OF χ^2

(Obtaining values for "Expected" and "Observed" frequencies from the above entries, test the hypotheses that none of the subgroup distributions varies significantly from the normal Q-Sort scale)

Intensity Category	Expected Moscow	Observed Moscow	D	D^2	D^2/E
1					
2					
3					
4					
5					
6					
7					
8					
9					

df = 8 $\chi^2 =$ _____

H_0: Moscow statements do not differ significantly from Q-sort norm

Significance level: .05

Value of χ^2 needed to reject: 15.5

Is H_0 accepted? _____

Intensity Category	Expected Hanoi	Observed Hanoi	D	D^2	D^2/E
1					
2					
3					
4					
5					
6					
7					
8					
9					

$\text{df} = 8$ $\chi^2 =$ _____

H_0: Hanoi statements do not differ significantly from Q-sort norm

Significance level: .05

Value of χ^2 needed to reject: 15.5

Is H_0 accepted? _____

Intensity Category	Expected Peking	Observed Peking	D	D^2	D^2/E
1					
2					
3					
4					
5					
6					
7					
8					
9					

$\text{df} = 8$ $\chi^2 =$ _____

H_0: Peking statements do not differ significantly from Q-sort norm

Significance level: .05

Value of χ^2 needed to reject: 15.5

Is H_0 accepted? _____

Intensity Category	Expected Manila	Observed Manila	D	D^2	D^2/E
1					
2					
3					
4					
5					
6					
7					
8					
9					

df = 8 $\chi^2 = $ _____

H_0: Manila statements do not differ significantly from Q-sort norm

Significance level: .05

Value of χ^2 needed to reject: 15.5

Is H_0 accepted? _____

Intensity Category	Expected Honolulu	Observed Honolulu	D	D^2	D^2/E
1					
2					
3					
4					
5					
6					
7					
8					
9					

df = 8 $\chi^2 = $ _____

H_0: Honolulu statements do not differ significantly from Q-sort norm

Significance level: .05

Value of χ^2 needed to reject: 15.5

Is H_0 accepted? _____

8-3.   In the exercise above we have used the chi-square test to compare our findings with a "normal" distribution. In addition, the chi-square test may be used to test our various sets of observations *for association* with one another. To make the computations simpler, we will use only a portion of each group, dichotomized into the frequencies above the mean and the frequencies below the mean, thus yielding a 2×2 table for each pair of groups. In one cell of each table we enter the sum of frequencies in intensity categories 1, 2, 3, and 4; in the other cell we enter the sum of frequencies in intensity categories 6, 7, 8, and 9. We omit the frequencies in intensity category 5. The work-sheet entries use the letters in the appropriate cells to guide your computations. For these exercises we will retain actual frequencies, not using those obtained by multiplying our results by four.

	Moscow	Peking	Total
Low Hostility (1, 2, 3, 4)	a	b	e
High Hostility (6, 7, 8, 9)	c	d	f
Total	g	h	T

Observed	Expected	D	D^2	D^2/E
$a =$	$ge/T =$			
$b =$	$he/T =$			
$c =$	$gf/T =$			
$d =$	$hf/T =$			

df $= 1$ $\chi^2 =$ _____

H_0: Hostility of Moscow and Peking not significantly different
Significance level: .05
Value of chi-square needed to reject H_0: 3.841
Is H_0 rejected? _____

	Moscow	Hanoi	Total
Low Hostility			
High Hostility			
Total			

	Peking	Hanoi	Total
Low Hostility			
High Hostility			
Total			

	Honolulu	Manila	Total
Low Hostility			
High Hostility			
Total			

	Moscow-Hanoi					Peking-Hanoi					Honolulu-Manila				
	O	E	D	D^2	D^2/E	O	E	D	D^2	D^2/E	O	E	D	D^2	D^2/E
a															
b															
c															
d															

$\chi^2 =$ $\chi^2 =$ $\chi^2 =$

df $= 1$ Significance level $= .05$

H_0: Hostility of Moscow and Hanoi not significantly different.   Accept?_____

H_0: Hostility of Peking and Hanoi not significantly different.   Accept?_____

H_0: Hostility of the three communist sources not significantly

different for the post-Honolulu and the post-Manila periods.   Accept?_____

ALTERNATIVE χ^2 WORKSHEET FOR 2×2 TABLES

(1) Without Yates' Correction, for the Type Table

a	b	e
c	d	f
g	h	T

$$\chi^2 = \frac{T(ad - bc)^2}{efgh}$$

Step	Computations	
1	$a + b = e =$	_____
2	$c + d = f =$	_____
3	$a + c = g =$	_____
4	$b + d = h =$	_____
5	$a + b + c + d = T$	_____
6	$ad - bc =$ (_____ $\times$ _____) $-$ (_____ $\times$ _____) $=$ _____	
7	(Yates' Correction here, if used)	
8	$(ad - bc)^2 =$	_____
9	$T(ad - bc)^2 =$ _____ $\times$ _____ $=$ _____ (Numerator)	
10	$efgh =$ _____ $\times$ _____ $\times$ _____ $\times$ _____ $=$ _____ (Denominator)	
11	$\chi^2 = \dfrac{\text{Numerator}}{\text{Denominator}}$	

(2) With Yates' Correction, for the Same Type Table

$$\chi^2 = \frac{T(\mid ad - bc \mid - T/2)^2}{efgh}$$

The worksheet is identical to that above, except that at Step 7, the absolute value $\mid ad - bc \mid$ is reduced by half the grand total ($T/2$) before squaring it in Step 8. "Absolute value" means the value without plus or minus sign—we were not concerned with this concept in the first formula because the value is squared in the next step—squaring always yields a positive product.

Reading List

Berelson, Bernard, *Content Analysis in Communication Research*. New York: Free Press, 1951.

Lasswell, Harold D., Daniel Lerner, and Ithiel de Sola Pool, *The Comparative Study of Symbols: An Introduction*. Stanford: Stanford University Press, 1952; Hoover Institute Studies, Series C: Symbols, No. 1.*

_____, N. Leites, and associates, *Language of Politics: Studies in Quantitative Semantics*. New York: George W. Stewart, 1949.

North, Robert C., Ole R. Holsti, M. George Zaninovich, and Dina A. Zinnes, *Content Analysis: A Handbook with Applications for the Study of International Crisis*. Evanston: Northwestern University Press, 1963.*

Osgood, Charles E., George J. Suci, and Percy H. Tannenbaum, *The Measurement of Meaning*. Urbana: University of Illinois Press, 1957.

Pool, Ithiel de Sola, *The "Prestige Papers": A Survey of Their Editorials*. Stanford: Stanford University Press, 1952; Hoover Institute Studies, Series C: Symbols, No. 2.*

_____, *Symbols of Democracy*. Stanford: Stanford University Press, 1952; Hoover Institute Studies, Series C: Symbols, No. 4.*

_____, *Symbols of Internationalism*. Stanford: Stanford University Press, 1951; Hoover Institute Studies, Series C: Symbols, No. 3.*

_____ (Ed.), *Trends in Content Analysis*. Urbana: University of Illinois Press, 1959.

* Paperback edition available.

9

EFFECTS OF A CONTROL VARIABLE

In a strictly scientific experiment, the *control* factor is literally controlled: it is the element in the analysis deliberately kept uncontaminated by the *causal* factor under test, so that the *effect* being examined can be attributed more confidently to the experimental "cause." It is the unfertilized plot of land, if we seek an explanation of high or low yield; it is the placebo pill group, if we seek a measure of effect on health of a new drug; it is the *status quo* industrial technique, if we are examining the relationship of the new technique to high or low production.

In political and social research we are usually not able to maintain so pure a control as in "hard" scientific work. Approximations to a clearly identified single control factor are illustrated in Table 5-1 (6) (where we examined the effect of a propaganda campaign for the British loan on two groups, those who initially trusted England and those who did not), and in Table 5-1(9) (where we saw the impact of Peace Corps experience on career goals). Other studies have isolated exposure to a specific TV program, to a mail campaign for voter registration, and to reading a particular newspaper. Perhaps it is the similarity of these "controlled" experiments to the basic "scientific control" which makes them somehow satisfying. We see at a glance that they indeed resemble the experimental method. The initial impression of satisfaction is, of course, a superficial one. With only a little thought, we realize that in any political or social process there are bound to be a multitude of complex causal factors besides the one we have so neatly "controlled"—indeed, this very "control" factor is almost always contaminated by a number of other factors. Some of these we can measure if we take the time, and others we realize are certain to be at work and equally certain to prove unmeasurable.

In political research we attempt to examine relationships between effect and "cause," response and stimulus, voter choice and influence on it, by comparing interactions of a large number of factors thought or previously found to be related. It is often possible to use one of these as a tentative "control"

just as a scientifically controlled factor is used in the purer sciences. We accomplish this by tabulation of one pair of associated variables with reference to a third. In this chapter we shall examine some of the effects of a tabulation on three variables. To simplify matters, we limit our discussion to dichotomous variables—that is, we do not refine any variable into more than two groups: High and Low, Democratic and Republican, North and South, Men and Women. The processes are the same in logic, if more complicated in format and mathematics, for comparison of relationships of variables when subdivided into more categories, as well as for comparison of more than three variables. Determination of exact statistical significance of the association of three variables would take us into the statistical topic known as analysis of covariance, which is beyond the scope of this workbook. Our examples present eight of the principal results of analysis of covariance for dichotomous arrays of three variables, but avoid the more complicated statistical work which would be required for a complete discussion.

9-1 An Example:
The "Nothing Happens" Effect

Perhaps the simplest result of controlling for a third variable is that which occurs when the original two-variable correlation remains unchanged under the control. As an illustration, you might test opinion on the United Nations as related to educational background of the respondents. The (hypothetical) results might be displayed in the dichotomized pattern of Table 9-1A, showing frequencies only. Both educa-

TABLE 9-1A. *Support of the United Nations, by Education*

Attitude	No College	Some College
Support	42	60
Oppose	30	12

tional groups support the United Nations, but respondents with some college education are more likely to support it than are those with no college background.

To refine your data, you might next proceed to control for sex of respondent, obtaining the results of Table 9-1B. As the percentage columns show, you find exactly the same degree of association in each control condition: men and women do not differ in support of the United Nations in either educational group.

immediately clear. You should examine the breakdown under the two control conditions in Table 9-1B to satisfy yourself that the frequencies are correct. The entries in Table 9-1D are the *column totals;* those in Table 9-1C are the *row totals.*

Some Terminology. We are now ready to summarize our analysis of the data in this hypothetical survey in the more formal pattern of Figure 9-1. First, however, we must identify the terms and abbreviations used there.

TABLE 9-1B. *Support of the United Nations, by Education, Controlled for Sex*

Attitude	No College		College		Men				Women			
					No College		College		No College		College	
	N	%	*N*	%	*N*	%	*N*	%	*N*	%	*N*	%
Support	42	58	60	83	21	58	30	83	21	58	30	83
Oppose	30	42	12	17	15	42	6	17	15	42	6	17
Total	72	100	72	100	36	100	36	100	36	100	36	100

In this example, the control variable has no influence at all. From one point of view it is irrelevant to the analysis. On the other hand, the result confirms the original correlation between the Support variable and the Education variable as probably sound—at any rate uncontaminated by this control. Another control, of course, might yield a different result, but for the data at hand the original correlation is *completely explained* by the relationship between Support and Education. The point is made more emphatic by a look at two other arrangements of the same data, shown in Tables 9-1C and 9-1D.

TABLE 9-1C. *Support of the United Nations, by Sex*

Attitude	Men	Women
Support	51	51
Oppose	21	21

TABLE 9-1D. *Educational Level of Respondents, by Sex*

Educational Level	Men	Women
No College	36	36
Some College	36	36

You see at a glance that the correlation is zero for each of these tables. Yule's *Q* test and the χ^2 test each yields a value of precisely 0.00. The source of the frequencies in Table 9-1C and 9-1D may not be

1. *The Variables.* The three associated variables are abbreviated as follows:

(1) D = *Dependent Variable.* This is the effect to be explained, the political attitude, decision, or other characteristic thought to be influenced by or to *depend on* the other variables. "D+" and "D−" are used for the two dichotomized categories of the Dependent Variable, appearing on the *rows.* In Figure 9-1, "D+" means "Support the United Nations," and "D−" means "Oppose the United Nations."

(2) I = *Independent Variable.* This is the initial explanatory or causal factor. "I+" and "I−" refer to its dichotomized categories, and appear in the *columns.* In Figure 9-1, "I+" means "No College," and "I−" means "Some College."

(3) C = *Control Variable.* This is the characteristic "held constant," under which we re-examine the original association between the Dependent Variable and the Independent Variable. We speak of the dichotomized categories of the Control Variable as the two *control conditions.* In Figure 9-1, "C+" means "Men" and "C−" means "Women."

2. *The Tables.* In Figure 9-1, as well as in the other seven summary displays of control variable effects which follow in this chapter, we show five 2 × 2 tabulations of the data in frequencies, with row totals and column totals supplied as aids to the analysis. For Figure 9-1, these five tables correspond to the arrangements of data in the hypothetical survey on

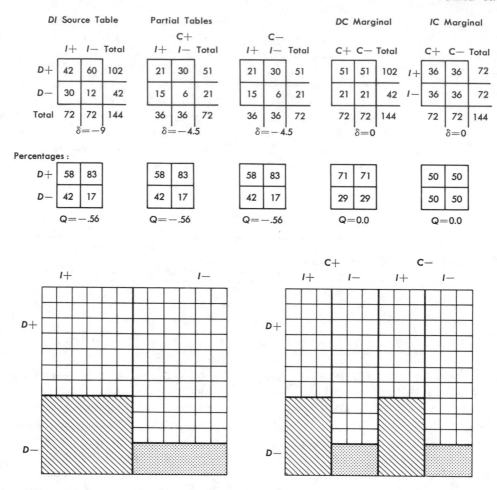

Association between the Dependent Variable and the Independent Variable in the Source Table remains exactly the same in each control condition.

FIGURE 9-1. *The "Nothing Happens" Effect*

Support of the United Nations in the same sequence as presented in Tables 9-1B, 9-1C, and 9-1D, as follows:

(1) *DI Source Table:* The Dependent-Independent variable association, as tabulated in the original uncontrolled 2 × 2 table.

(2) *Partial Tables:* These represent the effect of the dichotomized Control Variable under the two control conditions. The two partials "add up" to the DI Source Table, in that frequencies in the corresponding cells of the partials sum to the frequency in the equivalent cell of the source table. This is also true, of course, of the row sums, the column sums, and the grand totals of the partials. In fact, this is why they are called "partials." Each is simply a "part" of the source table.

(3) *DC Marginal.* The remaining two tables are called the "marginals" because the cell entries are obtained from the marginal totals of the partial tables. The first marginal table shown is the display of relationship between the original Dependent Variable and the Control Variable, and its entries are obtained from the row totals of the partials. In this table, the Control Variable simply replaces the Independent Variable as a single explanatory factor. It might have been tabulated in a separate operation directly from the source data.

(4) *IC Marginal:* The Independent-Control table shown in the last of the five 2 × 2 tabulations contains entries from the column totals of the partial tables. It tells us whether the two matched groups (I+ and I−) have the same proportional distribution under the two control conditions as under the

original DI tabulation. If the proportions change, the Control Variable has become *confounded* with the Independent Variable as part of the causal influence.

3. *Tests of Association.* Although we do not present here a statistical analysis of relationships among the source table, the partials, and the marginals, two simple statistics which we have already learned are shown for each of the five tables. Examination of their relative values will help us see the different patterns of relationship among the variables. The statistician calls our partials the "within groups" and our marginals the "between groups." Impact of the marginal associations on the partial associations is clarified by the process of computing a single value which represents the degree of association for the entire table.

(1) *The Delta Value* (δ). We learned the computation of this statistic in the χ^2 worksheets for 2×2 tables in Chapter 5. It is the "Observed minus Expected" value, which we called simply "difference" or "D." You will recall that for a 2×2 table, with only one degree of freedom, this value is the same for all four cells of the table, differing only in the plus or minus sign. This characteristic makes the delta value useful in itself as a measure of association in a 2×2 table. The "Expected" frequency for a given cell is computed by multiplying the cell's row total by its column total, and dividing the product by the grand total. The delta value is the difference between the actual frequency appearing in the table and the computed "Expected" frequency. By using the delta value with the sign it assumes in Row 1, Column 1 (the upper left-hand cell), we also identify the association as positive or negative. This was not done in the χ^2 worksheets of Chapter 5 because the value was later squared—the χ^2 test does not reveal whether an association is positive or negative.

(2) *The Q Value.* Below each of the five frequency tables in Figure 9-1 is a percentage display of the same frequency distribution, with the value for Yule's Q entered as an additional measure of association. You will recall that this statistic is often used as a quick preliminary test of association in a 2×2 table, and that it is *margin-free*—that is, it comes out the same whether the entries in the computation are frequencies or percentages, so long as the proportions are the same. Its value ranges from $+1.00$ to -1.00, with the value 0.00 meaning zero correlation. Unlike the delta value, the Q value is not sensitive to the size and proportions of the marginal totals. This means that two

tables having the same Q's will have delta values which vary in direct proportion to their grand totals.

The Graphs. The final display in Figure 9-1 (as well as in those which follow) shows the same data in graphic form. The first graph is based on the DI Source Table, and the second graph shows the breakdown under the two control conditions—it graphs the two partials. The data for the illustrative examples throughout this chapter are deliberately forced into a 12×12 graph grid for simplifying comparisons of one effect with another and to bring out more clearly the basic differences in the patterns. Our sample N, in other words, is always exactly 144. Though the illustrative tables and graphs are not based on actual surveys, each in fact represents a pattern found in actual surveys, if not with the precise frequency proportions we have chosen.

In the graphs, you should notice in particular the area relationships. The shaded portions of the DI source graph must exactly "fill up" the similarly shaded portions of the two partials. Think of each hatched area in the DI graph as a separate jar; then the content of each DI "jar" must exactly "fill up" its two counterparts in the control graph, where the hatched area is divided into the two partials. On the graph grids each small square represents exactly one respondent.

9-2 The Independent Effect

In actual tabulations, of course, so simple a control effect as that illustrated in Figure 9-1 will rarely occur. Almost always the control variable will in fact exercise some influence on the frequency distributions in the partial tables. A second example, which we call the "Independent" effect, is more common. Again, our illustrative survey is hypothetical, representing a poll of voter preference by religion, controlling for economic status. The distribution of Republicans and Democrats under the Religion variable represents the DI Source Table, and the same distribution divided into High Status religious groups and Low Status religious groups represents the two partials. The results shown in Table 9-2 are summarized for more detailed study in Figure 9-2.

In this tabulation, both the Independent Variable and the Control Variable exercise an influence on the Dependent Variable, and each association is in the same direction. Catholics are less likely to vote Republican than are Protestants, and voters of Low Economic Status are less likely to vote Republican than are voters of High Economic Status. The eco-

TABLE 9-2. *Vote by Religion, Controlled by Economic Status*

Vote	Protestant		Catholic		Status High				Status Low			
					Protestant		Catholic		Protestant		Catholic	
	N	%	N	%	N	%	N	%	N	%	N	%
Republican	56	58	12	25	32	67	8	33	24	50	4	17
Democratic	40	42	36	75	16	33	16	67	24	50	20	83
Total	96	100	48	100	48	100	24	100	48	100	24	100

nomic influence is about the same in each religious group, and the religious influence is about the same in each economic group. The two factors can be said to be *reinforcing* variables: each exercises an influence on the dependent variable, but independently.

Examining the delta and Q values of Figure 9-2, you will notice that both values of the DC Marginal Table are non-zero, and both are positive. The same is true of statistics for the DI Source Table and for both of the partials. This means that a separate 2×2 table showing voter preference by economic status would have shown an association in the same direction as the pattern of association in the original tabulation of voter preference by religion.

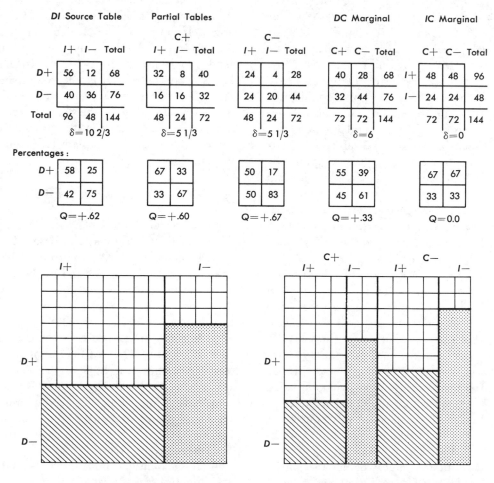

Both the Independent Variable and the Control Variable are associated with the Dependent Variable, and each association is in the same direction (each is positive or each is negative). The two factors may be considered reinforcing influences.

FIGURE 9-2. *The Independent Effect*

Holding Constant. Since in this example (as well as in all those which follow) the control variable is exercising an influence, a word is in order on just what we mean by holding the control constant, under the control conditions. The term "hold constant" means simply that we examine the original Dependent-Independent relationship under controlled conditions in which the characteristics of the control are as closely specified and distinguished as possible or useful. This meaning of "hold constant" is not immediately obvious for dichotomous cases. We speak of "holding age constant" when in fact we may pack all ages under 40 into one side of the dichotomy "Young-Old." The meaning may be easier to grasp if we think of "holding age constant" by a more elaborate cross-tabulation, listing the distribution of our two original variables under one age value at

a time—for example, vote choice by economic status for 21-year-olds (displayed in the first column), then for 22-year-olds, then for 23-year-olds, and so forth. When we use the simpler dichotomous breakdown we should be aware that we lose some of our data, unless the "constant" control condition is one of the two under an inherently dichotomous variable (Sex, Party in a two-party breakdown, Voter Turnout).

9-3 The "Stretch and Shrink" Effect

Our third hypothetical survey discloses a pattern similar to that just studied, in that the Control Variable and the Independent Variable both exercise an influence on the Dependent Variable. The difference is that although the association in the original table retains the same direction under each control condition, it is stronger in one condition and weaker in

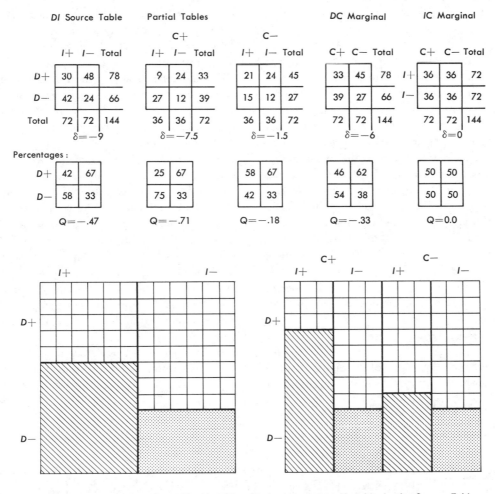

Association between the Dependent Variable and the Independent Variable in the Source Table remains in each control condition, but is greater in one condition than in the other.

FIGURE 9-3. *The "Stretch and Shrink" Effect*

TABLE 9-3. *Aggressiveness by Sex, Controlled for Region*

	Men		Women		South				North			
					Men		Women		Men		Women	
	N	%	N	%	N	%	N	%	N	%	N	%
Not Aggressive	30	42	48	67	9	25	24	67	21	58	24	67
Aggressive	42	58	24	33	27	75	12	33	15	42	12	33
Total	72	100	72	100	36	100	36	100	36	100	36	100

the other condition. All three correlations are negative (check the Q values in Figure 9-3), but one partial is more negative and the other is less negative than the DI Source Table.

For our illustration, we assume a survey on the personality characteristic of "Aggressiveness," initially showing that under the Independent Variable of Sex, men are more aggressive than women. When controlled for Region, the original correlation is still negative in both South and North, but the difference is much greater in the South than in the North. In the South, the correlation is greater than in the DI Source Table, while in the North it is less.

Again we see in the display of Figure 9-3 that the DC Marginal has a non-zero correlation, meaning that the Control Variable is at work on the initial Dependent Variable. We ordinarily expect this to be true, if the Control Variable is relevant to the analysis. A zero relationship here means that the original DI relationship we are trying to re-examine is identical in each condition of the control variable (as in Figure 9-1), so that (except for learning this and so confirming the validity of the original DI association) we may as well not have bothered to control for these conditions. Contrariwise, the more distant the DC correlation is from zero, the more relevant the control —the more important it is to the effect being studied.

9-4 The "Half-True" Effect

If the impact of the Control Variable in the "Stretch and Shrink" pattern is slightly increased, it

may result in the original association disappearing entirely in one control condition, and of course becoming even stronger in the other control condition. For one of the partials the correlation becomes zero and for the other it is greater than for the original DI Source Table.

Our illustrative hypothetical data, shown in Table 9-4, do not precisely follow McClosky's famous Leader-Follower survey, but are suggested by it. The ideological spread (Liberal-Conservative) for the entire sample of Republicans and Democrats is substantially increased for the party breakdown under the Leader control condition, and becomes relatively insignificant (in our example, it disappears) under the Follower control condition. Consensus is greater among followers than among leaders.

A close approximation to the "Half-True" effect is found in Durkheim's well known study of suicide. Durkheim's data showed that the suicide rate was higher for Protestants than for Catholics. With the data retabulated under the control of Type of Community (rural or urban), it was found that in urban communities suicide rates did not differ appreciably for the two religious groups, whereas in rural communities the difference was greater. This result does not exactly render the original correlation spurious, but it certainly emphasizes the impact of the control variable as greater than that of the original independent variable.

Relationship of the Association in the Five Tables. In the summary displayed in Figure 9-4, you will notice that the delta values for the two partials sum

TABLE 9-4. *Ideology by Party, Controlled for Leader-Follower Status*

Ideology	Republican		Democrat		Leader				Follower			
					Republican		Democrat		Republican		Democrat	
	N	%	N	%	N	%	N	%	N	%	N	%
Liberal	42	58	54	75	21	58	33	92	21	58	21	58
Conservative	30	42	18	25	15	42	3	8	15	42	15	42
Total	72	100	72	100	36	100	36	100	36	100	36	100

DI Source Table

	I+	I−	Total
D+	42	54	96
D−	30	18	48
Total	72	72	144

δ=−6

Partial Tables

C+

	I+	I−	Total
D+	21	33	54
D−	15	3	18
Total	36	36	72

δ=−6

C−

	I+	I−	Total
D+	21	21	42
D−	15	15	30
Total	36	36	72

δ=0

DC Marginal

	C+	C−	Total
D+	54	42	96
D−	18	30	48
Total	72	72	144

δ=+6

IC Marginal

	C+	C−	Total
I+	36	36	72
I−	36	36	72
Total	72	72	144

δ=0

Percentages:

	I+	I−
D+	58	75
D−	42	25

Q=−.36

D+	58	92
D−	42	8

Q=−.77

D+	58	58
D−	42	42

Q=0.0

	75	58
	25	42

Q=+.36

	50	50
	50	50

Q=0.0

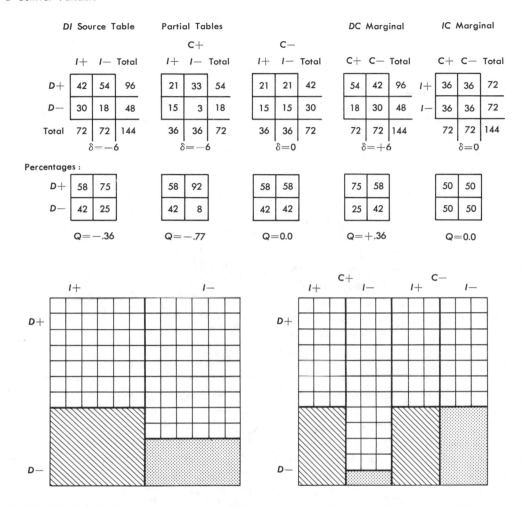

Association between the Dependent Variable and the Independent Variable in the Source Table disappears in one control condition and becomes stronger in the other.

FIGURE 9-4. *The "Half-True" Effect*

exactly to the delta value for the DI Source Table. You may already have guessed that this is a regularity of these patterns, since it was also true of the corresponding values in Figure 9-1, 9-2, and 9-3.

An exact mathematical equality indeed exists between the correlation for the DI Source Table and the correlations for its partials and their marginals. The five delta values in our displays may be used to state this equality precisely:

$$\delta \text{DI} = \delta \text{P1} + \delta \text{P2} + \left((N/N1 \cdot N2) \cdot \delta \text{DC} \cdot \delta \text{IC} \right)$$

in which:

δ = the delta value of the "$O − E$" computations for chi-square in the 2×2 table, with the sign it assumes in Row 1, Column 1.

DI = the 2×2 table displaying associa-

tion of the Dependent and Independent Variables, without the Control Variable.

P1, P2 = the two partials (each a 2×2 table) representing the relations of the Dependent and Independent Variables under the two "conditions" of the Control Variable.

DC = the 2×2 marginal table displaying relation of the Dependent and Control variables.

IC = the 2×2 marginal table displaying relation of Independent and Control variables.

N = Grand Total of frequencies in the DI source table.

N1, N2 = The two Grand Totals of frequencies in the two partials ($N1 + N2 = N$).

Four remarks will summarize the effects of the formula:

Remark 1. If *either* marginal table has zero correlation, *all* of the delta value of the DI Source Table must come from the partials.

Remark 2. If *both partials* have zero correlation, the DI correlation is *spurious*. All of its delta value must come from the marginals.

Remark 3. In turn, this means that if either marginal has zero correlation and one partial shows a stronger correlation than did the source DI table, then the other partial must show a lower correlation.

Remark 4. If the delta values in the two partials do not add up to the delta value of the source DI table, then *both* the Dependent Variable and the Independent Variable are correlated with the Control Variable.

9-5 The "Plus and Minus" Effect

An especially useful control effect occurs when the original DI correlation is zero (or near zero), but under the conditions of the Control Variable counteracting correlations are revealed. In one condition, association between the Dependent and Independent Variables proves to be positive, and in the other condition negative.

Hadley Cantril's World War II study of isolationism parallels our hypothetical data for the "Plus and Minus" effect. The initial tabulation on Isolationism and Age showed very little relationship: the Young and Old groups were about equal in isolationist sentiment. When Cantril controlled for Economic Status, however, he found that in the High Status group, young people were much more isolationist than old people, whereas the reverse was true in the Low Status group—the old were significantly more isolationist than the young.

Is the DI zero correlation spurious? The answer depends on the purpose of our investigation. Certainly it is significant that the original tabulation shows a majority are non-isolationist. For a politician counting potential votes, this is perhaps the most significant information. On the other hand if we are looking for hints about reaction of particular age groups to a foreign aid program, it is of obvious importance that the young are more isolationist than the old in certain elite circles, that the (presumably more influential) older persons of high economic status are predominantly internationalist, and that the (probably numerous and high in voting turnout) older persons of low economic status are rather evenly divided. None of this information was supplied by the original DI Source Table, which blithely reported a two-to-one split among both Young and Old on the isolationism variable. If not spurious, the Source Table is certainly deficient. Much more light is cast on the subject by the control.

Summary of the Five Effects. Careful study of the delta equation in Section 9-4 will teach you a great deal about the relationship of three variables. If you check it out in detail for our first five summary displays (Figures 9-1 to 9-5), you will find that all the effects thus far described have one feature in common—the delta value for the IC Marginal is always zero. This makes computation of the formula quite easy, since the zero cancels out the last (and most difficult) factor of the equation, leaving us only the task of adding the delta values for the two partials. The zero IC correlation also means that the five effects constitute a logical group—no change in proportions of the Independent Variable categories occurs under the two conditions. Computations for the five effects are listed here to emphasize their similarity on this point.

1. Nothing Happens Effect
   $$\delta\,DI = -9 = -4.5 - 4.5 + 0 = -9$$

TABLE 9-5. *Isolationism by Age, Controlled for Economic Status*

Attitude	Young		Old		Status High				Status Low			
					Young		Old		Young		Old	
	N	%	N	%	N	%	N	%	N	%	N	%
Internationalist	48	67	48	67	18	50	27	75	30	83	21	58
Isolationist	24	33	24	33	18	50	9	25	6	17	15	42
Total	72	100	72	100	36	100	36	100	36	100	36	100

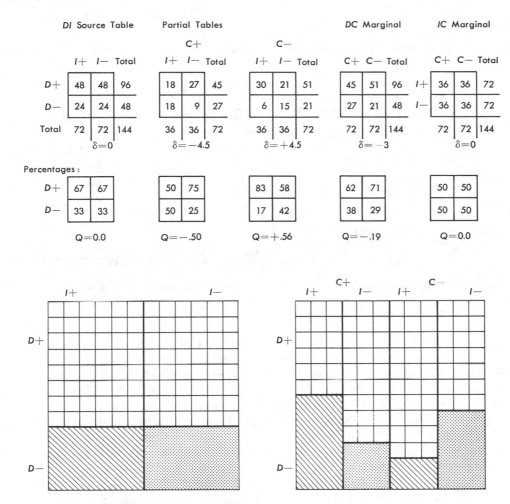

Association between the Dependent Variable and the Independent Variable in the Source Table is zero, but becomes positive in one control condition and negative in the other.

FIGURE 9-5. *The "Plus and Minus" Effect*

2. Independent Effect
   δ DI = 10 2/3 = 5 1/3 + 5 1/3 + 0 = 10 2/3

3. Stretch and Shrink Effect
   δ DI = −9 = −7.5 − 1.5 + 0 = −9

4. Half-True Effect
   δ DI = −6 = −6 + 0 + 0 = −6

5. Plus and Minus Effect
   δ DI = 0 = −4.5 + 4.5 + 0 = 0

Whereas we normally expect the DC Marginal to have a non-zero correlation, the IC Marginal should have a correlation at or near zero if the two matched groups under the two control conditions are essentially alike—*if their proportions do not change in the partials from what they were in the Source Table.*

The proportions of I+ and I− need not be equal as they are in most of our examples (note Figure 9-2 for an exception—Protestants outnumbered Catholics two to one). The important consideration is that whatever the proportions, they hold the same in the partials. If the proportions do change appreciably, our Control Variable has become *confounded* with the Independent Variable, and their association thus impairs the value of the control. It is as if we were using quite different populations to determine the effect of a given "cause"—for example, one group consisting of only 10 per cent Catholics and another in which Catholics constitute 90 per cent. What is true of the lace-curtain Irish may not be true of the more numerous shanty Irish.

the small society

Washington Star Syndicate. Inc.   BRICKMAN

Reprinted by permission of The Washington Star Syndicate, Inc.

For our last three examples of Control Variable effects, we turn to cases in which the proportions of the Independent Variable categories do change under the control conditions—in which the IC Marginal Table yields a non-zero correlation. None of these three effects is possible if the Independent Variable proportions remain the same under the control, a feature which sharply distinguishes them from the five effects we have examined.

9-6 The "Now You See It and Now You Don't" Effect

The similarity of our last three examples will become apparent if you look ahead at the graphs in Figures 9-6, 9-7, and 9-8. Notice that the width of the hatched areas which represent the two categories of the Independent Variable is different for the two control conditions. In all three cases, the Independent

Variable groups have changed proportions under the control.

Now, re-examine the delta equation of Section 9-4. The change in proportions means that the delta value for the IC Marginal will be non-zero, in turn meaning that the last ingredient of the equation does not cancel out. The explanation of the correlation in the DI Source Table *does not* come entirely from the partials; some of the explanation must come from the marginals.

In the hypothetical survey reported in Table 9-6, *all* of the explanation comes from the marginals, since both partials turn up a zero delta value. Here we find initially that voter preference is associated with union membership, non-union voters dividing exactly evenly and union members preferring the Democrats, though the correlation is not strong.

Controlling for Income, it is found—not surprisingly—that the High Income group contains rela-

TABLE 9-6.   *Vote by Union Membership, Controlled for Income*

Respondent Is	Not Union Member		Union Member		Income High				Income Low			
					Non-Union		Union		Non-Union		Union	
	N	%	N	%	N	%	N	%	N	%	N	%
Republican	36	50	30	42	28	58	14	58	8	33	16	33
Democrat	36	50	42	58	20	42	10	42	16	67	32	67
Total	72	100	72	100	48	100	24	100	24	100	48	100

tively few union members, the Low Income group relatively few non-union members. (Apparently we have here a thoroughly unionized community, and a year in which the Republicans are doing well.) The disproportionate grouping of union and non-union membership under the Income variable makes possible a result in which, for both income groups, voter preference is about the same.

It is instructive to compare this effect with the "Half-True" effect of Figure 9-4. In Figure 9-4, all of the DI Source Table's delta value had to come from the partials, since the marginal ingredient of the equation was zero. That being true, if the original DI correlation disappeared (became zero) in one partial, it necessarily increased in the other partial.

Is the original correlation between voter preference and union membership spurious? It is in part, at least, since the Income variable obviously is more strongly associated with voter preference than is union membership. Compare the relatively large delta values for both marginals in Figure 9-6 with the relatively small delta for the DI Source Table. Nevertheless, there remains the stubborn fact that for the entire sample union membership does correlate with voter preference. Why is this so? The Control Variable supplies the valuable information that union members in the low income group are twice as numerous as those in the high income group, and moreover are twice as numerous as low income non-members. However, low income union members are no more likely to vote Democratic than are low income non-members. If you were a Democratic party worker in this commu-

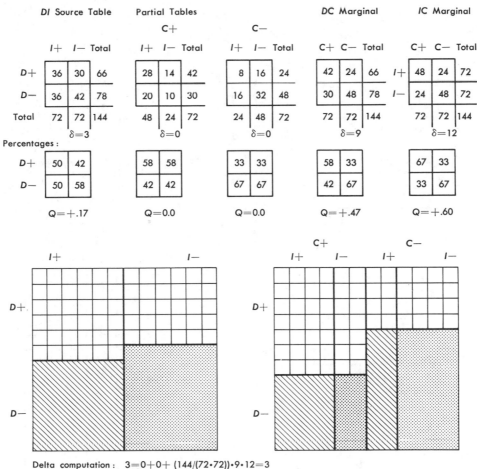

Delta computation: $3 = 0 + 0 + (144/(72 \cdot 72)) \cdot 9 \cdot 12 = 3$

Association between the Dependent Variable and the Independent Variable in the Source Table disappears in both control conditions, possible only if proportions of the Independent Variable categories change under the control.

FIGURE 9-6. *The "Now You See It and Now You Don't" Effect*

nity, planning a pre-election registration drive, you would have no doubt as to where you should concentrate your efforts.

Assuming you are alert to the political reality behind your data, it is certainly sound practice to deem the original DI correlation spurious if both partials under the control conditions have zero correlation. In our example, it is the Income variable which accounts for voter preference, union membership being essentially irrelevant.

9-7 The "Something from Nothing" Effect

In contrast to our last example, in which the original DI correlation was found spurious, we sometimes find the opposite effect. The original DI correlation may be zero, but when controlled, an association may

appear in both control conditions, and may be *in the same direction* in both. In Figure 9-7, the delta value for the DI Source Table is zero, but for *both* partials, it is negative. It is useful to compare this result with that of Figure 9-5—the "Plus and Minus" effect. In that example, without change in proportions of the Independent Variable groups under the control conditions, an original DI zero correlation, if changed under the control, could only result in correlations with *opposite signs* under the two partials. If a positive correlation developed under one control condition, then under the other control condition the correlation had to be negative.

Our hypothetical survey on Attitude Toward Urban Renewal is displayed in Table 9-7. Republicans and Democrats divide evenly on the question. When controlled for Income, the disproportionate

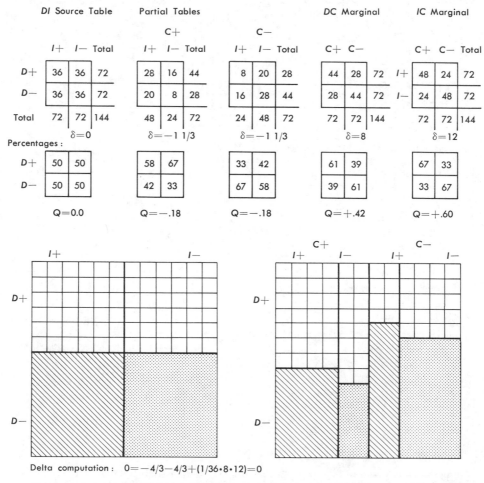

Delta computation: $0 = -4/3 - 4/3 + (1/36 \cdot 8 \cdot 12) = 0$

Association between the Dependent Variable and the Independent Variable in the Source Table is zero, but under the control an association in the same direction appears in each control condition (both are positive or both are negative).

FIGURE 9-7. *The "Something from Nothing" Effect*

TABLE 9-7. *Attitude Toward Urban Renewal, by Party, Controlled for Income*

Attitude	Republican		Democrat		Income High				Income Low			
					Republican		Democrat		Republican		Democrat	
	N	%	*N*	%	*N*	%	*N*	%	*N*	%	*N*	%
For Urban Renewal	36	50	36	50	28	58	16	67	8	33	20	42
Against Urban Renewal	36	50	36	50	20	42	8	33	16	67	28	58
Total	72	100	72	100	48	100	24	100	24	100	48	100

(relatively small) number of poor Republicans and rich Democrats makes possible a slight negative correlation in each control condition.

As with the "Now You See It and Now You Don't" effect, the explanation for this effect must be sought in the marginals, although in this case the non-zero correlations in the partials signify that the Independent Variable is also associated with the results. Again, examine the basic delta equation for the five 2 × 2 tables in Figure 9-7: the complicated computation is supplied just below the graphs. Where in Figure 9-6 the explanation for the original DI correlation was entirely from the marginal deltas, in this case it is a combination of non-zero correlations in both partials and marginals.

Again the question arises: Is the original DI zero correlation between support of urban renewal and party preference of respondent a spurious result? Since the total sample was exactly evenly divided on the question of support for urban renewal, the answer might be politically crucial were this an actual survey. If the community power structure were dominated by rich Republicans, the ultimate decision might swing in favor of urban renewal; if it were dominated by political leaders strongly based on support of poor Democrats, the decision would probably go against urban renewal. In a balanced power structure in a community with non-partisan city elections, we might expect the more typical political decision to postpone action until public opinion has time

to develop a clear-cut majority on one side or the other.

In any event, the results indicate that the original DI correlation of zero is not an adequate description of party division on the question. In this sense, the zero correlation is misleading, and may well be deemed spurious. In both income groups, Republicans do in fact differ from Democrats on the question.

9-8 The "Flip-Flop" Effect

A slightly more powerful impact of a non-zero IC Marginal correlation sometimes produces a result under the control conditions even more unusual than the two just examined. The original DI Source Table's correlation may actually be *reversed* in both conditions under the Control Variable, a result which is again impossible unless the proportions of the Independent Variable groups are changed under the control.

In our hypothetical illustration of this "Flip-Flop" effect, suggested by a student survey which was done as a class project, we have modified the frequencies to fit our standard sample of 144 respondents, but the pattern remains the same. Responses of a mixed group of career military officers and college students on attitude toward compulsory military service were first distributed by party preference (the DI Source Table). Republicans were found to be slightly more favorable to the draft than were Democrats. When

TABLE 9-8. *Attitude Toward Compulsory Military Service, by Party, Controlled for Occupation*

Attitude	Republican		Democrat		Career Military Officers				College Students			
					Republican		Democrat		Republican		Democrat	
	N	%	*N*	%	*N*	%	*N*	%	*N*	%	*N*	%
For	36	50	24	33	35	58	9	75	1	8	15	25
Against	36	50	48	67	25	42	3	25	11	92	45	75
Total	72	100	72	100	60	100	12	100	12	100	60	100

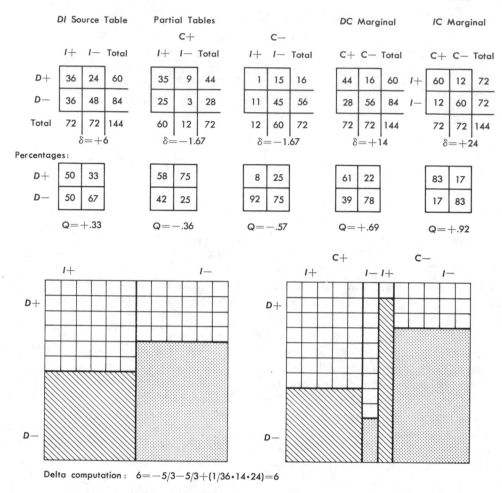

Delta computation: $6 = -5/3 - 5/3 + (1/36 \cdot 14 \cdot 24) = 6$

Association between the Dependent Variable and the Independent Variable in the Source Table is reversed (if positive, it becomes negative) in both control conditions.

FIGURE 9-8. *The "Flip-Flop" Effect*

controlled for occupation it turned out that there were so few Democratic career officers in the sample, and so few Republican students, that the original correlation was reversed for both occupational groups. The small number of Democratic career officers favored the draft by a larger proportion than did the Republicans, and the small number of Republican students opposed it by a larger proportion than did the Democrats.

A parallel example from Yule reports a survey of death rates in England during the 1930's.* British coal miners were found to have a lower death rate than Anglican clergymen. Considering the occupa-

---

* G. U. Yule and M. G. Kendall, *An Introduction to the Theory of Statistics* (New York: Hafner Publishing Company, 14th ed., 1950), p. 39–40.

tional hazards in the two professions, this initial result seemed difficult to believe. When the control of age was introduced, the explanation was found in the IC Marginal correlation. There were so few old coal miners and so few young clergymen that within each control condition the original correlation was reversed. Both young coal miners and old coal miners, respectively, had higher death rates than young and old clergymen.

9-9 Spuriousness

With this final example of effects of a control variable it becomes clear that an analysis is by no means wasted merely because the proportions of the Independent Variable are changed under the control conditions. Nor is the original DI correlation *neces-*

sarily entirely spurious merely because the IC Marginal yields a non-zero correlation. Indeed, one of the most important results of an analysis under a control variable occurs just in this event. If the IC correlation is non-zero, we have learned one of two things:

1. The control variable has helped us understand the original relationship of the DI Source Table by showing that the Control Variable itself, as well as the Independent Variable of the Source Table, is at work as an influence on the results.

2. Alternatively, the non-zero IC correlation may indicate that the Control Variable has contaminated the original tabulation to so great an extent that we should abandon the first Dependent-Independent correlation as spurious, the result being accounted for by the control.

These two conclusions seem diametrically opposite, but it is literally true that from the statistical analysis alone the two results are identical. This dilemma often seems frustrating to the devotee of quantitative methods in political research, although it is likely to amuse the traditionally oriented scholar who is cynical about the modern trend toward statistical approaches. Both the cynic and the devotee are partly right. We must depend on our substantive information about the subject under study to distinguish the two results—the figures alone do not supply the answer.

At this point you should review the short discussion of multiple causality in Chapter 2 (Section 2-6), with special attention to the three-point graphs in Figure 2-1. Paul Lazarsfeld has suggested a useful classification device (on which Figure 2-1 is partly based). The Control Variable may be chronologically *antecedent* to the Independent Variable of the DI Source Table, or it may be *intervening* (in time) between the Independent and the Dependent Variables. If the correlation of the DC Marginal is non-zero, and if the correlations in the two partials are zero, then the relationship of the Control Variable becomes crucial. If antecedent, we must deem the original DI association spurious. If intervening, we may consider it an essential link in the DI association. Thus the decision depends finally on our political information.

To emphasize the many and often unexpected results of a third variable, a story from the old West is apt. Most Americans, when young children, played the game of Cowboys and Indians. You will recognize this situational recreation as one involving a simple dichotomous variable. Few complications are possible: one side wins or a stalemate occurs, and a stalemate is not popular. The author's wife, born and bred in that romantic region of the United States known as the Indian Nations, never knew such a game. Her home territory was one in which Indians often were landowners or ranchers, and in a later age senators or governors. Her version of the game—her standard school playground contest—was "Cowboys, Indians, and Mean Men." In her community the Indian could not be the villain, so a third (and readily available) variable had to be introduced. The Mean Man—the present-day TV antagonist—made the children's game more real-to-life by forcing the multiplicity of results possible from the interaction of three variables.

We conclude this discussion of control effects, appropriately, with the same comment with which we concluded the first chapter. The wise political analyst is the master, not the slave, of his quantitative methodology. Helpful as statistical analysis can be, it cannot stand alone. The more we know about the substance of politics, the more effectively we can use these methods.

Exercise Set 9. What Happened Under the Control?
(or, Get Out Your Slide Rule!)

Tables in this exercise contain frequencies only, retrieved from problems in Chapters 2, 5, and 6. To present each table in the same format—a display of three dichotomized variables—we have omitted some categories, collapsed others, and added categories by use of percentages complementary to those shown in the original tables.

Following each table is a simplified version, with N's often drastically reduced to facilitate computations. Reduction ratios of 1/3, 1/10, 1/30, and 1/150 have been applied, but approximate proportions are retained. Since both delta values and chi-square values (and significance levels) vary with N, a formal statistical test should use the original frequencies. Here we are concerned only with the relationships among the three variables.

For each table, you are asked to carry out a brief analysis, in five steps:

1. Fill in marginal totals for both rows and columns of the DI Source Table and the two Partial Tables. The grand totals are shown, but check that your results crossfoot.

2. Fill in the DC and IC Marginal Tables, and write a short title for each, using the same descriptions of variables as were used in the original title.

3. Compute the four delta values for the partials and marginals, and then compute the delta equation. The delta value for the DI Source Table is supplied. Recall that all four deltas in a 2×2 table are the same except for the sign. Since we desire the sign of the delta value for the upper left cell, we use the formula:

$$\delta = a - (ge/T)$$

The letters refer to entries in the type table:

a	b	e
c	d	f
g	h	T

The computation (multiplying the column total by the row total and dividing the product by the grand total) yields the frequency which would appear in the cell if there were zero correlation. The difference between this value and the frequency which actually appears is our delta. On the worksheets, the computation of $N/(N1 \cdot N2)$, the multiplier for the product of the deltas of the marginal tables, is supplied to facilitate your work.

4. Try to identify the pattern of association with one of the eight principal effects of a control variable displayed in this chapter. All the effects are illustrated, but few in "pure" form, since these are actual tables, not deliberately arranged to display theoretical patterns.

5. Make a brief comment about the results, similar to those used for the "real world" examples of this chapter. Look for any spurious association, particularly in terms of antecedent or intervening variables. Re-examine Figure 2-1 and try to associate the relationship of the three variables with one of the three-point directed graphs.

Note. Computations for this set of exercises may prove rather time-consuming if done by hand. Rounding and approximations will yield sufficiently accurate results to demonstrate the pattern of relationships of the three variables. Depending on your own objectives and interests, you may prefer to work only a few of the exercises—but you should not abandon them until you feel you have a grasp of the patterns.

Computations for the first exercise are supplied as a guide. The FORTRAN program for delta computations

in Appendix C will run for these tables and is followed by a printout of the results for the first exercise in this set.

9-1. *Reported Presidential Vote in 1964, by Political Activism, Controlled for Party Preference of Respondent*
(Independents and Nonvoters omitted)

Voted For	Activist	Non-Activist	Respondent Republican		Respondent Democrat	
			Activist	Non-Activist	Activist	Non-Activist
Goldwater	52	102	50	87	2	15
Johnson	76	268	6	36	70	232

Source: Exercise Set 2 (4).

DI Source Table
Total

17	34	51
25	89	114
42	123	165

$\delta = 4.02$

Partial Tables
Total

16	29	45
2	12	14
18	41	59

$\delta = 2.27$

Total

1	5	6
23	77	100
24	82	106

$\delta = -.36$

DC Marginal
Total

45	6	51
14	100	114
59	106	165

$\delta = 26.77$

IC Marginal
Total

18	24	42
41	82	123
59	106	165

$\delta = 2.98$

Delta Computation:

$$\delta DI = \delta P1 + \delta P2 + \left((N/N1 \cdot N2) \cdot \delta DC \cdot \delta IC\right)$$
$$4.02 = 2.27 + -.36 + (.0264 \cdot 26.77 \cdot 2.98) = 4.02$$

Pattern: _____

Title for the DC Marginal: _____

_____

Title for the IC Marginal: _____

_____

Comment: _____

_____

9-2. *Voter Turnout in 1964, by Political Activism, Controlled for Respondent Identification as Partisan or Independent*

Turnout	Activist	Non-Activist	Partisan (Dem. or Rep.)		Independent	
			Activist	Non-Activist	Activist	Non-Activist
Voted	136	411	128	369	8	42
Did Not Vote	24	125	21	102	3	23

Source: Exercise Set 2 (4).

DI Source Table	Partial Tables		DC Marginal	IC Marginal
Total	Total	Total	Total	Total

DI Source Table

46	137	
8	42	
		233

$\delta = 3.59$

Partial Tables

43	123	
7	34	
		207

$\delta = $ _____

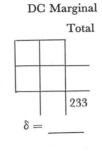

3	14	
1	8	
		26

$\delta = $ _____

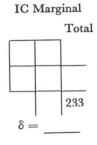

DC Marginal

		233

$\delta = $ _____

IC Marginal

		233

$\delta = $ _____

Delta Computation:

$$\delta DI = \delta P1 + \delta P2 + \big((N/N1 \cdot N2) \cdot \delta DC \cdot \delta IC\big)$$

$$3.59 = \text{\_\_\_\_} + \text{\_\_\_\_} + (.043 \cdot \text{\_\_\_\_} \cdot \text{\_\_\_\_}) = \text{\_\_\_\_}$$

Pattern: _____

Title for the DC Marginal: _____

_____

Title for the IC Marginal: _____

_____

Comment: _____

9-3. *Voter Turnout in 1956, by Intensity of Respondent Preference, Controlled for Perception of Closeness of Election*

Turnout	Preference Weak or Moderate	Preference Strong	Election Seen as One-Sided		Election Seen as Close	
			Weak or Moderate	Strong	Weak or Moderate	Strong
Voted	710	265	212	64	498	201
Did Not Vote	251	49	88	24	163	25

Source: Exercise Set 2 (5).

DI Source Table   Partial Tables   DC Marginal   IC Marginal

		Total
71	26	
25	5	
		127

$\delta = -2.32$

		Total
21	6	
9	2	
		38

$\delta = \underline{\quad}$

		Total
50	20	
16	3	
		89

$\delta = \underline{\quad}$

DC Marginal

		Total
		127

$\delta = \underline{\quad}$

IC Marginal

		Total
		127

$\delta = \underline{\quad}$

Delta Computation:

$$\delta DI = \delta P1 + \delta P2 + \left((N/N1 \cdot N2) \cdot \delta DC \cdot \delta IC\right)$$

$$-2.32 = \underline{\quad} + \underline{\quad} + (.0376 \cdot \underline{\quad} \cdot \underline{\quad}) = \underline{\quad}$$

Pattern: _____

Title for the DC Marginal: _____

_____

Title for the IC Marginal: _____

_____

Comment: _____

_____

9-4. *Presidential Preference in 1944 Reported by Members of Political Organizations, by Religion, Controlled for Income*

Preference	Catholic or Jew	Protestant	Low Income		High Income	
			Catholic or Jew	Protestant	Catholic or Jew	Protestant
Roosevelt	24	4	15	0	9	4
Dewey	2	7	2	0	0	7

Source: Exercise Set 2 (6).

DI Source Table	Partial Tables		DC Marginal	IC Marginal

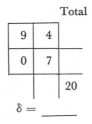

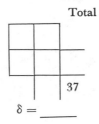

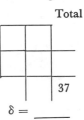

DI Source Table
Total
24 | 4
2 | 7
37
$\delta = 4.32$

Partial Tables
Total
15 | 0
2 | 0
17
$\delta = \underline{\hspace{1cm}}$

Total
9 | 4
0 | 7
20
$\delta = \underline{\hspace{1cm}}$

DC Marginal
Total
37
$\delta = \underline{\hspace{1cm}}$

IC Marginal
Total
37
$\delta = \underline{\hspace{1cm}}$

Delta Computation:

$$\delta DI + \delta P1 + \delta P2 + ((N/N1 \cdot N2) \cdot \delta DC \cdot \delta IC)$$

$$4.32 = \underline{\hspace{1cm}} + \underline{\hspace{1cm}} + (.1088 \cdot \underline{\hspace{1cm}} \cdot \underline{\hspace{1cm}}) = \underline{\hspace{1cm}}$$

Pattern: _____

Title for the DC Marginal: _____

_____

Title for the IC Marginal: _____

_____

Comment: _____

_____

9-5. *Membership in Political Organizations in 1944, by Income, Controlled for Religion*

Membership	Low Income	High Income	Catholic or Jew		Protestant	
			Low Income	High Income	Low Income	High Income
Member	17	20	17	9	0	11
Not Member	171	182	139	136	32	46

Source: Exercise Set 2 (6).

DI Source Table

Total

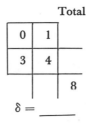

$\delta = .05$

Partial Tables

Total   Total

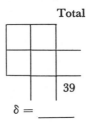

$\delta =$ _____ $\delta =$ _____

DC Marginal

Total

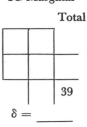

$\delta =$ _____

IC Marginal

Total

$\delta =$ _____

Delta Computation:

$$\delta DI = \delta P1 + \delta P2 + \left((N/N1 \cdot N2) \cdot \delta DC \cdot \delta IC\right)$$

$$.05 = \underline{\quad\quad} + \underline{\quad\quad} + (.1573 \cdot \underline{\quad\quad} \cdot \underline{\quad\quad}) = \underline{\quad\quad}$$

Pattern: _____

Title for the DC Marginal: _____

_____

Title for the IC Marginal: _____

_____

Comment: _____

_____

9-6. *Discussion of Politics in Germany, by Sex, Controlled for Education*

Discussion Role	Men	Women	Primary Education or Less		Secondary Education or More	
			Men	Women	Men	Women
Discuss Politics	340	230	260	185	79	44
Do not Discuss Politics	102	269	92	255	11	15

Source: Exercise Set 2 (9).

DI Source Table
Total

34	23
10	27
	94

$\delta = 7.32$

Partial Tables
Total

26	19
9	26
	80

$\delta = $ _____

Total

8	4
1	1
	14

$\delta = $ _____

DC Marginal
Total

$\delta = $ _____

IC Marginal
Total

$\delta = $ _____

Delta Computation:

$$\delta DI = \delta P1 + \delta P2 + ((N/N1 \cdot N2) \cdot \delta DC \cdot \delta IC)$$

$$7.32 = \underline{\quad} + \underline{\quad} + (.0839 \cdot \underline{\quad} \cdot \underline{\quad}) = \underline{\quad}$$

Pattern: _____

Title for the DC Marginal: _____

_____

Title for the IC Marginal: _____

_____

Comment: _____

_____

9-7. *Acknowledgment of Duty To Participate in Local Community (in Germany), by Sex, Controlled for Education*

Attitude	Men	Women	Primary Education or Less		Secondary Education or More	
			Men	Women	Men	Women
Have Duty	138	83	102	70	36	13
Do not Have Duty	304	416	250	370	54	46

Source: Exercise 2–10.

DI Source Table — Total

14	8	
30	42	
		94

$\delta = 3.7$

Partial Tables — Total

10	7	
25	37	
		79

$\delta =$ _____

Total

4	1	
5	5	
		15

$\delta =$ _____

DC Marginal — Total

$\delta =$ _____

IC Marginal — Total

$\delta =$ _____

Delta Computation:

$$\delta DI = \delta P1 + \delta P2 + ((N/N1 \cdot N2) \cdot \delta DC \cdot \delta IC)$$
$$3.7 = \underline{\hspace{1cm}} + \underline{\hspace{1cm}} + (.0793 \cdot \underline{\hspace{1cm}} \cdot \underline{\hspace{1cm}}) = \underline{\hspace{1cm}}$$

Pattern: _____

Title for the DC Marginal: _____

Title for the IC Marginal: _____

Comment: _____

9-8. *Acknowledgment of Duty To Participate in Local Community (Great Britain), by Sex, Controlled for Education*

Attitude	Men	Women	Primary Education or Less		Secondary Education or More	
			Men	Women	Men	Women
Have Duty	195	182	119	112	76	70
Do not Have Duty	264	321	158	228	106	93

Source: Exercise 2–10.

DI Source Table
Total

20	18	
26	32	
		96

$\delta = 1.8$

Partial Tables
Total

12	11	
16	23	
		62

$\delta = $ _____

Total

8	7	
10	9	
		34

$\delta = $ _____

DC Marginal
Total

$\delta = $ _____

IC Marginal
Total

$\delta = $ _____

Delta Computation:

$$\delta DI = \delta P1 + \delta P2 + ((N/N1 \cdot N2) \cdot \delta DC \cdot \delta IC)$$
$$1.8 = \underline{\quad} + \underline{\quad} + (.0455 \cdot \underline{\quad} \cdot \underline{\quad}) = \underline{\quad}$$

Pattern: _____

Title for the DC Marginal: _____

_____

Title for the IC Marginal: _____

_____

Comment: _____

9-9. *Acknowledgment by German and British Respondents of Duty To Participate in Local Community, by Sex, Controlled for Nation*

Attitude	Men	Women	British		German	
			Men	Women	Men	Women
Have Duty	333	265	195	182	138	83
Do not Have Duty	568	737	264	321	304	416

Source: Exercise 2–10.

DI Source Table	Partial Tables		DC Marginal	IC Marginal
Total	Total	Total	Total	Total

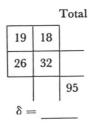
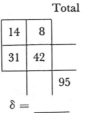
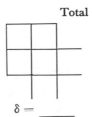
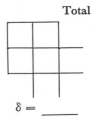

$\delta = 5.05$ $\delta = \underline{\quad}$ $\delta = \underline{\quad}$ $\delta = \underline{\quad}$ $\delta = \underline{\quad}$

Delta Computation:

$$\delta DI = \delta P1 + \delta P2 + ((N/N1 \cdot N2) \cdot \delta DC \cdot \delta IC)$$
$$5.05 = \underline{\quad} + \underline{\quad} + (.0211 \cdot \underline{\quad} \cdot \underline{\quad}) = \underline{\quad}$$

Pattern: _____

Title for the DC Marginal: _____

_____

Title for the IC Marginal: _____

_____

Comment: _____

_____

9-10.   *Party Preference in a Japanese Community, by Leadership Role, Controlled for Age*

Preference	Leaders	Advisers	Over 45		45 and Under	
			Leaders	Advisers	Leaders	Advisers
Conservative	20	3	20	3	0	0
Socialist	1	6	0	0	1	6

Source: Exercise 5–1 (3).

DI Source Table	Partial Tables		DC Marginal	IC Marginal

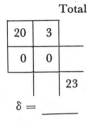

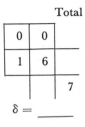

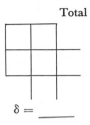

DI Source Table — Total — 30 — $\delta = 3.9$

Partial Tables — Total — 23 — $\delta = $ _____ — Total — 7 — $\delta = $ _____

DC Marginal — Total — $\delta = $ _____

IC Marginal — Total — $\delta = $ _____

Delta Computation:

$$\delta DI = \delta P1 + \delta P2 + ((N/N1 \cdot N2) \cdot \delta DC \cdot \delta IC)$$

$$3.9 = \underline{\hspace{1cm}} + \underline{\hspace{1cm}} + (.1863 \cdot \underline{\hspace{1cm}} \cdot \underline{\hspace{1cm}}) = \underline{\hspace{1cm}}$$

Pattern: _____

Title for the DC Marginal: _____

_____

Title for the IC Marginal: _____

_____

Comment: _____

_____

9-11. *Government Expenditures, by Voting Turnout, Controlled for Development (Number of countries)*

Expenditures	Voting High	Voting Low	Development High		Development Low	
			Voting High	Voting Low	Voting High	Voting Low
High	10	6	8	3	2	3
Low	2	8	2	1	0	7

Source: Exercise 5–1 (8).

DI Source Table	Partial Tables		DC Marginal	IC Marginal

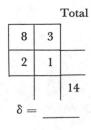

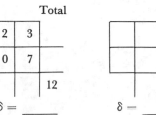

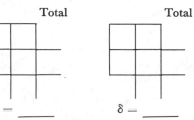

Delta Computation:

$$\delta DI = \delta P1 + \delta P2 + \left((N/N1 \cdot N2) \cdot \delta DC \cdot \delta IC\right)$$
$$2.6 = \underline{\quad} + \underline{\quad} + (.1548 \cdot \underline{\quad} \cdot \underline{\quad}) = \underline{\quad}$$

Pattern: _____

Title for the DC Marginal: _____

_____

Title for the IC Marginal: _____

_____

Comment: _____

_____

9-12. *Pre-Convention Goldwater Support by Respondents in the Midwest and South, by Religion, Controlled for Region* (N's *rounded*)

Candidate Preferred	Protestant	Catholic	South		Midwest	
			Protestant	Catholic	Protestant	Catholic
Goldwater	690	95	440	45	250	50
Others	3310	755	1560	205	1750	550

Source: Exercises 5–3 (5) and 5–3 (6).

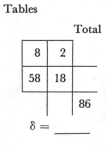

DI Source Table
Total

23	4
110	25
	162

$\delta = .83$

Partial Tables
Total

15	2
52	7
	76

$\delta = \underline{\quad}$

Total

8	2
58	18
	86

$\delta = \underline{\quad}$

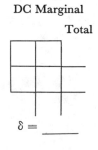

DC Marginal
Total

$\delta = \underline{\quad}$

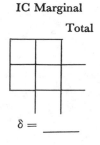

IC Marginal
Total

$\delta = \underline{\quad}$

Delta Computation:

$$\delta DI = \delta P1 + \delta P2 + ((N/N1 \cdot N2) \cdot \delta DC \cdot \delta IC)$$

$$.83 = \underline{\quad} + \underline{\quad} + (.0248 \cdot \underline{\quad} \cdot \underline{\quad}) = \underline{\quad}$$

Pattern: _____

Title for the DC Marginal: _____

_____

Title for the IC Marginal: _____

_____

Comment: _____

_____

9-13. *Party Preference of University Students in London, by Parental Party Preference, Controlled for Social Class of Family*

Student's Preference	Parents Vote Conservative	Parents Vote Labour or Liberal	Middle Class Family		Working Class Family	
			Conservative	Labour or Liberal	Conservative	Labour or Liberal
Conservative	162	33	143	19	19	14
Labour or Liberal	98	117	82	81	16	36

Source: Table 6-J.

DI Source Table	Partial Tables		DC Marginal	IC Marginal

DI Source Table
Total

16	3
10	12

Total 41

$\delta = 3.95$

Partial Tables
Total

14	2
8	8

Total 32

$\delta = \underline{\hspace{1cm}}$

Total

2	1
2	4

Total 9

$\delta = \underline{\hspace{1cm}}$

DC Marginal
Total

$\delta = \underline{\hspace{1cm}}$

IC Marginal
Total

$\delta = \underline{\hspace{1cm}}$

Delta Computation:

$$\delta DI = \delta P1 + \delta P2 + \left((N/N1 \cdot N2) \cdot \delta DC \cdot \delta IC \right)$$

$$3.95 = \underline{\hspace{1cm}} + \underline{\hspace{1cm}} + (.1424 \cdot \underline{\hspace{1cm}} \cdot \underline{\hspace{1cm}}) = \underline{\hspace{1cm}}$$

Pattern: _____

Title for the DC Marginal: _____

_____

Title for the IC Marginal: _____

_____

Comment: _____

_____

9-14. *Support of the United Nations, by Party of Respondent, Controlled for Respondent's Role as Political Leader or Follower*

Respondent Feels UN Role Should Be	Respondent Is Democrat	Respondent Is Republican	Leaders		Followers	
			Democrat	Republican	Democrat	Republican
Increased or Same (& n.c.)	2152	1306	1473	803	679	503
Decreased	457	549	315	429	142	120

Source: Table 6-A. The sample is overweighted for leaders, there being 3020 leaders to 1444 followers.

DI Source Table

Total

14	9
3	4

30

$\delta = .97$

Partial Tables

Total

10	6
2	3

21

$\delta = $ _____

Total

4	3
1	1

9

$\delta = $ _____

DC Marginal

Total

$\delta = $ _____

IC Marginal

Total

$\delta = $ _____

Delta Computation:

$$\delta DI = \delta P1 + \delta P2 + ((N/N1 \cdot N2) \cdot \delta DC \cdot \delta IC)$$

$$.97 = \underline{\quad} + \underline{\quad} + (.1587 \cdot \underline{\quad} \cdot \underline{\quad}) = \underline{\quad}$$

Pattern: _____

Title for the DC Marginal: _____

_____

Title for the IC Marginal: _____

_____

Comment: _____

9-15. *Attitude Toward U.S. Policy in Southeast Asia, by Party Preference of Respondent, Controlled for Occupation*

Attitude	Republican	Democrat & Other	Political Science Graduate Students		Career Military Officers	
			Republican	Democrat & Other	Republican	Democrat & Other
Dove	4	10	2	9	2	1
Other	14	23	2	13	12	10

Source: Exercise 10-3, with one respondent added to the student Republican Doves for the purpose of this illustrative exercise.

DI Source Table

Total

4	10	14
14	23	37
18	33	51

$\delta = -.94$

Partial Tables

Total

2	9	
2	13	
		26

$\delta = $ _____

Total

2	1	
12	10	
		25

$\delta = $ _____

DC Marginal

Total

11	3	
15	22	
		51

$\delta = $ _____

IC Marginal

Total

4	14	
22	11	
		51

$\delta = $ _____

Delta Computation:

$$\delta DI = \delta P1 + \delta P2 + ((N/N1 \cdot N2) \cdot \delta DC \cdot \delta IC)$$

$-.94 = $ _____ $+$ _____ $+ (.0785 \cdot$ _____ $\cdot$ _____ $) = $ _____

Pattern: _____

Title for the DC Marginal: _____

_____

Title for the IC Marginal: _____

_____

Comment: _____

_____

9-16. *Attitude Toward U.S. Policy in Southeast Asia, by Party Preference of Respondent, Controlled for Occupation (Democrats and Republicans Only)*

Attitude	Republican	Democrat	Political Science Graduate Students		Career Military Officers	
			Republican	Democrat	Republican	Democrat
Dove	3	5	1	4	2	1
Other	14	23	2	13	12	10

Source: Exercise 10–3, with one student Democratic Dove switched to "Other" for the purpose of this illustrative exercise.

DI Source Table

Total

3	5	8
14	23	37
17	28	45

$\delta = -0.02$

Partial Tables

Total

1	4
2	13
		20

$\delta = $ ____

Total

2	1
12	10
		25

$\delta = $ ____

DC Marginal

Total

5	3
15	22
		45

$\delta = $ ____

IC Marginal

Total

3	14
17	11
		45

$\delta = $ ____

Delta Computation:

$$\delta DI = \delta P1 + \delta P2 + ((N/N1 \cdot N2) \cdot \delta DC \cdot \delta IC)$$

$$-0.02 = \underline{\quad\quad} + \underline{\quad\quad} + (.09 \cdot \underline{\quad\quad} \cdot \underline{\quad\quad}) = \underline{\quad\quad}$$

Pattern: _____

Title for the DC Marginal: _____

_____

Title for the IC Marginal: _____

_____

Comment: _____

Reading List

Alker, Hayward R., Jr., *Mathematics and Politics*. New York: The Macmillan Co. 1965.*

Blalock, Hubert M., *Social Statistics*. New York: McGraw-Hill Book Co., Inc., 1960.

Hyman, Herbert, *Survey Design and Andlysis*. New York: Free Press, 1965.

Lazarsfeld, Paul F., and Morris Rosenberg (Eds.), *The Language of Social Research*. New York: Free Press, 1955.*

Zeisel, Hans, *Say It With Figures*. New York: Harper and Row, Publishers, 1957.

* Paperback edition available.

10

REPORTING YOUR PROJECT:

What Have You Proved and What Difference Could It Make?

No single format can be prescribed for a research report. Each project has its special features and is designed for a special purpose—whether that purpose be the propounding of a new theory of politics or the simple satisfaction of a term report requirement. The guidelines suggested here should be interpreted with the flexibility suitable to your particular report.

Even so, reference to a standard checklist is helpful, particularly for the beginner. Many a potentially valuable project has lost much of its usefulness by inadequate reporting, lack of attention to relevant reports by other researchers, incomplete analysis of the data, or unwarranted conclusions. This chapter is such a checklist, tailored to the preparation of reports of quantitative research, with special attention to surveys.

10-1 Your Prefatory Statement

1. *The general theme* of your project should be described briefly but clearly at the outset, with specific mention of the particular segment you have investigated. You have spent considerable time on the project and are saturated with its detail. This is a good point at which to re-examine its broadest aspects and to consider just how your study was designed to contribute to knowledge of the subject.

2. *The major hypotheses* under investigation should be stated, though probably not in rigorous statistical language. Say simply what general concept or idea you set out to examine, and list the several phases of it you have covered.

3. *Reasons for your choice* of this topic are appropriate in the prefatory section of your report. You may have read an article in one of the political science journals which suggested the need for further investigation, or which struck you as having drawn some doubtful conclusions which needed testing. Perhaps you were interested in examining some widely accepted generalization about politics which you felt lacked sufficient empirical evidence in its support. Or there was some current political issue or con-

troversy—national, state, or local—you wanted to study.

4. *Mention of previous research* related to yours should be included. You presumably have searched the literature in planning your work. Without labored detail, give the significant findings of at least one or two reported investigations of the theme most nearly relevant to your own. If you have searched and found nothing on your subject, it is a good idea to ask your teachers and fellow students: one of them may have seen an item you missed, or have an unpublished study available.

5. *The area of political science* in which your project lies should be established, whether it be one of the traditional fields (political theory, public law, comparative politics, international politics, popular government) or an area of focus in the behavioralism spectrum (political socialization, reference groups, analysis of political systems, political acculturization, judicial behavior, legislative behavior, political elites). Your study may well involve material which applies to more than one of these fields. It almost certainly involves work of interest to psychologists, sociologists, economists, or other social scientists. You should look beyond the literature of political science proper for research concepts and published studies which may bear on your project.

10-2 The Procedural Statement

1. *The source data* (the sample, if a survey) should be described in some detail. Give reasons for your selection (if limited by mere convenience, or lack of time or money, say so). If the project entails incomplete sources or a restricted sample—and this is usually true—make some effort to suggest what additional data would be desirable for fuller treatment. In a survey report, compare your sample's structure with what you know about random and stratified sampling. Mention any particular bias relevant to your study which you suspect your sample contains.

2. *The method of analysis—for example, the survey instrument*—should be briefly described, and

compared with similar methods or test instruments used in prior studies. You may have adapted a questionnaire or interview schedule from a major survey, or used a mixture of original and tested questions in a new setting. The value of your study may well depend on replication of another survey. If so, you have no apologies; the scientific study of political behavior is in its infancy and there is no research publication, no matter how distinguished the sponsorship, which cannot profit from verification or rebuttal by a new examination. Even if you use exactly the same instrument, you may cast new light; at least, the all-important variables of time and place are original with you.

Do not include your entire research design or questionnaire at this early stage; the appendix is the proper place for such detail. A few key items may well be listed, especially if they attack some of your basic hypotheses. A more extensive description may be desirable if you have included a novel method. If your further exposition uses an index based on a scaled or grouped set of questions, the procedure for deriving the index should be given, either with a display of the questions on which it is based or with reference to the footnoted or appended section of the questionnaire which serves as the basis for the index.

3. *For a survey report, the time, place, and manner of administration* of the survey should be stated succinctly, together with mention of any special problems or difficulties encountered. This information is important to appraisal of your results, and you should show awareness of its relevance. If respondents were reluctant to answer certain questions, there may be some significant factor behind their hesitancy. Even the most sophisticated and expertly administered surveys have encountered problems of this kind. Your report may well be suspect if you leave the impression that all was clear sailing.

4. *Special features.* Even though you do not have the resources to carry out a major project at this time, with care, advance planning, and ingenuity you may nevertheless make your project interesting and valuable. Some examples of student surveys displaying the attribute of "extra effort" will be suggestive of what can be accomplished.

A Filipino graduate student surveyed attitudes toward the Supreme Court's right-to-counsel cases. By sending his questionnaire to a colleague at the University of the Philippines, where he had taught, he was able to compare student opinion in the United States with student opinion in the Philip-

pines, as well as including an American sample of non-students representing the lay public, lawyers, judges, and police officers.

A student with political contacts was able to interview all twenty members of the county central committee of the Republican party in a metropolitan county, scaling responses on a liberal-conservative scale with respect to foreign policy and domestic policy.

During a political campaign, a student polled a sample of passers-by on the courthouse square of his home town on their knowledge of and attitudes toward the incumbent congressman, who was the leading contender for election to the office.

A Spanish-American student developed a bilingual questionnaire and administered it to samples of respondents with similar socio-economic characteristics in the lower-income sections of two cities, one with a large Spanish-American population and one with a large Negro population.

A journalism graduate student compared attitudes on democracy in a class of high-school seniors and a class of college sophomores (the latter having the common characteristic of having completed a required course in American government).

Rather than being content with an all-freshman sample from a "captive" discussion class, one student carefully sought out a sufficiently representative sample for comparing such dichotomous attributes as men and women, Greek and non-Greek, freshmen and graduate students, Democrat and Republican.

Two students cooperated in helping a faculty member conduct an international relations simulation, and reported on a "before and after" questionnaire aimed at showing the effect of the simulation exercise on the participant's information and attitudes about a variety of foreign policy and international issues.

By taking inventory of your own assets in the way of contacts, language skills, special access to interest groups, or lines of communication abroad, you may be able to add a dimension to your survey which will make it outstanding.

5. *Limitations.* Do not disguise the limitations of your project. You are probably dissatisfied with the small size or lack of representativeness of your sample, inadequacies in the responses, or what seems an excessive proportion of "Don't Know's." Without being apologetic, state these limiting features clearly. Awareness of such limitations will safeguard you against the common error of claiming too much for

your results, and at the same time will identify you as a careful researcher and give the reader confidence in your analysis.

10-3 Analysis of Your Results

Only a very general pattern can be suggested for the analytical section of your report, since each project will have its individual variations. Most complete studies, however, will contain almost all the items listed here, though not in the same order.

1. *The general trend* shown by your results might be stated briefly, particularly if it seems to verify or to differ from a finding in some of the published surveys you have examined.

2. *Your variables* should be clearly described. You are trying to explain some political attitude, opinion, action, or decision—perhaps a number of related attitudes. Your project has been designed to seek some explanation or combination of explanations of why the dependent variable varies as it does: why respondents think or act in different ways. The dependent variable is what you are trying to explain —the variable attitude, vote, attribute, or action which is thought to be influenced by or to *depend on* some other factor or combination of factors.

3. *The independent variable or variables* used as explanatory or causal factors should be discussed in some detail, with your reasons for selecting them. The list will often include such identification characteristics as religion, education, economic status, party affiliation, nationality, age, sex, and the like. Or you may discover some interesting association between respondents' attitudes on two different subjects, the one attitude perhaps in part explaining the other ("of respondents who trust England, 70 per cent approve the British loan"). In this event your independent variable is the "causal" or explanatory attitude, your dependent variable the attitude which it explains. Your ingenuity in seeking significant relationships between the dependent variable and various combinations of independent variables will determine to a large extent the value of your study.

4. *The control variable or variables.* Your data will almost certainly permit at least one tabulation under a control variable—a factor you "hold constant" in order to examine refinements and alternative explanations for the variation in the dependent variable. The principal effects possible when a control variable is introduced were outlined in the last chapter, which you should review before completing the

final tabular presentations for your report. In spite of the complexities of tabulating the association of three variables, the process of doing so is profitable experience, and will add a dimension of depth to your findings (as well as a dimension of difficulty to the work).

For a beginning project, it is suggested that you keep your control categories simple. In fact, it is probably best to use a naturally dichotomous variable for your control—keeping in mind of course that there should be a logical reason for selection of the control variable, not merely simplicity of format.

5. *Style of statements about association.* In writing statements about your results, recall the warning in Chapter 2 that we always interpret a table in terms of the categories which add to 100 per cent. This is a rule of even more importance in preparing the verbal interpretation of your own results than in translating a table done by another. No other error can get you into trouble more quickly or lead to valid criticism of your report more often than mistakened comparisons of categories which are not comparable.

An easy way to remember this principle is to express it in terms of sentence structure: for our format tables, *use the boxhead categories as the subjects of your sentences; use the stub categories as predicates.* For any format of any table, use the independent and control variable categories as subjects of sentences; use the dependent variable categories as predicates. You may make statements in terms of the dependent variable categories—that is, you may use the dependent variable categories as subjects of sentences—*only if you reconstruct the table from the original data,* so that the dependent variable categories add up to 100 per cent. In this case you have switched the roles of the variables: you are using the original dependent variable to explain the original independent variable.

Brief review of the examples of correct statements in Chapter 2 will help you keep your variables straight in writing up your own survey report. You may find it awkward and repetitious to follow the correct form in statement after statement about your tabulated results. You will probably have an uneasy feeling that you are violating the basic canons of essay writing which you learned in your courses on English style. On this problem, however, accuracy is more important than graceful prose, and you should plunge right ahead, no matter how repetitious and dull your sentences seem. After completing the task of translating your figures into correct prose statements, you may then turn your ingenuity to the secondary problems of smoothing them out, introducing variations on the repetitive phrases, and experimenting with different combinations of words which mean the same thing.

10-4 Tabular Presentation

The tables should be interspersed throughout your analysis as appropriate to the verbal context. A few mechanical points should be borne in mind.

1. *Position.* It is good practice to include a given table immediately after the first specific mention of it in the text, though spacing may require its postponement until the next page.

2. *Large tables.* A table so large as to require almost an entire page to itself should be given the entire page, rather than crowded with a few lines of text. A table more than eight columns wide must usually be placed sideways on the page; in this case the table should always appear alone, or with another table, even if its vertical dimension is quite short and considerable space is left. A table positioned sideways *always* has its top at the left-hand side of the page either in typescript or in print. Unusually elaborate tables, such as one in which you try to include almost all your data, had best be reserved for the appendix.

3. *Format.* As to format, we suggest the pattern of the tables in Exercise Set 10, or a suitable variation, unless your breakdown of categories dictates another arrangement, either in terms of physical space limits or clarity of presentation. In a table showing effects of a control variable, include the "totals" summation of the uncontrolled data for convenience in comparing relationships. If inclusion of the "totals" portion makes the table too unwieldy for your space on the page, add it as a separate table either immediately before or after the controlled breakdown.

4. *Titles.* Use special care in wording titles, avoiding the common tendency to overgeneralize. Make the title *informative*: it is the first thing the reader sees. It should describe succinctly but exactly what the table contains *and no more.* "Interest in World Affairs Expressed by Male College Freshmen, by ROTC Status" is more accurate than "Interest in World Affairs of College Students." The student group questioned is more closely defined, and the word "expressed" makes clear that respondents' interest was determined merely by asking them rather than by testing their extent of information or in some other way.

The title should be *neutrally worded,* avoiding phrases which suggest conclusions from the data. Do not use titles to state your findings (as in "Greater Interest in World Affairs of ROTC Students").

While the title should be as complete as possible, do not burden it with *excessive detail.* Do not use the title as a vehicle for a full description of your sample ("Interest in World Affairs Expressed by Two Hundred Male College Freshmen in Two Sections of Political Science Courses and Two Sections of ROTC Courses at the University of Oklahoma in May 1966"). While not wrong, such a title is cumbersome; specification of the sample is better listed in text or in footnotes to the table. Size of the sample is shown by including your "N's" in appropriate cells of the table itself.

10-5 Statistical Test

Even with the brief introduction to statistical inference presented in these lessons, you will derive satisfaction and your report will be more authoritative if you include at least one statistical test of your results. Those who have taken a standard statistics course will be able to carry out a more sophisticated analysis than that suggested here. The suggestions here are directed to those with the more limited equipment supplied in this workbook.

1. *Dichotomize your tabulations.* This is not very orthodox statistical advice, but it is an excellent practice for the beginner. You may miss some significant relationship by concentrating on twofold crosstabulations, but you are less likely to become confused by the complexities of the more elaborate computations needed for testing an $n \times m$ table. Some of your categories will be naturally dichotomous in any event (sex, voter status, home-ownership, party identification in a two-party breakdown, student status). When relevant, the state, national, or world mean obtained from census data is commonly used as a basis for dichotomizing such variables as family income, years of formal education, size of family, and type of housing. Or you may dichotomize your sample at a line nearest its own mean on the variable tabulated (greater than average, less than average).

2. *Preliminary analysis: Yule's Q test.* Having developed a series of 2×2 tabulations, each displaying the association of a dichotomized dependent variable with a dichotomized independent or putative explanatory variable, you need a quick method of testing the general significance of the results. This is probably best done by use of Yule's Q test. Simpli-

city and ease of computation (difference of cross-products divided by their sum) makes it an ideal device for preliminary identification of those associations likely to be significant. Remember, however, that *no specific statistical significance* can be attached to the Q test, since it is margin-free—unaffected by the size of the sample. Each of your 2×2 tabulations will presumably involve approximately the same total N, however, so the Q test will supply a *relative* guide to the comparative significance of your several tabulations. For the same total N, a Q value of greater magnitude reflects greater significance than one of lesser magnitude. For example, a tabulation of preference for Goldwater by income level, controlled for region, might be Q-tested separately for two regions, leading to the valid statement that "In the West, preference for Goldwater was somewhat associated with high socio-economic status, though no similar association was found in the East."*

3. *Significance level:* χ^2 *test.* Having identified certain of your tabulations as highly likely to show significant associations, you can then run the chi-square test to determine the precise probability level for each pair of tabulated variables. Use the worksheet layout for the 2×2 table given in Chapter 5; for greater accuracy you may wish to apply Yate's correction if your total N is small.

As with the Q test, you can use the χ^2 test to compare the two sections or "partials" of a table showing the association of two variables under the different categories of a control variable. Following the formats of Chapter 9, you should run three χ^2 computations—one for the 2×2 totals table, and one for each of the two "partials." This procedure will enable you to make accurate statements about the significance of association of the two variables without the control, as well as with it. You will be able to say, for example: "Nationally, Protestants favored Goldwater to a statistically significant degree more than did Catholics, but...when region is controlled, only in the Midwest is there a statistically significant difference."† Alternatively, with different distributions, you might say, "There was no statistically significant difference overall in Protestant and Catholic support of Goldwater, but when region was controlled, Midwestern Protestant Goldwater support was significantly greater than Catholic." Statements about other effects of a control variable will occur

to you as you review the displays in Chapter 9.

The phrase "statistically significant" should be more specifically defined, either in text, footnote, or accompanying table, by stating the test used and the probability level of the "significance": "statistically significant at the .05 level by the χ^2 test."

4. *Report negative results.* It is important to keep in mind that a finding that the statistical test discloses *no significant association* (at the probability level you have set) is just as important as a finding that a highly significant association exists. The word "significant," as used in statistics, has only a technical meaning: it means merely that the null hypothesis (of no association other than random) may be rejected at the chosen probability level. Actually, of course, it is just as "significant" to our knowledge of political reality to learn that two variables are essentially independent of one another as to learn that they are closely associated. A student who laboriously runs computations on all his tabulations, only to find that the χ^2 test yields values too small to permit rejection of the null hypothesis at any reasonable probability level, should not despair that "none of his results are significant." On the contrary, such negative results may go just as far as statistically "significant" ones toward upsetting an accepted principle or establishing a new one or supplying hints for future research.

10-6 Conclusions

The closing paragraphs of your report should summarize briefly in non-technical language the principal findings of your research. These should be related to the opening statement describing the hypotheses which you set out to explore, and to other relevant findings in the published literature. Often it will be appropriate to add suggestions for further investigations growing out of your results (as though you were preparing an application for a grant which would permit you to devote sufficient time, money, and travel to explore further the interesting leads you have uncovered).

Above all, avoid bias in favor of your original presumptions, as well as the bias of others whose work you have followed. Avoid attaching exaggerated importance to your results. A solid job of research speaks for itself. You probably have not opened a new frontier in political science, but you have discovered a new pebble on the shore of the vast sea of knowledge. Place it proudly on the cairn which others have started and to which still others will add.

---

* Irving Crespi, "The Structural Basis for Right-Wing Conservatism: The Goldwater Case," *Public Opinion Quarterly*, 29:4, p. 543.

† Crespi, *op. cit.*, p. 529.

Exercise Set 10. Is the Conclusion Valid?

These final exercises are planned as practice in making correct statements about tabulated data and drawing valid conclusions in reporting a quantitative project. Each is drawn from a student term project, which is described briefly. You are asked to check for validity the statements which appear following each table. In preparation, you should review the discussion of verbal statements about percentage tables in Chapter 2, with special attention to the point that a statement may be *true* in terms of the source data but *invalid* in terms of the percentage computations presented in a particular table. Since both valid and invalid statements are included deliberately in the lists, you should understand clearly that these have been reworded from the original reports for the purpose of this exercise—invalid statements are *not* to be attributed to the student authors whose names appear as sources.

The last statement in each exercise calls for your verification of a simple statistical computation, after which you are asked to express verbally your interpretation of the result. An additional problem for the last exercise provides experience in detecting groups of items with similar and unlike response patterns.

1. *Democratic Consensus and Frame of Reference.* In 1964 McClosky published an analysis of the extent of agreement in the United States by "political influentials" and the "general electorate" on a series of questions relating to "rules of the game" in democratic politics. A basic finding was that the American electorate is often divided on fundamental democratic values and procedural rules of the game, but that political influentials are in substantial agreement. Questions were worded so that a response of "Agree" represented an essentially undemocratic attitude (for example: "The majority has the right to abolish minorities if it wants to"; "I don't mind a politician's methods if he manages to get the right things done"). The full questionnaire and the results appear in Herbert McClosky, "Consensus and Ideology in American Politics," *American Political Science Review*, Vol. lviii, June 1964.

The student survey from which the table is taken does not attempt to refute McClosky's basic conclusions, but is designed to determine whether the questions were sufficiently general and ambiguous to have allowed for differences in interpretation, depending on whether they were perceived as statements of social fact or of social norm. The questionnaire was given to two classes of college freshmen, the first being instructed to consider them abstract principles (the "Idealistic" frame of reference) and the second to consider them operational practices (the "Realistic" frame of reference). In the table, "Agree" means that the respondent agreed with a majority of the nine "undemocratic" propositions.

TABLE 10-1. *Student Agreement on Democratic "Rules of the Game," by Political Orientation, Controlled for Frame of Reference (in percentages)*

Response	Respondent Identifies as		Idealistic Frame of Reference (Rules are Social Norm)		Realistic Frame of Reference (Rules are Social Fact)	
	Liberal	Conservative	Liberal	Conservative	Liberal	Conservative
Agree	43	43	7	28	68	59
Disagree	57	57	93	72	32	41
Total	100	100	100	100	100	100
(N)	(37)	(47)	(15)	(25)	(22)	(22)

Source: Arnold Kaufman, "The Influence of Frame of Reference on the Response of College Students to the McClosky Democratic Consensus Questionnaire," unpublished report, January 1967.

Is the statement valid?

1. Liberals and Conservatives divide in about the same proportions on agreement with rules of the game. _____

2. A negligible percentage of Liberals but more than one in four Conservatives agreed with the rules of the game when asked to respond as Idealistic. _____

3. Whether Liberal or Conservative, respondents were substantially more likely to agree with the rules of the game in the Idealistic Frame of Reference than in the Realistic Frame of Reference. _____

4. In either Frame of Reference, Liberals were less likely than Conservatives to agree. _____

5. More Liberals than Conservatives disagreed with the rules of the game if asked to respond as Idealists. _____

6. Respondents' frame of reference significantly biased their responses to these questions. _____

7. Retrieving frequencies for a new 2×2 table with "Agree-Disagree" as rows and "Idealistic-Realistic" as columns, Yule's Q is found to be $-.75$. _____

8. This value for Q indicates that _____

2. *Legal Representation of an Accused Person: Attitudes of Occupational and National Groups.* Controversy over the issue of police practices in dealing with those they arrest has been sharpened by two major decisions of the United States Supreme Court: *Escobedo* v. *Illinois* (1964) and *Miranda* v. *Arizona* (1966). In *Escobedo* the Court held that a person brought in for questioning by the police in a criminal matter should have the assistance of a lawyer if he so requests. In *Miranda* the Court went a step further, invalidating a conviction for rape on the grounds that the police had obtained a confession from the accused without specifically informing him that he had a right to have a lawyer present during the interrogation.

The survey on which Table 10-2 is based was administered after the *Escobedo* ruling, but before *Miranda*. It consisted of ten questions, varying from quite general ones ("Society needs the services of lawyers") to specific formulations of the *Escobedo* ruling. The results acquire added interest from the fact that the author was able to have the same questionnaire administered to a group of Filipino college students in addition to his American sample. Only two items from the survey are reported here.

TABLE 10-2. *Attitudes on Right to Counsel, by Occupation and Nation (in percentages)*

Response	American Sample			American College Freshmen ($N = 55$)	Filipino College Sophomores ($N = 53$)
	Students ($N = 98$)	Lawyers ($N = 11$)	Policemen ($N = 10$)		
Item (a)					
Strongly agree	76	73	70	76	23
Agree	22	18	30	22	36
Undecided	1	9	0	0	17
Disagree	1	0	0	2	17
Strongly disagree	0	0	0	0	7
Total	100	100	100	100	100
Item (b)					
Strongly agree	3	9	0	4	38
Agree	15	18	0	15	48
Undecided	18	9	10	12	7
Disagree	44	27	30	54	5
Strongly disagree	20	27	60	15	2
Total	100	100	100	100	100

(a) Every person brought in for questioning by the police in connection with a crime should have the assistance of legal counsel upon his request.

(b) The government should assign counsel to indigent drunks, breachers of the peace, speed and parking meter violators.

Source: Orlando M. Hernando, "A Survey of Local Attitudes on Legal Representation of the Accused Person," unpublished report, May 1966.

Is the statement valid?

1. On the basis of the sample, policemen fully accept *Escobedo*. _____

2. Students, lawyers, and police support *Escobedo* in about equal proportions. _____

3. More students than policemen support government assignment of counsel to indigent drunks. _____

4. More lawyers than policemen support government assignment of counsel to indigent drunks. _____

5. A majority of all three occupational categories in the American sample support the right to counsel of an accused person who requests it, but oppose government assignment of counsel in misdemeanor cases. _____

6. The strongest contrast shown in the table is that between American policemen and Filipino college sophomores with respect to the issue of government assignment of counsel in misdemeanor cases. _____

7. Retrieving frequencies and collapsing categories for a new 2×2 table, with "Agree-Disagree" as rows (omitting "Undecided") and "American Freshmen-Filipino Sophomores" as columns for the results on government assignment of counsel in misdemeanor cases, we obtain a value for Yule's Q of $-.96$. _____

8. This value for Q indicates that _____

3. *Political Science Graduate Students and Military Officers: Views on Foreign Policy*. General opinion polls on United States policy in Southeast Asia are published with some frequency, but rarely is the opportunity available to conduct a survey into the views of career military officers on foreign policy questions. The student survey on which Table 10-3 is based was carried out as a class assignment by a senior officer who had recently returned from Vietnam and was doing graduate work toward a master's degree in political science. His access to two groups with different career orientations and in different age groups, both presumed well informed on the issues, prompted this study, in which 25 political science graduate students and 25 career military officers constituted the sample.

One feature of the questionnaire was a "militancy scale" based on a set of questions designed to classify respondents by their score on specific policies into six groups ranging from "aggressive" to "non-militarist." The scale was used to compare respondents' self-identification as Hawk, Dove, or Other with how they chose among definite policy alternatives. In the table, results of the military policy scale are dichotomized, the Hawk label being used for those classed as favoring policies called "Aggressive," "Strong," and "Moderate;" the Dove label for those called "Moderately Weak," "Weak," and "Non-Militarist."

TABLE 10-3. *Militancy of Graduate Students and Military Officers Compared with Respondents' Self-Identification, by Career and Party Preference (in percentages)*

| | Military Policy Scale | | Self-Identification as Hawk, Dove, or Other | | | | | | | |
| | | | | | Graduate Student | | | Military Officer | | |
Attitude	Graduate Student	Military Officer	Graduate Student	Military Officer	Dem.	Rep.	Other	Dem.	Rep.	Other
Hawk	32	76	32	84	29	67	20	91	79	—
Dove	68	24	28	12	12	33	80	9	14	—
Other			36	4	53	0	0	0	7	—
Don't Know			4	0	6	0	0	0	0	—
Total	100	100	100	100	100	100	100	100	100	—
(*N*)	(25)	(25)	(25)	(25)	(17)	(3)	(5)	(11)	(14)	

Source: George S. Lokken, "Opinions of United States Military Officers and Political Science Graduate Students Toward the United States Policy in Southeast Asia," unpublished report, January 1967.

Is the statement valid?

1. For Student Hawks, the military policy scale value corresponds exactly to their proportions in the self-identification listing, but the Officer Hawks were fewer. _____

2. More Graduate Students identified themselves as "Other" than in any other category.* _____

3. All of the Students who identified as "Other" were Democrats. _____

4. Republican Officer Doves outnumber Democratic Officer Doves. _____

5. Republican Student Hawks outnumber Democratic Student Hawks. _____

6. For the 2 × 2 Military Policy table, the χ^2 value, computed with Yate's correction, is about 8.04. _____

7. This value shows that at the _____ probability level, we reject a null hypothesis that _____

---

* One student identified himself as an Owl—defined as someone who takes neither side, but likes just to sit back, look, listen, and hoot!

4. *Cuban Policy: Midwestern and Florida Opinion.* To see whether he could verify the plausible assumption that persons in Florida were likely to be more concerned than Midwesterners with the question of United States policy toward Cuba, the author of the survey from which Table 10-4 is drawn developed a questionnaire which was administered to college students in both places in December 1966. The interesting results for two items shown here seem to indicate less concern with Cuba in Miami than in Oklahoma.

TABLE 10-4(A). *Attitudes of Oklahoma and Florida College Students on United States Cuban Policy, by Party (in percentages)*

	University of Oklahoma		Miami Dade Junior College	
	Democrats	Republicans	Democrats	Republicans
Effective	33	20	71	73
Ineffective	67	80	29	27
Total	100	100	100	100
(*N*)	(15)	(10)	(17)	(11)

(B). *Views on Ousting Castro, by Region And Party*[a]

Agree	44	50	29	18
Disagree	56	50	71	82
Total	100	100	100	100
(*N*)	(16)	(10)	(17)	(11)

[a] Agreement with the statement "Our best strategy in the Vietnamese war would be to help the Cuban people to oust Castro."

Source: Roberto E. Villarreal, "Attitudes of University of Oklahoma Students and Miami Dade Junior College Students on United States Policy toward Cuba," unpublished report, January 1967.

Is the statement valid?

1. Both Democrats and Republicans in the Miami sample are more likely to deem U.S. Cuban policy effective than are the corresponding groups in Oklahoma. _____

2. The regional factor accounts for more variation than the party factor as an explanation of attitude toward effectiveness of Cuban policy. _____

3. Democrats generally feel administration Cuban policy effective and Republicans generally feel it ineffective. _____

4. More Republicans than Democrats in the Oklahoma sample agree that ousting Castro is a good way to win in Vietnam. _____

5. Florida Republicans feel U.S. Cuban policy is effective in larger proportions than is true of any other group in the sample. _____

6. As an explanatory factor, party preference is positively associated with attitude in one region but negatively in the other. This is true of both issues. _____

7. Retrieving frequencies and reconstructing a 2 × 2 table for the data in Table 10-4 (A), with Effective-Ineffective" as the rows and "Oklahoma-Florida" as the columns, we obtain a χ^2 value on regional difference of about 8.31. _____

8. This value would permit us to reject, at the _____ probability level, the null hypothesis

that _____

5. *Internationalism: American and Swiss Student Opinion.* To determine how national cultural differences affect attitudes on broad political issues, a student who had resided in Europe for several years developed a series of scaled questions to tap the attitude dimensions of Internationalism, East-West Reconciliation, and European Neutralism. These were administered to 20 American and 20 Swiss college students, at Oklahoma and Lausanne, in December 1966. The questions for the Internationalism scale are listed here, each with American and Swiss responses (+ is Agree, − is Disagree). Rank order for each question is determined by support percentage accorded it in the two groups (+'s only), ties being broken where possible by recomputing the support percentages with "Don't Know" responses omitted.

TABLE 10-5. *Responses of U.S. and Swiss Students on Questions of Internationalism, Ranked by Percentages of Support in the Two Groups*

Question	U.S. Responses (%)			Swiss Responses (%)			Support Rank	Support Rank
	+	−	DK	+	−	DK	(U.S.)	(Swiss)
	(N = 20)			(N = 20)				
1. Approve of the United Nations	95	5	0	60	30	10	1	5
2. The eventual political unification of Europe is important	80	5	15	80	15	5	2	1
3. The United Nations is effective as a world political forum	80	15	5	30	65	5	3	8
4. National interest should not be the main reason for participation in the UN	70	25	5	60	35	5	4	6
5. The UN Specialized Agencies (technical, economic, social) are effective	65	10	25	75	10	15	5	2
6. U.S. and USSR should support a European community of both East and West Europe	60	20	20	75	25	0	6	3.5
7. International cooperation should take precedence over national interest	35	60	5	75	25	0	7	3.5
8. Nation state is outmoded and should be replaced by international organizations	30	65	5	45	45	10	8	7

Source: Paul R. Petty, "Political Attitudes of U.S. and Swiss Students," unpublished report, January 1967.

Is the statement valid?

1. American students in the sample are more internationalist than Swiss students. _____

2. Support for the United Nations is stronger in the American sample than in the Swiss sample. _____

3. Consistency of support ranking by the two groups may be tested by Spearman's coefficient of rank correlation, yielding a value of about +0.11. _____

4. This value indicates that we may reasonably accept a null hypothesis that the two groups are essentially similar in their support of the eight issues. _____

5. An alternative hypothesis suggested by the rank correlation test is _____

6. To select questions from the Internationalism Scale for further exploration, identify those on which the U.S.-Swiss response patterns are significantly similar and significantly different. Use Yule's Q for this preliminary identification, running your computations from the condensed 2×2 frequency tables showing agreement and disagreement (columns) by the two groups (rows) on the eight issues.

	1 +	1 −	2 +	2 −	3 +	3 −	4 +	4 −	5 +	5 −	6 +	6 −	7 +	7 −	8 +	8 −
U.S.	19	1	16	1	16	3	14	5	13	2	12	4	7	12	6	13
Swiss	12	6	16	3	6	13	12	7	15	2	15	5	15	5	9	9

$Q =$ _____ _____ _____ _____ _____ _____ _____ _____

Tentative List of Similar Associations   Tentative List of Different Associations

_____   _____

_____   _____

_____   _____

_____   _____

Reading List

The best guide to preparing a report is a good model. Literally hundreds of good models are found in the articles and research notes which appear in the volumes and current issues of the professional scholarly journals listed in Part 1. Many of the best articles from these and other journals have been selected for inclusion in the edited collections and "readers" in the reading list of Chapter 6. Part 2 concludes our reading lists with a selection of major reference works containing data series of value to political scientists.

1. *Professional Journals in Political Science and Allied Fields*

1–1. Journals of political science associations

American Political Science Review, journal of the American Political Science Association.

Journal of Politics, Southern Political Science Association.

Midwest Journal of Political Science, Midwest Conference of Political Scientists.

Polity, scheduled to appear in 1968 as the journal of the Northeastern Political Science Associations.

Western Political Quarterly, Western Political Science Association.

1–2. Political science and others

Annals of the American Academy of Political and Social Science.

Political Science Quarterly, edited for the Academy of Political Science by the faculty of political science of Columbia University.

Review of Politics, University of Notre Dame.

Southwestern Social Science Quarterly, Southwestern Social Science Association.

World Politics, Princeton University Center of International Studies.

1–3. Related fields

American Journal of Sociology, University of Chicago.

American Sociological Review, American Sociological Association.

International Social Science Bulletin, UNESCO.

Gallup Opinion Index—Political, Social and Economic Trends. Princeton: Gallup International, monthly.

Public Opinion Quarterly, published by Princeton University for the American Association for Public Opinion Research.

2. *Reference Works Useful in Political Research*

2–1. Recurrent Publications of the United States Bureau of the Census

Congressional District Data Book (*Districts of the 88th Congress*) and *Supplements, Redistricted States* (published in 1964; supplements in 1965 and 1966. Most of the census items contained in the *Abstract* and the *County and City Data Book* are re-computed for the 435 congressional districts; $4.75).

County and City Data Book (latest editions 1962 and 1966; $5.25).

Historical Statistics of the United States, Colonial Times to 1957 and *Continuation to 1962 and Revisions* (more than 8000 statistical time series; $6.00 and $1.00).

Statistical Abstract of the United States (annual, $3.75).

2–2. Recurrent Publications of the United Nations

Demographic Yearbook ($15.00).

Statistical Yearbook ($15.00).

World Economic Survey ($4.50).

Yearbook of International Trade Statistics ($11.50).

Yearbook of National Accounts Statistics ($7.00).

Yearbook of the United Nations ($21.75).

2–3. Unofficial publications

America Votes. Washington: Governmental Affairs Institute, biennial. Election results by county since 1948.

Atlas of Economic Development, by Norton Ginsburg. Chicago: University of Chicago Press, 1961. Rankings of up to 140 political units on 47 variables, each with world map and graph hatched by sextiles.

Britannica Book of the Year. Chicago: Encyclopedia Britannica, Inc., annual. Contains a statistical supplement on the States, and reproduces many statistical items from the publications of the U.S. Census Bureau, the United Nations, and private sources.

Congress and the Nation: 1945–1964, by the Congressional Quarterly staff. Washington: Congressional Quarterly, Inc., 1965. Key roll-calls in both Senate and House for each Congress.

A Cross-Polity Survey, by Arthur S. Banks and Robert B. Textor. Cambridge: M.I.T. Press, 1963. Tabulations of 194 characteristics for 115 independent polities.

The Military Balance, 1966/1967. London: Institute of Strategic Studies, 1966.

World Handbook of Political and Social Indicators, by Bruce M. Russett, Hayward R. Alker, Jr., Karl W. Deutsch, and Harold D. Lasswell. New Haven: Yale University Press, 1964. All available data for independent countries on 75 characteristics; correlations of each pair of variables and other analysis.

APPENDIX

A. List of Lecture Sources

B. Speed in Computations

C. Computer Programs

D. Table of Reciprocals to 100

E. Values for Q for Percentage Deciles

F. Significance Levels for Spearman's Coefficient of Rank Correlation

G. Abridged Table of Critical Values of Chi Square

A. List of Lecture Sources

These topics and sources are suggested for the teacher who wishes to develop an introductory course in empirical methods to accompany this workbook. The list is tailored to the beginning student in quantification and ruthlessly excludes difficult items or identifies the more approachable segments of advanced treatments. Excellent alternative sources exist for most of the topics. This is a minimal yet wieldy kit of materials with which to begin. The topic on data sources, listed last for convenience, should be introduced at a point suitable to the level of advancement of the class, preferably with many of the reference books and journals physically available for student use throughout the course.

1. **Politics and Data**

   1.1. What Political Science Studies
   Perspectives on Political Science, by Frank J. Sorauf. Columbus: Charles E. Merrill Books, 1965. Chapters 1 and 2.

   1.2. The Behavioral Emphasis in Political Science
   The Behavioral Persuasion in Politics, by Heinz Eulau. New York: Random House, Inc., 1963.

   1.3. The Place of Data in Political Science
   Mathematics and Politics, by Hayward R. Alker, Jr., New York: The Macmillan Company, 1965. Chapters 1 and 2.

2. **Tables**

   2.1. Formats of Tabular Presentation
   Say It With Figures, by Hans Zeisel. New York: Harper and Row, Publishers, 1957. Chapters 2 and 4.

   2.2. Variables
   Social Statistics, by Hubert M. Blalock. New York: McGraw-Hill Book Company, 1960. Chapter 2.

   2.3. The Concept of Property Space
   The Language of Social Research, eds. Paul F. Lazarsfeld and Morris Rosenberg. Glencoe: Free Press, 1955. Pages 40–53.

3. **Graphs and Charts**

   3.1. Graphs as Mappings of Property Space
   Handbook of Graphic Presentation, by Calvin F. Schmid. New York: The Ronald Press Company, 1954.

   3.2. Directed Graphs
   Graphs and Their Uses, by Oystein Ore. New York: Random House, Inc., 1963. Chapters 5 and 8.
   Mathematical Models in the Social Sciences, by John G. Kemeny and J. Laurie Snell. New York: Ginn and Company, 1962. Chapter 8.

   3.3. Venn Diagrams
   Modern Logic, by Norman L. Thomas. New York: Barnes and Noble, 1966. Chapter 2.

Introduction to Finite Mathematics, by John G. Kemeny, J. Laurie Snell, and Gerald L. Thompson. Englewood Cliffs, N.J.: Prentice-Hall, 1956. Chapters 2 and 3.

4. **Data Processing**

    4.1. The Logic of Coding
    Data Processing, by Kenneth Janda. Evanston: Northwestern University Press, 1965. Chapters 2 and 5.

    4.2. Methods of Processing Data
    Survey Design and Analysis, by Herbert Hyman. New York: Free Press, 1955. Appendix, C and D.

    4.3. Hardware for Data Processing
    Textbook on Mechanized Information Retrieval, by Allen Kent. New York: John Wiley & Sons, Inc., 1962. Also Janda, Chapters 3 and 4.

5. **Statistics**

    5.1. Basic Concepts of Descriptive Statistics
    The Conduct of Inquiry, by Abraham Kaplan. San Francisco: Chandler Publishing Co., 1964. Chapter 27.

    5.2. The Logic of Statistical Inference
    Social Statistics, by Hubert M. Blalock (cited above). Chapters 8 and 9.

    5.3. Three Non-Parametric Tests: *Q,* Rho, and Chi-Square
    A Basic Course in Sociological Statistics, by Morris Zelditch, Jr. New York: Holt, Rinehart, & Winston, Inc., 1959. Chapters 7, 10, and 11.

6. **Survey Research**

    6.1. The Role of Surveys in Political Science
    Political Behavior in America: New Directions, ed. Heinz Eulau. New York: Random House, Inc., 1966. Introduction and prefatory notes at pages 17, 201, and 335.

    6.2. How to Ask Questions
    Survey Research, by Charles H. Backstrom and Gerald D. Hursh. Evanston: Northwestern University Press, 1963. Chapter 3.

    6.3. Your Own Survey
    The Focused Interview, by Robert K. Merton, Marjorie Fiske, and Patricia L. Kendall. Glencoe: Free Press, 1956.

7. **Indexes and Scaling**

    7.1. Indexes and Scales in Social Research
    Handbook of Research Design and Social

Measurement, by Delbert C. Miller. New York: David McKay Co., Inc., 1964.

    7.2. Roll-Call Scaling
    Legislative Roll-Call Analysis, by Lee F. Anderson, Meredith W. Watts, Jr., and Allen R. Wilcox. Evanston: Northwestern University Press, 1966. Chapters 2, 3, and 4.

    7.3. Planning a Scaling Project
    Legislative Behavior: A Reader in Research and Theory, eds. John C. Wahlke and Heinz Eulau. New York: Free Press, 1959.

8. **Content Analysis**

    8.1. Political Uses of Content Analysis
    Trends in Content Analysis, ed. Ithiel de Sola Pool. Urbana: University of Illinois Press, 1959. The editor's summary of the conference papers, pp. 189–233.

    8.2. A Specific Technique of Content Analysis: The *Q*-Sort
    Content Analysis: A Handbook with Applications for the Study of International Crisis, by Robert C. North, Ole R. Holsti, M. George Zaninovich, and Dina A. Zinnes. Evanston: Northwestern University Press, 1963. Pages 55–77.

    8.3. A Look at Advanced Methods of Content Analysis
    The Measurement of Meaning, by Charles E. Osgood, George J. Suci, and Percy H. Tannenbaum. Urbana: University of Illinois Press, 1957.

9. **Effects of a Control Variable**

    9.1. Causality and Controls
    Social Statistics, by Hubert M. Blalock (cited above). Chapter 8.

    9.2. The Logic of Three Variables
    The Language of Social Research, eds. Lazarsfeld and Rosenberg (cited above). Pages 115–125.

    9.3. Identification of Spurious Association
    Mathematics and Politics, by Hayward R. Alker, Jr. (cited above). Chapter 6.

10. **Reporting A Project**

    10.1. The Logic of Hypotheses
    The Conduct of Inquiry, by Abraham Kaplan (cited above). Part III on "Laws" and IV on "Experiments."

    10.2. Reporting a Survey
    The best guide is a set of good reports: for example those in *Political Behavior in*

America: New Dimensions, ed. Heinz Eulau (cited above).

10.3. Data Sources: Reference Books and Archives

In addition to the journals and reference volumes in the reading list of Chapter 10, an account of the collections and services of the leading social science data archives is given by Ralph L. Bisco in "Social Science Data Archives: A Review of Developments," *American Political Science Review,* March 1966 (Vol. IX, No. 1), pages 93–109. Machine-readable data (on punchcards or tape) are maintained at these centers in a form usable for research by individual scholars. Processing facilities of the centers are available to qualified persons, or duplicates of material desired for a special project may be prepared at cost. Of special interest to teachers is the series of instructional laboratory manuals in preparation by the Political Behavior Laboratory of the University of Minnesota. Drawing on the archive of the Inter-University Consortium for Political Research, supplemented by that of Minnesota's comparative government data file, these manuals are tailored to specially prepared "analysis decks" planned for undergraduate instruction in political behavior, judicial behavior, international politics, and comparative government.

The Consortium, established in 1962, is a cooperative enterprise of the Survey Research Center of the University of Michigan and more than sixty affiliated universities and research organizations in the United States and abroad. Its archive contains all of the major political surveys done in the United States, and is being expanded to include historical data of American elections since 1824, a complete set of all roll-call votes in Congress since 1775, and major foreign sample surveys.

Two other major data collections of value for political research are those of the Roper Public Opinion Research Center at Williamstown, Massachusetts, containing more than 4000 polls and surveys from the United States and forty-one foreign countries; and of the International Data Library and Reference Service, University of California, Berkeley, which gives special emphasis to survey and poll data from the countries of Latin America and Asia.

B. Speed in Computations

Difficulty in doing computations "by hand" is a serious obstacle for the newcomer to statistics. Even if interested in the processes he often gives up when confronted with a series of involved calculations. The following comments describe three aids which any interested student can master with relative ease. Of these, the desk calculator is the most versatile and accurate, the adding machine (with repeater key) is a slower but useful substitute, and the slide rule is the most easily available, least expensive, and accurate enough for practically any problem.

1. *The Desk Calculator.* By far the best statistical aid for beginning study, if available, is a good desk calculator. A few hours of careful experiment, with careful attention to the manufacturer's instruction manual, will be most rewarding. Almost every campus has such machines and you can usually make arrangements to use them. A good practice is to prepare in advance a written list of the basic multiplication and division problems in your exercise, and take it with you to the statistics lab. Study carefully the manual's explanation of simple multiplication and division, experimenting first with problems involving small numbers, on which you can do mental arithmetic easily. Though the variety of calculators makes uniform specific instructions impossible, almost all involve features which make useful the following points about division problems:

(1) The machine typically yields a quotient in two sections, usually on two lines. Only the first line is in decimal digits; the second is the numerator of a fractional remainder. The process is identical to that of deciding on the "number of places" to use in dividing by hand. Example: in dividing 10 by 3, the machine will print or display:

10	the dividend you have punched
3	the divisor you have punched
3	the quotient to the nearest place possible
1	the remainder, meaning in this case 1/3

In a percentage problem, you need to provide a suitable number of extra zeroes after your dividend. Allow one more zero than the number of decimal digits you require in your answer, to simplify rounding. Example:

10000	the dividend you have punched
3	the divisor you have punched
3333	the quotient to the nearest place possible
1	the remainder, meaning in this case 1/3 of .001

This method permits you to record directly the result, 33.3%, after checking that the last digit in the quotient rounds down rather than up.

(2) Most machines do not provide for "locking in" a divisor for repeated division. The need for a constant divisor frequently arises in preparing tables which show each item in a list as a percentage of the total, obtained by dividing the item by the total. The particular machine manual will probably explain how to take the *reciprocal* of the divisor. With this reciprocal locked in as a constant multiplier, you can do repeated multiplications which yield the same result as repeated divisions, but usually with only half the work.

Example:

N	%	
3	_____	%
8	_____	
2	_____	
4	_____	
Total 17	100	%

You wish to fill in the percentage which each *N* constitutes of the total, 17. This means each item must be divided by 17. To do this more quickly you proceed as follows:

Step 1: Obtain the reciprocal of 17 (that is, 1/17), either by dividing 100,000 by 17 on the machine, or by consulting a table of reciprocals. To the fourth significant digit, this value is .05882.

Step 2: Lock 5882 in the machine as a constant multiplier.

Step 3: Multiply in turn by each *N* in your list. On a printing calculator, the result will read:

5882	the constant multiplier you have punched
3	the first *N* in your list
17646	product of 5882 × 3
8	the second *N* in your list
47056	product of 5882 × 8
2	the third *N* in your list
11764	product of 5882 × 2
4	the last *N* in your list
23528	product of 5882 × 4

You now complete your table, with the percentages yielded by these products: 17.6%, 47.1%, 11.8%, and 23.5%, which actually add to 100.0%, though a small rounding error often results. Such rounding error may be explained in a footnote, or may be avoided by using more significant digits in the computations.

(3) *Never* try to divide by zero, and be careful that accidental punching of keys does not produce this result. Modern machines usually have built-in safety devices which will halt operations in this event, but many older models still in use will keep churning until they burn up. If this happens to you, pull the cord from the electric outlet and report the problem.

2. *Adding Machines.* Simple adding machines are much less expensive than calculators and thus more commonly available. Most modern ones are equipped with a repeater key whereby repeated additions yield the same result as multiplication (and thus the same result as division if you multiply by the reciprocal). The procedure will go more rapidly if the number entered in the machine for repeated adding is the one whose digits add to the larger total. The example below is from Exercise 5-3(7). To obtain the first "Expected" value in the worksheet, we need the result of the computation 112/160ths of 129. This is the same problem as (112 × 129)/160. The reciprocal of 160 being .00625, we obtain the result by multiplying 129 first by 112, and the resulting product by 625. The tape shows:

129	Set 129 on the machine, with repeater key engaged
129	Push adder bar for two cycles
1290	Press the zero, then the adder bar for one cycle
12900	Press the zero, then the adder bar for one cycle
	Press clear key, press subtotaler
14448 S	Subtotal is sum of 129 × 100 plus 129 × 10 plus 129 × 2 (that is, it equals 129 × 112).
14448	Reset 14448 in the machine. Press adder
14448	bar for four additional cycles (you need
14448	5 and have one already)
14448	This operation yields the result of 5 × 14448
144480	Press the zero, then the adder bar for
144480	two cycles. This results in the product 20 × 14448
1444800	Press the zero, then the adder bar for
1444800	six cycles. This results in the product
1444800	600 × 14448, so that you have succes-
1444800	sively obtained the units, tens, and
1444800	hundreds ingredients of the desired
1444800	multiplication
	Press clear key, disengage repeater, press totaler
9030000 T	Desired "Expected" value is 90.3

3. *The Slide Rule.* Familiarity with the slide rule is one of the most useful skills you can acquire. Even the simplest, least expensive rule you can find will give sufficient accuracy for most statistical problems,

and serves as an excellent check on more precise computations even in advanced work. Its use is easy to learn, and a little experience with the elementary manipulations for multiplication and division will add to your confidence in your results.

If you have not used the slide rule before, the best approach is to concentrate on the basic C and D scales. The C scale is usually located on the lower side of the slide, and the D scale immediately below it on the body of the rule. The two scales are identical; each is the fundamental slide rule scale. Other scales are used for convenience in some computations or for specialized applications beyond our interest.

Use of the C and D scales together involves the two basic slide rule principles. (1) multiplication is done by adding logarithms, and (2) division is done by subtracting the logarithm of the divisor (denominator) from that of the dividend (numerator).

C scale graduated illustration

Notice that the graduated lines on the scale are not uniformly spaced: the two major intervals between 1 and 3 at the left of the scale occupy nearly half its length—nearly as much as the remaining seven major intervals from 3 to 10. This variation in spacing is the key to how the rule works. The actual lengths over which the successive numbered ticks are marked correspond to the logarithms of the marked numbers. You can check this point easily if your rule has an L scale (L for logarithm), which is divided into ten equal sections. In computations with the C and D scales, we use the C scale as a measuring device to add or subtract logarithm distance-values on the D scale. A firm grasp of this basic principle will be of great help in learning the correct manipulations, as well as giving a sense of confidence that the results are what should be expected.

The basic operations may be briefly outlined, but ease of use will come only with sufficient practice to make them second nature. Start with simple problems, to which you know the answers, and after each do more complicated but closely related ones (for example, multiply 2×3, then 25×35, then 215×335).

3.1. TO MULTIPLY $x \cdot y$

Step 1: Put one end (the index "1") of the C scale over x on the D scale.

Step 2: Read the answer on the D scale directly under y on the C scale.

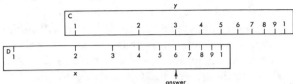

Note: You have *added* log x to log y in terms of the spacing used on the two scales. Starting at the point on the D scale corresponding to log x, you have used the distance on the C scale corresponding to log y to "step off" this added logarithmic distance on the D scale.

Use Either Index. A major source of confusion develops when you find the C scale number under which you expect the answer extending out into space beyond the end of the D scale. Either index (the "1" on either end) may be used; a little practice will teach you where the break-off point comes. This feature of the rule results from the basic logarithmic principle: the numbers on the scales may be read in any multiple of 10: they may be located any number of spaces to the left or right of the decimal point. The reading "2" is used for 2000, 200, 20, 2, .2, .02, etc. Thus the reading "1" at the left end of the rule corresponds to the reading "1" at the right end except for appropriate adjustment of the decimal point. The easiest way to handle location of the decimal point is to "do in your head" the nearest easy rounded computation. Thus for the multiplication 567×342, "do in your head" $500 \times 300 = 150,000$. Your slide rule result of about 194 is then interpreted to represent 194,000—a close approximation to the computed answer of 193,914. Three significant digit accuracy is about all you can obtain with most rules. Use of the right index in multiplication is illustrated below.

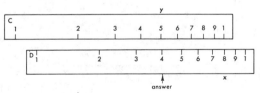

3.2. TO DIVIDE x/y

Step 1: Put y on the C scale directly over x on the D scale.

Step 2: Read the answer on the D scale directly under the end (index "1") of the C scale.

Note: You have *subtracted* log y from log x in terms of the spacing used on the two scales. The distance between the index "1" of the C scale and the index of the D scale after Step 1 represents the space corresponding to the difference between the logarithms of *x* and *y*. In practicing division with single digits (for example 3/4), it will help to remember that at the initial setting of Step 1 they will appear "upside down," since the divisor (the denominator in a fraction) is located on the C scale. To divide 3 by 4, bring the "4" of the C scale directly *above* the "3" of the D scale. The answer (.75) is then read on the D scale directly beneath the right index "1" of the C scale. As with multiplication, the index "1" at either end may be used. Go back to the first illustrative setting under multiplication, and check that it is also set to divide 8 by 4. The "4" on C has been brought directly over the "8" on D. Here the answer to the division 8/4 = 2 appears under the *left* index of C.

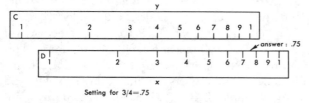

Setting for 3/4 = .75

3.3. PERCENTAGES.

The problem "*x*% of *y*" is exactly the same as multiplying *x* by *y*, except that we interpret the answer as *xy*/100.

The problem "*x* is what per cent of *y*?" is exactly the same as dividing *x*/*y*, except that we interpret the answer as 100 *x*/*y*.

3.4. RATIOS.

To find the value of *x* in a problem such as *x*/300 = 500/2000, we simply multiply and then divide. Notice that the problem is the same as *x* = (500 × 300)/2000. This is the same computation as that needed in the chi-square worksheet of Exercises 5-3 to 5-7 for expected values in the 2 × 2 table:

E		300
		1700
500	1500	2000

To find E *in the χ² computation for 2 × 2 or larger tables:*

E = (Column Total) times (Row Total) divided by Grand Total

Step 1: Find the Column Total on the C scale and locate it over *N* (Grand Total) on the D scale. (In the example, find 500 on C and locate it over the 2000 on D.)

Step 2: Read the answer (*E*) on the C scale directly *above* the Row Total on the D scale. (In the example, read *E* (75) directly over 300 on the D scale.)

Note: You have *subtracted* log 2000 from log 500 and then *added* log 300 to the result. Notice that in the ratio problem we locate the answer on the C scale, where in the other problems we located the answer on the D scale. The reason for this will become clear if you examine the relationship between all C scale marks and the corresponding D scale marks once the "5" has been drawn over the "2."

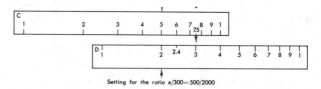

Setting for the ratio x/300 = 500/2000

Not only does this setting locate the ratio 75/300 sought for the answer, but *every* pair of marks displays the C/D ratio which is equivalent to the same 500/2000 ratio. With the same setting you can read such ratios as 3/12, 4/16, 45/180, 6/24, 8/32, 9/36, and at the right index the smallest such fractional ratio, 1/4. The setting of 6/24 is shown above to illustrate the principle.

Use Either Index. As with multiplication, your desired answer may be located in outer space, beyond the end of the D index. In this event you simply use the slide to "shift gears":—replacing the C index "1" which is in the D scale range by the C index "1" at the other end of the C scale. This operation is easier with the cursor and hairline: place the hairline over the "1" on C; pull the C scale across its complete length to locate the "1" at the opposite end of the C scale under the hairline (where the other "1" was originally). You then read the desired answer as in Step 2 above. Your "gear shifting" adds or drops a decimal place, depending on whether you have geared up (by a ratio of 10 to 1) or down—that is, moved the slide left or right.

Example: to find *E* in the chi-square computation

E		900
		1100
500	1500	2000

Shifted Setting for 500/2000 = x/900

C. Computer Programs

Although this workbook is deliberately planned to avoid the need for advanced computational hardware, an increasing number of students have acquired some skill in computer programming. If you continue an interest in quantification, you will inevitably find need for computer processing of your data. Political science research is able to tap great quantities of data which in the past could hardly be used at all because of their sheer volume, but which can now be organized in manageable patterns and forced to reveal significant associations by virtue of the great capacity and speed of electronic computers and the developing sophistication of statistical methods for their use.

The most important breakthrough in making the power of computers available to political scientists was the development of the powerful FORTRAN (for FORmula TRANslation) language, which allows the beginner to instruct the computer with statements and symbols already familiar or easily learned. The machine itself will translate the FORTRAN statements into "machine language", meaning a series of detailed step-by-step instructions for manipulating any set of data to which the FORTRAN program is tailored. The program is the computer's worksheet. Just as you follow the logical sequence of a good worksheet for a series of computations of the same kind of problem with different sets of data, so the computer stores a given program and uses it as often as you please as an exact computational guide for any defined set of numbers. Once the proper program is "on the machine" you may supply merely one set of four data items representing the four cells of a 2 × 2 table, and obtain as answers the values for chi-square and Yule's Q, as in Program 1, or a thousand sets of four numbers, obtaining a thousand pair of these values. Or with a longer program you may supply a set of 10,000 data items (say 100 characteristics of 100 countries, 100 roll-call votes of 100 members, or 100 elections in 100 countries) and the machine will supply the 5050 correlation coefficients needed for each of a series of matrices which it then uses to "squeeze out" factors to account for the variance in your data.

The simple FORTRAN programs which follow are meant as an "instant introduction" for the beginner and as an aid or refresher for those who have had only elementary work in programming—beginning courses often give slight attention to computational routines useful in the social sciences. Each is designed to handle computations used in this workbook, and the line-by-line explanations of the FORTRAN statements cover most of the features of this powerful language. Careful perusal of these listings will not make you a programmer but should enable you to discuss your problems with programmers or to undertake a beginning course in programming with more confidence.

A Word on Use of the Programs. These programs were prepared deliberately for the simplest computer equipment commonly available—the IBM 1620 with punchcard input and output, using 1620 FORTRAN WITH FORMAT—but will run on almost any machine. For the printouts, cards containing the programs, the input data, and the output data were run through a lister. To use the programs in your own computer center, either as a class demonstration or just to work problems, you should check them out carefully with a staff programmer to be sure any necessary housekeeping instructions or variations needed for his equipment are added. The programs are so simple that a minimum of such modification will be required.

An interesting demonstration can be arranged by packaging all five programs into a single "Rocket Problem Solver." This master program requires that, prior to each set of input data, an instruction be entered informing the computer which program is to be used in processing it. The Rocket Solver could be expanded by including a rank correlation routine to provide programs for solving almost all the problems in this workbook in a few minutes.

PROGRAM 1. CHI SQUARE AND YULE'S Q

1 FORMAT and 2 FORMAT

The FORMAT statement specifies the kind, size, and spacing of numbers (or alphabetic information) to be used for the data which the program will read into the machine and print out as answers. In this program, 1 FORMAT is used for the input data card specification and is used by the READ statement (READ 1). The expression 4F10.0 means that the data cards will each contain four numbers in decimal notation (F is "floating point") written in a right-justified field 10 spaces wide (including leading blank spaces, decimal point and + or − sign), with zero

```
***** PROGRAM LISTING WITH 1620 MONITOR CONTROL CARDS *****          =


ZZFORX    Z                  1620 FORTRAN RUN CARD

C      PROGRAM 1.

C      CHI SQUARE AND YULES COMPUTATION FOR 2X2 TABLES

C

     1 FORMAT(4F10.0)

     2 FORMAT(2(20X,2F10.0//),25X,11HCHI SQUARE= ,F10.5/40X,2HQ=,F5.2)

     3 READ 1,A,B,C,D

       CHISQ=(A+B+C+D)*((A*D-B*C)**2)/((A+B)*(C+D)*(A+C)*(B+D))

       Q=(A*D-B*C)/(A*D+B*C)

       PUNCH 2,A,B,C,D,CHISQ,Q

       STOP

       END


***** INPUT DATA FOLLOWS END CARD *****                              =

       8.        52.        28.         3.

ZZZZ                         1620 END OF JOB CARD


***** LISTING OF OUTPUT CARDS *****                                  =

                 8.        52.



                28.         3.



           CHI SQUARE=   50.66981

                    Q= -.96
```

places after the decimal point. "F5.3" would define a field five spaces wide with three spaces following the decimal point: that is, allowing one space for the sign and one place for the decimal point, a number of the form + .123. "F5.4" is invalid, since a field five spaces wide can have only three places after the decimal. Comment on the complicated 2 FORMAT statement is given with the discussion of the output.

3 READ 1, A, B, C, D

The program is directed to read four numbers by the specification given in FORMAT statement 1, and to store them under the labels A, B, C, and D. These are the four entries of our 2×2 table for which chi-square and Q are to be computed.

CHISQ = and Q =

These are the arithmetic statements, in notation much like that of ordinary formulas. In a FORTRAN arithmetic statement, = means that the expression on the left becomes the future label for the expression on the right, * means multiplication, ** means exponentiation, and / means division. Parentheses are used for grouping exactly as in ordinary notation.

The CHISQ = ... statement will cause the computer first to compute the value $(a + b + c + d)$ $(ad - bc)^2/(a + b) (c + d) (a + c) (b + d)$, and then to store it in a location labelled CHISQ for future reference. The Q = ... statement will cause the computer to find the value $(ad - bc)/(ad + bc)$ and to store it in a location labelled Q.

PUNCH 2 is the output statement, causing the computer to use the specification of FORMAT statement 2 for an output unit containing the successive values A, B, C, D, CHISQ and Q. PUNCH, PRINT, and TYPE are all output statements, the choice depending on the equipment.

Referring back to the specification listing in 2 FORMAT, you should follow each item by comparing it with the output listing which appears after the program and the input data. A FORMAT statement performs the same function as setting stops on a typewriter:

( ) enclose the entire specification, within which each unit is set off by commas.

2(20X, 2F10.0//) defines the two lines of the 2×2 table containing the original four entries. The initial 2 means that what follows is used twice; 20X means 20 leading blanks—to center the table on the page: 2F10.0 specifies what kind of numbers to use; and // means to double space after each of the two lines.

25X means 25 leading blanks—to center the equation which follows.

11HCHI SQUARE=, means to print an alphabetic expression 11 spaces wide containing exactly what appears in the 11 spaces following the H (H is used in honor of Hollerith, who invented the punchcard). In that portion of output defined by a Hollerith field, letters, blanks, numbers, and characters will appear exactly as entered.

F10.5/ specifies the form of the number used for the chi-square value; the / means to space before the next step.

40X, 2HQ=, F5.2 defines the spacing for the last output line, the Hollerith field for "Q=" being only two spaces and F5.2 allowing the Q value to range from −1.00 to +1.00.

PROGRAM 2. CHI SQUARE for $M \times N$ TABLES

This more complex program introduces four new FORTRAN expressions—DIMENSION, IF, DO, and GO TO, as well as the use of subscripted variables. If you have difficulty following the logic, you might first study Programs 3, 4, and 5. However, the comment on the DO statement given here should be absorbed before you look at Programs 3 and 4.

DIMENSION is a storage reserve instruction. It informs the computer that we will need space in storage for a 16×16 matrix containing numbers for values of a variable to be labelled FRQCY (these are the cell entries in our table), 16 spaces for a variable to be labelled ROW (we will use these for row totals), and 16 spaces for a variable to be labelled COL (used for column totals).

9 FORMAT(3I3) specifies the form of the first data card, which is read at "1 READ 9" and lists three *I*ntegers, each occupying a 3-space field. These three integers (no decimal point) inform the program (1) how many rows are in our table, (2) how many columns, and (3) what Problem Number to use— this is a repeating program.

10 FORMAT "sets stops" for the input listing, and introduces no new terms. The 16F specification is used to allow the maximum permitted input of 16 frequencies for each row, but since M and N are defined on the first data card, the program will actually read only the number of entries in the problem before it at each successive run.

7 FORMAT is the spacing and alphabetic specification for the output lines. You should compare it with the actual listings at the end of the program.

```
***** PROGRAM LISTING WITH 1620 MONITOR CONTROL CARDS *****                    =
                                                                               =
ZZFORX    Z                     1620 FORTRAN RUN CARD
C       PROGRAM 2.
C       CHI SQUARE COMPUTATION FOR MXN TABLE (MAXIMUM 16X16)
C       REPEATING PROGRAM WITH SHUT OFF CONTROL CARD
C       M=NUMBER OF ROWS, N=NUMBER OF COLUMNS, NO= PROBLEM NUMBER
C
        DIMENSION  FRQCY(16,16),ROW(16),COL(16)
      9 FORMAT(3I3)
     10 FORMAT (16F5.0)
      7 FORMAT(12H PROBLEM NO.,I3,13H  CHI SQUARE=,F12.5,5X,3HDF=,I4)
      1 READ 9,M,N,NO
        IF (NO) 8,8,2
      2 DO 3 J=1,N
      3 COL(J)=0.
        GRTOT=0.
        DO 5 I=1,M
        READ 10,(FRQCY(I,J),J=1,N)
        ROW(I)=0.
        DO 4 J=1,N
        ROW(I)=ROW(I)+FRQCY(I,J)
      4 COL(J)=COL(J)+FRQCY(I,J)
      5 GRTOT=GRTOT+ROW(I)
        CHISQ=0.
        DO 6 I=1,M
        DO 6 J=1,N
        EXPTD=COL(J)*ROW(I)/GRTOT
        DELTA=FRQCY(I,J)-EXPTD
      6 CHISQ=CHISQ+DELTA**2/EXPTD
        JFD=(M-1)*(N-1)
        PUNCH 7,NO,CHISQ,JFD
        GO TO 1
      8 STOP
        END

***** INPUT DATA FOLLOWS END CARD *****                                        =
                                                                               =
  4   3   1
    3.    3.    1.
126.   61.   38.
 71.   93.   69.
 19.   14.   27.
  2   2   2
    8.   52.
   28.    3.
  0   0   0
ZZZZ                            1620 END OF JOB CARD

  ***** LISTING OF OUTPUT CARDS *****                                          =
PROBLEM NO.   1  CHI SQUARE=      44.46460        DF=    6
PROBLEM NO.   2  CHI SQUARE=      50.66980        DF=    1
```

IF (NO) 8, 8, 2

This is the extremely useful IF, or branching statement, but here has only the housekeeping function of stopping the machine when all problems supplied are completed. We may translate this IF to mean: "If the value of variable NO—used here for the Problem Number—is negative or zero, go next to Statement 8 (that is, STOP); if it is positive, go next to Statement 2 (that is, do the problem)." In this repeating program, we must include a "shut-off control card" at the end of our data. You can verify by glancing at the last input line that the value zero is supplied for NO on the last card, after the data to be used in the problems. Thus at this point, the IF statement will send the program to Statement 8 STOP. So long as there is a positive Problem Number, the program will continue computations. If the shut-off card were not used, the computer would simply repeat the last problem over and over again or note error.

DO 3 J = 1, N
3 COL(J) = 0.

The DO statement is the most powerful in FORTRAN: it is the instruction to "loop" or iterate a sequence of following instructions until "the DO is satisfied." Iteration is the key to the computer's great advantage over hand methods. We may translate DO 3 (J) = 1, N to read: "Iterate all instructions from here to Statement 3, repeatedly, with the value of J set first to 1, and continue iterations with the value of J increasing by 1 each time until completion of the iteration at which J has attained the value N." This simple DO loop iterates only one instruction, since Statement 3 is the only one in its range. Its function in the program is to set an initial value of zero for each of the column totals, to be identified as COL(J), which we will need in our computation of chi-square. The term COL(J) is a *subscripted variable* for which (J) is the subscript. Later in the program, we will add to this series of 0.'s the frequencies of each column in turn to obtain the totals.

GRTOT = 0.

This sets the initial value for the grand total at zero, to which the program will later add each frequency in the table. The decimal point is required, since our data will be in "floating point," or decimal notation—used because the computations will involve division. FORTRAN can add, subtract, and multiply integers up to maximum values of 9999, but in division, all fractional remainders are lost. The division

of 2 by 3, for example, yields 0 as the quotient, whereas 2./3. yields .6666 if F6.4 or wider space is provided.

DO 5 I = 1, M
5 GRTOT = GRTOT + ROW(I)

This DO loop contains six statements, including another DO loop, within its range. All six will be iterated for each *row* in our table. The data for each row are contained on a single input card, so each iteration of the DO 5 handles one card. Notice exactly what happens on one iteration: at READ 10, the program stores the frequencies for the row; at ROW(I) = 0, it sets the row total initially to zero for later summing; at DO 4 it prepares the inner or "nested" loop for adding up the frequencies on the row; at ROW(I) = ... and 4 COL(J) = ..., the inner loop adds these frequencies to the initial zero values for the row and column totals; and finally, at 5 GRTOT = ..., the row total obtained by the inner DO 4 loop is added to the initial zero value for the grand total. After completing the first iteration, the program continues to return to the READ 10 instruction for each data card—each row of the table. The DO is "satisfied" when it has processed *m* cards. (You must, of course, be sure that *m* data cards are actually supplied).

CHISQ = 0.

...

6 CHISQ = CHISQ + DELTA**2/EXPTD

If you have followed the logic of the DO 5 and its nested DO 4 (to grasp it fully you may need to read it through several times, with hand computations of totals from the sample data listings), you will have little difficulty with the remainder of the program. The value CHISQ is set to zero, and the double DO 6 loop provides for iterating the $m \times n$ computations of each "expected" value. The expected value is then subtracted from its corresponding "observed" value—FRQCY(I, J)—to obtain DELTA. DELTA is then squared and divided by the expected value, yielding the number to be added to the initial zero value of CHISQ at the end of each iteration of computations for each cell.

JFD = (M–1)*(N–1)

The final arithmetic statement performs the simple calculation for number of degrees of freedom in the $m \times n$ table, using the integer values for *m* and *n* supplied at the first READ. JFD is used for our mnemonic, rather than DF, because these numbers are integers (FORTRAN reserves the letters *I, J, K, L, M, N* for use as initial letters of integer variables;

all other letters indicate floating-point variables in decimal-point notation).

> GO TO 1
> 8 STOP

The GO to 1 statement is used to repeat the program for successive problems, as described at the IF statement. STOP and END need not concern you otherwise; they are housekeeping statements not connected with the computational logic.

PROGRAM 3. TRANSLATION OF A FREQUENCY TABLE INTO A PERCENTAGE TABLE

Similar to Program 2 in its use of DO loops, this routine causes the input data to be read as one *column* of frequencies per card, the contents of each card to be translated into percentages, and then printed in columns parallel with corresponding percentages, with a totals line for both frequencies and percentages at the end.

DIMENSION

Storage space is reserved for a maximum of 5×10 percentages and the same number of frequencies, with five spaces each for totals. Additional space is reserved for the same frequencies and their totals translated into integer notation (INT and ITOT) so they may be listed in the output without decimal points.

FORMAT

The three format statements specify the form of numbers for:

(1) The data cards containing frequencies (10F8.0, floating point being used to facilitate computations).

(2) The initial data card read at READ 1, M, N, telling the computer the number of rows and columns (10I8), and

(3) The output lines (5(I6, F10.3) meaning that up to five pair of values may appear on each line, each pair consisting of a frequency in integer notation and its corresponding percentage. Notice that the FORMAT statements need not be entered in the program in the order used, and that no harm is done if a FORMAT expression provides for more entries on a card than the card actually contains. The expression 10I8, which defines ten entries, is used to read only two.

> DO 3 I = 1, M
> ...
> 3 PCTOT (I) = PCTOT(I) + PCT(I, J)

The range of the DO 3 loop includes the next eleven statements and provides all steps needed for reading the table and for the computations and transformations. It contains three short nested DO loops within its range—DO 2, which sums the frequencies for each column; DO 4, which transforms each frequency into integer notation as well as into percentages; and DO 3, which adds the percentages in each column for a percentage total. One iteration of DO 3 processes one card, preparing results for two columns of output. DO 3 is "satisfied" when *m* cards have been processed.

During each iteration, DO 3 first sets a zero value in TOTAL and PCTOT, to which the inner DO's will add to obtain the two column sums. At READ 7 it provides for storing the values for one column of frequencies in locations labelled FRQCY (I, J). You will recall that the expression (I, J) is a double subscript indicating that the value for FRQCY is the one listed in Row I, Column J. The value for I, or the row number, moves from 1 to M, increasing by one at each DO 3 iteration. The value for J, or the column number, moves from 1 to N, increasing by one at each iteration of the nested loops DO 2, DO 4, and DO 3.

Why two DO 3's? Recall that the number following DO specifies the last instruction in the range of the DO. In this case, both the outer DO loop, with its eleven statement iteration cycle, and the short nested DO, with only one statement in its range, end at Statement 3.

> DO 5 J = 1, N
> PUNCH 6...
> 5 CONTINUE
> PUNCH 6...

The DO 5 loop initiates the short output routine for printing (or punching, in this program) *n* lines of the table, each line containing *m* frequencies and *m* percentages. The range of DO 5 actually includes only the first PUNCH 6 statement. However, FORTRAN does not allow a DO loop to end with an output instruction, so that the dummy 5 CONTINUE statement is inserted to satisfy the rules. After the DO 5 iterations are completed by punching the output lines of the table proper, the final PUNCH 6 statement causes the totals line to be added.

One source of confusion in following this program lies in the fact that we read the table one column at a time, but print the results one row at a time, so that the roles of *m* and *n* (and of the subscripts I and J) are reversed in the output routine. Though

```
***** PROGRAM LISTING WITH 1620 MONITOR CONTROL CARDS *****                    =

ZZJOB            JOB 03226Z              1620 JOB CARD
ZZFORX     Z                        1620 FORTRAN RUN CARD
C       PROGRAM 3.
C       TRANSLATION OF AN MXN FREQUENCY TABLE INTO A PERCENTAGE TABLE
C            (5X10) MAX)
C
        DIMENSIONINT(5,10),PCT(5,10),FRQCY(5,10),ITOT(5),PCTOT(5),TOTAL(5)
      7 FORMAT(10F8.0)
      1 FORMAT (10I8)
      6 FORMAT(5(I6,F10.3))
        READ 1,M,N
        DO 3 I=1,M
        TOTAL(I)=0.0
        PCTOT(I)=0.
        READ 7,(FRQCY(I,J),J=1,N)
        DO 2 J=1,N
      2 TOTAL(I)=TOTAL(I)+FRQCY(I,J)
        DO 4 J=1,N
        INT(I,J)=FRQCY(I,J)
      4 PCT(I,J)=FRQCY(I,J)/TOTAL(I)
        ITOT(I)=TOTAL(I)
        DO 3 J=1,N
      3 PCTOT(I)=PCTOT(I)+PCT(I,J)
        DO 5 J=1,N
        PUNCH 6, (INT(I,J),PCT(I,J) ,I=1,M)
      5 CONTINUE
        PUNCH 6, (ITOT(I),PCTOT(I) ,I=1,M)
        STOP
        END
                                                                               =
                                                                               =
***** INPUT DATA FOLLOWS END CARD *****                                         =
                                                                               =
         3         3
       10.       20.       20.
       10.       30.       60.
      123.       23.      235.
ZZZZ                                1620 END OF JOB CARD

***** LISTING OF OUTPUT CARDS *****                                             =

       10       .200       10       .100      123       .322
       20       .400       30       .300       23       .060
       20       .400       60       .600      235       .616
       50      1.000      100      1.000      381       .999
```

387

useful as a device to permit flexibility in ordering your listings of input and output, reversal of subscripts is always tricky work and requires careful checking.

PROGRAM 4. RETRIEVAL OF FREQUENCIES FROM A PERCENTAGE TABLE

Reversing the problem of Program 3, here we program the computation of the original frequencies from which a percentage table was constructed, a procedure often necessary before a statistical test may be used. The program provides for a basic READ unit of one card, listing first the total number of frequencies as an integer (maximum size 9999), and then the series of percentages into which that number was divided in the original percentage table. Up to ten percentages are provided for. If all categories are included, these percentages should add to 100.00. In short, each input card corresponds to a *column* of a standard survey table constructed as recommended in Chapter 2, but this retrieval program will deal with it as a *row* both for input and output.

Do not be disturbed that some of the sample input percentages given below the program are obviously faked (e.g., there is no such frequency as 5 per cent of 10). This was done purposely to illustrate a useful programming device explained below.

DIMENSION

Storage space is reserved for up to 10×10 percentages, up to 10 N's, and up to 10×10 resulting frequencies.

FORMAT

The three format statements specify numbers only, but in both I (integer) and F (decimal point) mode, as follows:

(1) 2I3 for the two integers read at READ 9, giving the number of rows and columns.

(2) 10I7, I9 for each line of output at PUNCH 6, each line containing up to 10 frequencies expressed as integers and one integer total.

(3) I5, 10F7.2 for input of the table at READ 2, one card at a time, each containing an integer for the total number of frequencies and up to 10 percentages in decimal notation.

DO 1 I = 1, M

The DO 1 loop includes the rest of the program in its range, including the output at PUNCH 6. Each iteration reads one input card, computes frequencies, and produces an output line containing the frequencies and their total, iterations being repeated

until m cards have been processed and m lines of output produced.

READ 2, NE, (PCT (I, J), = 1, N)

At the first statement in the DO 1 loop, a line of data on one card is read by the 2 FORMAT specification: one integer (NE) and as many percentages as were specified at READ 9. The NE integer is actually the total N to which the percentages refer. We spell it backwards for input, but change it to EN at the next step to permit decimal computations (recall that in FORTRAN the letters I through N are reserved for integers).

DO 4 J = 1, N

The inner nested DO 4 loop has a range of two statements, the first running the retrieval of frequencies for each cell and the second totalling them by adding each to the zero initially set for ITOT just before this DO.

The actual retrieval of a single frequency is done by the single arithmetic statement INT(I, J) = (PCT (I, J)/100.) *EN(I) +.5 and a word about this computation is needed. It does exactly what you do in handwork: multiply the N by the percentage in the given cell of the table, and round. In this program we accomplish rounding by adding the .5 to our result. FORTRAN automatically truncates a number at the decimal point when translating it into an integer. The trick of adding the .5 in the FORTRAN arithmetic statement has the same effect as rounding by hand—if the decimal fractional remainder is less than .5 it is dropped but if more than .5 the value is "rounded up." The device is not infallible but it will serve to avoid serious losses by truncation. Even with our faked percentages, the computed totals miss by a maximum of 1, and for the large N of 1234 the computed total comes out precisely right. You should verify that with truncation, the third line (N = 10) would yield a total of only 8.

PUNCH 6 . . .

1 CONTINUE

As in Program 3, a DO loop which logically ends with an output statement must add the dummy CONTINUE as the last statement in its formal range to comply with FORTRAN rules.

PROGRAM 5. DELTA COMPUTATION FOR A 2×2 CONTINGENCY TABLE WITH A DICHOTOMIZED CONTROL VARIABLE.

This longer program is crude but effective, and the simplest in logic of all five. It avoids DO loops, subscripted variables, and DIMENSION, but since it

```
***** PROGRAM LISTING WITH 1620 MONITOR CONTROL CARDS *****          =
                                                                     =
ZZFORX    Z                   1620 FORTRAN RUN CARD
C     PROGRAM 4.
C     RETRIEVAL OF FREQUENCIES FROM A PERCENTAGE TABLE
C     OF M ROWS AND N COLUMNS          (10X10 MAX)
C
      DIMENSION PCT(10,10),EN(10),INT(10,10)
    9 FORMAT(2I3)
    6 FORMAT(10I7,I9)
    2 FORMAT(I5,10F7.2)
      READ 9 ,M,N
      DO 1 I=1,M
      READ 2,NE,(PCT(I,J),J=1,N)
      EN(I)=NE
       ITOT =0
      DO 4 J=1,N
      INT(I,J)=(PCT(I,J)/100.)*EN(I)+.5
    4 ITOT=ITOT+INT(I,J)
      PUNCH 6,(INT(I,J),J=1,N),ITOT
    1 CONTINUE
      STOP
      END
                                                                     =
***** INPUT DATA FOLLOWS END CARD *****                              =
                                                                     =
  6  5
1234  19.00   21.00   35.15    4.85   20.00
 135  50.00   15.00   10.00   10.00   15.00
  10  60.00   10.00    5.00    6.00   19.00
  25  60.00   10.00    5.00    6.00   19.00
  50  60.00   10.00    5.00    6.00   19.00
  75  60.00   10.00    5.00    6.00   19.00
ZZZZ                          1620 END OF JOB CARD

***** LISTING OF OUTPUT CARDS *****                                  =

   234     259     434      60     247    1234
    68      20      14      14      20     136
     6       1       1       1       2      11
    15       3       1       2       5      26
    30       5       3       3      10      51
    45       8       4       5      14      76
```

389

```
***** PROGRAM LISTING WITH 1620 MONITOR CONTROL CARDS *****                    =
ZZFORX    Z                      1620 FORTRAN RUN CARD
C     PROGRAM 5.
C     DELTA COMPUTATION FOR A 2X2 CONTINGENCY TABLE
C     WITH A DICHOTOMIZED CONTROL VARIABLE
    1 FORMAT(8F5.0)
    2 FORMAT(5(F6.0,2F5.0))
    3 FORMAT(66H DELTA DI= DELTA P1 + DELTA P2 + (N/(N1*N2))*(DELTA DC)*
     1(DELTA IC))
    4 FORMAT( 16H WGHT=N/(N1*NI)=, F12.6)
    5 FORMAT(F8.2,3H = ,F8.3,3H + ,F8.3,4H + (,F7.3,2H)(,F12.6,2H)(,F7.3
     1,2H)=,F6.2)
    6 FORMAT(72H DI SOURCE TABLE   C+PARTIAL    C-PARTIAL    DC MARGINAL
     1    IC MARGINAL)
    7 FORMAT(5(11X,5HTOTAL))
      READ 1, A,B,C,D,AP,BP,CP,DP
      EN=A+B+C+D
      ENP1=AP+BP+CP+DP
      ENP2=EN-ENP1
      WGHT=EN/(ENP1*ENP2)
      AP2=A-AP
      BP2=B-BP
      CP2=C-CP
      DP2=D-DP
      E=A+B
      FX=C+D
      G=A+C
      H=B+D
      EP=AP+BP
      FP=CP+DP
      GP=AP+CP
      HP=BP+DP
      EP2=AP2+BP2
      FP2=CP2+DP2
      GP2=AP2+CP2
      HP2=BP2+DP2
      DLTDI=A-G*E/EN
      DLTP1=AP-GP*EP/ENP1
      DLTP2=AP2-GP2*EP2/ENP2
      DLTIC=GP-ENP1*G/EN
      DLTDC=EP-ENP1*E/EN
      DLTCP=DLTP1+DLTP2+WGHT*DLTDC*DLTIC
      PUNCH 6
      PUNCH 2,A,B,E,AP,BP,EP,AP2,BP2,EP2,EP,EP2,E,GP,GP2,G
      PUNCH 2,C,D,FX,CP,DP,FP,CP2,DP2,FP2,FP,FP2,FX,HP,HP2,H
      PUNCH 7
      PUNCH 2,G,H,EN,GP,HP,ENP1,GP2,HP2,ENP2,ENP1,ENP2,EN,ENP1,ENP2,EN
      PUNCH 4,WGHT
      PUNCH 3
      PUNCH 5,DLTDI,DLTP1,DLTP2,WGHT,DLTDC,DLTIC,DLTCP
      STOP
      END


***** INPUT DATA FOLLOWS END CARD *****                                         =

                                                                                =

   17.   34.   25.   89.   16.   29.    2.   12.

ZZZZ                             1620 END OF JOB CARD
```

```
***** LISTING OF OUTPUT CARDS *****                                                =

DI SOURCE TABLE    C+PARTIAL       C-PARTIAL      DC MARGINAL      IC MARGINAL

   17.  34.  51.    16.  29.  45.    1.   5.   6.    45.   6.  51.    18.  24.  42.

   25.  89. 114.     2.  12.  14.   23.  77. 100.    14. 100. 114.    41.  82. 123.

         TOTAL           TOTAL           TOTAL           TOTAL           TOTAL

   42. 123. 165.    18.  41.  59.   24.  82. 106.    59. 106. 165.    59. 106. 165.

WGHT=N/(N1*NI)=       .026383

DELTA DI= DELTA P1 + DELTA P2 + (N/(N1*N2))*(DELTA DC)*(DELTA IC)

    4.01 =     2.271 +    -.358 + (   .026)(   26.763637)(  2.981)=  4.01
```

deals entirely with 2×2 tables it will work with less complication and chance of error than a more elegant program. Its chief complications are the lengthy FORMAT and PUNCH statements, which could have been simplified by subscription. Its chief advantage is that almost any beginner can follow its logic by occasional reference to one of the displays in Chapter 9.

FORMAT

The seven format statements at the outset include five mainly devoted to alphabetic lines meant to clarify the eventual printout. The only crucial FORMAT is the first, 8F5.0, which at READ 1 causes the computer to store the eight frequencies of the 2×2 DI Source Table and its first Partial Table (A, B, C, D are the four entries of the Source Table; AP, BP, CP, DP are the four entries of the first Partial Table).

The statement 6 FORMAT, used for the alphabetic line of table titles in the printout, does not quite fit all the tables. A single alphabetic specification is restricted to 72 spaces, though the alignment could be remedied by more complex programming.

ARITHMETIC STATEMENTS:
EN = A + B + C + D to DLTCP...

These 26 computations do exactly what you do by hand in Exercise Set 9. The successive steps may be grouped in worksheet form as follows:

(1) We obtain the grand total for the Source Table (EN) by adding cells A, B, C, and D; the total for the first Partial Table (ENP1) by adding its cells; and the total for the second Partial (ENP2) by subtracting ENP1 from EN. We then compute the weighting factor for the delta equation by dividing EN by the product ENP1 $\times$ ENP2.

(2) We obtain values for the four cells of the second Partial Table by subtracting cells of the first Partial (AP, ...) from corresponding ones of the Source Table (A, ...), yielding the entries AP2, BP2, CP2, and DP2.

(3) We obtain values for the three sets of four marginal entries in the next twelve statements (E, FX, G, H, for the DI Source Table; EP, FP, GP, HP, for the first Partial; EP2, FP2, GP2, and HP2, for the second Partial). Note that all cells of the two marginal tables (IC and DC) of the problems in Exercise Set 9 are found in these twelve marginal totals—that is why IC and DC are called marginal tables. We do not need to compute them directly, although we must keep a sharp eye on our labels in writing the statements for their deltas.

(4) The six delta equations which conclude the computations should follow readily from the pattern set out in Chapter 9. DLTCP is our code for "Computed Delta," and its value is to be inserted at the end of the output line called for at PUNCH 5 for comparison with the separately computed delta of the original DI Source Table (DLTDI) which it is supposed to equal. Small differences between DLTDI and DLTCP may occur as a result of rounding and loss of values beyond the decimal places allowed in the program, but in our sample problem they match exactly.

D. Table of Reciprocals To 100

1	10000	21	47619	41	24390	61	16393	81	12346
2	50000	22	45455	42	23810	62	16129	82	12195
3	33333	23	43478	43	23256	63	15873	83	12048
4	25000	24	41667	44	22727	64	15625	84	11905
5	20000	25	40000	45	22222	65	15385	85	11765
6	16667	26	38462	46	21739	66	15152	86	11628
7	14286	27	37037	47	21277	67	14925	87	11494
8	12500	28	35714	48	20833	68	14706	88	11364
9	11111	29	34483	49	20408	69	14493	89	11236
10	10000	30	33333	50	20000	70	14286	90	11111
11	90909	31	32258	51	19608	71	14085	91	10989
12	83333	32	31250	52	19231	72	13889	92	10870
13	76923	33	30303	53	18868	73	13699	93	10753
14	71429	34	29412	54	18519	74	13514	94	10638
15	66667	35	28571	55	18182	75	13333	95	10526
16	62500	36	27778	56	17857	76	13158	96	10417
17	58824	37	27027	57	17544	77	12987	97	10309
18	55556	38	26316	58	17241	78	12821	98	10204
19	52632	39	25641	59	16949	79	12658	99	10101
20	50000	40	25000	60	16667	80	12500	100	10000

The table shows only the decimal portion of the reciprocals. For numbers from 11 to 99 the reciprocal shown also drops the first zero following the decimal point. In computations, multiplying a number by the reciprocal of a divisor is equivalent to dividing by the divisor.

E. Values for *Q* for Percentage Deciles

Since Yule's *Q* is "margin-free" and comes out the same regardless of whether computed with frequencies or percentages, it is possible to tabulate for quick reference the *Q* values for a 2 × 2 table if the table is in percentages. In the table below this computation has been performed for even deciles. The captions *a* and *b* refer to cells in the type table:

a	*b*
c	*d*
100%	100%

Since we are dealing with a 2 × 2 percentage table, *c* is of course determined by *a* and *d* is determined by *b*. If *a* is 100%, *c* must be 0%; if *a* is 90%, *c* must be 10%.

In using the table, you need only examine the first percentage listed in each column. For example, in the table

70	50
30	50

you will simply check the entry on the row following 70 at the column headed "50." The *Q* value shown there is +.40, indicating positive association of the two variables, though not a very strong one. (You will recall that *Q* values do not disclose a precise probability ordering).

Use of the Table. An examination of the table reveals several important characteristics of the *Q* values:

1. *The Diagonal.* The diagonal line running from Row 0 to Column 100 consists of eleven cells all

with the value 0.00. This means that $Q = 0.00$ if the contingency table is of the type (for percentages):

a	a
100−a	100 − a

or if the table contains frequencies, and is of the type

a	b
c	d

$Q = 0.00$ if the proportions of each row are the same, that is if $a/b = c/d$. (In which case, of course, $ad = bc$, so that the formula yields zero as the numerator.)

2. *The Edges.* $Q = +1.00$ only if $b = 0$ or $c = 0$, or both.
   $Q = -1.00$ only if $a = 0$ or $d = 0$, or both.

3. *Above Diagonal.* Q lies between 0.00 and $+1.00$ if a is greater than b (in percentages).

4. *Below Diagonal.* Q lies between 0.00 and -1.00 if b is greater than a (in percentages). In using the table for rough estimates, the conservative policy is to use the even decile nearest the value in the source table *in the direction of 50%*. Thus if the value in cell a is 65, round to 60, but if it is 35, round to 40. This results in an underestimate of the degree of association rather than an overestimate.

Values for Q for Percentage Deciles.

a \ b	0	10	20	30	40	50	60	70	80	90	100
100	1.00	1.00	1.00	1.00	1.00	1.00	1.00	1.00	1.00	1.00	0.00
90	1.00	.98	.95	.91	.86	.80	.71	.59	.38	0.00	−1.00
80	1.00	.95	.88	.81	.71	.60	.45	.26	0.00	−.38	−1.00
70	1.00	.91	.81	.69	.56	.40	.22	0.00	−.26	−.59	−1.00
60	1.00	.86	.71	.56	.38	.20	0.00	−.22	−.45	−.71	−1.00
50	1.00	.80	.60	.40	.20	0.00	−.20	−.40	−.60	−.80	−1.00
40	1.00	.71	.45	.22	0.00	−.20	−.38	−.56	−.71	−.86	−1.00
30	1.00	.59	.26	0.00	−.22	−.40	−.56	−.69	−.81	−.91	−1.00
20	1.00	.38	0.00	−.26	−.45	−.60	−.71	−.81	−.88	−.95	−1.00
10	1.00	0.00	−.38	−.59	−.71	−.80	−.86	−.91	−.95	−.98	−1.00
0	0.00	−1.00	−1.00	−1.00	−1.00	−1.00	−1.00	−1.00	−1.00	−1.00	−1.00

F. Significance Levels for Spearman's Coefficient of Rank Correlation in Even Tenths for 4 to 30 Paired Rankings (one direction from zero).

N \ p =	.10	.05	.02	.01	.001
4	1.0	1.0	—	—	—
5	.8	.9	1.0	1.0	—
6	.6	.8	.9	1.0	—
7	.6	.7	.9	1.0	—
8	.5	.7	.8	.9	—
9	.5	.6	.8	.9	—
10	.5	.6	.7	.8	—
11	.5	.6	.7	.8	1.0
12	.4	.5	.7	.8	1.0
13	.4	.5	.6	.7	.9
14	.4	.5	.6	.7	.9
15	.4	.5	.6	.7	.9
16	.4	.5	.6	.7	.9
17	.4	.5	.6	.6	.8
18	.4	.4	.5	.6	.8
19	.4	.4	.5	.6	.8
20	.3	.4	.5	.6	.8
21	.3	.4	.5	.6	.7
22	.3	.4	.5	.6	.7
23	.3	.4	.5	.5	.7
24	.3	.4	.5	.5	.7
25	.3	.4	.5	.5	.7
26	.3	.4	.5	.5	.7
27	.3	.4	.5	.5	.7
28	.3	.4	.4	.5	.6
29	.3	.4	.4	.5	.6
30	.3	.4	.4	.5	.6

G. Abridged Table of Critical Values of Chi Square*

p =	.50	.10	.05	.02	.01	.005	.001
df							
1	0.455	2.71	3.841	5.42	6.635	7.879	10.83
2	1.386	4.61	5.991	7.83	9.210	10.60	13.82
3	2.366	6.25	7.815	9.84	11.341	12.84	16.27
4	3.357	7.78	9.488	11.67	13.277	14.86	18.47
5	4.351	9.24	11.070	13.39	15.086	16.75	20.52
6	5.348	10.65	12.592	15.04	16.812	18.55	22.46
7	6.346	12.02	14.067	16.63	18.475	20.28	24.33
8	7.344	13.37	15.507	18.17	20.090	21.96	26.13
9	8.343	14.69	16.919	19.68	21.666	23.59	27.88
10	9.342	15.99	18.307	21.17	23.209	25.19	29.59
11	10.34	17.28	19.675	22.62	24.725	26.76	31.27
12	11.34	18.55	21.026	24.06	26.217	28.30	32.91

* The table of chi-square values is taken from Table III of Fisher & Yates, *Statistical Tables for Biological, Agricultural and Medical Research*, published by Oliver & Boyd Ltd., Edinburgh, and by permission of the authors and publishers.

How to Use the Table

Enter the table on the *row* determined by the degrees of freedom (*df*) and in the *column* determined by the significance level (*p*). If the value of χ^2 you have obtained equals or exceeds the value in the table, reject the null hypothesis.

Example. In Exercise 5–3(2) there is only one degree of freedom, and the significance level set is .05. The value in the table on the "*df* = 1" row and in the "*p* = .05" column is 3.841, which is the value of χ^2 which must be equalled or exceeded to justify rejection of the null hypothesis.

Degrees of freedom. The number of degrees of freedom is the number of entries in a table which can be determined by chance, assuming both row and column totals are fixed. In a 1×2 table, for example, only one entry is "free," since its value controls the other. This is also true of a 2×2 table, as the example below illustrates:

a	b	a + b
c	d	c + d
a + c	b + d	a + b + c + d

Given the marginal totals, once *a* is "freely" determined, *b* is automatically determined (by subtracting *a* from the marginal total *a* + *b*, *c* is determined by subtracting *a* from the marginal total *a* + *c*, and *d* is determined by subtracting either *b* or *c* from the appropriate marginal total.

In general, for a table of *R* rows and *C* columns, with both *R* and *C* greater than one, degrees of freedom = (*R-1*) (*C-1*).

Index

Abrams, Mark, 225
Action and affect statements, 271
Adding machines, use of, 377
Affect and action statements, 271
Agriculture and party (U.S.), (table), 181
Alker, Hayward R., Jr., 8n, 21, 169, 197, 353, 373
Alliances shown by Venn diagrams, 87, 103–4
Almond, Gabriel A., 51–57, 63, 175, 181, 191, 233, 331–37
America Votes, 373
American Journal of Sociology, 373
American Political Science Review, 373
  number of graphic and tabular displays (*table*), 22
American Sociological Review, 373
Amos, Jimmy R., 197
Analysis of variance, 158
Anderson, Lee F., 197, 267
Anglican clergymen and coal miners, 316
Annals of the American Academy of Political and Social Science, 373
Apter, David E., 233
Area graphs, 70, 74
Atlas of Economic Development, 73, 373
Atomic energy, support of public control (*table*), 219
Australian elections, 101–2
Austrian and British elections (*graph*), 80
Automatic data processing, 121–3

Backstrom, Charles H., 147, 200, 204–5, 233
Bailey, Harry A., Jr., 233
Banks, Arthur S., 3n, 373
Bar graphs, 67–71
Behavioralism, 1n, 2, 4–6
  objections to, 4–7
Bennett, James O. (Racial conservatism scale), 237
Berelson, Bernard R., 69, 169, 233, 301
Berlin party officials (*table*), 59
Beyle, Herman C., 267
Blalock, Hubert M., 197, 353
Bogardus, Emory S. (Racial distance scale), 239
Boxhead (of a table), 25
Brickman, Morrie (Small Society cartoons), 149, 312
Britain, duty to community (*table*), 335–7
Britannica Book of the Year, 373
British and Austrian elections (*graph*), 80
British loan (exercises), 167, 189
British students, political attitudes (*table*), 225, 345
Bromley, David, 225
Brown, Foster L., 197
Buchanan, William, 233

Burke, Edmund, theory of representation (*tables*), 221

Calculator, use of, 376
California and Nevada, population growth (*graph*), 78
Calvert, Robert, Jr., 171
Campbell, Angus, 63, 233
Cantril, Hadley, 233, 310
Captions in a table, 25
Card:
  Hollerith, 113, 122
  IBM, 113
  Keysort, 123
  marginal hole, 123
  punched, 113–15, 121
Cartesian coordinates, 71
Cartwright, Dorwin, 233
Category identification in content analysis, 270
Catholicism and communist vote (*table*), 179
Causality, multiple, 33–34, ch. 9
Central limit theorem, 149
Charlesworth, James, 1n, 21
Chaudhuri, Joyotpaul, 2n
Chernoff, Herman, 197
Chi-square, 154–58
  alternative formula for 2 × 2 tables, 299
  computer programs, 380–85
  table of critical values, 394
  worksheets, 156–57
  with Yates' correction, 299
Children and politics (*tables*), 223
Circle graphs, 79–81, 101
Civic Culture, The, 51–57, 63, 175, 181, 191, 233, 331–37
Clusters, roll-call voting, 245–46
Coal miners and clergymen, 316
Codebook, 110–12
Coding, 110–14
  Survey Research Center codes, 111–12
  of verbal statements, 270–71
Coding exercises, 127–45
Coding sheet, 112–14, 141–43
Coefficient of rank correlation, 152–54
Cohesion, index of, 245
Communication and community political activity in five nations (*table*), 181
Communication index, 85
Communist vote:
  compared with Catholicism (*table*), 179
  compared with industrialization (*table*), 185
  compared with socialist vote (*table*), 177, 185

Computations, speed in, 376–80
Computer programs, 114, 116, 380–90
    FORTRAN language, 380–90
Concept, 3
Conceptual framework, 1
Conceptual graphs, 74–76
Conclusions:
    in research report, 208, 358
    in statistical test, 151, 358
Confidence limits in statistical test, 150–51
Congress (U.S.), scaling votes, 251–65
Congress and the Nation: 1945–1964, 259, 267
Congressional District Data Book, 373
Congressional Quarterly, 267
Consensus, democratic (*table*), 361
Consensus and the affluent society (*tables*), 221
Consensus patterns (*graph*), 75
Content analysis, 268–74
Converse, Philip E., 63, 233
Coordinate graphs, 71–79
Coordinates, Cartesian, 71
Correlations, epistemic, 1
Counsel, right to (*table*), 363
Counter-sorter, 123
County and City Data Book, 373
Covariance, 158
Cowden, Dudley J., 109, 197
Crespi, Irving, 165, 191–93, 358
Crick, Bernard, 21
Criminals, right to counsel (*table*), 363
Cross-Polity Survey, A, 3, 154, 373
Croxton, Frederick E., 109, 197
Cuban policy (*table*), 367
Cube law of representation, 76–77, 97; (*graph*), 77
Cultural fallacy, 5
Curve:
    bell-shaped, 149
    in coordinate graphs, 71
    cube law curve, 77
    Gini index curve, 8–11

Dahl, Robert A., 21, 74–5, 109, 233
    consensus patterns (*graph*), 75
Data, 1, 6–8
    relevant, 3
Data processing, 110–47
Data sorting, 115–19
Davies, James C., 76
Davies' J-curve of revolution (*graph*), 76
Decile, 148
Deduction, 2
Degrees of freedom, 154–55
Delta value, 319
    association in 2 × 2 tables, 310–11
    computer program, 387–90
    role in control variable, 305
Demographic Yearbook, U.N., 373
Demonstration cities (bad question examples), 204–5
Descartes, René, 71
Descriptive-connective in content analysis, 271
Deutsch, Karl W., 373
Developing nations, rank correlation example, 153
Development, expenditures and voting (*table*), 169, 341
Diamond, Solomon, 197
Dice, random values (*graph*), 72
DIMENSION statement, 382
Directed graphs, 81–86, 103
Dirksen amendment (*table*), 161
DO statement, 384

Dominance graph, 103
Dominance index, 83
Dominance patterns (*graph*), 83
Durkheim, Emile, 308

Easton, David, 21
Editorial apparatus in a table, 23–25
Education, secondary and higher (*graph*), 73
Eisenhower, D., scale of attitudes toward (*graph*), 74
Eldersveld, Samuel J., 233
Electoral college votes and cube law, 97
Elmira voting study, 69, 169
Empiricism, 1
Epistemic correlations, 1
Epistemology, 1
Epstein, Leon D., 41–5
Equality, Gini index, 8–12
Equations, *see* Formulas
Error, statistical, 151
Error, Type I and Type II paradigm, 151
Escobedo v. *Illinois,* 363
Eulau, Heinz, 1*n*, 8*n*, 21, 221, 233, 267
Expenditures, U.S. governmental (*graph*), 80

Farrell, R. Barry, 233
Ferguson, Leroy C., 233
Filipino students' attitudes (*table*), 363
Fisher, Ronald A., 394
Fiske, Marjorie, 233
"Flip flop" effect, 315–16
Florida student attitudes (*table*), 367
Flow chart for tallying, 116
Food preference by sex (*table*), 30
Footnotes in a table, 24
FORMAT statement, 380
Formulas:
    Bogardus' racial distance quotient, 240
    chi-square, 154
        alternative formula for 2 × 2 tables, 299
        worksheets, 156
        with Yates' correction, 299
    coefficient of rank correlation, 153
    communication index, 85
    cube law of representation, 76
    degrees of freedom, 155
    delta value in 2 × 2 tables, 319
        association of delta values, 309
    dominance index, 83
    equality, Gini index, 9
    Guttman coefficient of reproducibility, 241
    index of cohesion, 245
    index of interagreement, 245
    index of likeness, 246
    intensity index in content analysis, 272
    judging, reliability in content analysis, 273
    Landau's hierarchy index, 83
    Spearman's *rho,* 153
    transition probability vector, 85
    Yule's *Q,* 151
FORTRAN, 380
Free, Lloyd A., 233
French and British colonies (*table*), 4, 154
Frequency counts in content analysis, 269
Frequency polygons, 72

Galileo, 7
Gallup sample, 199
Galtung, Johan, 61
Gamma, 158

Gaudet, Hazel, 233
Germany:
    discussion of politics (*table*), 55, 331
    duty to community (*table*), 57, 333, 337
    party officials in Berlin (*table*), 59
Gini index, 8–12
Ginsberg, Norton, 73, 273
GNP (U.S.) and population growth (*graph*), 79, 93
Goldrich, Daniel, 225
Goldwater, B., vote for president, 41–45, 91–93, 137–45, 165, 191–93, 343
Goldwater support in Midwest and South (*table*), 191–93, 343
Gorow, Frank F., 197
Gosset, W. S., 149
GO TO statement, 385
Government levels shown by Venn diagrams, 88
Graphs:
    area graphs, 74
    bar graphs, 67–71
    circle and half-circle graphs, 79–81
    compound bar, 69–71, 73
    conceptual use of, 74–76
    coordinate graphs, 71–79
    directed graphs, 81–86
    frequency polygons, 72
    good qualities of, 64
    ratio graphs, 77–79
    relationship graphs, 81–88
    time series graphs, 71
    Venn diagrams, 86–88
Greenstein, Fred I., 223, 233
Grievances, confidence in redress (*table*), 175
Gurin, Gerald, 233

"Half true" effect, 308–10
Hanoi broadcasts, 275–97
Harris, L. Dale, 147
Hartkemeier, Harry P., 147
Hawkins, David, 21
Headnote in a table, 24
Heisenberg, Werner, 6
Hernando, Orlando M., 363
Hierarchy index, 83–84
Historical Statistics of the United States, 373
Hollerith alphabetic field (computers), 382
Hollerith card, 113, 122
Holsti, Ole R., 301
Honolulu conference, broadcasts about, 275–97
Hostility, measurement in content analysis, 272–73
Huntington, Samuel P., 233
Hursh, Gerald D., 147, 233
Hyman, Herbert, 147, 167, 205, 233, 353
Hyneman, Charles S., 21
Hypothesis, 3
    for a survey, 206
    null, 150–51
    testing, 3–4
    tests of statistical, 150–51

IBM card, 113–15, 122
Ideology, political, 206
IF statement, 114, 384
Immigration (*table*), 101
Incumbency, effect of in voting 229–30.
Independent effect, 305–07
Indexes (*see also* Scales, Formulas)
    example of simple index, 236
    good qualities, 235

index values, 236
Induction, 2
Inequality, Gini index, 8–12
Inference, statistical, 148
Intensity in content analysis, 270, 272
Interagreement index, 245
International politics, 207
International Social Science Bulletin, 373
Internationalism, Swiss and U.S. students (*table*), 369
Interpreter, 122
Interquartile range, 148
Intersection in Venn diagrams, 86
Isolationism, Cantril study of, 310
Israel example, 6

J-curve of revolution (*graph*), 76
Janda, Kenneth, 110
Janowitz, Morris, 233
Japan, party preference (*table*), 161–63, 339
Johnson, L. B.
    support by freshman congressmen, 195
    vote for president, 41–45, 91–93, 165
Journal of Politics, 373
Judging, consistency in content analysis, 273

Kaplan, Abraham, 21, 197
Katz, Daniel, 233
Kaufman, Arnold, 361
Kemeny, John G., 109
Kendall, Patricia L., 233
Kent, Allen, 147
Key, V. O., Jr., 88, 181, 197, 233
Keypunch machine, 121
Keysort card, 123
Khrushchev example, 271
Korean example, 271
Kornberg, Allan, 225
Kuroda, Yasumasa, 161–63

Lambda, 158
Landau, H. G., 83–84
Landau's hierarchy index, 83–84
Lane, Robert, 221, 233
Large numbers, law of, 149
Lasswell, Harold, 1, 21, 301, 373
Lazarsfeld, Paul F., 5, 63, 233, 353
Leaders and followers (*table*), 219
League of Women Voters of Pennsylvania, score card for citizen political action, 237
Lecture sources, 374–76
Lee, Alfred McClung, 233
Leites, N., 301
Lerner, Daniel, 301
Likeness, index of, 246
Lines in a table (*see* Rules)
Linkage patterns (*graph*), 82
Literacy and colonial ruler (*table*), 4, 154
Literary Digest, 6, 198
Living standards in four nations (*graph*), 66, 68
Local government:
    duty to participate in five nations (*table*), 57
    estimates of impact in five nations (*table*), 51
Logarithmic scale (*graphs*), 78–79
Logic tree for tallying, 117
Lokken, George S., 365
Loops in computer programs, 384

McClosky, Herbert, 31, 68, 219, 361
Machine data processing, 121–23

McPhee, W. N., 233
MacRae, Duncan, Jr., 242–44, 267
Manila conference, broadcasts about, 275–97
March, James G., 76
Marginal tables, 25–26, 304
Marvick, Dwaine, 233
Marxist theory, tests of (*tables*), 183–85
Matrix representation of relationships, 83, 85
Mean, 148
Median, 148
Medical personnel and infant mortality (*graph*), 68
Merton, Robert K., 233
Midwest Journal of Political Science, 373
Military Balance, 1966/1967, The, 373
Military forces:
    Gini index, 17–19
    graphs of magnitude, 64, 67, 70
Military officers and students (*table*), 315, 349–51, 365
Miller, Delbert C., 147, 233
Miller, W. (cartoon), 201
Miller, Warren E., 63, 233
Mink, Oscar G., 197
Miranda v. *Arizona,* 363
Mode, 148
Morgenstern, Oscar, 7
Moroney, M. J., 7, 197
Moscow broadcasts, 275–97
Moses, Lincoln E., 197
Multiple causality, 33–34, ch. 9

N:
    importance of, 26, 30
    small *N,* 119
NASA expenditures (*graph*), 70
National government, impact in five nations (*table*), 53
Nature, 1
Negation, in Venn diagrams, 86
Negro integration in schools (*table*), 221
Nevada and California population growth (*graph*), 78
Newspaper circulation, Gini index, 15
Newton, 7
Non-voter:
    analysis of, 229
    education of, 231
    political concerns of (*table*), 227
Non-voting (*table*), 47
Norms, 7
    political, 206
North, Robert C., 268, 271, 301
Northrop, F.S.C., 2
Norway, attitudes toward religion and UN (*table*), 61
"Nothing happens" effect, 302–04
"Now you see it..." effect, 312–14
Null hypothesis, 148, 150

Oklahoma:
    agriculture and party (*table*), 181
    runoff primaries (*table*), 179
    scaling votes of congressional delegation, 259–65
    student attitudes (*tables*), 367–69
Oklahoma University Bureau of Government Research, 179, 181
Ore, Oystein, 109
Osgood, Charles E., 269, 301
Owls, 365

Panamanian students, political attitudes of (*table*), 225
Parameter and statistic, 149

Partial tables, 304
Party organization shown by Venn diagrams, 88
Party preference:
    by intensity of partisanship (*tables*), 45
    by parental preference (*tables*), 39, 68, 169
Pascal, Blaise, 72
Peace Corps volunteers, (*table*), 171
Peking broadcasts, 275–297
Perceived in content analysis, 271
Perceiver in content analysis, 271
Percentage table (computer program), 385–387
Percentages:
    number of places, 26–27
    problem of reading, 27–28
    in a table, 26–28
    table for converting degrees, 81
Perception unit in content analysis, 271
Petty, Paul R., 369
Phenomenology, 1
Phenomenon, 3
Phi and phi-square, 158
Philippines, student attitudes (*table*), 363
"Plus and minus" effect, 310–12
Political science:
    behavioralism, 1
    study of, 1
Political Science Quarterly, 373
Political values, 7–8, 206
Politics:
    discussion in five nations (*table*), 55
    science of, 4–6
Polity, 373
Polygons, frequency, 72–73
Pool, Ithiel de Sola, 268–69, 301
Population, statistical, 148
Power index, 103
Prefatory statement in report, 354
Presidential elections, U.S. (*see* Vote for president, U.S.)
Presidential vote:
    and activism (*table*), 45, 321
    and organization membership (*table*), 49, 327, 329
    and population (*graph*), 78, 93, 99
Presidents (U.S.), age of (*graph*), 72
Pride in government in five nations (*table*), 175, 191
Primary, runoff, and closeness of election (*table*), 179
Probability, 148
Procedural statement in report, 354–56
Property space, 34–39, 119–121
Proposition, 3
Public Opinion Quarterly, 207, 373

Q, Yule's, 151
    use in scaling roll-calls, 242–244
    values for percentage deciles, 392
Q-Sort distribution (*table*), 272
Q-Sort scale in content analysis, 271–74
Quantification, 6–8
Quartile, 148
Questionnaire, 202–03
    pre-test of, 208
Questions:
    bad, 204–05
    decision, 201–03
    identification of respondent, 200
    motivation, 201
    role of respondent, 201
    structure of, 202–04
    structured and unstructured, 203–04
Quota sample, 150

Racial Distance Quotient (Bogardus), 240
Random sample, 198
Range, 148
Rank correlation, 152–54, 393
Ranney, Austin, 41–45
Ratio graphs, 77–79, 99
Ratios, *see* Formulas, Indexes
Realism, logical, 1
Reciprocals (*table*), 391
Reduction of property space, 119–21
Registrations, chi-square test, 189
Relationship, 1
Relationship graphs, 81–88
Relevant data, 3
Religion and party preference, Elmira (*graph*), 69
Religion and vote (*graph*), 69; (*table*), 327
Reporting research, 354–58
Representation:
   Burke's theory of (*tables*), 221
   cube law of, 76–77
Reproducer, 123
Reproducibility, Guttman Coefficient of, 241
Research expenditures and doctorates (*table*), 99
Research reporting, 354–58
Retrieval of frequencies:
   computer program, 387
   procedure in reading a table, 32
   worksheet, 93
Review of Politics, 373
Revolution, Davies' J-curve of, 76
Rho, table of significance levels, 393
Rice, Stuart A., 245–46, 267
Rieselbach, Leroy N., 247–48
Roberts, Harry V., 63, 197
Roll-call clusters, 245–46
Roosevelt and Dewey voters (*table*), 49
Rose, Richard, 233
Rosenau, James N., 234
Rosenberg, Morris, 63, 233, 353
Ross, H. Laurence, 234
Ross, Ralph, 21
ROTC students and interest in world affairs, 131–35, 231
"Rules of the game" in a democracy, 361
Rules (printer's) in a table, 26
Russett, Bruce M., 177–85, 373
Russian revolution (*graph*), 76

Saenger, Gerhart H., 49
Sample:
   Gallup, 199
   quota, 150
   random, 198
   statistical, 148–50
   stratified, 198
   survey, 198–200
Scales (*see also* Formulas, Indexes)
   Bogardus scale, 239
   citizen political action scale, 236
   Galtung social position scale, 61
   Guttman scales, 240–242
   McClosky support ratio, 218, 235
   Q-sort scale in content analysis, 272–275
   racial conservatism scale, 237–239
   racial distance scale, 239
   Senate roll-call scale, 242–245
   social distance scale, 239
   social mobility index, 31, 235
   Supreme Court civil liberties scale, 246
   UN colonial issue scale, 247

Schmid, Calvin F. 109
Schubert, Glendom, 234, 267
Scientific method, 2–4
Scott, Edward W., 225
Semantic differential, 202
Senate (U.S.), scaling votes, 242–46
Senators, rank correlation example, 153
Sets in Venn diagrams, 86–88
Shao, Stephen P., 147, 197
Sheatsley, P. B., 167
Significance level in statistics, 150
Singer, J. David, 234
Slide rule, use of, 377–79
Smith, Joel, 225
Snell, J. Laurie, 109
Social mobility, voter stability and family preference (*tables*),
   31–34; (*graphs*), 34, 68
Socialist and communist vote (*tables*), 177, 185
Socialization, political, 206
Sociogram, 82–83
"Something from nothing" effect, 314–15
Somit, Albert, 1, 21
Sorauf, Francis J., 2
Sorting, efficient procedure, 115–19; (*table*), 118
Source citation in a table, 25
Southwestern Social Science Quarterly, 373
Spearman's *rho*, 152–54
   table of significance levels, 393
Spuriousness, 316
Standard deviation, 148
Stanford University, content analysis projects, 268–71
Statistic and parameter, 149–50
Statistical Abstract of the United States, 373
Statistical inference, 148
Statistical reference works, 373
Statistical test in research report, 357–58
Statistical Yearbook, UN, 373
Stimulus-response, paradigm of structure in questionnaire,
   203–04
Stokes, Donald E., 63, 234
Storing, Herbert J., 5, 21
Stratified sample, 198
   table of U.S. census, 199
Strauss, Leo, 5
"Stretch and shrink" effect, 307–08
Structured question paradigm, 204
Stub (in a table), 25
Student's *t*-test, 149
Substruction of property-space, 119–21
Suci, George J., 301
Suicide and religion, 308
Supreme Court, scalogram of civil liberty votes, 246
Survey:
   briefs of, 209–27
   planning your own, 205–08
   reporting, 354–58
   sample, 198–200
   student survey briefs, 359–71
Survey research, 198–208
Survey Research Center (University of Michigan), 111–12
Swiss students, internationalism (*table*), 369

t test, 149
Table:
   anatomy of, 23–26
   causality in, 33–34
   construction of, 34–38
   key relationship in, 22–23
   percentages in, 26–28

reading, 22–34
   use in research report, 357
   variable in, 28–31
   variation in, 22–23
Tabulator, 123
Tally flow chart, 116
Tanenhaus, Joseph, 1, 21
Tannenbaum, Percy H., 301
Target in content analysis, 271
Textor, Robert B., 3, 373
Theory, 1
Thomas, Norman L., 109
Thompson, Gerald L., 109
Time series graphs, 71–72
Title of a table, 23–24
Totals in a table, 25
Transition probability vector, 85
Truman, David B., 234, 267
Turnout (voter) and partisanship (*table*), 323–25

U-2 example, 271
Ulmer, S. Sidney, 246
Uncertainty principle, 6
Unidimensionality, Guttman scale criteria, 240–41
Union, in Venn diagrams, 86
Union membership (*table*), 312–14
Unit records in data processing, 114–15
Unit statement in content analysis, 271
United Nations:
   caucusing groups (*graph*), 88
   forces, attitude of Norwegians, 61
   publications, 373
   scalogram of colonialism votes, 247–48
   support by education and sex (*table*), 302–05
   support by leaders and followers (*table*), 219, 347
   voting (Gini index), 11, 13
Universal set, 86
Universe of discourse, 86
Urban renewal, party attitudes (*table*), 314–15

Valence in content analysis, 269
Values, political, 7–8, 206
Van Dyke, Vernon, 21
Variables:
   control, 30, 302–18
   dependent, 29
   dichotomous, 29
   independent, 29
   interval, 29, 65
   nominal, 29, 65
   ordinal, 29, 65
   in a table, 28–31

third, 30, 302–18
Variance, 148, 158
Venn diagrams, 86–88
Verba, Sidney, 51–57, 63, 175, 181, 191, 233, 331–37
Verifier, 123
Viet Nam policy, 30, 119–21, 127–35, 349, 351, 365
Villarreal, Roberto E., 367
von Neumann, John, 7
Vote and religion (*graph*), 69; (*table*) 305–06
Vote for president (U.S.):
   by party activism, 1964 (*table*), 45
   by age, 1964 (*table*), 43
   by perceived closeness of election, 1956 (*table*), 47
   and congressional elections (*graph*), 72
   by education, 1964 (*table*), 41
   and attitude toward Eisenhower (*graph*), 74
   and organization membership, 1944 (*table*), 49
   and population growth, 1900–1964 (graph), 78; 1820–1860 (*table*), 93
   turnout by region, 1964 (*table*), 24; (*graph*), 65
   by religion, Elmira, 1948 (*graph*), 69
Voter stability, family preference, and social distance, (*tables*), 31–34; (*graphs*) 34, 68
Voting, intention by fathers and spouses (*table*), 169

Wahlke, John C., 221, 233, 267
Wallis, W. Allen, 63, 197
Watts, Meredith W., Jr., 197, 267
Western Political Quarterly, 373
Wilcox, Allen R., 197, 267
Women, political attitudes of (*table*), 225
World Economic Survey, U.N., 373
World Handbook of Political and Social Indicators, 373
World Politics, 373
Wright, William E., 59

Yates, Frank, 158, 299, 394
Yearbook of International Trade Statistics, UN, 373
Yearbook of National Accounts Statistics, UN, 373
Yearbook of the United Nations, 373
Yule, G. U., 269
Yule's *K*, 269
Yule's *Q*, 151
   computer program, 380–82
   values for percentage deciles, 392

Zaninovich, M. George, 301
Zeisel, Hans, 63, 353
Zelditch, Morris, Jr., 197
Zero test, 114, 384
Zinnes, Dina A., 301